# Learning Hyper-V

Learn how to design, deploy, configure, and manage virtualization infrastructure using Hyper-V

**Vinícius R. Apolinário**

[PACKT] enterprise
PUBLISHING        professional expertise distilled

BIRMINGHAM - MUMBAI

# Learning Hyper-V

First published: May 2015

Production reference: 1260515

Published by Packt Publishing Ltd.
Livery Place
35 Livery Street
Birmingham B3 2PB, UK.

ISBN 978-1-78439-986-3

www.packtpub.com

# Credits

# Foreword

Few other areas of knowledge have had so many technological revolutions as hardware abstraction and virtualization in such a short period.

In this new scenario, Vinícius R. Apolinário showcases the newest advances in the area of virtualization. In his own unmistakable style, he explains complex issues through examples that introduce important concepts in a simple and didactic way.

This book is intended for anyone who wants to learn Hyper-V. If you have basic knowledge of virtualization or a competing technology, such as VMware, it will help, but it is not a requirement. The book begins with a fundamental understanding of each technology and then discusses more advanced topics such as High Availability, replication, Disaster Recovery, storage, networking, templates, and a special chapter that deals with the best practices of using virtualization Domain Controllers. If you are an architect, a consultant, a network administrator, or really anyone who just wants a better understanding of Hyper-V, this book is for you.

Vinícius R. Apolinário knows a lot about his subject, and this book is a step forward in the knowledge of this vast field. He endeavored to study it, and he has become an expert since then. I witnessed the beginning of his career and his growth as a network administrator for a small company when I interviewed him for a job while he was still attending the university. He was hired as a Microsoft technical evangelist, sharing his knowledge with thousands of professionals through blogs, webcasts, and live events.

Considering all of this, this book is indispensable to professionals who wish to not only monitor the most important advances of Hyper-V technology, but also to acquire a solid background in an area as dynamic as computer virtualization.

Happy is the person who transfers what you know and learns what you teach.

Enjoy reading!

**Gilson Banin**

Microsoft Premier Field Engineer

# About the Author

**Vinícius R. Apolinário** is a professional with more than 13 years of experience in information technology. He has worked with Microsoft and in other industries, managing servers and environments of small, medium, and large companies. With a strong background in managing servers for directory services and client infrastructure, he has focused on virtualization and data center management in recent years.

Vinícius is a Microsoft Certified Trainer and system engineer on Windows Server 2012 and Private Cloud. Besides this, he holds a cloud computing certification from EXIN and teaches this technology. He also holds a certification of Extension Course in Product Marketing Manager by Fundação Getúlio Vargas (FGV). His last achievement was becoming a VMware Certified Associate and a VMware Certified Professional for data center virtualization.

Currently, Vinícius works for Microsoft in Brazil as a technical evangelist, presenting new technologies on Windows Server, Hyper-V, System Center, and Microsoft Azure to customers. Prior to this book, he reviewed *Hyper-V Cookbook* and *Hyper-V Cluster Design*.

I would like to start by thanking my wife. As always, her support and understanding were essential in helping me accomplish this. Thank you, little girl, for always being by my side and for all the love.

I thank my manager, Danilo Bordini, for supporting this project, for all the tasks I have in my current role, and for supporting the rest of my career. Thanks to my coworker and friend Fabio Hara for all the knowledge shared over the time we have worked together.

I would also like to thank my great friend Gilson Banin, who has always helped me in my career and has always been an inspiring professional for me and many others.

Additional thanks to Rafael Bernardes and Leandro Carvalho, the reviewers of this book and excellent professionals, for accepting the challenge and all the feedback!

# About the Reviewers

**Rafael Bernardes** is the founder of CooperaTI, one of the most recognized IT portals in Brazil. He is well-known personality and holds recognitions by Microsoft with the MVP, MiVP, and TechNet IT Hero titles.

Rafael also holds an MCSE (Microsoft Certified Solutions Expert) certification in Private Cloud as well as the most recent cloud and virtualization certifications.

> First, I must thank my wife, Renata. Without her support, I wouldn't have been the professional I am today. I would like to thank Vinícius R. Apolinário for the excellent challenge of contributing to the technical review of this book. The book is awesome and goes straight to the point. I recommend it to everybody.

**Leandro Carvalho** is a well-known virtualization specialist, who writes and presents sessions on virtualization and cloud computing. He works as a system engineer on Microsoft solutions, such as Windows Server, Hyper-V, App-V, VDI, System Center, Exchange, Lync Server, SharePoint, Project Server, security, and client systems. He also helps the community frequently with articles, forums, videos, and lectures about his passion — Microsoft virtualization. Leandro has the certifications of Certified Ethical Hacker, MCP, MCSA+M+S, MCSE+S, MCTS, MCITP, MCT, and MVP. In 2009, he received the Trainer of the Year award from MCT Awards, Latin America. He has won the Microsoft MVP award as a virtualization specialist every year since 2010. He has also worked on *Windows Server 2012 Hyper-V Cookbook*.

Leandro can be contacted at `http://leandroesc.wordpress.com`, and his Twitter handle is `@LeandroEduardo`.

I would like to thank my wife, Juliana, and my son, Eduardo, for their ongoing support, understanding, and encouragement. You are the source of my inspiration and happiness.

I also wish to thank Vinícius R. Apolinário for the invitation to be the reviewer of this book. It was a real pleasure because in 2012, he was the reviewer of my book. Here we are now — history repeating itself — with me as the reviewer of your book, so thanks again!

**Tomas Dabasinskas** started his career in the IT field during his days at the university, where he was studying software engineering. He started working as a developer, but a few years later, he moved into the IT Pro field. For a few years, Tomas worked on implementing and deploying a number of different solutions based on Microsoft technologies, including SharePoint, Exchange, and Hyper-V. Now, he is working as a lead for a Windows support team in a large enterprise organization. He also has to deal with virtualization technologies (both VMware ESXi and Microsoft Hyper-V).

**David Luu** is a quality assurance engineer, software developer, and technical writer. His professional experience and interests include working with technologies such as virtualization, networking, Microsoft Windows, .NET, cloud computing, and more. He primarily tests software products and services, occasionally workin on software development, documentation review, and technical writing/editing.

David also contributes to open source software and has released a .NET library to facilitate the management of Hyper-V virtual machines programmatically. It is available at `http://code.google.com/p/robotframework-hypervlibrary/`.

**James Murray-Curtis** has a BSc (Hons) degree in computing and information systems from London Metropolitan University. Through the course of his continual professional development, he has acquired numerous Cisco and Microsoft certifications. He has worked in the IT field for the last 10 years and has been involved in multiple projects for large organizations as a systems engineer. James is currently employed as an IP network engineer for a leading on-demand mobile virtual network enabler (MVNE). When he is not supporting, fixing, and maintaining core network infrastructure, he works as an MCT for a local training academy. This is of great benefit to his students, as he uses not only his academic knowledge but also his practical experience in high-availability systems in production environments and core networks. James has experience in teaching Windows Server, Exchange Server, and virtualization.

I would like to thank my fiancée, Trisha, for the continual support and love she has had for me throughout my career development and studies.

**Federico Tonelli** was born on June 3, 1985. He lives in Livorno (Leghorn in English), Tuscany, Italy, and he also studied there up to high school. Then, he studied information technology at the University of Pisa and obtained his bachelor's degree in 2009, with a thesis on security of P2P networks through virtual machines. Then, he studied security information at La Spezia, a wing of the University of Pisa, where he obtained his master's degree (110 cum laude) in 2012. After gaining his master's degree, he was a scholarship holder, and his research was about vulnerability analysis in SCADA systems, funded by Enel Engineering and Services. Finally, he got a call for becoming a PhD student and secured the first place, with a score of 99/100.

Federico's main research interests in the computer security field are formal approaches to risk assessment and management of complex ICT infrastructures. He has been involved in risk assessment and management of several systems, and he has worked on industrial control systems with SCADA components. He has authored several papers on ICT security. Federico is currently developing a suite of tools, named Haruspex, to automatize risk assessment and management of any ICT infrastructure.

# www.PacktPub.com

## Support files, eBooks, discount offers, and more

For support files and downloads related to your book, please visit www.PacktPub.com.

Did you know that Packt offers eBook versions of every book published, with PDF and ePub files available? You can upgrade to the eBook version at www.PacktPub.com and as a print book customer, you are entitled to a discount on the eBook copy. Get in touch with us at service@packtpub.com for more details.

At www.PacktPub.com, you can also read a collection of free technical articles, sign up for a range of free newsletters and receive exclusive discounts and offers on Packt books and eBooks.

![PACKT™ logo]

https://www2.packtpub.com/books/subscription/packtlib

Do you need instant solutions to your IT questions? PacktLib is Packt's online digital book library. Here, you can search, access, and read Packt's entire library of books.

## Why subscribe?

- Fully searchable across every book published by Packt
- Copy and paste, print, and bookmark content
- On demand and accessible via a web browser

## Free access for Packt account holders

If you have an account with Packt at www.PacktPub.com, you can use this to access PacktLib today and view 9 entirely free books. Simply use your login credentials for immediate access.

## Instant updates on new Packt books

Get notified! Find out when new books are published by following @PacktEnterprise on Twitter or the *Packt Enterprise* Facebook page.

# Table of Contents

# Preface

Hyper-V is gaining market share over its competitors, and is already the leader in some markets. With the release of Windows Server 2012, Hyper-V is positioned not only as a low cost alternative, but also as a featured virtualization platform. Therefore, every day, an increasing number of administrators take the first step to acquiring Microsoft virtualization technologies. As a step-by-step guide, this book will take you through a journey that involves learning about the Hyper-V platform from scratch. This will prepare you to become a more versatile Hyper-V admin.

## What this book covers

*Chapter 1, Getting Started with Hyper-V Architecture and Components*, covers the Hyper-V architecture and takes a deep dive into how its basic components, such as the processor and memory, can influence a host's performance and utilization.

*Chapter 2, Deploying Hyper-V Hosts*, covers multiple Hyper-V deployment options and provides you with the pros and cons of each option.

*Chapter 3, Licensing a Virtualization Environment with Hyper-V*, provides an overview of licensing a virtualization environment with Hyper-V for Windows Server, Windows Client, and Linux VMs. You will also be given tips and tricks regarding licensing Microsoft virtualization environments.

*Chapter 4, Managing Networking*, focuses on networking configuration for hosts and Virtual Machines (VMs), allowing you to understand how to configure physical and virtual networks for better performance.

*Chapter 5, Managing Storage*, covers storage and its influence on a host and VM performance, and presents you with techniques to optimize storage.

*Chapter 6, Virtual Machines and Virtual Machine Templates*, covers multiple components of a VM and its templates to optimize creation of a VM with Hyper-V.

*Chapter 7, Implementing High Availability*, provides an overview of Microsoft failover clusters that are used to support Hyper-V with High Availability (HA).

*Chapter 8, Implementing Live Migration and Replica*, covers how to prepare a virtualization environment for scheduled maintenance and Site Disaster Recovery.

*Chapter 9, Virtualizing Active Directory Domain Controllers*, covers the best practices used to virtualize Domain Controllers, avoid replication problems, and get around configuration mistakes.

*Chapter 10, Implementing a Virtual Desktop Infrastructure*, covers the basics involved in Virtual Desktop Infrastructure (VDI) and Remote Desktop Services (RDS), and how Hyper-V can support them.

*Chapter 11, Protecting Your Virtualization Environment*, gives an overview of the protection used for hosts and VMs in a virtualized environment. The chapter will also provide an overview of other tools that are used for backup and restore.

# What you need for this book

This book is based on the Hyper-V and Windows Server technology. If you want to reproduce the labs in this book, you will need a computer (a server, workstation, or laptop) that meets the Hyper-V requirements described in *Chapter 1, Getting Started with Hyper-V Architecture and Components*, and a Windows Server trial license or a Hyper-V Server to install on the computer you will be using.

# Who this book is for

This book focuses on readers starting their journey with Hyper-V, assuming they have minimal or no knowledge of virtualization. You are given your first steps into Microsoft virtualization technology, and you will need to install, configure, and maintain Hyper-V Hosts and VMs to prepare their environments for next-generation technologies.

# Conventions

In this book, you will find a number of text styles that distinguish between different kinds of information. Here are some examples of these styles and an explanation of their meaning.

Code words in text, database table names, folder names, filenames, file extensions, pathnames, dummy URLs, user input, and Twitter handles are shown as follows: "If you do not wish to restart the server right away, you can remove the `-Restart` option and run the `Restart-Computer` later."

Any command-line input or output is written as follows:

```
Install-WindowsFeature –Name Server-Gui-Mgmt-Infra –Restart
```

**New terms** and **important words** are shown in bold. Words that you see on the screen, for example, in menus or dialog boxes, appear in the text like this: "From **Server Manager**, select **Hyper-V group**, right-click the server you want to manage, and select **Hyper-V Manager**."

> Warnings or important notes appear in a box like this.

> Tips and tricks appear like this.

# Reader feedback

Feedback from our readers is always welcome. Let us know what you think about this book—what you liked or disliked. Reader feedback is important for us as it helps us develop titles that you will really get the most out of.

To send us general feedback, simply e-mail feedback@packtpub.com, and mention the book's title in the subject of your message.

If there is a topic that you have expertise in and you are interested in either writing or contributing to a book, see our author guide at www.packtpub.com/authors.

# Customer support

Now that you are the proud owner of a Packt book, we have a number of things to help you to get the most from your purchase.

# Errata

Although we have taken every care to ensure the accuracy of our content, mistakes do happen. If you find a mistake in one of our books—maybe a mistake in the text or the code—we would be grateful if you could report this to us. By doing so, you can save other readers from frustration and help us improve subsequent versions of this book. If you find any errata, please report them by visiting http://www.packtpub.com/submit-errata, selecting your book, clicking on the **Errata Submission Form** link, and entering the details of your errata. Once your errata are verified, your submission will be accepted and the errata will be uploaded to our website or added to any list of existing errata under the Errata section of that title.

To view the previously submitted errata, go to https://www.packtpub.com/books/content/support and enter the name of the book in the search field. The required information will appear under the **Errata** section.

# Piracy

Piracy of copyrighted material on the Internet is an ongoing problem across all media. At Packt, we take the protection of our copyright and licenses very seriously. If you come across any illegal copies of our works in any form on the Internet, please provide us with the location address or website name immediately so that we can pursue a remedy.

Please contact us at copyright@packtpub.com with a link to the suspected pirated material.

We appreciate your help in protecting our authors and our ability to bring you valuable content.

# Questions

If you have a problem with any aspect of this book, you can contact us at questions@packtpub.com, and we will do our best to address the problem.

# 1
# Getting Started with Hyper-V Architecture and Components

Hyper-V has evolved since its release back in 2008. At that time, Hyper-V was released as an update to Windows Server 2008, KB950050 to be more precise (which can be found at `https://support2.microsoft.com/kb/950050/en-us`). Many of the features available today were not present at that point. If you take a look, you can actually see that virtualization has been one of the areas of major investments by Microsoft, not only with Hyper-V, but also to ensure that all its major products would be able to run perfectly on a virtualization environment. As an example of how Hyper-V has evolved, Microsoft Azure runs entirely on it. In the first release, Hyper-V did not have Live Migration, Storage Live Migration, Replica, Dynamic memory, and many other features. It also had support for only four virtual processors and 64 GB of virtual RAM per **Virtual Machine** (**VM**). At first, Hyper-V's only appeal was its price, or the fact that it is not charged at all.

Nowadays, Hyper-V is the leading virtualization solution in many markets and is rapidly gaining market share over its competitors. The reason behind this is actually simple. Hyper-V combines a solution that meets the higher expectations of large enterprises and since it's delivered free, even small companies can benefit from all Hyper-V features. Moreover, Microsoft Hyper-V Server is a totally free virtualization platform with no restrictions, compared to the Hyper-V from Windows Server, and is a perfect scenario for open source users too. Licensing and Utilization options will be explained in detail in *Chapter 3, Licensing a Virtualization Environment with Hyper-V*, so for now, all you have to keep in mind is that Microsoft delivers all its virtualization technologies at no cost.

However, before we go through all the Hyper-V features that this book will cover, it's important to understand the architecture and components of Hyper-V, so you'll have a better understanding on how all this works and will be able to make better decisions when planning your virtualization environment.

In this chapter, we will cover the following topics:

- Hypervisor architecture
- Type 1 and 2 Hypervisors
- Microkernel and Monolithic Type 1 Hypervisors
- Hyper-V requirements
- Processor and memory configuration

Looking back in history, Hyper-V is not the first virtualization technology from Microsoft. Actually, virtualization, emulation, and other techniques have been used since the first computer was released. Even mainframes use these techniques. Specifically, virtualization, as we know today, was imagined to solve a common problem, that is, the average utilization of a server is extremely low. Even though some components are used more than others, the total utilization of a server is minimal. That happens because when you plan for a server that will run an application, you have to plan for the higher utilization moment, when an application is stressed. But this utilization peak will occur just a few times during the month. For all other times, your server will be either idle or using 5 to 10 percent of all its capacity. That is the average. Before virtualization, another technique was also used: **server consolidation**. This technique consists of running multiple applications on the same server. The problem with this option is that you have no isolation between the application environment, and often, you can't combine too many different applications on the same server as they may have totally different requirements. Another problem of the server consolidation is that the utilization peak will create another problem of two concurrent applications on the same server. This technique is hardly used today, as virtualization addresses these issues in a much better way.

Microsoft has played in this field of better hardware utilization since its first operating system. Even Microsoft DOS had some options for doubling RAM. Windows 3.X introduced paging, also known as virtual memory, on later Operating Systems (OS). The game started to change in 2003, when Microsoft bought two products called Virtual PC, which already had released versions for Mac OS and Windows, and Virtual Server, which was in the development phase at that moment, from Connectix. With the acquisition, part of the staff from Connectix came to Microsoft, and, in 2004, Microsoft released Microsoft Virtual Server 2005.

Compared to the first version of Hyper-V, Microsoft Virtual Server is a dinosaur. That's not only because Hyper-V implements new features, but also because there is a major architectural difference between these products. This is the Hypervisor architecture.

# Hypervisor architecture

If you've used Microsoft Virtual Server or Virtual PC, and then moved to Hyper-V, I'm almost sure that your first impression was: "Wow, this is much faster than Virtual Server". You are right. And there is a reason why Hyper-V performance is much better than Virtual Server or Virtual PC. It's all about the architecture.

There are two types of Hypervisor architectures. Hypervisor Type 1, like Hyper-V and ESXi from VMware, and Hypervisor Type 2, like Virtual Server, Virtual PC, VMware Workstation, and others. The objective of the Hypervisor is to execute, manage and control the operation of the VM on a given hardware. For that reason, the Hypervisor is also called **Virtual Machine Monitor** (**VMM**). The main difference between these Hypervisor types is the way they operate on the host machine and its operating systems. As Hyper-V is a Type 1 Hypervisor, we will cover Type 2 first, so we can detail Type 1 and its benefits later.

# Type 1 and Type 2 Hypervisors

Hypervisor Type 2, also known as **hosted**, is an implementation of the Hypervisor over and above the OS installed on the host machine. With that, the OS will impose some limitations to the Hypervisor to operate, and these limitations are going to reflect on the performance of the VM.

To understand that, let me explain how a process is placed on the processor: the processor has what we call **Rings** on which the processes are placed, based on prioritization. The main Rings are 0 and 3. Kernel processes are placed on Ring 0 as they are vital to the OS. Application processes are placed on Ring 3, and, as a result, they will have less priority when compared to Ring 0. The issue on Hypervisors Type 2 is that it will be considered an application, and will run on Ring 3. Let's have a look at it:

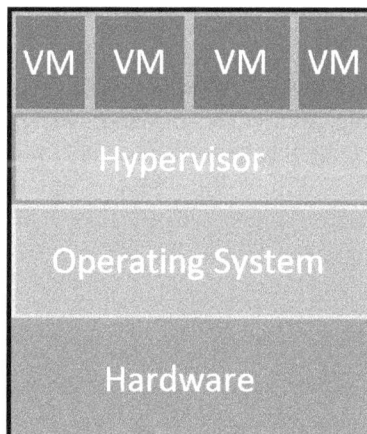

As you can see from the preceding diagram, the hypervisor has an additional layer to access the hardware. Now, let's compare it with Hypervisor Type 1:

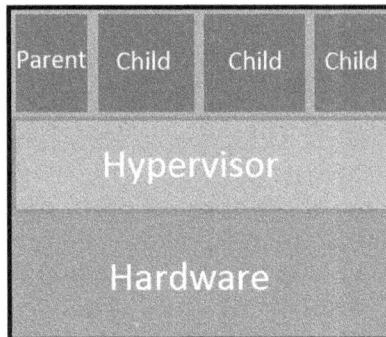

The impact is immediate. As you can see, Hypervisor Type 1 has total control of the underlying hardware. In fact, when you enable **Virtualization Assistance (hardware-assisted virtualization)** at the server BIOS, you are enabling what we call Ring -1, or Ring decompression, on the processor and the Hypervisor will run on this Ring.

The question you might have is "And what about the host OS?" If you install the Hyper-V role on a Windows Server for the first time, you may note that after installation, the server will restart. But, if you're really paying attention, you will note that the server will actually reboot twice. This behavior is expected, and the reason it will happen is because the OS is not only installing and enabling Hyper-V bits, but also changing its architecture to the Type 1 Hypervisor. In this mode, the host OS will operate in the same way a VM does, on top of the Hypervisor, but on what we call parent partition. The parent partition will play a key role as the boot partition and in supporting the child partitions, or guest OS, where the VMs are running. The main reason for this partition model is the key attribute of a Hypervisor: isolation.

> For Microsoft Hyper-V Server you don't have to install the Hyper-V role, as it will be installed when you install the OS, so you won't be able to see the server booting twice.

With isolation, you can ensure that a given VM will never have access to another VM. That means that if you have a compromised VM, with isolation, the VM will never infect another VM or the host OS. The only way a VM can access another VM is through the network, like all other devices in your network. Actually, the same is true for the host OS. This is one of the reasons why you need an antivirus for the host and the VMs, but this will be discussed later.

The major difference between Type 1 and Type 2 now is that kernel processes from both host OS and VM OS will run on Ring 0. Application processes from both host OS and VM OS will run on Ring 3. However, there is one piece left. The question now is: "What about device drivers?"

# Microkernel and Monolithic Type 1 Hypervisors

Have you tried to install Hyper-V on a laptop? What about an all-in-one device? A PC? A server? An x64 based tablet? They all worked, right? And they're supposed to work. As Hyper-V is a Microkernel Type 1 Hypervisor, all the device drivers are hosted on the parent partition. A Monolithic Type 1 Hypervisor hosts its drivers on the Hypervisor itself. VMware ESXi works this way. That's why you should never use a standard ESXi media to install an ESXi host. The hardware manufacturer will provide you with an appropriate media with the correct drivers for the specific hardware.

The main advantage of the Monolithic Type 1 Hypervisor is that, as it always has the correct driver installed, you will never have a performance issue due to an incorrect driver. On the other hand, you won't be able to install this on any device.

The Microkernel Type 1 Hypervisor, on the other hand, hosts its drivers on the parent partition. That means that if you installed the host OS on a device, and the drivers are working, the Hypervisor, and in this case Hyper-V, will work just fine.

> There are other hardware requirements. These will be discussed later in this chapter.

The other side of this is that if you use a generic driver, or a wrong version of it, you may have performance issues, or even driver malfunction. What you have to keep in mind here is that Microsoft does not certify drivers for Hyper-V. Device drivers are always certified for Windows Server. If the driver is certified for Windows Server, it is also certified for Hyper-V. But you always have to ensure the use of correct driver for a given hardware. Let's take a better look at how Hyper-V works as a Microkernel Type 1 Hypervisor:

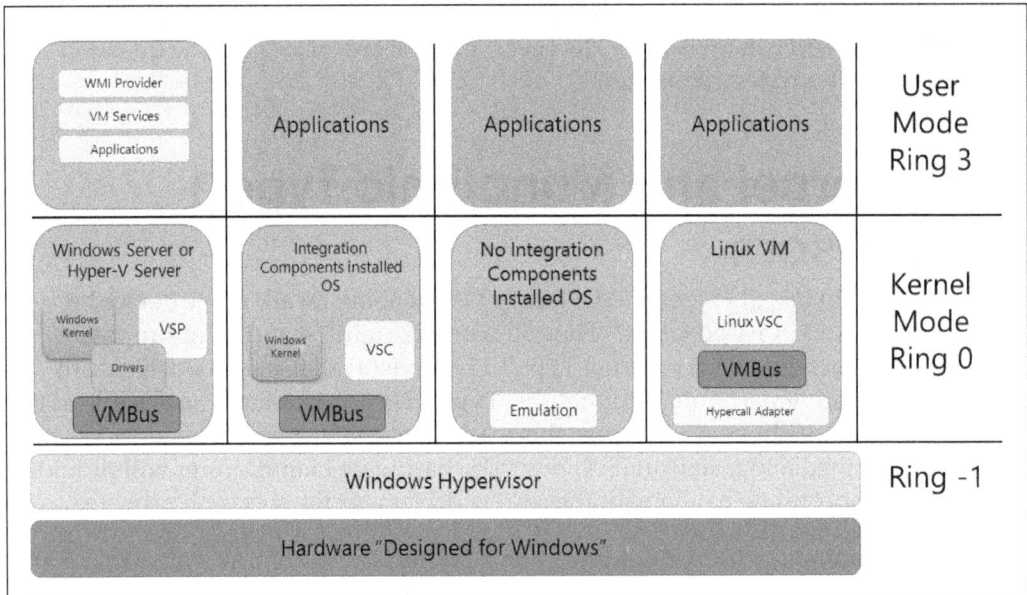

As you can see from the preceding diagram, there are multiple components to ensure that the VM will run perfectly. However, the major component is the **Integration Components** (IC), also called Integration Services. The IC is a set of tools that you should install or upgrade on the VM, so that the VM OS will be able to detect the virtualization stack and run as a regular OS on a given hardware.

To understand this more clearly, let's see how an application accesses the hardware and understand all the processes behind it.

When the application tries to send a request to the hardware, the kernel is responsible for interpreting this call. As this OS is running on an **Enlightened Child Partition** (Means that IC is installed), the Kernel will send this call to the **Virtual Service Client** (**VSC**) that operates as a synthetic device driver. The VSC is responsible for communicating with the **Virtual Service Provider** (**VSP**) on the parent partition, through VMBus, so the VSC can use the hardware resource. The VMBus will then be able to communicate with the hardware for the VM. The VMBus, a channel-based communication, is actually responsible for communicating with the parent partition and hardware.

For the VMBus to access the hardware, it will communicate directly with a component on the Hypervisor called **hypercalls**. These hypercalls are then redirected to the hardware. However, only the parent partition can actually access the physical processor and memory. The child partitions access a virtual view of these components that are translated on the guest and the host partitions.

New processors have a feature called **Second Level Address Translation** (**SLAT**) or Nested Paging. This feature is extremely important on high performance VMs and hosts, as it helps reduce the overhead of the virtual to physical memory and processor translation. On Windows 8, SLAT is a requirement for Hyper-V.

It is important to note that Enlightened Child Partitions, or partitions with IC, can be Windows or Linux OS. If the child partitions have a Linux OS, the name of the component is **Linux Integration Services** (**LIS**), but the operation is actually the same.

Another important fact regarding ICs is that they are already present on Windows Server 2008 or later. But, if you are running a newer version of Hyper-V, you have to upgrade the IC version on the VM OS. For example, if you are running Hyper-V 2012 R2 on the host OS and the guest OS is running Windows Server 2012 R2, you probably don't have to worry about it. But if you are running Hyper-V 2012 R2 on the host OS and the guest OS is running Windows Server 2012, then you have to upgrade the IC on the VM to match the parent partition version. Running guest OS Windows Server 2012 R2 on a VM on top of Hyper-V 2012 is not recommended. For Linux guest OS, the process is the same. Linux kernel version 3 or later already have LIS installed. If you are running an old version of Linux, you should verify the correct LIS version of your OS. To confirm the Linux and LIS versions, you can refer to an article at `http://technet.microsoft.com/library/dn531030.aspx`.

Another situation is when the guest OS does not support IC or LIS, or an Unenlightened Child Partition. In this case, the guest OS and its kernel will not be able to run as an Enlightened Child Partition. As the VMBus is not present in this case, the utilization of hardware will be made by emulation and performance will be degraded. This only happens with old versions of Windows and Linux, like Windows 2000 Server, Windows NT, and CentOS 5.8 or earlier, or in case that the guest OS does not have or support IC. Now that you understand how the Hyper-V architecture works, you may be thinking: "Okay, so for all of this to work, what are the requirements?"

# Hyper-V requirements and processor features

At this point, you can see that there is a lot of effort for putting all of this to work. In fact, this architecture is only possible because hardware and software companies worked together in the past. The main goal of both type of companies was to enable virtualization of operating systems without changing them.

Intel and AMD created, each one with its own implementation, a processor feature called virtualization assistance so that the Hypervisor could run on Ring 0, as explained before. But this is just the first requirement. There are other requirement as well, which are as follows:

- **Virtualization assistance** (also known as **Hardware-assisted virtualization**): This feature was created to remove the necessity of changing the OS for virtualizing it.

    ◦ On Intel processors, it is known as Intel VT-x. All recent processor families support this feature, including Core i3, Core i5, and Core i7. The complete list of processors and features can be found at http://ark.intel.com/Products/VirtualizationTechnology. You can also use this tool to check if your processor meets this requirement which can be downloaded at: https://downloadcenter.intel.com/Detail_Desc.aspx?ProductID=1881&DwnldID=7838.

    ◦ On AMD Processors, this technology is known as AMD-V. Like Intel, all recent processor families support this feature. AMD provides a tool to check processor compatibility that can be downloaded at http://www.amd.com/en-us/innovations/software-technologies/server-solution/virtualization.

- **Data Execution Prevention (DEP)**: This is a security feature that marks memory pages as either *executable* or *nonexecutable*. For Hyper-V to run, this option must be enabled on the System BIOS. For an Intel-based processor, this feature is called **Execute Disable bit** (Intel XD bit) and No Execute Bit (AMD NX bit). This configuration will vary from one System BIOS to another. Check with your hardware vendor how to enable it on System BIOS.

- **x64 (64-bit) based processor**: This processor feature uses a 64-bit memory address. Although you may find that all new processors are x64, you might want to check if this is true before starting your implementation. The compatibility checkers above, from Intel and AMD, will show you if your processor is x64.

- **Second Level Address Translation (SLAT)**: As discussed before, SLAT is not a requirement for Hyper-V to work. This feature provides much more performance on the VMs as it removes the need for translating physical and virtual pages of memory. It is highly recommended to have the SLAT feature on the processor ait  provides more performance on high performance systems. As also discussed before, SLAT is a requirement if you want to use Hyper-V on Windows 8 or 8.1. To check if your processor has the SLAT feature, use the **Sysinternals** tool — **Coreinfo** — that can be downloaded at `http://technet.microsoft.com/en-us/sysinternals/cc835722.aspx`.

 There are some specific processor features that are not used exclusively for virtualization. But when the VM is initiated, it will use these specific features from the processor. If the VM is initiated and these features are allocated on the guest OS, you can't simply remove them. This is a problem if you are going to Live Migrate this VM from a host to another host; if these specific features are not available, you won't be able to perform the operation. Live Migration and Share Nothing Live Migration will be covered in later chapters. At this moment, you have to understand that Live Migration moves a powered-on VM from one host to another. If you try to Live Migrate a VM between hosts with different processor types, you may be presented with an error.

Live Migration is only permitted between the same processor vendor: Intel-Intel or AMD-AMD. Intel-AMD Live Migration is not allowed under any circumstance. If the processor is the same on both hosts, Live Migration and Share Nothing Live Migration will work without problems.

But even within the same vendor, there can be different processor families. In this case, you can remove these specific features from the Virtual Processor presented to the VM. To do that, open **Hyper-V Manager | Settings... | Processor | Processor Compatibility**. Mark the **Migrate to a physical computer with a different processor version** option. This option is only available if the VM is powered off.

Keep in mind that enabling this option will remove processor-specific features for the VM. If you are going to run an application that requires these features, they will not be available and the application may not run.

Now that you have checked all the requirements, you can start planning your server for virtualization with Hyper-V. This is true from the perspective that you understand how Hyper-V works and what are the requirements for it to work. But there is another important subject that you should pay attention to when planning your server: memory.

# Memory configuration

I believe you have heard this one before: "The application server is running under performance". In the virtualization world, there is an obvious answer to it: give more virtual hardware to the VM. Although it seems to be the logical solution, the real effect can be totally opposite.

During the early days, when servers had just a few sockets, processors, and cores, a single channel made the communication between logical processors and memory. But server hardware has evolved, and today, we have servers with 256 logical processors and 4 TB of RAM. To provide better communication between these components, a new concept emerged. Modern servers with multiple logical processors and high amount of memory use a new design called **Non-Uniform Memory Access** (**NUMA**) architecture.

# Non-Uniform Memory Access (NUMA) architecture

NUMA is a memory design that consists of allocating memory to a given node, or a cluster of memory and logical processors. Accessing memory from a processor inside the node is notably faster than accessing memory from another node. If a processor has to access memory from another node, the performance of the process performing the operation will be affected. Basically, to solve this equation you have to ensure that the process inside the guest VM is aware of the NUMA node and is able to use the best available option.

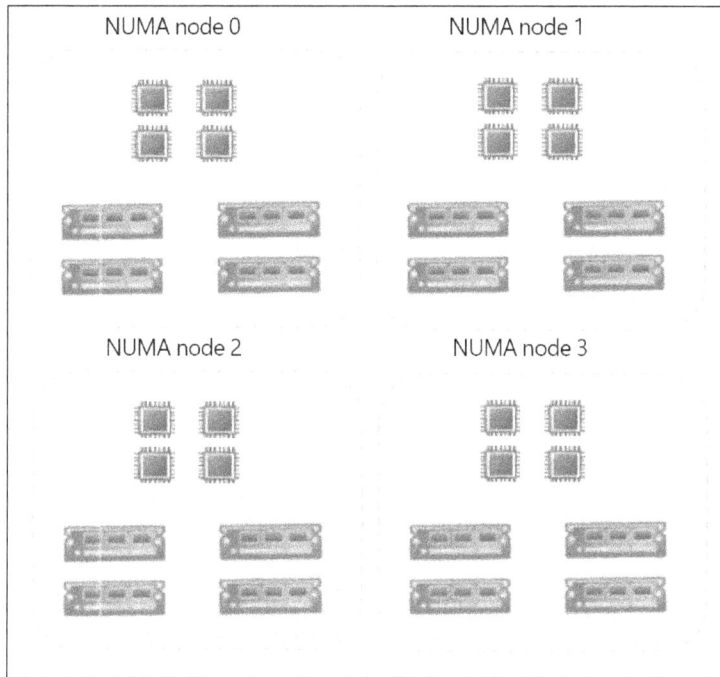

When you create a virtual machine, you decide how many virtual processors and how much virtual RAM this VM will have. Usually, you assign the amount of RAM that the application will need to run and meet the expected performance. For example, you may ask a software vendor on the application requirements and this software vendor will say that the application would be using at least 8 GB of RAM. Suppose you have a server with 16 GB of RAM. What you don't know is that this server has four NUMA nodes. To be able to know how much memory each NUMA node has, you must divide the total amount of RAM installed on the server by the number of NUMA nodes on the system. The result will be the amount of RAM of each NUMA node. In this case, each NUMA node has a total of 4 GB of RAM.

Following the instructions of the software vendor, you create a VM with 8 GB of RAM. The Hyper-V standard configuration is to allow NUMA spanning, so you will be able to create the VM and start it. Hyper-V will accommodate 4 GB of RAM on two NUMA nodes. This NUMA spanning configuration means that a processor can access the memory on another NUMA node. As mentioned earlier, this will have an impact on the performance if the application is not aware of it. On Hyper-V, prior to the 2012 version, the guest OS was not informed about the NUMA configuration. Basically, in this case, the guest OS would see one NUMA node with 8 GB of RAM, and the allocation of memory would be made without NUMA restrictions, impacting the final performance of the application.

Hyper-V 2012 and 2012 R2 have the same feature—the guest OS will see the **virtual NUMA (vNUMA)** presented to the child partition. With this feature, the guest OS and/or the application can make a better choice on where to allocate memory for each process running on this VM.

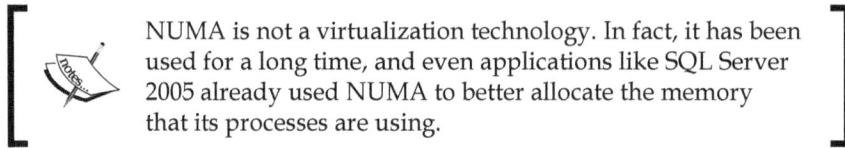

> NUMA is not a virtualization technology. In fact, it has been used for a long time, and even applications like SQL Server 2005 already used NUMA to better allocate the memory that its processes are using.

Prior to Hyper-V 2012, if you wanted to avoid this behavior, you had two choices:

- Create the VM and allocate the maximum vRAM of a single NUMA node for it, as Hyper-V will always try to allocate the memory inside of a single NUMA node. In the above case, the VM should not have more than 4 GB of vRAM. But for this configuration to really work, you should also follow the next choice.

- Disable NUMA Spanning on Hyper-V. With this configuration disabled, you will not be able to run a VM if the memory configuration exceeds a single NUMA node. To do this, you should clear the **Allow virtual machines to span physical NUMA nodes** checkbox on **Hyper-V Manager | Hyper-V Settings... | NUMA Spanning**. Keep in mind that disabling this option will prevent you from running a VM if no nodes are available.

You should also remember that even with Hyper-V 2012, if you create a VM with 8 GB of RAM using two NUMA nodes, the application on top of the guest OS (and the guest OS) must understand the NUMA topology. If the application and/or guest OS are not NUMA aware, vNUMA will not have effect and the application can still have performance issues.

At this point you are probably asking yourself "How do I know how many NUMA nodes I have on my server?" This was harder to find in the previous versions of Windows Server and Hyper-V Server. In versions prior to 2012, you should open the Performance Monitor and check the available counters in **Hyper-V VM Vid NUMA Node**. The number of instances represents the number of NUMA Nodes.

In Hyper-V 2012, you can check the settings for any VM. Under the **Processor** tab, there is a new feature available for **NUMA**. Let's have a look at this screen to understand what it represents:

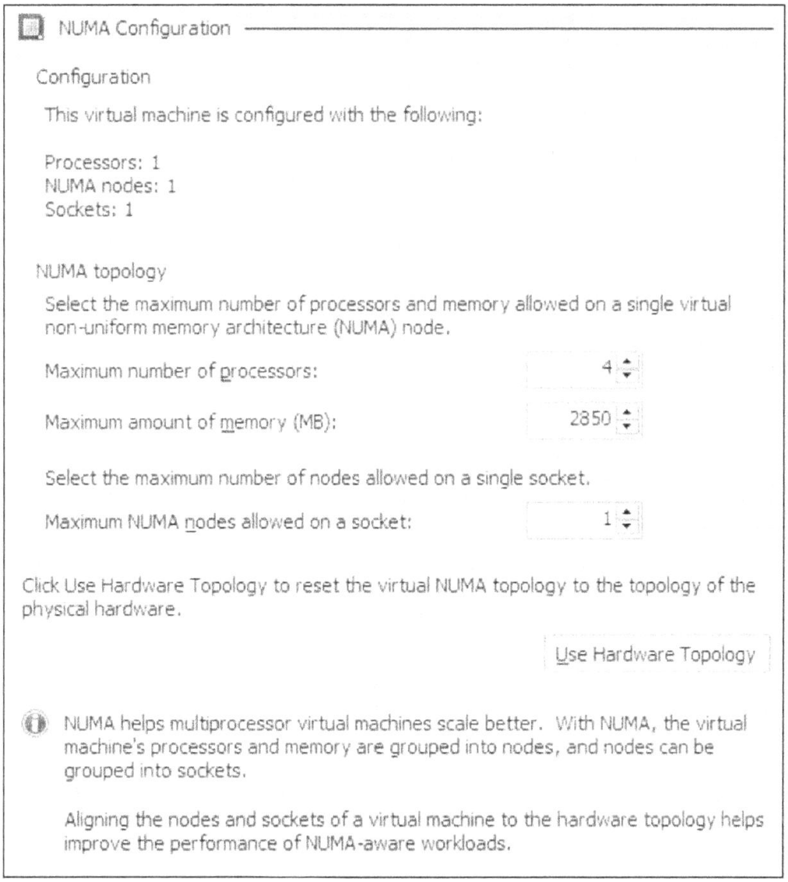

NUMA Configuration ─────────────────────────

Configuration

This virtual machine is configured with the following:

Processors: 1
NUMA nodes: 1
Sockets: 1

NUMA topology

Select the maximum number of processors and memory allowed on a single virtual non-uniform memory architecture (NUMA) node.

Maximum number of processors:                               4 ↕

Maximum amount of memory (MB):                          2850 ↕

Select the maximum number of nodes allowed on a single socket.

Maximum NUMA nodes allowed on a socket:                    1 ↕

Click Use Hardware Topology to reset the virtual NUMA topology to the topology of the physical hardware.

Use Hardware Topology

ⓘ NUMA helps multiprocessor virtual machines scale better. With NUMA, the virtual machine's processors and memory are grouped into nodes, and nodes can be grouped into sockets.

Aligning the nodes and sockets of a virtual machine to the hardware topology helps improve the performance of NUMA-aware workloads.

In **Configuration**, you can easily confirm how many NUMA nodes the host running this VM has. In the case above, the server has only 1 NUMA node. This means that all memory will be allocated close to the processor.

> Multiple NUMA nodes are usually present on servers with high amount of logical processors and memory.

In the **NUMA topology** section, you can ensure that this VM will always run with the informed configuration. This is presented to you because of a new Hyper-V 2012 feature called Share Nothing Live Migration, which will be explained in detail later. This feature allows you to move a VM from one host to another without turning the VM off, with no cluster and no shared storage. As you can move the VM turned on, you might want to force the processor and memory configuration, based on the hardware of your worst server, ensuring that your VM will always meet your performance expectations.

The **Use Hardware Topology** button will apply the hardware topology in case you moved the VM to another host or in case you changed the configuration and you want to apply the default configuration again.

To summarize, if you want to make sure that your VM will not have performance problems, you should check how many NUMA nodes your server has and divide the total amount of memory by it; the result is the total memory on each node. Creating a VM with more memory than a single node will make Hyper-V present a vNUMA to the guest OS. Ensuring that the guest OS and applications are NUMA aware is also important, so that the guest OS and application can use this information to allocate memory for a process on the correct node.

NUMA is important to ensure that you will not have problems because of host configuration and misconfiguration on the VM. But, in some cases, even when planning the VM size, you will come to a moment when the VM memory is stressed. In these cases, Hyper-V can help with another feature called Dynamic memory.

# Dynamic memory

Dynamic memory is a feature that was released in Service Pack 1 for Windows Server 2008 R2 and Hyper-V Server 2008 R2. It was a long awaited feature for Hyper-V as its major competitors had other features for managing VM memory, and, until that point, Hyper-V option was the static VM memory.

This feature allows you to configure not only the amount of memory for a VM, but also define a Minimum and Maximum of vRAM. In case the VM memory is stressed, Hyper-V can provide more memory to the VM, as long as the host has physical memory. An important point for Dynamic memory is that it only uses physical memory. Other memory management techniques in the market use processors (page sharing) or disks (Second Level Paging) to address memory issues. Microsoft decided not to use these techniques as they bring overhead to the host or drag the performance of the VM, except for some VM restart operations with **Smart Paging** that will be explained later in this section. Instead, Dynamic memory uses another technique from the market called **ballooning**.

To better understand the ballooning technique, imagine the air companies' ticketing and sales process. Let's say an aircraft has 200 seats. The company will sell a given percentage above those 200 seats. In the end, only 200 passengers are allowed to check-in. With Dynamic memory, you can create any number of VMs with a maximum that exceeds the physical memory on the host, but only the available physical memory will be allocated to these VMs. If a VM requires more memory and there is no available memory on this host, the VM will have to wait for the ballooning process to work on other VMs and for the host to reclaim unused memory.

# Dynamic memory configuration

The Dynamic memory configuration is made on a per-VM basis. Open the VM Settings and select **Memory**. Let's take a look at the **Dynamic Memory** configuration, as seen in the following screenshot:

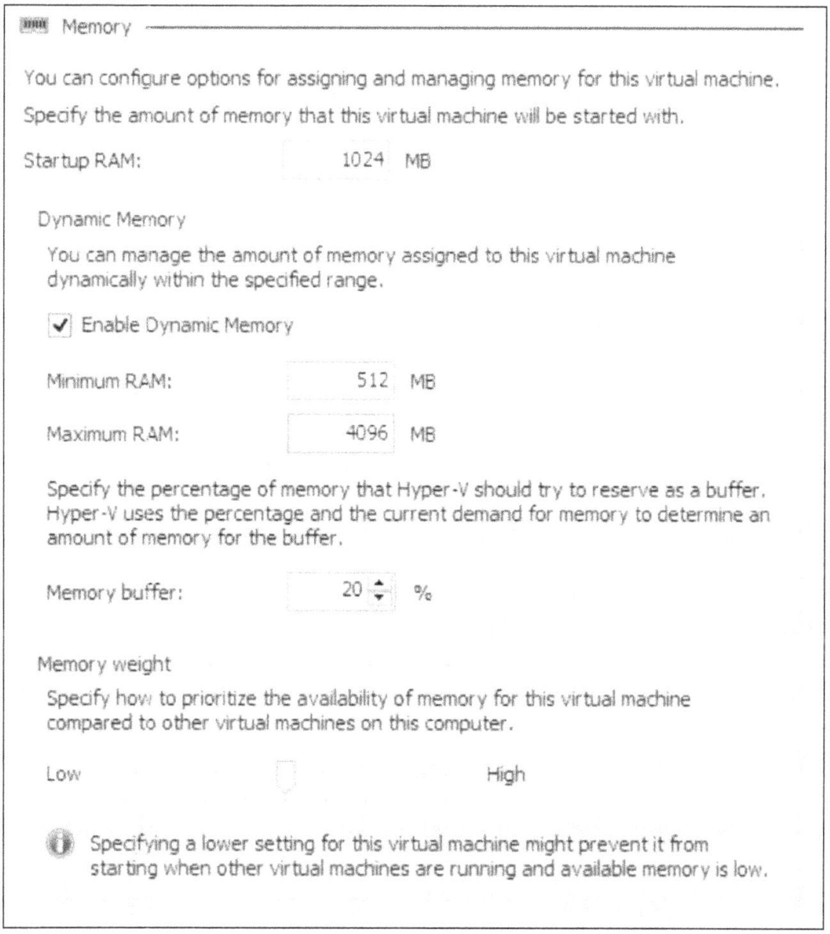

The standard configuration, unless you changed it during VM creation, has the **Enable Dynamic Memory** checkbox cleared. With that configuration, you can specify the **Startup RAM** size and the VM will run with this amount of RAM all the time. This is what we call static memory.

> Keep in mind that static memory is the recommended option. Dynamic memory is an alternative that can be used for consolidating VMs on environments with idle or low-load VMs. Dynamic memory is only recommended for **Virtual Desktop Infrastructure** (**VDI**) with Pooled VMs scenario. Additionally, some applications, such as SharePoint, do not support Dynamic memory.

If you enable Dynamic memory, you can also specify the Minimum RAM and Maximum RAM. This is a new configuration for Dynamic memory since Hyper-V 2012. Prior to that, you were able to set the Startup and Maximum RAM. This change enables you to set a Startup RAM that will be set to the VM at the moment of the VM startup. As the VM continues to run, and if it doesn't need that amount of RAM, Hyper-V will reclaim that memory up to the value configured on Minimum RAM. This reclaimed memory will be available for use by other VMs. This new configuration of startup and minimum memory creates a scenario issue that will be explained in detail later in this section.

The Maximum RAM will limit how much memory a VM can allocate as the application inside the VM requests more memory. When the limit is reached, Hyper-V stops giving memory to the VM.

# Memory buffer

The two remaining options are as important as the other ones. **Memory buffer** and **Memory weight** are usually overlooked, but require attention as they influence the operation of the VM. The **Memory buffer** option is important because it is the definition of how much memory Hyper-V will try to reserve and assign for the VM on the host. When the VM requests more memory, Hyper-V will deliver the reserved memory for the VM based on the percentage and the memory requested by the application. After that, Hyper-V will reserve the percentage again. To validate the amount of memory that will be assigned to the VM, Hyper-V uses **performance counters** to identify the committed memory. You can check this performance counter by opening Performance Monitor and adding the *Hyper-V Dynamic memory VM / Average Pressure* performance counter. With that information, Hyper-V uses the following formula to determine how much memory to assign to the VM:

Amount of Memory Buffer = How much memory the virtual machine actually needs / (Memory Buffer value / 100)

For example, suppose that the memory allocation is 2000 MB and the memory buffer is 20 percent. In this case, Hyper-V will try to allocate 400 MB of RAM, with a total of 2400 MB, for the VM. But all of this will only make sense if you also configure Memory weight.

# Memory weight

Memory weight is the configuration that confirms the reserved memory. Once the VM requests memory and Hyper-V delivers it, Hyper-V is unable to remove the memory from the VM as this can crash the VM operation. If the Memory weight is the same for all VMs, then all VMs can actually request all available memory on the host, as long as the maximum memory allows it, even if this memory is reserved to another VM. If a VM is more important in your environment, and you want to ensure that the reserved memory is not consumed by other VMs, you can increase the Memory weight. This configuration will ensure that VMs with a lower configuration of Memory weight do not use the reserved memory from VMs with higher Memory weight configuration.

After configuring Dynamic memory, you can verify the VM memory on Hyper-V Memory, as seen in the following screenshot:

**Virtual Machines**

| Name | State | CPU Usage | Assigned Memory | Uptime | Status |
|------|-------|-----------|-----------------|--------|--------|
| VM-Win | Running | 11% | 1024 MB | 00:00:58 | |

**Checkpoints**

The selected virtual machine has no checkpoints.

**VM-Win**

| | | | |
|---|---|---|---|
| Startup Memory: | 1024 MB | Assigned Memory: | 1024 MB |
| Dynamic Memory: | Enabled | Memory Demand: | 911 MB |
| Minimum Memory: | 512 MB | Memory Status: | Low |
| Maximum Memory: | 4096 MB | | |

Summary   Memory   Networking

As you can see from the image above, there is some important information on Hyper-V Manager for you to take note of, and to verify that your VM is correctly configured. If you need more details on Dynamic memory, there are other performance counters under Hyper-V Dynamic Memory VM in **Performance Monitor**.

As mentioned earlier, this Dynamic memory configuration can cause another problem in a specific scenario. Check the following Hyper-V and VMs configuration:

| VMs | Startup RAM | Minimum RAM | Maximum RAM |
|-----|-------------|-------------|-------------|
| Host | 4 GB | N/A | N/A |
| VM01 | 1 GB | 512 MB | 4 GB |
| VM02 | 1 GB | 512 MB | 4 GB |
| VM03 | 1 GB | 512 MB | 4 GB |
| VM04 | 1 GB | 512 MB | 4 GB |

With the configuration above, if all VMs are turned on at the same time, Hyper-V will be able to allocate the correct amount of memory for each VM.

> The preceding configuration is an example. In fact, due to memory management overhead, you need more memory on the host to be able to turn on the VMs with the VM configuration illustrated in this table. A minimum of 512 MB is recommended to be reserved on the host.

In case you turn off VM04 and VM01 requests more memory, VM01 will be able to use 2 GB of RAM. In this case, if you try to turn on VM04 again, you won't be able to power on as there are not enough resources. The following error will be presented:

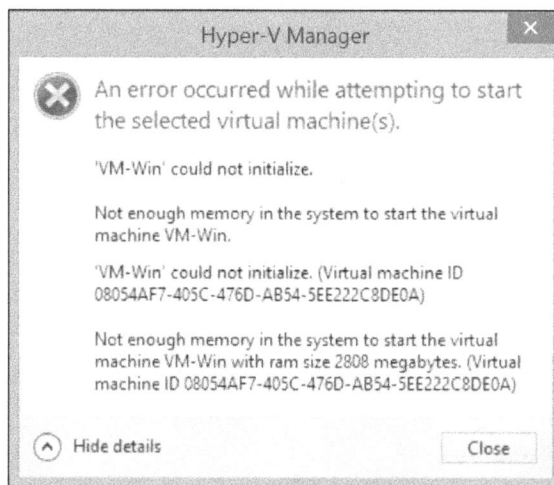

Hyper-V Manager

An error occurred while attempting to start the selected virtual machine(s).

'VM-Win' could not initialize.

Not enough memory in the system to start the virtual machine VM-Win.

'VM-Win' could not initialize. (Virtual machine ID 08054AF7-405C-476D-AB54-5EE222C8DE0A)

Not enough memory in the system to start the virtual machine VM-Win with ram size 2808 megabytes. (Virtual machine ID 08054AF7-405C-476D-AB54-5EE222C8DE0A)

Hide details                    Close

But there is another case where a situation like this can happen even without turning any VM off. With the same configuration from the previous table, imagine that after a while, Hyper-V tries to reclaim memory from the VMs, and VM01 is with low utilization. As VM01 is configured to use 512 MB of Minimum RAM, Hyper-V will reclaim another 512 MB of RAM. At this moment, VM04 is stressed and requests more memory. Hyper-V will then allocate the available 512 MB of RAM to VM04.

Everything is okay until VM01 begins to restart. As VM01 is configured to use 1 GB of startup RAM, the VM won't be able to initialize. To avoid this scenario, Microsoft introduced Smart Paging.

# Smart Paging

Smart Paging is a feature released in Hyper-V 2012. It creates a Smart Paging file on the host disk for allocating memory to the VM so that the VM can use the correct Startup memory configuration. This feature can be used only under certain conditions (all must be true), which are as follows:

- The virtual machine is being restarted
- There is no available physical memory
- No memory can be reclaimed from other virtual machines running on the host

If all of the above are true, Smart Paging will work to allow the VM to restart. You can configure the Smart Paging location by navigating to **Hyper-V Manager** | VM **Settings...** | **Smart Paging File Location**. It is recommended to use a Solid-State Disk (SSD), or disks which are not over-utilized, for better performance.

With all the Dynamic memory configuration in place, it is important to understand its behavior from the architectural perspective and guest OS limitations. As you were probably able to figure out, for Hyper-V to be able to reclaim unused memory, the guest OS will be prompted to return this memory. This can only be achieved by using IC or LIS, so it is extremely important to have IC/LIS updated on the guest OS.

The IC will create the balloon driver and this driver will be utilized by the VSC on the guest OS. This driver will *inflate* when an application requests memory and Hyper-V delivers it. For this driver to work, there are some requirements for the guest OS. When using a Windows Server 2012 or 2012 R2, both Standard and Datacenter versions will support it. But some versions of previous releases of Windows Server, the Standard and Datacenter versions did not support it. For Windows Server 2008 and 2008 R2, the Standard version did not support Dynamic memory. For Windows 8 and 8.1, only Professional and Enterprise support it. For a complete list of guest OS, that support Dynamic memory, check the official article at http://technet.microsoft.com/en-us/library/hh831766.aspx.

# Summary

After understanding all the information on architecture presented in this chapter, you must now be equipped to understand how Hyper-V works, and to make a better choice of your physical servers for virtualization. To summarize, a physical server must attend to some requirements to be able to run Hyper-V. When you install the Hyper-V role, the architecture will be modified to a Microkernel Type 1 Hypervisor. The processor families on all hosts must be identified to allow VM Live Migration. Memory configuration must be examined to avoid the misconfiguration of VMs leading to NUMA issues, and Dynamic memory can help in memory allocation among VMs for idle or low-load VMs.

In the next chapter, we will cover the installation of Hyper-V on multiple scenarios, and options for Windows Server and Hyper-V Server, so you will be able to see all of the information presented here in action.

# 2
# Deploying Hyper-V Hosts

So far, you have seen how important it is to understand the Hyper-V architecture and the impact it will have on the VM and host performance. Planning the virtualization environment is crucial as most of the time, you are unable to make a major change in the environment without interruptions. New technologies like **Shared Nothing Live Migration**, which will be discussed in detail in *Chapter 8, Implementing Live Migration and Replica*, can minimize the impact of infrastructure changes and host management to the VM. Nevertheless, changing your environment during production is always painful. Deploying your host the right way from the start is just as important.

Hyper-V can be implemented in three different ways—Windows Server with **graphical user interface** (**GUI**), Windows Server without GUI, and Hyper-V Server. In *Chapter 3, Licensing a Virtualization Environment with Hyper-V*, we will cover the licensing impact of each model, so, for now, we will focus on the technical aspects of each option and the impact on the environment and management.

In this chapter we will cover the following topics:

- Different options for installing a Hyper-V host
- How to ensure your Hyper-V host is correctly configured
- How to perform basic operations on a host without GUI
- How to install the Remote Management Tools on a Windows client
- Understanding the difference between Hyper-V on a server and client
- Planning your server for Microsoft support

# Considerations before installing a Hyper-V Host

Keep in mind that the host installation and maintenance is extremely important from the following perspectives:

- **Usability**: Hyper-V Server and Windows Server without a GUI will offer only Command Prompt and PowerShell as administration tools on the server console. Although you can connect from any other machine with a GUI, and perform maintenance and day-to-day operations, if connectivity is lost you should be familiarized with these tools, so you can at least recover the machine to an acceptable state where you can connect to it or even recover it.

- **Security**: Windows Server with GUI is the primary choice for someone unfamiliar with Hyper-V or even Windows Server. That's because the GUI offers a more friendly interface, and, even if you are installing Hyper-V for the first time, you will be able to accomplish basic tasks, without much help. But the installation of a GUI comes with some cons too. One example is Internet Explorer (IE). Although you may never use it on a virtualization host, if an update for IE is available, you should install it so that you can keep your server up-to-date. Additionally, not using a GUI results in less footprints, services, opened ports, and so on.

- **Updates**: Not only from a security perspective, but updates have another impact on the environment: reboots. Another important issue in the GUI interface is that the number of updates is higher compared to the one without a GUI. Hyper-V Server has even less updates to be applied, reducing the numbers of reboots.

- **Performance**: As more features are present on the host, the more reservations you should apply for it. Running a server without a GUI will make your server run with fewer resources. In fact, the requirements for running Hyper-V Server, and Windows Server with and without GUI, are different, as you will see later in this chapter.

Consider all of the above before installing your virtualization host on a production environment. But, if you are running a **lab environment** and just want to familiarize yourself with Hyper-V, its components and features, then you should probably use the Windows Server with a GUI. Learning how to use Hyper-V with a GUI will give you the confidence to perform the necessary tasks. The next step will be to learn how to perform these tasks without a GUI.

The other important point that you should consider for your virtualization host independently is the option for OS installation. If you want to verify all the recommendations for Hyper-V, regardless of the installation option, you can use the **Best Practices Analyzer (BPA)**. This tool is built-in on Windows Server 2012 R2 and you can run it locally or on a remote host. BPA will be covered later in this chapter.

In a production environment, you probably want to follow the vendor recommendations, so the question you might have now is "What does Microsoft recommend for installing on the Host OS?"

The answer is not that simple. The basic and simplistic answer is to install the Microsoft Hyper-V Server. But this is not true if some requirements from your environment are not met by the Hyper-V Server. Suppose you have an antivirus software that only runs with a GUI. In this case, you can surely use Windows Server with a GUI and Hyper-V role enabled; you just have to be sure that you configure your server following all the best practices. The so called *better choice* for your environment is the one that meets all your pre-requisites for a host. Having said that, let's see how to implement all the options, so that you can verify which one will be the *better choice* for your environment.

# Windows Server with a GUI

This is probably the main choice for someone starting with Hyper-V. It is not a case of being better or worse than other options, but you have to keep in mind that this is the option that you'll have to look at for more details on security, updates, and so on.

Since the 2008 version, Windows Server works as the foundation for many roles and features. Everything is modularized, so you can choose to enable or disable a role or a feature, for example, you can install **Internet Information Services (IIS)** on a server and choose to enable the CGI component on that server. With this approach, you'll be sure that only specific components will be running, so your attack surface is minimal to the services you need. Remember, though, that even a role or a feature that is not installed must be updated in case an update is available.

With Windows Server 2012 R2 with a GUI, all possible Windows Server roles and features are available for you to install. This will give you as much flexibility on a Windows Server and Hyper-V host as possible. Not only for Windows Server roles and features, there are also some cases where the GUI is necessary.

A Hyper-V host, by definition, is supposed to run only the minimal tools necessary for running the VMs. Windows Server by itself will do that. But in a production environment, there are other important tools which you might want to use: backup tools, antivirus, **management agents,** and others. Microsoft has made significant progress in Hyper-V Server and Windows Server without a GUI so that all your other software works with these options. But, in case you're not using only Microsoft software, you may find that other vendor software still requires a GUI to work correctly. In these cases, you have no other alternative than to use the Windows Server with a GUI.

It is not part of the scope of this book to show you how to install a traditional Windows Server on a host, so we will assume that you have your host in place. The next question is "How to enable Hyper-V on a host with Windows Server with a GUI?"

# Enabling the Hyper-V role

Since Windows Server 2008, Microsoft provides a central administration tool called Server Manager for administrators.

In Server Manager, you will find that all host configurations are few clicks away, including the roles and features installation. To install Hyper-V role, select **Manage** on the top-right corner and select **Add Roles and Features**.

On **Add Roles and Features Wizard**, click **Next >**. Select **Role-based or feature-based installation** and click **Next >**. If you are managing multiple servers, select the server where you want to install the Hyper-V feature and click **Next >**. On the **Roles** page, check the **Hyper-V** option.

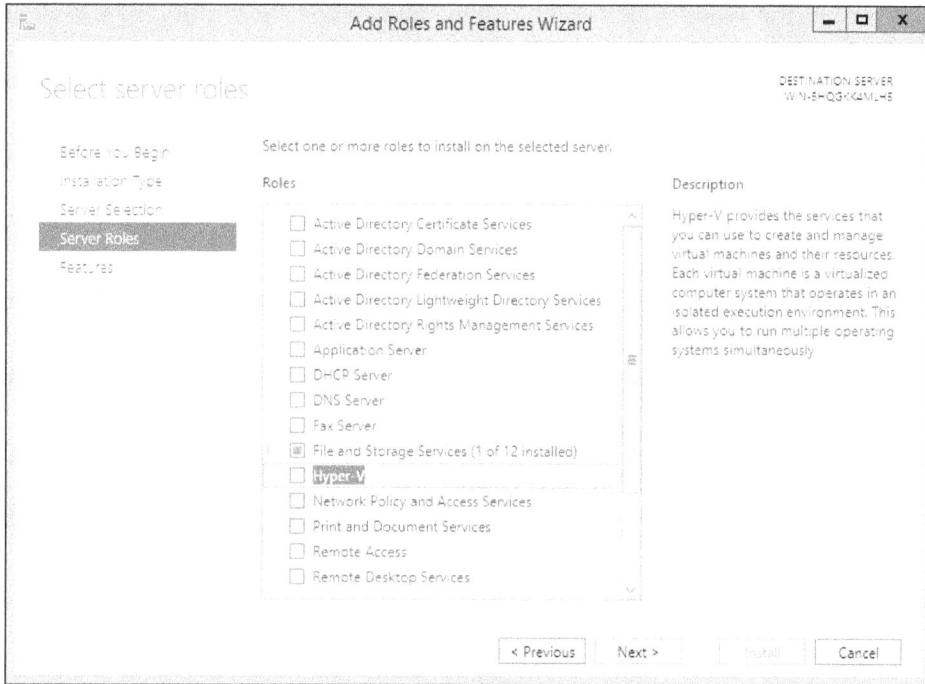

When you marked the **Hyper-V** option, Windows Server suggests that you install other features required by Hyper-V. You can actually choose not to install them, as these are management tools. You would choose not to install them if you are going to manage this Hyper-V host from another computer. However, it is recommended that you install it, as you may need to perform some tasks from the console. Click **Add Features** and then click **Next >**.

If on the previous screen, you kept the **Hyper-V Management Tools**, you can click **Next >** on the **Features** screen. Click **Next >** on the Hyper-V information screen. On **Network Adapter**, you can choose to create a **Virtual Switch** with an uplink to one of the present **Network Interface Cards** (**NIC**). This configuration will be covered in *Chapter 4, Managing Networking*, so leave the defaults and click **Next >**.

On the next screen, you can enable Shared-Nothing Live Migration. As this topic will be covered in *Chapter 8, Implementing Live Migration and Replica*, leave the defaults and click **Next >**. Now you have the option to choose the default location for creating the virtual machines and VM Disks. Storage configuration will be covered on *Chapter 5, Managing Storage*, but keep in mind that when you create a VM, you can always change the default location for the VM and VM disks. Click **Next >**.

On the **Confirmation** screen, you will finish the installation. As already mentioned in *Chapter 1, Getting Started with Hyper-V Architecture and Components*, Hyper-V requires the server to restart twice after installation, so before clicking on **Install**, mark the option **Restart the destination server automatically if required** and click **Install**. This will restart the server as required, and after installation, you can log on to the server and confirm that the installation succeeded. In case you clicked **Install** without marking this option, you can restart the server manually once the installation is complete.

After rebooting, Hyper-V is installed. That means that the foundation for virtualizing is done, but your work is not. Let's see which components are installed and where to find each of them.

# Hyper-V Manager

Hyper-V Manager is a **Microsoft Management Console (MMC)** installed as a part of the Management Tools for Hyper-V. To open Hyper-V Manager on Windows Server 2012 R2, you can try the following three ways:

- Open it from **Server Manager** by clicking on **Tools** on the top right corner:

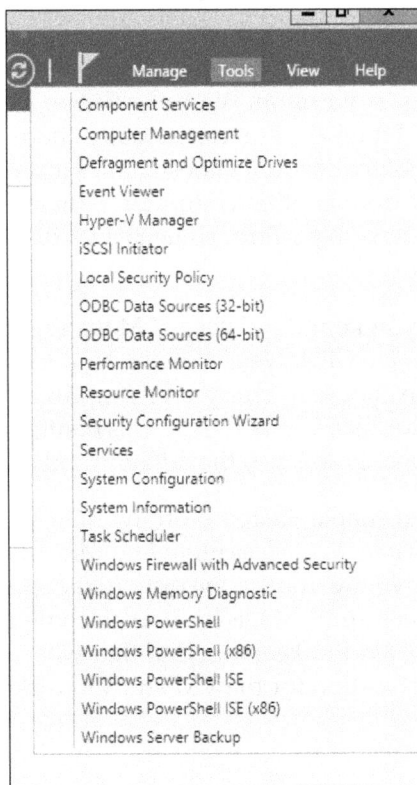

- From **Server Manager**, select **Hyper-V** group, right-click the server you want to manage, and select **Hyper-V Manager**:

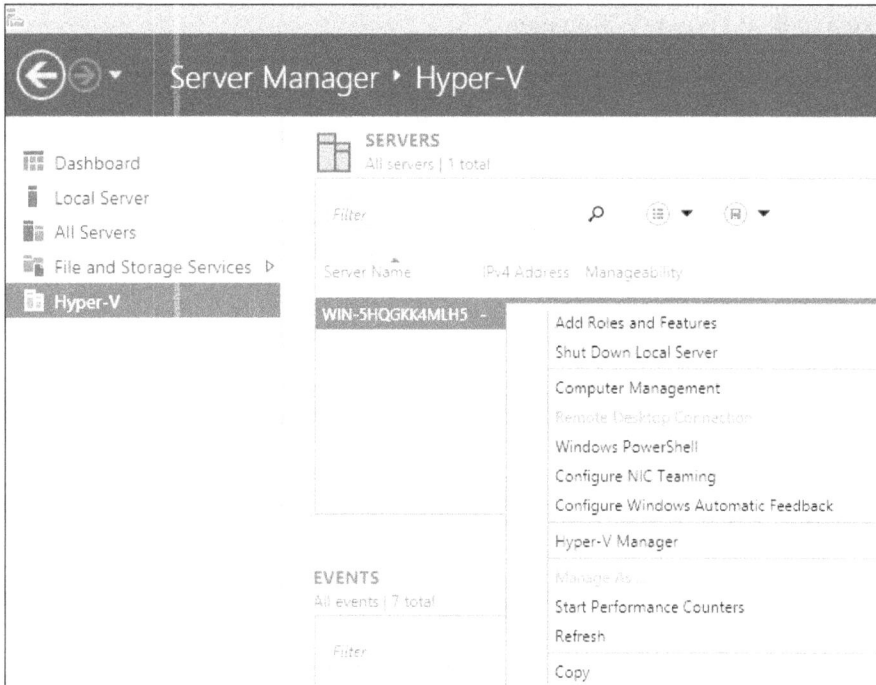

- Click WinKey (this will open the Start screen) and just type Hyper-V Manager:

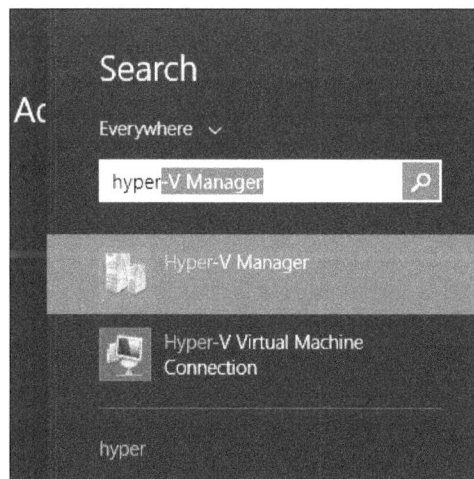

Once you have the Hyper-V Manager open, it is important to get familiar with this screen, as this will be your main console using Hyper-V, unless you're using another virtualization management tool, such as **System Center Virtual Machine Manager**. Let's take a look at Hyper-V Manager:

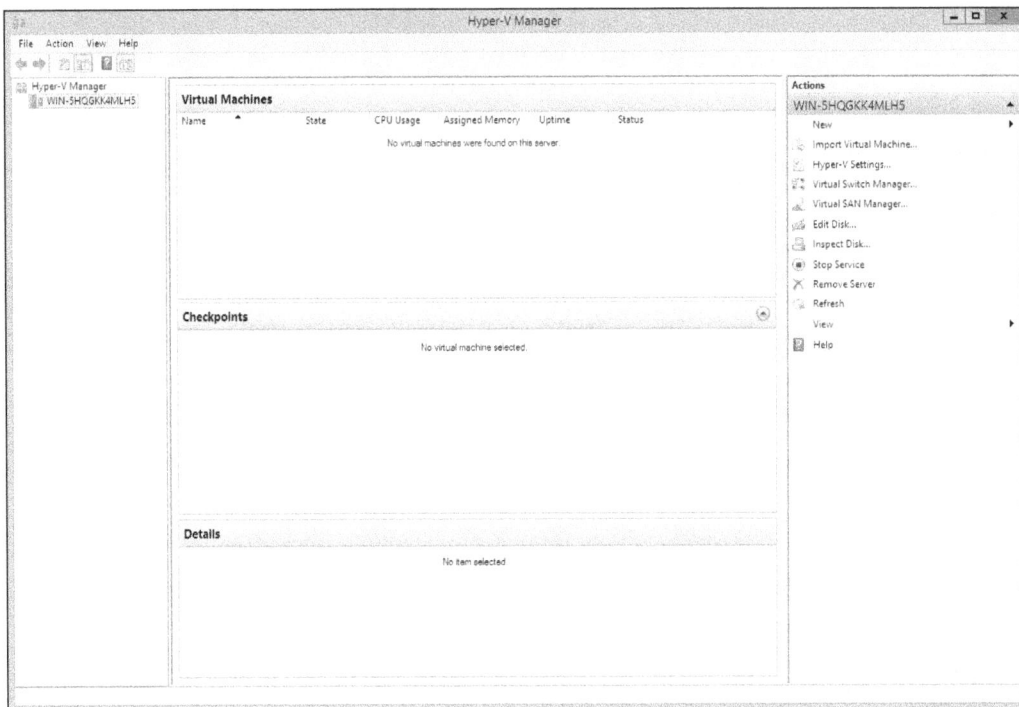

On the left, you have a list of servers that you are managing. Right now, you have one server, but you can add another server to this console. To do that, right-click **Hyper-V Manager** and select **Connect to Server....** Type the name or IP of the server you want to manage and click **OK**. After adding the server, you can perform the operations on the selected server.

> On the Hyper-V Manager, you are always performing the operation on the server and server alone. On Hyper-V Server, you can't perform an action on multiple servers at once. Throughout this book, we will show you how to perform operations on multiple servers through PowerShell.

With the server selected, you have the center pane that shows you from, top to bottom, your VMs, the VM **Checkpoints** (in preceding screenshot), and VM **Details** such as Memory, Network and Replication information.

On the right, you have the contextual menu for the host and VM. On the host contextual menu, you can modify the Hyper-V settings by selecting **Hyper-V Settings...**:

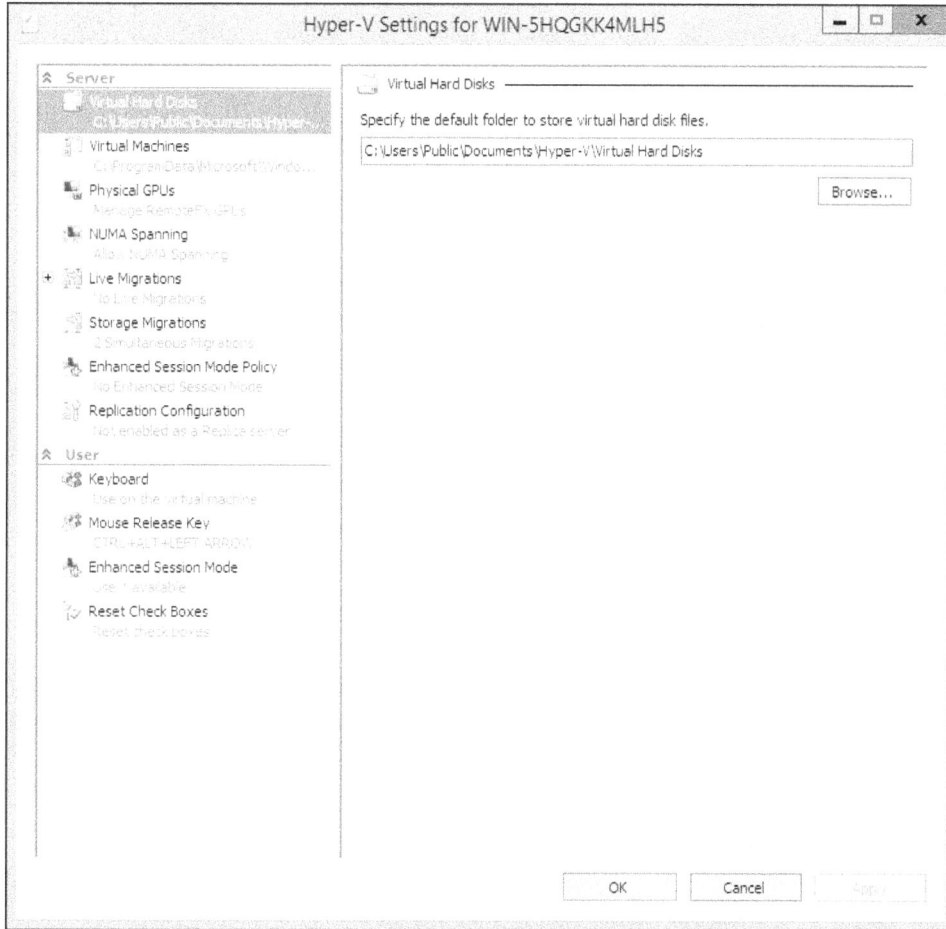

In the preceding screenshot, you have multiple configurations, as follows:

- **Virtual Hard Disks**: You can specify the default location for creating new VM disks. This option is true for new VM disks. The virtual disk created when you create a VM will be, by default, created in the VM folder under the `Virtual Hard Disk` folder within the VM folder.

- **Virtual Machines**: This is the default location for new VMs. Although, you can choose a different folder when creating a VM, you might want to change the default location so that another administrator does not create a VM in a different folder.

- **Physical GPUs**: One of the Hyper-V features is to present the VM with a virtual GPU installed on the host. This feature is designed to VDI scenarios and will be explained in *Chapter 10, Implementing a Virtual Desktop Infrastructure*.

- **NUMA Spanning**: As discussed in *Chapter 1, Getting Started with Hyper-V Architecture and Components*, Hyper-V can allow VMs to access memory from different NUMA nodes. The NUMA Spanning option will enable or disable this behavior. Keep in mind that once you disable it, you'll won't be able to have VMs using more memory than the NUMA node capacity.

- **Live Migrations**: The Shared Nothing Live Migration feature allows you to move a VM from one host to another without interruption on the VM and on shared storage. This topic will be covered in *Chapter 8, Implementing Live Migration and Replica*.

- **Storage Migrations**: This feature allows you to move the VM storage from one place to another without interruptions for the VM. You can also choose how many simultaneous storage migrations are allowed on this host. This topic will also be covered in *Chapter 8, Implementing Live Migration and Replica*.

- **Enhanced Session Mode Policy**: This feature allows you to use local resources inside the VM session, but only for the given session. This is a new feature in Hyper-V 2012 R2 and will be explained in detail in *Chapter 6, Virtual Machines and Virtual Machine Templates*.

- **Replication Configuration**: Hyper-V Replica can be enabled for this host on this screen. Remember that the configuration presented here is to allow this host to receive replicas. You also have to enable each VM to replicate to another Hyper-V replica enabled host. Hyper-V Replica will be discussed in *Chapter 8, Implementing Live Migration and Replica*.

The configurations above are server configurations. You also have user configurations as follows:

- **Keyboard**: With the VM console open, you can choose where the Windows Key combination (such as WinKey + *Tab*) will take effect. In Windows Server 2012 R2, the default configuration is **Use on virtual machine**.

- **Mouse Release Key**: On the VM console for guest OS without Integration Services, the mouse will be locked inside the session. To release the mouse, you can choose a combination of keys that will release it. The default release key combination is *Ctrl* + *Alt* + LEFT ARROW.

- **Enhanced Session Mode**: If the **Enhanced Session Mode Policy** allows, you can configure to use or not the Enhanced Session Mode in VM connections.

- **Reset Check Boxes**: This option will reset all other configurations to their defaults.

These are the server and user configurations for a Hyper-V Server. There are other configurations that will be shown throughout the book. One thing that you have to remember is that if you are connected to multiple servers on the Hyper-V Manager, these configurations apply to only one server at a time. If you want to configure multiple servers through Hyper-V Manager, you will have to repeat the operation on each server that you connect to, on the left pane.

# Windows Server without a GUI

Windows Server without a GUI, or Server Core, was introduced in Windows Server 2008. The main goal for this feature is to have a server with a minimal attack surface, better performance, minimal updates, and reboots. But, you still may think: "If **Server Core** is a better option than Server with a GUI, why do so few use it?"

There are two main reasons:

- On Windows Server 2008 and 2008 R2, Server Core is an installation option. Even on Windows Server 2012 and 2012 R2, during installation, the wizard will prompt you to choose between the GUI or without the GUI:

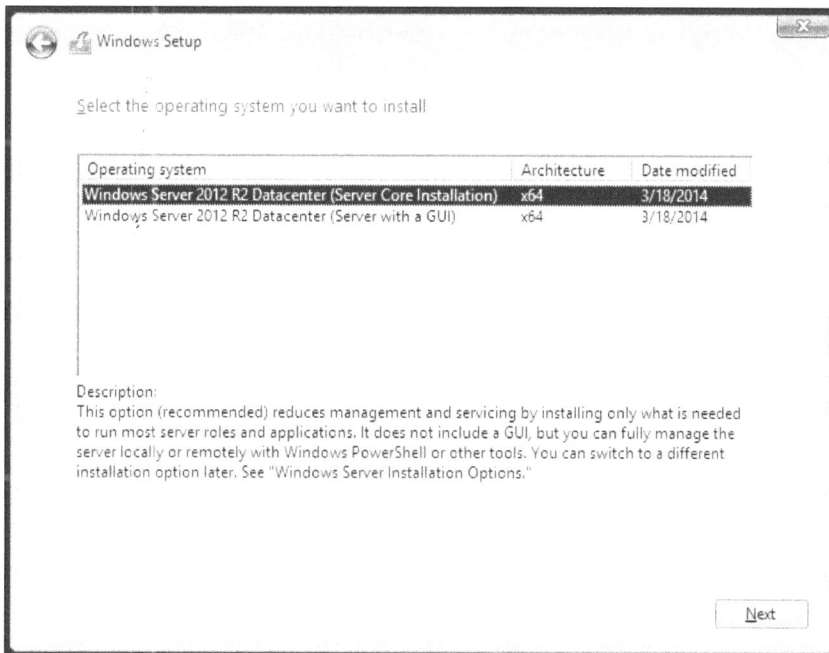

The problem with installing Server Core in the previous versions of Windows Server is that you cannot just enable the Graphical Interface. If you installed an option and wanted to change it later, you would have to reinstall the server.

> The description for the first (Server Core) option in the preceding screenshot reminds you that this is the recommended option.

- The other reason is that not all administrators are familiar with Server Core, which provides the Command Prompt and PowerShell only. In some cases, you can even install and configure the server, but in case of a problem, you might not have the necessary time to understand how to perform the necessary maintenance tasks on the server.

The good news is that in Windows Server 2012 and 2012 R2, you can enable or disable the GUI at any time. More than that, you have different stages for Server Core.

# Windows Server Core

As seen in the preceding screenshot, you can install the Windows Server as a Server Core. The other possibility is to install Windows Server with a GUI and remove the Graphical Interface when needed.

> You will have to restart the server to apply the configuration change, so plan your installation or configuration before going to production.

To remove the Graphical Interface, open **Server Manager**, click **Manage** on the top right corner and select **Remove Roles and Features**. In the wizard, click **Next >**, select the server you want to perform the operation on, click **Next >** and click **Next >** on Roles.

On the **Features** screen, expand **User Interfaces and Infrastructure**, as shown in the following screenshot:

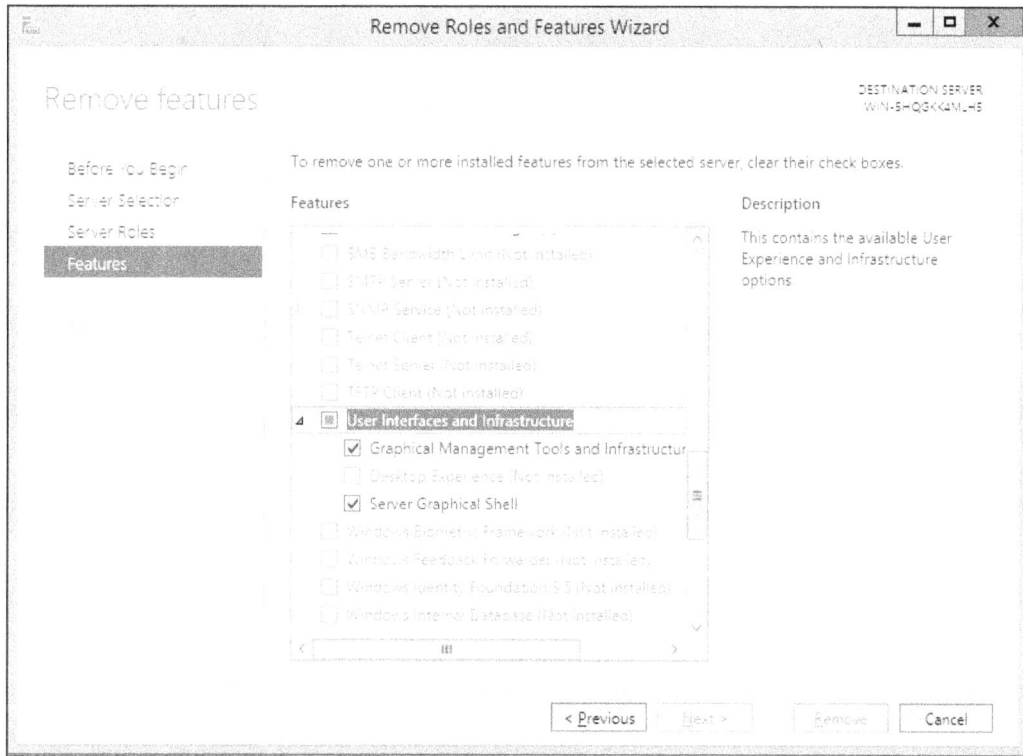

To remove all GUIs and turn your server into a Server Core, remove all options. You will note that when you remove the Graphical Interface, the Management Interface for Hyper-V, which is the Hyper-V Manager, is also removed. But if you look closely, you will note that the PowerShell module for Hyper-V is not. Proceed with the wizard to remove this as well. Remember to restart the server for the configuration to take effect.

When you remove all of the options, you will have the Command Prompt and PowerShell only. Take a look at how your server looks like on a Server Core:

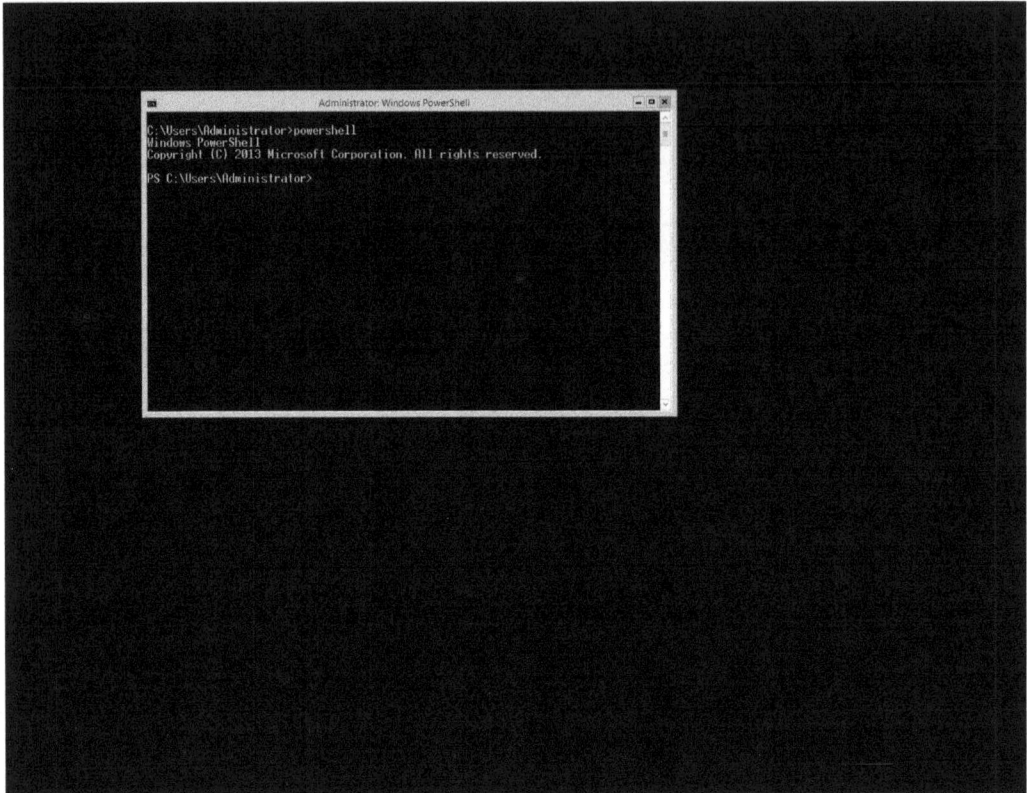

This is it. There is no Start menu (Start screen), no desktop, no IE, nothing. When you log on to the server, you see a Command Prompt window and from there, you can open PowerShell.

As the Hyper-V module for PowerShell is present, you can run Hyper-V commands to test as follows:

```
Get-VMHost | fl
```

The preceding command will show the configuration of the host server.

```
Get-VM | fl
```

The preceding command will show the VMs on the host, if any.

Throughout this book, you'll see many PowerShell commands for managing your host and VMs, so, for now, keep in mind that all administration can be done from the GUI or Server Core as well.

But managing your server from PowerShell can be a hard challenge if you need to get things done quickly. Therefore, the question is "Is there an easier way to manage a server without a GUI?"

# Windows Server Minimal Server Interface (MiniShell)

Windows Server MiniShell is a bridge between the Server Core and the GUI. The main difference between Server Core and MiniShell is that MiniShell also adds Server Manager and MMCs, like the Hyper-V Manager.

If you are on the GUI installation screen and want to enable MiniShell, remove the **Server Graphical Shell**, as explained in the *Windows Server Core* section in this chapter. You will have to restart your server.

But if you're running on a Server Core, you'll have to use PowerShell to enable MiniShell by issuing the following command:

```
Install-WindowsFeature -Name Server-Gui-Mgmt-Infra -Restart
```

> If you do not wish to restart the server right away, you can remove the -Restart option and run the Restart-Computer cmdlet later.

This will only enable MiniShell on top of the Server Core mode and restart the server. But there is something missing. When you removed the GUI, you also removed the Hyper-V Manager MMC, as the Server Core will not support it. To install Hyper-V Manager MMC on a MiniShell Server, you can either use Server Manager, as it is available on MiniShell, or through PowerShell:

```
Install-WindowsFeature -Name Hyper-V-Tools
```

After installing the Hyper-V Manager, your server will look similar to the following screenshot:

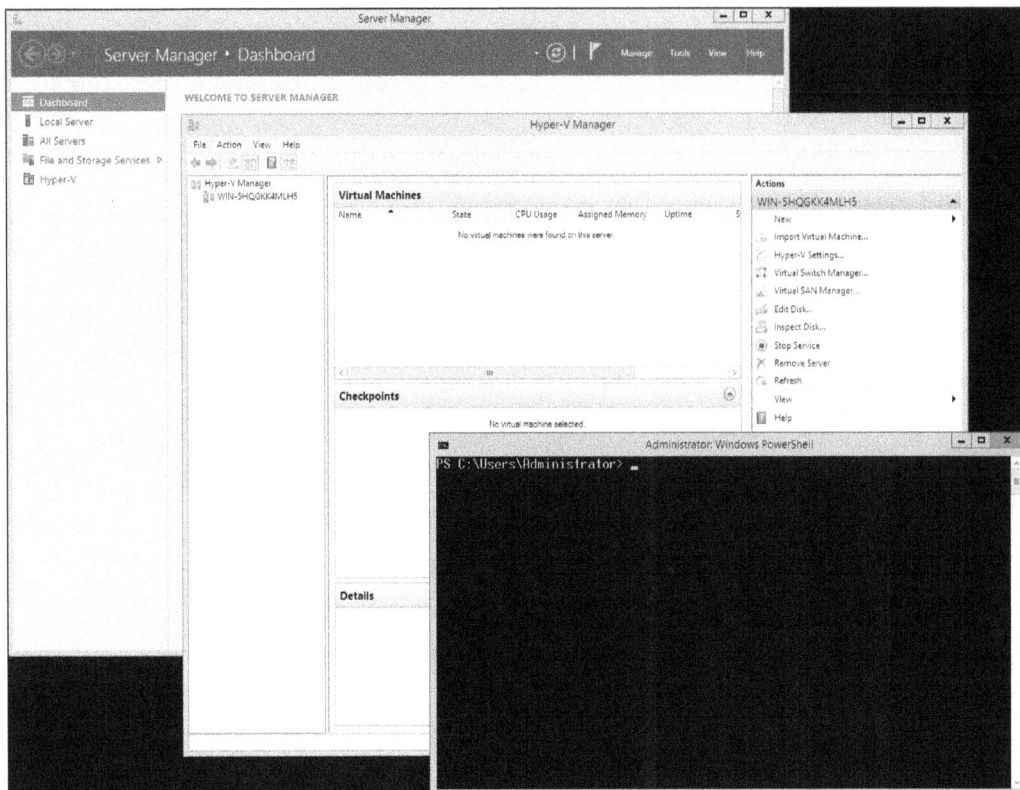

Remember that Server Core and MiniShell will support not only Hyper-V, but also other roles and features for Windows Server. However, as a recommendation, try to run the least amount of software on your Hyper-V Host, so you can have a better performance on your host and minimal attack surface.

With MiniShell, you have an optimal interface as you can use Server Manager to configure your server (or multiple servers), Hyper-V Manager to manage your Hyper-V Hosts, and VMs and PowerShell to perform all other operations and bulk operations.

However, the configuration above assumes that you installed Hyper-V on Server Manager. You might then ask "How to install Hyper-V without a GUI?"

To perform this operation on PowerShell, run the following command:

```
Install-WindowsFeature -Name Hyper-V -IncludeAllSubFeature -
IncludeManagementTools -Restart
```

The preceding command will install Hyper-V on the localhost and enable all sub features and the necessary management tools. After the installation, the server will restart automatically. You can choose to remove all the options for sub features, management tools, and the restart option, as you can run these options later, as explained in the earlier sections of this chapter.

When running Server Core or MiniShell, you might have to install the GUI in some cases. To do that, you can use Server Manager on MiniShell or PowerShell on both:

```
Install-WindowsFeature -Name Server-Gui-Shell -Restart
```

The preceding command will install, on Server Core, the GUI and the GUI components from MiniShell. If you run the command in MiniShell, the remaining components will be installed. The server will restart after the installation completes.

Remember that all the options are running on Windows Server. As said earlier, all other roles and features are available and must be updated in case of an update. If you don't want this administrative overhead, you can use Microsoft Hyper-V Server.

# Microsoft Hyper-V Server

Hyper-V Server was released as an option for admins to run their VMs on a robust virtualization platform, with all the available features at absolutely no cost. Licensing will be covered in the next chapter, but imagine the following scenario:

You are running Linux VMs on a Hyper-V Host. If you use Windows Server (GUI, Server Core or MiniShell), you must license your OS for the host, because Windows Server will always require a license. If you use Hyper-V Server, you can run without a Windows Server License. In this case, you can have all Hyper-V features and run as many VMs as your hardware is able to run (Microsoft supports 1024 VMs per host) at absolutely no cost.

Additionally, you can use the Hyper-V Server for any supported guest OS with multiple benefits:

- Minimal attack surface, as all other roles and features are not available (other features to support Hyper-V, such as Failover Clustering, are available)

- Less updates, as only Hyper-V updates, and few other updates, will apply for this OS

- More performance, as without a GUI, the server will run with less requirements

The installation of the Hyper-V Server is the same as a Windows Server. Like Windows Server, you must change the local administrator password. When you log on to the server, it'll feel like Server Core, with the major difference being that Hyper-V Server will present Sconfig for the initial configuration, as shown in the following screenshot:

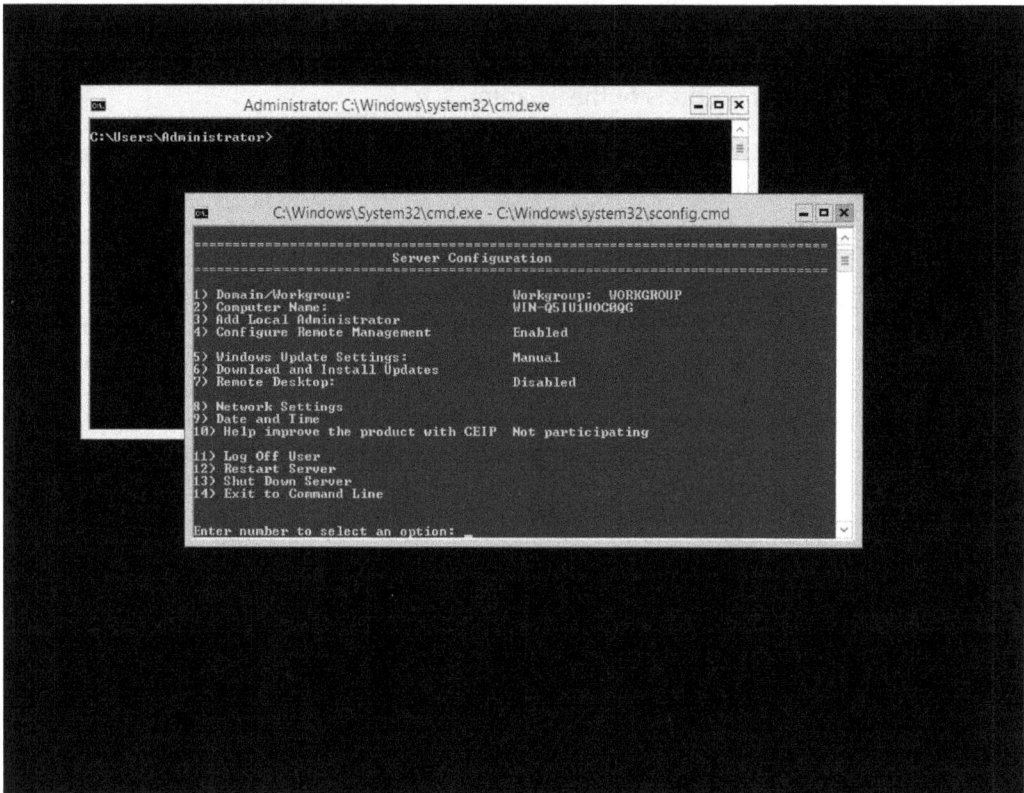

Sconfig is a command line tool that will help you to configure your server without an interface. With Sconfig, you can join a Domain/Workgroup, change Computer Name, enable or disable Remote Management, change Windows Update Settings to Automatic or Manual, force the download and installation of updates, enable or disable Remote Desktop for this server, change Network Settings such as IP configuration, change Date and Time, and other configurations for the local server. To open Sconfig at any time, just type sconfig at the Command Prompt and press *Enter*.

The difference between the Hyper-V Server and Windows Server is that Hyper-V is already enabled on Hyper-V Server, so you do not have to install it. The administration, on the other hand, is the same for PowerShell commands. Remember, though, that Hyper-V Server does not have the option of enabling MiniShell or GUI. All the administration must be made through PowerShell.

PowerShell is an extremely powerful tool, but using it for every task can be painful. To avoid this, you can also install all the management tools on a client machine.

# Remote Server Administration Tools (RSAT) and Hyper-V Manager for Windows

RSAT is a set of components for managing a server locally or remotely. When you install a role or feature on a server through Server Manager, it will suggest that you install the Management Tools, or you can install it from Server Manager later. From PowerShell, you can include the `-IncludeManagementTools` option on the installation command, or use the `Install -WindowsFeature` command to install the Management Tools later.

But if you're running Hyper-V Server only, you don't have this option, as Hyper-V Server doesn't have Server Manager or MMC (Hyper-V Manager). In this case, you can install RSAT, Hyper-V Manager, and Hyper-V module for PowerShell for Windows 8.1 and manage your servers remotely.

RSAT is not native to Windows Client; you can download it from `http://www.microsoft.com/en-us/download/details.aspx?id=39296`.

RSAT is a standalone update for Windows 8.1, and, after installing it, you have to enable the consoles that you want to use. To do that, open **Programs and Features** from Start screen and select **Turn Windows features on or off**. On the **Windows Features** page, you can select the necessary components. For the Hyper-V Manager and Hyper-V modules for PowerShell, expand **Hyper-V** and select the necessary components. For all other components, expand **Remote Server Administration Tools** and select the components you need:

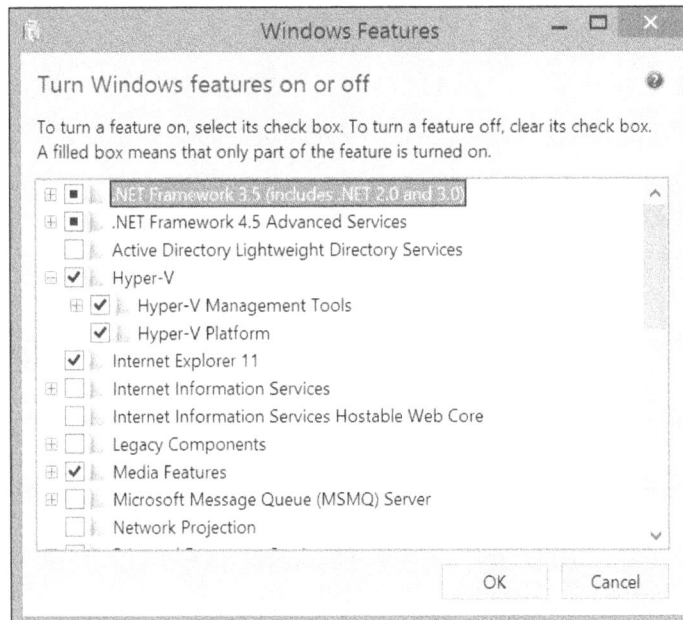

With that, you can have on your Windows Client the same Management Tools as on Windows Server: Server Manager, Hyper-V Manager, and Hyper-V module for PowerShell. Remember that you'll have to connect to the server when using any of these tools. For Server Manager, click **Manage** at the top right corner and select **Add Servers** to add the servers you want to manage remotely.

In Hyper-V Server, repeat the steps as explained earlier in the *Hyper-V Manager* subsection of the *Windows Server with a GUI section* in this chapter. For PowerShell, you'll have to indicate the destination server every time you run a command. For example, to list the VMs on a Remote Host, give the following command:

```
Get-VM -ComputerName HostName
```

Another important aspect of Hyper-V Manager and RSAT is that the client used must be compatible with the server. The following table lists the compatibility of each client:

| Client Version | Server Compatible Version |
| --- | --- |
| Windows 8.1 | Windows Server 2012 R2 |
| Windows 8 | Windows Server 2012 |
| Windows 7 | Windows Server 2008 R2 |
| Windows Vista | Windows Server 2008 |

It is possible to use a different version on a server or client, but some features may not work properly or may not be available. During the configuration of Hyper-V Manager for Windows 8.1, you might have seen that Hyper-V is also available for Windows Client. This is true, but there are some considerations.

# Hyper-V for Windows

Although Hyper-V Manager is the same on Windows and Windows Server, there are different requirements for running the Hyper-V platform, and some features are not available.

As discussed in *Chapter 1*, *Getting Started with Hyper-V Architecture and Components*, Hyper-V on Windows 8 and 8.1 requires a processor feature called SLAT. This is not a requirement for Hyper-V on Windows Server, although it is highly recommended; in Windows 8 and 8.1, it is obligatory.

Following are the features that are not available on Windows Client:

- RemoteFX is not capable of virtualizing GPUs
- Live Migration and Hyper-V Replica
- Virtual Fiber Channel (**Virtual SAN Manager**)
- 32-bit SR-IOV
- Shared `.vhdx`
- Virtual Network Adapter moving from wireless to wired connection

Keep in mind that Hyper-V on Windows 8 and 8.1 was designed for running test and POC scenarios. With Hyper-V on Windows Client, you can run a VM of a different guest OS, export a VM from Hyper-V on Windows Client, and import it to Windows Server, and many other applications, except running a production environment of servers on your laptop or desktop environment.

Now that you have your host up and running, it's important to understand that Microsoft will have some recommendations based on the configuration of your host and environment. The question now is "Is my Hyper-V Host configured correctly?"

# Microsoft Best Practices Analyzer (BPA)

Microsoft BPA is a native tool on the Windows Server that can be started from Server Manager or through PowerShell. With BPA, you can scan your server to check the configuration of multiple components and verify their compliance with Microsoft recommendations.

BPA will analyze the following components:

- Configuration
- Operation
- Policy

After analysis, the report can show three possible states for each validation:

- **Information**: In this case, BPA validated the compliance, and your server meets the required configuration. No action needed.
- **Warning**: In this case, BPA verified that the item is not fully compliant, but the item is not critical. For example: a Hyper-V Host should be domain-joined. This is a recommendation, not mandatory. Check the warning, and verify if it applies to your environment.
- **Error**: In this case, BPA verified that a compliance rule is not met and the configuration is critical/important for the host. The recommended action it to change the configuration or apply the necessary correction to meet the compliance rule.

To start the BPA scan, open **Server Manager** and select **Hyper-V** on the left pane. On the right pane, select the Hyper-V Host where you want to run the BPA scan and scroll down to **BEST PRACTICES ANALYZER**. At the top right corner of the BPA window, click **TASKS** and click Start BPA Scan. Wait for the process to finish.

> After clicking **Start BPA Scan**, the BPA wizard will ask for the servers you want to run the BPA against. It is possible to run the BPA on multiple servers at a time.

When finished, the BPA window will show the following:

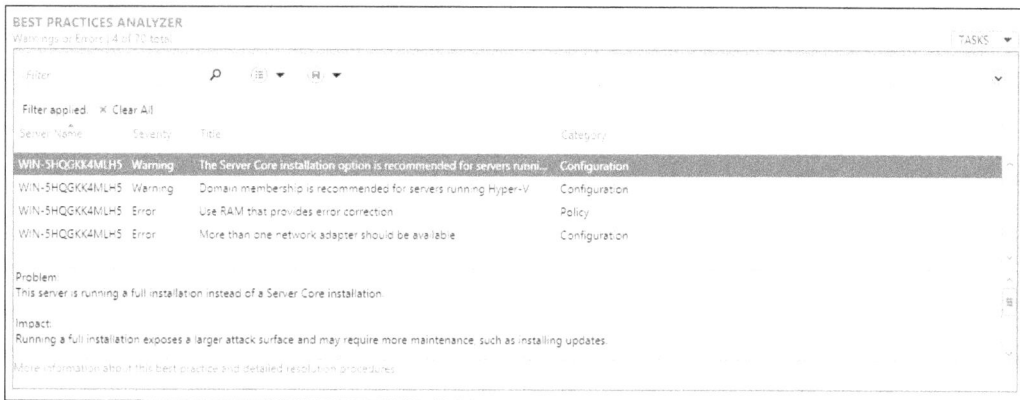

As you can see from the preceding screenshot, only **Warning or Error** logs are shown. You can see the other logs by clicking on the list icon and selecting **Compliant results**. The link at the bottom will take you to the Microsoft website with more details about the compliance rule and possible resolutions for each rule.

You can also run BPA on PowerShell, which is ideal for Server Core. To do that, run the following command:

```
Invoke-BpaModel -ComputerName HostName -ModelId
Microsoft/Windows/Hyper-V -RepositoryPath "C:\BPA"
```

The preceding command will run the Hyper-V BPA process on the localhost and save the results in the C:\BPA folder (the folder must exist, as BPA will not create it).

To show the results, run the following command:

```
Get-BpaResult -ComputerName HostName -ModelId
Microsoft/Windows/Hyper-V -RepositoryPath "C:\BPA"
```

The preceding command will show all the results from the report saved in the C:\ BPA folder. The problem with this approach is that all results are shown and that makes it difficult to understand the priorities. To view only specific results, you can filter the results by running the following command:

```
Get-BpaResult -ComputerName HostName -ModelId
Microsoft/Windows/Hyper-V -RepositoryPath "C:\BPA" -filter
Noncompliant
```

The preceding command will filter the `Noncompliant` results, making it easier to understand what should be analyzed right away. You can also run a variation of the preceding command, filtering by type:

```
Get-BpaResult -ComputerName HostName -ModelId
Microsoft/Windows/Hyper-V -RepositoryPath "C:\BPA" | Where-Object
{$_.Severity -eq "Warning"}
Get-BpaResult -ComputerName HostName -ModelId
Microsoft/Windows/Hyper-V -RepositoryPath "C:\BPA" | Where-Object
{$_.Severity -eq "Error"}
```

In the preceding commands, the first command will show only the results with **Warning Severity**. The second command will show results with **Error Severity**. Another option is to export the results to a CSV file for later inspection and use:

```
Get-BpaResult -ComputerName HostName -ModelId
Microsoft/Windows/Hyper-V -RepositoryPath "C:\BPA" | Export-Csv
C:\bpa\results.csv
```

As you can see, there are multiple ways to use BPA and verify if your host is correctly configured. But there is one topic that is always a cause of some confusion — antivirus.

# Antivirus – to be or not to be?

You may have noted that BPA did not point out as an error that an antivirus wasn't running. This is actually because the Hyper-V module of BPA will focus only on Hyper-V settings. But the question remains "Should I install an antivirus software on my Hyper-V Host?" Actually, the question is not complete. You should also question yourself if you should install an antivirus on your VMs. To understand that, let's take a look at the following a diagram from *Chapter 1, Getting Started with Hyper-V Architecture and Components*:

| | | | | User Mode Ring 3 |
|---|---|---|---|---|
| WMI Provider / VM Services / Applications | Applications | Applications | Applications | User Mode Ring 3 |
| Windows Server or Hyper-V Server — Windows Kernel / VSP / Drivers — **VMBus** | Integration Components installed OS — Windows Kernel / VSC — **VMBus** | No Integration Components Installed OS — Emulation | Linux VM — Linux VSC — **VMBus** — Hypercall Adapter | Kernel Mode Ring 0 |
| Windows Hypervisor | | | | Ring -1 |
| Hardware "Designed for Windows" | | | | |

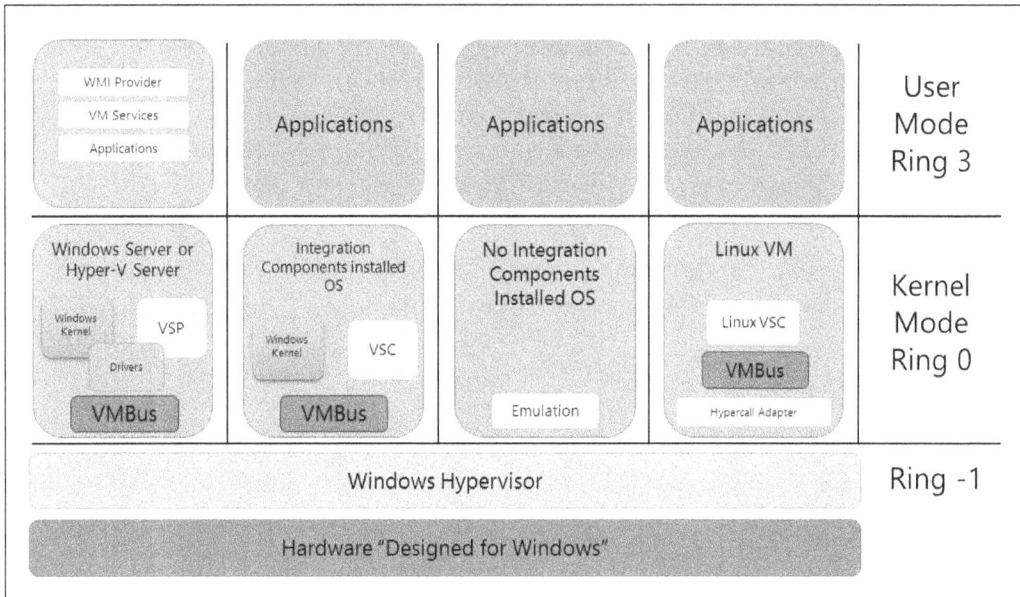

As explained in *Chapter 1, Getting Started with Hyper-V Architecture and Components*, the main function of a Hypervisor is to isolate the partitions, parent and child. That means that if you install an antivirus software on any partition, the antivirus software will be able to scan only the partition it is installed in. Also, the parent partition is running an OS in the same way as the child partition. However, the parent partition has no access to the child partitions at all.

Having said that, you must install an antivirus on the parent partition, because the OS running on the parent partition is exposed to regular malwares like any other OS. It is true that Hyper-V Server has a minor attack surface and some companies run it without an antivirus software and have never run through problems. Nevertheless, Microsoft recommends installing an antivirus, even on Hyper-V Server. The good news is that since Windows Server 2012, Windows Defender works as an anti-malware and antivirus software, so you don't have to worry about it on the host. On the guest OS, if you're running an OS other than Windows Server 2012 and 2012 R2, or Windows 8 and 8.1, you should install an antivirus on this guest OS.

In some cases, your company may decide that you should use a specific antivirus software. For most of the recent versions of antivirus, you'll have no problems. However, in some cases, you might find that your software is not compatible with Hyper-V. You can find that for a few reasons, such as slow performance on the host and/or VM, Hyper-V files in quarantine and the VMs stopping for no apparent reason. To avoid this, let's understand how Hyper-V works when a VM is up and what can be done to avoid antivirus problems.

When Hyper-V is running, a Windows service is started. The service is **Hyper-V Virtual Machine Management** or vmms.exe as shown in the following screenshot:

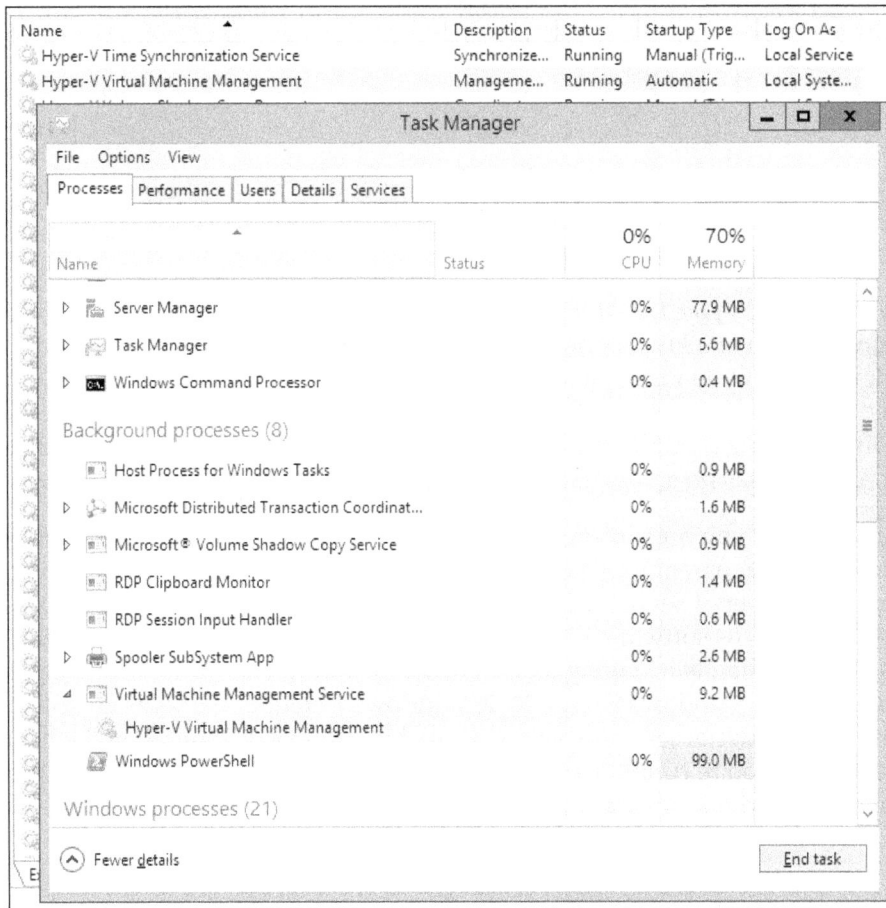

To avoid problems with the antivirus, you should configure an exception for this service on your antivirus software, so that the antivirus will not stop Hyper-V Service.

Another service problem occurs when you start a VM. The virtual BIOS for the VM will run a service called VMWP.exe or **Virtual Machine Worker Process**. Each VM will have its own process. In some cases, your antivirus might stop this service, which will stop the VM inadvertently. Include the process on the exclusion list of the antivirus.

Finally, yet importantly, your antivirus should understand the VM files so that the antivirus will never put these files in quarantine. A VM is composed of five file types:

| File Type | Description |
|---|---|
| XML | This file holds the configuration details and is always named by the VM GUID. When you create a Checkpoint, another XML file is created, one per VM and one per Checkpoint. |
| BIN | This file is used when the VM or snapshot is in a saved state. |
| VSV | This file holds the configuration for devices of the VM. |
| VHDX / VHD | This is the file that represents the Virtual Disk for the VM. Windows Server 2012 introduced the VHDX file type, which will be discussed in detail in *Chapter 5, Managing Storage*. |
| AVHDX / AVHD | This is a differencing disk created when you create a Checkpoint. Each Checkpoint will have its own AVHDX disk. All changes on the VM will be made to the differencing disk in use. When you delete a snapshot, a merge is made between the AVHDX and the VHDX disks. |

If, for any reason, your antivirus understands that one of these files is a potential malware, and puts the file in quarantine, the VM will stop, and, in some cases, can crash the disk file to an unrecoverable state. To avoid this, you can exclude the files, or the whole VM path, from the scan.

All of the configurations that we just discussed are host configurations. You still need to install an antivirus software on the guest OS of the VM. This is because of the isolation between the partitions. In some cases, some companies use an antivirus on the parent partition and the antivirus scans the disk file of the VM for malware. This approach is incorrect for the following two reasons:

* For this approach to work correctly, the VM must be in a paused state or off. If the VM is on and an antivirus starts scanning the disk file, the VM can run slow or even crash.

* The antivirus on the host won't be able to scan the VM memory, which can be infected by some malwares.

In a nutshell, if you use Windows Server 2012 or 2012 R2, and Windows 8 or 8.1, you don't have to install an antivirus, as it is native to these Windows versions. In case you're not using these versions, or you have a third-party antivirus software, be sure to configure all of the above.

Now that you know how to use the BPA, and you know for sure if your antivirus is not going to cause troubles to Hyper-V, there is one last important point for you to be good-to-go with your Hyper-V Hosts — **Hyper-V Limits**.

# Hyper-V Hosts and VM Limits

Hyper-V Limits is important for two reasons:

- Host configuration
- VM configuration

This is because you might be in a situation where high scale is important, but you have to be sure that you do not exceed the limits to which Microsoft will support your environment. There are multiple aspects of limits for a virtualization environment. Let's take a look at some of the Hyper-V Limits for the host:

| Component | Maximum |
|---|---|
| Logical Processors (LPs) | 320 (Same as Windows Server) |
| Virtual Processors (VPs) per LPs | No ratio imposed by Hyper-V |
| Running VMs per host | 1024 |
| VPs per host | 2048 |
| Memory | 4 TB |
| Nodes per Cluster | 64 |

In previous versions of Windows Server, these limits were extremely low as compared to the limits preceding table. However, even with these numbers, it is important to keep in mind that your host has some requirements to run. Hyper-V Server has a minimum memory requirement of 512 MB of RAM, dedicated to the host OS. Windows Server has a minimum requirement of 1 GB to 2 GB, depending on the installation option. You also have to consider other applications running on your server, such as a management application, backup application, and so on.

Another important aspect is that, in the previous versions of Hyper-V, a VP versus LP ratio should be considered for Microsoft to support the environment. This ratio is not mandatory, but, again, it can influence the host and VM performance.

the following table shows VM Limits:

| Component | Maximum |
|---|---|
| VPs per VM | 64 |
| Memory per VM (vRAM) | 1 TB |
| Virtual disk capacity | 64 TB per VHDX / 2 TB per VHD |
| Virtual IDE controller | 2 |
| Virtual IDE disks per controller | 2 |
| Virtual SCSI controllers | 4 |
| Virtual SCSI disks per controller | 64 |
| Checkpoints per VM | 50 |
| Virtual network adapters per VM | 12 |

Some of the numbers indicated in the preceding table will be discussed in the following chapters. However, it is worth pointing out some things regarding VM Limits:

- Although the maximum number of VPs and vRAM on a single VM is absurd, it is important to always determine the requirements for the applications running on the VM to configure the VM accordingly.

- In some cases, the guest OS might not support that number of VPs and vRAM, plan your VM before configuring it to avoid wasting hardware on the Host.

- You can have 64 disks per SCSI controller, with a total of 256 disks of 64 TB (VHDX) each. You'll probably run out of physical storage before virtual storage, so plan accordingly.

- If you need more than 64 TB of storage space per disk, you can do that by directly attaching a disk to a VM. There is no limit imposed by Hyper-V for the size of the disk in this case.

- Virtual SCSI controller requires Integration Components to be installed on the guest OS.

- Although you can have up to 50 Checkpoints per VM, the performance can be reduced when using multiple Checkpoints. In addition, Checkpoints are recommended for testing purposes, and should be deleted right after the test is done.

- You can have a total of 12 virtual network adapters, but only 8 are regular network adapters, which require Integration Components, and 4 Legacy network adapters, which do not require IC, but have several limitations, which will be discussed in *Chapter 4, Managing Networking*.

Planning your VM is important so you can have the optimal performance, while keeping support from Microsoft and a third-party software vendor. For a detailed list of Hyper-V Limits, check the updated URL at `http://technet.microsoft.com/en-us/library/jj680093.aspx`.

# Summary

In this chapter, you were able to understand the differences between a Hyper-V Server and Windows Server. Moreover, you understood the difference between a Windows Server with a GUI and without a GUI, and the importance of planning your deployment. You are now able to deploy Hyper-V on all of the scenarios that we discussed and manage it locally and remotely.

You now understand the difference between Hyper-V on Windows Server and Windows Client version, and how to use Windows Client to manage remote servers in a centralized manner.

Additionally, you now have the necessary information to install an antivirus or use the native one on your virtualization host and VMs, and will plan your host accordingly so you can maintain Microsoft Support.

In the next chapter, we will cover licensing your virtualization environment to meet the needs of your company for server and client virtualization.

# 3

# Licensing a Virtualization Environment with Hyper-V

Licensing a virtualization environment has never been an easy task, either because of the Microsoft licensing model, or because of the applications running on a virtual environment. But when virtualization became popular, and more and more companies started to virtualize their workloads, vendors started facilitating the licensing model for virtualization. Microsoft followed this trend, and in the Windows Server 2012, Microsoft changed the licensing model for Windows Server completely, directly impacting virtualization.

In this chapter we will cover the following topics:

- Virtualization licensing in the early days of Windows Server 2008 and 2008 R2
- Virtualization licensing on Windows Server 2012 and 2012 R2
- Benefits of Software Assurance on virtualization
- Hyper-V Replica impact on virtualization
- Licensing Linux VMs on Hyper-V
- Licensing models for **Virtual Desktop Infrastructure** (VDI)

Before we go through any details on licensing itself, it is important to understand some of the terms that will be used throughout this chapter:

| Terms | Description |
| --- | --- |
| Processor | The physical processor installed on the host machine. Microsoft does not count cores or hyper threads from a licensing perspective. |
| OSE | Operating System Environment. OSE is the environment where you install an OS: virtual (guest OS) or physical. |

| Terms | Description |
|---|---|
| Hypervisor | In this context, Hypervisor is the software installed on the host machine. It may be the OS itself or a software running on the OS installed on the host machine. |
| Software Assurance (SA) | SA is an SKU available on some Microsoft Contracts that have multiple benefits. Some of these benefits will influence the final license of the virtualization environment. |

If you're new to Hyper-V, you probably don't know it, but licensing a virtualization environment with Hyper-V prior to Windows Server 2012 was a bit confusing. But one thing remains the same: in a virtualization environment, you do not license the host; you have to license the VM. To begin the conversation, let's understand how licensing used to work before Windows Server 2012.

# Licensing a virtual environment prior to Windows Server 2012

It is important to understand how licensing used to work before Windows Server 2012, as understanding it will show how easy it is today to license your environment. In addition, if you come to manage a legacy environment one day, you will be able to verify if the licensing for this environment is correct.

One aspect of Windows Server 2008 and 2008 R2 that is different from Windows Server 2012 and 2012 R2 is that 2008 and 2008 R2 had more editions available for purchase. At that time, you were able to license the following editions:

- Standard Edition
- Enterprise Edition
- Datacenter Edition

There are actually other editions for 2008 and 2008 R2, but they focus on specific scenarios such as **Small Business Server** Edition and **Foundation** Edition, and will not be covered here.

One important aspect of Windows Server 2008 and 2008 R2 is that these editions had differences between them, not only from the virtualization licensing perspective, but also on the features and hardware capacity. For example, **Failover Clustering** was only available for Enterprise and Datacenter Editions. Standard had support for only 32 GB of RAM. Datacenter Edition did not have the Remote Desktop role, but, on the other hand, was the one that supported the highest hardware configuration. In short, to purchase the correct edition, you had to check what feature and hardware configuration matched the needs of your company.

After understanding the minimum requirements regarding features and hardware support, you had to check if the given version had the correct number of licenses for the VMs running in your environment, but there is a trick difference in the way you apply the license on the host. Standard and Enterprise were applied considering the physical server, the box on which it was licensed. Datacenter, on the other hand, was applied considering the number of physical processors on the host.

# Standard and Enterprise Editions of Windows Server 2008 and 2008 R2

As the Standard and Enterprise Editions were applied for the host, the box where you're running the Hypervisor, you did not have to count the processors. It was a facilitator for small and medium companies that run a few number of VMs.

The difference between the Standard and Enterprise Editions is that Standard licensed only one instance of a Windows Server VM, and Enterprise licensed up to four Windows Server VMs.

As you can see, Standard was not exactly focused on virtualization. But, in some cases, is still worth it. Imagine the following environment: you have a virtualization server and you run only two Windows Server VMs. In this case, you were able to buy two licenses of Windows Server Standard which allowed you to virtualize those two machines.

However, there are other caveats in this model. The Standard Edition will give you actually two OSE instances, one for the VM and one for the host machine. It means that you can install the same license two times, but keep in mind that the host machine can run only the virtualization stack and nothing more. If you install any other software on the host OS, you lose the right to run a VM with the same license. In the previous example, if you have two licenses of the Windows Server Standard Edition, and you install another software on the host, you'll be able to license only one VM OSE and the host OSE. You could buy another license of the Standard Edition, but then you get to a moment where the Enterprise Edition is better.

The Enterprise Edition was the so-called entry level for virtualization. This is because the Enterprise Edition allowed you to run up to four OSEs, plus the host OSE. It means that you can have four VMs with the Windows Server and still install Windows Server on the Host, with the same concept of using it for virtualization purposes only. In fact, in most cases, acquiring an Enterprise Edition had more benefits than Standard, because, even if you don't have more than two VMs, you are better prepared for scaling in the future.

To summarize the Standard and Enterprise licensing on the Windows Server 2008 and 2008 R2 , Standard will allow you to license only one VM OSE and the host OSE. Enterprise would allow you to run up to four VM OSEs and the host OSE.

# Datacenter Edition of Windows Server 2008 and 2008 R2

Different from Standard and Enterprise, the Datacenter Edition on Windows Server 2008 and 2008 R2 was the only one licensed per processor. Each license of the Datacenter Edition would license up to two processors. However, the real benefit of the Datacenter Edition was that it would license an unlimited number of Windows Server VMs.

The Datacenter Edition was an option for the companies that were running virtual environments with high consolidation, on host servers. With that, you only had to account for the number of processors per server and verify the number of licenses that each host required. If a virtualization server had four processors, you had to buy two licenses, but, with that, you were able to run as many VMs as the host was able to run.

Although you can run as many VMs you want per host, Hyper-V on Windows Server 2008 R2 supports 384 VMs per host.

That model was perfect for companies that did not want to worry about licensing, as all you had to do was account for the number of processors per host and licensing these processors.

With that, it was clear to customers that licensing a virtualization environment was not an easy task. It required some help from the licensing partner, and, before acquiring the Windows Server License, it was necessary to verify multiple details like: which features are available on each edition? Which of these features does the company really need? How many VMs is the company going to run on each host? Is it better to license per host or per processor? To summarize the licensing perspective, let's have a look at the following table:

| Edition | Licensed by | Processors covered | Editions allowed to install on VMs | Number of VMs licensed |
|---|---|---|---|---|
| Standard | Host | - | Standard only | 1 |
| Enterprise | Host | - | Standard and Enterprise | 2 |
| Datacenter | Processor | 2 | Standard, Enterprise and Datacenter | Unlimited |

With the release of the Windows Server 2012, and the new version of Hyper-V, it was clear that virtualization was a point of no return. With that, Microsoft radically changed its licensing model on Windows Server 2012 and 2012 R2 to make it easy for the customers to license their environment.

# Licensing a virtual environment with Windows Server 2012 and 2012 R2

With Windows Server 2012 and 2012 R2, Microsoft decided to focus its licensing all over virtualization. Of course, you can choose not to virtualize, but there are benefits in the virtual environments.

The first big change was the retirement of the Enterprise Edition, leaving the Standard and Datacenter Editions as the available choices. Again, there are other options for small businesses, but they are not the focus here. With only two options available, customers have now a simple scenario to choose.

The other big change is that the Standard and Datacenter Editions are exactly the same regarding technical features. It means that all features are available on both editions, such as cluster, RDS, and so on. Also, both editions have the same support for hardware. In conclusion, the only difference (apart from licensing) between the Standard and Datacenter Editions is the Windows Server logo.

The question you might have now is: if both versions are exactly the same, why will a customer choose one over the other? I'm glad you asked.

The most impacting change on the Windows Server 2012 and 2012 R2, besides the number of editions available, is that Standard will license up to two VM OSEs, and Datacenter will license an unlimited number of VM OSEs. Moreover, both editions are licensed by the processor, covering up to two processors for each license, which facilitates the accounting of the servers in the environment.

Basically, all you have to ask is: is my company going to have a virtual or a physical environment? If the answer is physical, you can choose to use the Standard Edition as it will have all the features and will license the server to run with all the features and scalability available on the Windows Server 2012 and 2012 R2. If the answer is virtual, then the best choice is the Datacenter Edition. This is because all you have to do is check the number of processors on the hosts and buy the necessary licenses for them. Having a Datacenter license on the host allows you to scale without problems with a number of VMs. You just have to make sure that the number of licenses covers the number of processors. Let's take a look at some scenarios.

# Virtualizing with Standard or Datacenter Editions

The Standard Edition, as the Datacenter, will cover up to two processors per server. In the case where you have a virtualization server with only one processor, you can associate the Standard license to this server. In the future, you can add a new processor to the server without acquiring a new license because the Standard license associated with the server is already in place. If you add three new processors, the server now has four processors and you have to buy one new Standard license for this server. On the other hand, with only one license, you can have two VMs with the licensed Windows Server. With two Standard licenses, you can have four VMs with the Windows Server.

> Keep in mind that for licensing the Windows Server, Microsoft count processors as sockets and cores are not considered. In case you have a processor with one socket and four cores, it is still only one processor. You can have two processors with four cores each, and it will still be accounted as two processors.

In *Chapter 2, Deploying Hyper-V Hosts*, we discussed that you have the option of installing the Hyper-V Server as the OS for the host, but in some cases, you still need Windows Server. The point that causes more confusion is when you have a Windows Server installed on the host. That's because with Windows Server and all its available features, some companies end up using the host server for additional purposes, like File Server, DHCP, and others. This is not recommended, as the Windows Server OSE installed on the host machine should be dedicated to virtualization if you want to make use of the two OSEs available for the VMs.

Another example of licensing a server is when you have a host with two processors, which requires only one license, but you have six VMs running Windows Server. In this case, although the processor count requires only one license, you actually need six licenses because of the VMs.

As the Standard and Datacenter Editions have the same technical limits, you can simply associate Standard licenses to a host to comply with the number of VMs running Windows Server. However, as you can imagine, at some point there is no benefit in using the Standard Edition. As we are not covering the actual price of each license, it's recommended to verify if your company has any valid contract and what the prices is of the Standard and the Datacenter Editions. This price may vary because of the Volume Licensing benefits that each company has. Nevertheless, at some point, when you reach an $X$ number of VMs you will find that the Datacenter Edition is cheaper than the Standard.

That's because, as mentioned earlier, the Datacenter Edition requires you to just check the number of processors of the host. For example, if a host has eight processors, you will need four licenses of the Datacenter Edition, but you can run as many VMs as the host is able to run.

> Hyper-V on the Windows Server 2012 and 2012 R2 supports up to 1024 VMs per host.

At this point, I believe you are able to see how easy licensing a virtual environment with Hyper-V and Windows Server VMs is. To summarize:

- Windows Server 2012 and 2012 R2 have two editions for virtual environments: Standard and Datacenter
- Standard and Datacenter have the same features available and support the same hardware limits
- Standard covers up to two processors and up to two VMs with Windows Server, while Datacenter covers up to two processors with no limits of VMs running Windows Server

One important aspect of both the editions is that the edition you purchase will allow you to run the edition itself and the edition lower. For example, if you buy the Standard Edition, you can run the Standard Edition on the VMs, but if you buy the Datacenter Edition, you can run the Datacenter or the Standard Editions on the VMs. This is a general rule that comes since Windows Server 2008 and 2008 R2 when it would make a difference to run a different edition. On Windows Server 2012, it is still valid but makes no effect. Let's have a look at the following table that summarizes all this:

| Edition | Licensed by | Processors covered | Editions allowed to install on VMs | Number of VMs licensed |
|---|---|---|---|---|
| Standard | Processor | 2 | Standard only | 2 |
| Datacenter | Processor | 2 | Standard and Datacenter | Unlimited |

As expected, Datacenter is always the easy way, and also the recommended way to license a virtual environment with Windows Server. That's because the Standard Edition can bring many questions. Let's have a look at some of them.

# Specific scenarios with Standard Edition

The Standard Edition can be used for virtualization without any restrictions from the technical perspective, but on the licensing side there are some caveats that you should know about before going to production. The first question you might have with what was said earlier is: if the Standard Edition allows only two VMs per host, and I'm able to move the VMs between them, what about the licensing in this scenario? To understand this point, take a look at the following scenario:

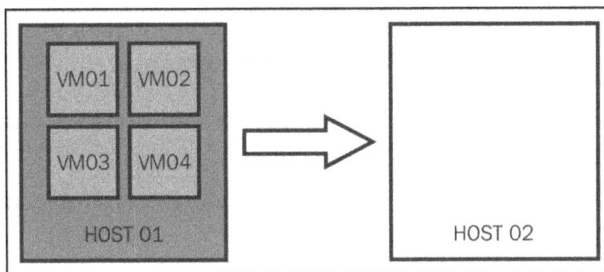

In the scenario depicted in the preceding diagram, **Host 01** has four processors and four VMs running Windows Server. You then associate two licenses of the Windows Server 2012 R2 Standard Edition. You're all set, but after some time, your company acquires a new server named **Host 02**. This server also has four processors. You install the Hyper-V Server on this host. Right now, there is absolutely no need to associate a license to this host, but when you move one VM from **Host 01** to **Host 02**, you have to license **Host 02** as well. In this case, you will need two licenses of the Windows Server 2012 R2 Standard Edition, because of the processors. This is the case where both servers are working together. It is valid for a cluster or a standalone environment. However, there is another case. See the following figure:

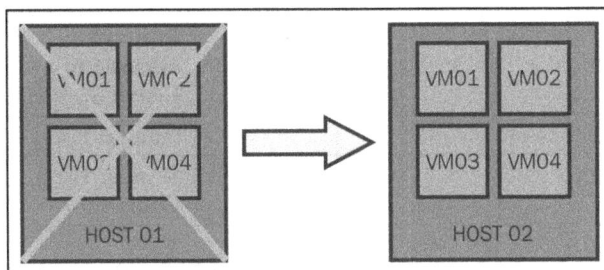

In the preceding case, your company bought **Host 02** to replace **Host 01**, either because **Host 01** presented a hardware failure or because it is obsolete. In both cases, you don't have to buy a new license of the Windows Server 2012 R2 Standard Edition. In this case you can re-associate the licenses which you already have to this new host. Keep in mind that this is valid only if you retire **Host 01** and don't use it again.

This case is valid only if the license you bought to **Host 01** is not an OEM license. An OEM license is cheaper than the regular licenses but OEM license locks the license to the host and you cannot re-associate that license to another host.

At this point, you understand the basic concepts of licensing a virtual environment with Hyper-V for Windows Server. Notice how I discuss Windows Server all the time. This is important for two other scenarios that you might have imagined already: what about Windows Client and other non-Microsoft OS?

Before we go into that, there is one missing piece on the host that we already mentioned in *Chapter 2, Deploying Hyper-V Hosts*, but now we can go into details.

# Virtualization host licensing and its impacts

This is the most common question: if I'm licensing the Windows Server to run VMs with Windows Server, do I have to install the same Windows Server on the host?

The simple answer is no. As already discussed in *Chapter 2, Deploying Hyper-V Hosts*, you should consider the option that best fits your company's needs. Besides technical aspects, there is one important licensing point to consider.

As you know, you should always consider the Hyper-V Server as the first option for your virtualization host. However, Hyper-V Server is a free OS. It still includes all the Hyper-V features, but is different from the Windows Server as it does not include any Windows Server usage rights. Let's see an example.

Following what you learned so far, you checked all the prerequisites for your virtualization host and you concluded that the Hyper-V Server is a suitable option for your company. You then install the Hyper-V Server on a host with two processors. On the other hand, the Hyper-V Server does not include any virtualization rights for the Windows Server.

In the first scenario, your company wants to run four VMs with the Windows Server 2012 R2. In this case, you can run the Hyper-V Server on the host and associate the necessary licenses to the host to run the number of VMs you wish; in this case, two licenses of the Windows Server Standard or one license of the Windows Server Datacenter.

See that you're not installing the Windows Server that you have the license for on the host. You're associating these licenses to this host. This association allows you to cover the processors and run these Windows Server OSEs on the VMs. You still have the ability to install the Windows Server on the host, in case the Hyper-V Server does not meet your needs.

Right now, you're probably wondering: if the Windows Server license is just an association, and I'm able to install the Hyper-V Server on the host, what about other Hypervisors?

# Licensing Windows Server VMs with other Hypervisors

Let's have a look at another scenario: you have a virtualization host, but for any given reason, you decide not to use Hyper-V as your Hypervisor, or you have a mix of hosts with different Hypervisors. For the hosts using other Hypervisors, the licensing rule remains the same.

You'll have to associate the Windows Server license to a host to cover the processors and the VMs running Windows Server OSEs. Let's say that you have a host with four processors and six VMs running Windows Server. In this case, you're running any other Hypervisor, like VMware ESX or Citrix XenServer. You still have to associate either three Windows Server Standard licenses or two Windows Server Datacenter licenses to this host.

The only point that you should keep in mind is that these Hypervisors may have their own licensing terms which will not be covered here.

One important and common mistake is that the Windows Server Standard license allows you to have three OSEs in total — two for the VMs and one for the host. In the scenario where you're using another Hypervisor with its own OS on the host, you lose the Windows Server OSE license for the host and you cannot convert it into three Windows Server VMs. This is also true for another scenario.

If you're familiar with VMware ESX, Citrix XenServer, and many other Hypervisors, you know that these Hypervisors have their own OS, and you don't need to install Windows Server on the host. This is true for Type 1 Hypervisors, as seen in *Chapter 1, Getting Started with Hyper-V Architecture and Components*. For Type 2 Hypervisors, on which you'll run the Hypervisor software on top of Windows Server, you need the Windows Server OSE license, the same way you need it when you're installing Windows Server with Hyper-V. Examples of these scenarios include VMware Workstation, Oracle VirtualBox, and many others.

# Host licensing with Hyper-V Replica

Hyper-V Replica will be explained in detail in *Chapter 8, Implementing Live Migration and Replica*, but there is a licensing issue with that technology. Basically, Hyper-V Replica allows you to have a replica of a VM on another Hyper-V Host. This host can be on the same or another site. See the following figure:

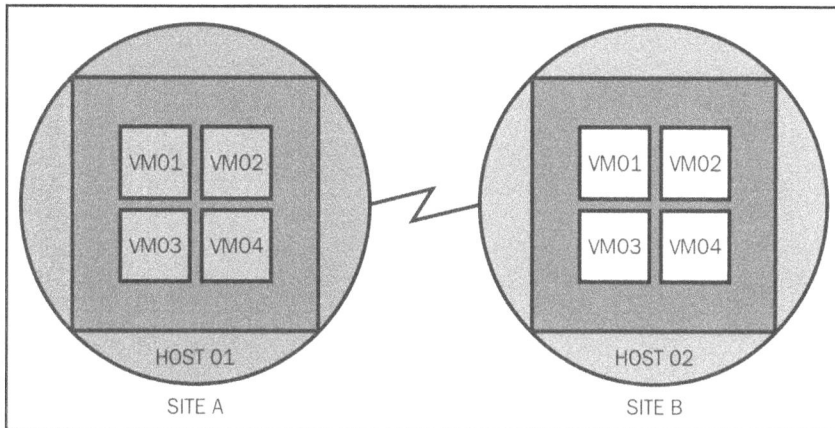

One important question about Hyper-V Replica is that the VMs on the Replica Server will always be turned off. As the VMs are turned off, many customers believe it is not necessary to license this environment. The question about this is that, although they are off, these VMs are being changed, as the goal of Hyper-V Replica is to asynchronously update the Replica VMs.

In the preceding scenario, you'll have to license both **Host 01** and **Host 02**. You can even use the Hyper-V Server as the OS for both the hosts, but you have to associate the necessary licenses to both the hosts considering the processors and VMs.

There is, however, a benefit for the customers with a contract with Microsoft. Such customers can include the Software Assurance (SA) in their contracts. An SA has multiple benefits the customers who have a contract for the complete period that the contract is valid for. The most important one is the ability to upgrade from the previous versions to new versions of software. For example, you can automatically upgrade from Windows Server 2012 to 2012 R2 if you have SA enabled in your valid contract. The reason we are explaining all this is because if you have SA enabled in your contract, and the hosts and VMs are licensed with the Windows Server license included in the contract, you don't have to license the Replica Server and Replica VMs. In this case, you would have to license **Host 01** only.

This is true for all contracts with SA enabled and the contract is still valid, but there are the following restrictions:

- The VMs on the Replica Server must be turned off all the time, unless for testing, disaster recovery, and patching (patching is not the case in Hyper-V Replica as the VMs are updated from the source VM).

- If **Host 01** is a cluster node, and the VM is highly available, the replica VMs cannot be part of the same cluster. It is possible to replicate the VM on another cluster. The other way around is also true. The source VM can be on a standalone host and the Replica VM on a cluster node.

- This benefit is not valid when the contract ends. The company has the option to renew the contract and the SA benefit. If the contract or the SA benefit is not renewed, the company will have to license the Replica Server and the Replica VMs.

Now it is time to take a look at the VMs and the impact of using other operating systems other than Windows Server.

# Hyper-V licensing with Linux VMs

Licensing VMs with Linux is actually the simplest scenario for Hyper-V. So far, you've seen that, from the licensing perspective, if you have a Windows Server VM, all you have to do is to associate the correct number of Windows Server licenses according to the number of VMs and processors on the host.

If you're running only Linux VMs, you actually don't need any license from Microsoft. The most obvious option is to use the Hyper-V Server that requires no Windows Server licenses.

Let's see an example: you have two virtualization hosts. Host 01 will run four Windows Server VMs and Host 02 will run 04 Linux VMs. Both hosts have four processors. In this case, you will need only two Windows Server licenses for the whole environment, and you will associate these licenses with Host 01 where the Windows Server VMs are. There is a caveat here, however: if you move any Windows Server VM from Host 01 to Host 02, you will have to license Host 02 as well. This is not true the other way: if you move a Linux VM from Host 02 to Host 01, you do not need any additional license to Host 01.

The same rule applies in the case that you have only one host with the Windows Server and Linux VMs. Let's take the same previous example where you have two hosts; Host 02 is where the Linux VM is in maintenance, and you move the Linux VMs to Host 02. In every case, all you have to license are the Windows Server VMs, not the Linux VMs. You can actually create even more Linux VMs, as long as the Windows Server VMs are licensed.

Another interesting point is the re-association. Considering the same example, imagine if Host 01 fails and it is irreversible. You can re-associate the licenses from Host 01 to Host 02, where the Linux VMs resides, and move the Windows Server VMs to Host 02, respecting processors counting.

Keep in mind that all the explanation above is focusing Windows Server licensing on a mixed environment of Windows Server and Linux. Some Linux distributions are not totally free to use and you must verify with the software vendor the licensing terms of each distribution. Those will not be covered here.

As in *Chapter 1*, *Getting Started with Hyper-V Architecture and Components*, you should also check which Linux distributions are supported on Hyper-V. You can check it at `http://technet.microsoft.com/library/dn531030.aspx`.

Now you know how to license your environment for the Windows Server, and even with previous versions of Windows Server, you know how to choose the best option for your host, and you know how using Linux with Hyper-V is easy. Now, let's take a look at Windows Client.

# Windows Client licensing on Hyper-V

If you are a server person, a data center manager, you're probably not familiar with Windows Client licensing, although this is not new stuff. Using virtualization to host Windows Client is not as common as hosting Windows Server or Linux VMs. This scenario will be explained in more detail in *Chapter 10*, *Implementing a Virtual Desktop Infrastructure*, but, for now, what you need to know is that some companies use the data center processing power to host the users' OS. Instead of using high performance devices for users, they virtualize the Windows Client on the virtualization hosts of the data center and use this processing for the customer's applications. The users will access these VMs remotely from their devices. However, the licensing of Windows Client is different from Windows Server.

As the licensing for Virtual Desktop Infrastructure (VDI) has not changed much from Windows 7 to Windows 8 and 8.1, we will cover the concepts of VDI for Windows 8 and 8.1 and if necessary point out what has changed.

The main difference between licensing on Windows Server and Windows Client is that on Windows Server, you associate the Windows Server License to the host, respecting the number of processors and the VMs you are running, but you are still associating it to the virtualization host. In the VDI scenario, the license that you use is called **Virtual Desktop Access** (**VDA**) and you have to actually license the device used to access the Windows Client VM. That changes everything and let me point it out, as this will be the core of everything in this section:

- The VDA license is accounted for by the devices used to access the Windows Client VM. Having said that, you can create as many VMs with Windows Client that you need to support your environment, and you can also have as many users you want, as long you license all the devices they are going to use with a VDA license.

I'm pretty sure that you have a lot of questions right now, so I'll try to answer them. I believe the first one is "If my company already bought a Windows Client version for the users' machines, do I need to buy the VDA license?" To better answer that, and all other questions, let's see all the scenarios covered by the licensing terms.

# Windows PCs and VDI

In this case, we are talking about a PC that is running a Windows Client version that is not the RT version. In such a case, the company has the following two options, depending on who is the owner of the device:

- **Scenario 1**: The company owns the Windows PC and has already bought a Windows Client license for it. In this case, the company will provide a VDI infrastructure for the users to access their VMs and the applications within the VMs.

- **Scenario 2**: The user owns the Windows PC and the PC is used at home by the user. This PC will never come to the company, but the user is able to access the VDI infrastructure provided by the company.

The answer for both the given scenarios is *Yes*. The company will have to associate a VDA license for all the devices accessing the VDI environment.

Despite the fact that we have two scenarios as mentioned, the company has the following three to choose from:

- **Option 1 for Scenario 1**: The company can acquire a VDA license for all the company's PCs. This will allow all Windows PCs to access the VDI environment.

- **Option 2 for Scenario 1**: The company can choose to add the Software Assurance (SA) to the contract. As said before, SA has multiple benefits. One of the benefits of SA is the VDA license for the Windows Clients in the contract.

- **Option 1 for Scenario 2**: The only option in this case is to acquire a VDA license for all the PCs that are going to access the VDI environment.

# Company-owned Windows RT tablets

Some companies are acquiring new devices for the workforce, focusing on production and freedom for the user. When using a tablet, the user can work from anywhere and still be as productive as on a PC. In many cases, as the tablet is not able to perform tasks like a PC, the companies provide the VDI environment to the users.

In this case, we are talking about a Windows RT device accessing the VDI environment, but the company has already provided the user with a company PC and the Windows PC is the primary device. Both the Windows PC and the Windows RT tablet belong to the company.

In this case, the company has the following two options:

- **Option 01**: Assign a VDA license to each Windows RT tablet. This will allow the tablet to access the VDI environment as any other device.

- **Option 02**: Assign SA to the contract. The SA has a new benefit called **Windows RT Companion VDA Rights**. This benefit allows the company to assign a VDA license to the Windows RT tablets for users who have a Windows PC owned by the company and a Windows RT tablet.

There is a caveat here, however: the company must own the Windows RT tablet. If the user owns the tablet, the SA will not apply and the company will have to buy the VDA license for the user's device.

As you can see, the licensing for VDI is very specific for each scenario, and you might be thinking "There are other scenarios not mentioned here. What about them?" These options are new to Windows 8 and 8.1 licensing. Let's explore them.

# User devices inside or outside the company network

This is a little bit more challenging. Let's first define what is inside and outside the company network. From the licensing perspective, inside the company is every device accessing the company resources from inside the company firewall. Everything behind the company firewall, or on the public network, is considered outside the company network.

This is important to understand as there are two ways of licensing your environment based on that information. In both scenarios, the user owns the device and will access the VDI environment. Let's take a look at the following scenarios:

- **Scenario 01**: A user owns the device and will access the VDI environment from outside the company network

  In this case, there is another benefit from SA called Roaming Use Rights. This is only available when the company has a primary device (Windows PC and Windows Client license) in a contract with SA. This benefit was created for users working out of office, like in a hotel, accessing the VDI environment from their own machines or a kiosk.

  If the company does not have an SA, the only alternative is to acquire the VDA license for every device accessing the VDI environment.

- **Scenario 02**: A user owns the device and will access the VDI environment from inside the company network

  This scenario is also known as **Bring Your Own Device (BYOD)**. It is becoming very popular and is the trickiest one. The reason why this is so is because, depending on the type of contract you have, the VDA license is already covered.

According to the **Product User Rights** (**PUR**), the document defined by Microsoft stating all the licensing terms, if your company has Select, Enterprise Agreement, Enrollment for Education Solutions, or a School Enrollment contract, and the SA is enabled in the contract for the users' primary device, the company can also acquire a **Companion Subscription License** (**CSL**). The CSL allows the user to bring up to four devices (owned by the user), and use it to access the VDI environment.

If the company has any other type of contract, or does not have SA, or even does not acquire the CSL, the company will have to acquire a VDA license for each user owned device that will access the VDI environment.

So far, we've seen how to license the VDI environment for Windows devices, both company or user-owned. The next question is "What about non-Microsoft devices?"

# Non-Microsoft smartphone and tablet licensing for VDI

More and more often, we can see that users are using multiple devices to work with, other than their primary PC-smartphones, tablets, and now even smartwatches. From the VDI licensing perspective, every device that was not covered in the earlier sections, and which can access the VDI environment, must have a VDA licensing.

From a technical perspective, the device must have the capability to access the VDI environment, which is a Remote Desktop client, in other words. Today the iOS, Android, and the Windows Phone have the ability to access the VDI environment with clients provided by Microsoft on the AppStore, Google Play, and the Windows Phone Store. There are other non-Microsoft clients for Remote Desktop access, but regardless of the software used to access the VDI environment, a VDA license is required.

For any other question regarding VDA, I highly recommend that you contact your re-seller. You can also check the official documentation at `http://www.microsoft.com/licensing/about-licensing/windows8-1.aspx`.

> Although they have a Windows license, thin clients are categorized in this context, as Windows Embedded is not eligible for VDA in an SA.

# VDI licensing, RDS, and virtualization host licensing

Another important aspect of the VDI licensing is that it is not sure which Hypervisor you will decide to use on the virtualization host and which component you will use to provide access to the Windows Client VMs.

From the Hypervisor perspective, you can use either Hyper-V Server, Windows Server with Hyper-V on the Microsoft stack, or you can choose to use another VDI solution, such as VMware Horizon or Citrix XenDesktop.

In the Microsoft stack, the recommendation is the same as the Windows Server virtualization. The first option should be to use the Hyper-V Server as it does not need any additional license and provides all Hyper-V capabilities and features. However, on most of the VDI scenarios, there are other necessary software, like GPU drivers, that are not available for the Hyper-V Server. In these cases, you can use the Windows Server with Hyper-V, but an additional Windows Server license will be necessary for the host OSE.

For other VDI products from other vendors, there are additional licenses which will not be covered here.

In addition to the Microsoft virtualization, RDS is also used on the VDI stack to provide access to the Windows Client VMs. RDS have a totally different approach for licensing in **Session Host** environments. Session Host environments consist of delivering applications to users through RDS. An RDS Session Host has the option not to expose the underlying OS of the application to the user. It is different from VDI as it is less flexible in exposing the entire OS. VDI, on the other hand, exposes the OS to the user so that the user can have a better experience, but it requires more administrative overhead.

The RDS Session Host must be licensed through RDS **CAL**. This license is not necessary for VDI and will not be covered here.

As the VDI licensing is more complex than the regular Hyper-V Licensing, it is possible that right now you have more questions than before. To try and answer these questions, let's take a look at a few scenarios and how to license it.

# VDI scenarios and licensing options

The following are the most frequently asked questions, from customers implementing a VDI environment. It will help you better understand the options for licensing a VDI environment. Remember, all the following scenarios apply to other VDI software using the Windows Client VMs:

- The company has a hundred devices accessing the VDI environment and 150 users. How many VDA licenses does this company need to acquire?

  The VDA license is associated to the device. In this case, the company has the option to enable the SA in the contract. If not, the company will have to acquire 100 VDA licenses.

- The company has the VDI environment already licensed. This company is using RDS to support the VDI environment and is planning to use a Session Host for some applications. Is there any other license to acquire?

  Yes. The RDS for the Session Host must be licensed apart from the VDI environment. For a Session Host, an RDS CAL must be acquired.

- The company has 150 users. 100 users are using Windows PC devices. 50 users are using iPad. How many VDA licenses does the company need?

  If the company has SA enabled in the contract, the 100 Windows PC devices are covered. In this case, the company has to acquire only 50 VDA licenses. If the SA is not enabled, the company has to acquire 150 VDA licenses.

- The company has retired 50 Windows PC devices and replaced them with Windows RT devices. Which license does the company need?

  As the company has retired the Windows PC devices, the only option is to acquire 50 VDA licenses. If the company had only added the new Windows RT devices as a second device, the SA would license the Windows RT devices.

- The company has 50 remote users with their own devices, and 50 users based in the office with their devices as well. How many, and which licenses does the company need?

  For the remote users, the company can use the benefit of the Roaming Use Rights in the SA, if it is available in the contract. For the office based users, it will depend on the contract. If the contract allows it, the company can acquire CSL on top of the SA. If SA is not available, in both cases, the company will have to acquire a VDA license for each device.

# Summary

Licensing a virtualization environment is relatively simple. In this chapter, you learned that licensing a virtualization environment for Windows Server VM is based on accounting the number of processors and VMs in order to decide between the Standard and the Datacenter Editions. You can choose to use Hyper-V Server as a Hypervisor for the virtual environment, especially for Linux VMs. In addition, you can choose to use another Hypervisor, but the Windows Server VM will remain the same.

For the Windows Client VMs in VDI environments, the licensing is relatively simple. Unlike the Windows Server, you have to associate a VDA license for each device accessing the VDI environment. If the company has an SA, there will be benefits for licensing both the Windows Server VMs and the VDI environment.

For the VDI environment, there are some caveats for user-owned devices, and for users from inside and outside the company network.

In the next chapter, we will come back to the technical matter focusing on networking for the host and the VM.

# 4
# Managing Networking

Networking, along with storage, is one of the most critical subsystems for virtualization. Planning your hardware accordingly is extremely important and failure in the planning phase can result in a virtualization environment with poor performance. Furthermore, changing your hardware during production, either network or storage, is not that simple.

From the networking point of view, there are two important aspects to be considered. These are the hardware networking, the physical network installed on the host machine, and the VM networking, the virtual network on which the VM accesses the network resources.

Another important aspect of Hyper-V in Windows Server 2012 and 2012 R2 are the new features available on **Hyper-V Switch**. These new features allow you to have a new hardware configuration, which was not supported by Microsoft in the previous versions of Windows Server. It also allows you to have not only a better VM density, but a variety of new workloads running on virtualization, still achieving the performance needs. Through this chapter, you'll be able to understand which feature requires a specialized hardware on the host.

In this chapter we will cover the following topics:

- Host network configuration
- Hardware Networking
- Hyper-V Switch
- VM network features
- Converged Networking

Before we go into the details about networking, it is important to understand the basic concepts of the Hyper-V Switch and how a VM can access the network. To understand that, let's start with the basics of the Hyper-V Switch.

# Hyper-V Switch basics

When you create a VM on Hyper-V, by default the VM will have a virtual network (vNIC or Virtual Network Interface Card) to access the network. You can add other vNICs to this VM later, but the point here is that this VM must have a connection with a switch, or in this case a Virtual Switch.

Hyper-V has three types of Virtual Switch which you can choose from, depending on the traffic and destinations you want this VM to reach. The three types of Virtual Switch are:

- **Private**: The Private Virtual Switch is a Virtual Switch that is not connected to the external network or the host itself. This means that a VM connected to this Virtual Switch can only reach VMs at the same Virtual Switch, as shown in the following figure:

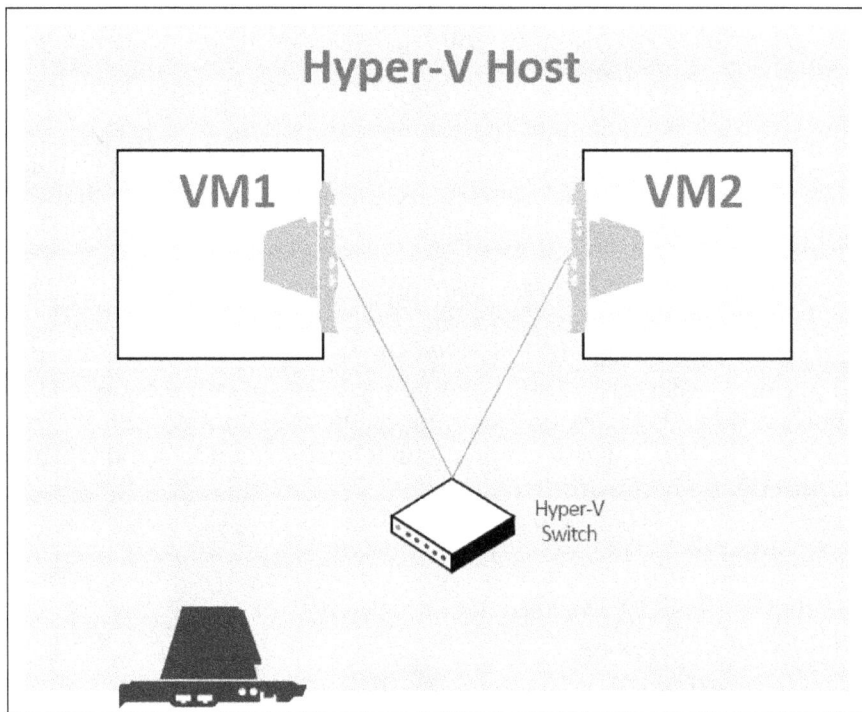

- **Internal**: The Internal Virtual Switch has an additional component for the host machine. This Virtual Switch allows you to connect a virtual network on the host to the itself. With that, the VMs can reach other VMs on the same Virtual Switch and the host, through the virtual network on the host connected to the Virtual Switch. See the details in the following figure:.

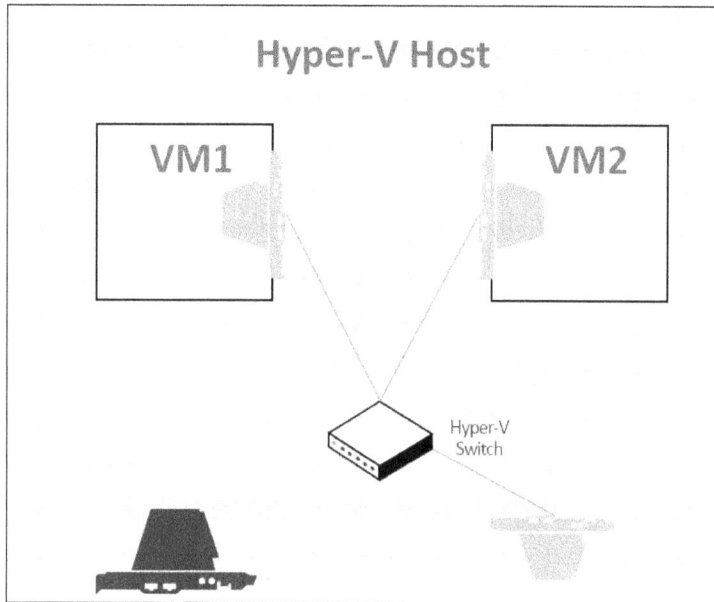

- **External**: This Virtual Switch has all the characteristics of the other ones, and adds an uplink on the Virtual Switch to the physical NIC on the host. The host will use the virtual network that is connected to the Virtual Switch to access the external LAN. See the following figure:

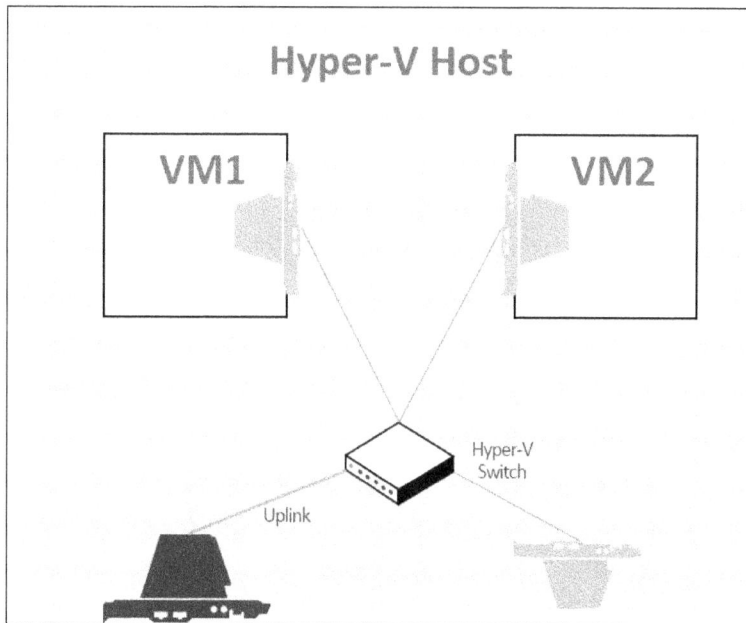

An important aspect of the External Switch is that, by default, all the configurations of the physical NIC, such as IP address, are inherited by the virtual network. With that, the host machine will remain connected to the network after applying the changes, when creating the External Virtual Switch.

> You can choose not to create the virtual network when creating an External Virtual Switch, either because you don't want the host to connect to the Virtual Switch or because you want to add it later. However, the process of creating a virtual network for the host must be done by PowerShell. The process to do that will be shown later in this chapter.

Now that the basic concepts of the Hyper-V Virtual Switch are clear, let's see how we apply it.

# Creating a Hyper-V Virtual Switch

To create a Hyper-V Virtual Switch, open **Hyper-V Manager** and select **Virtual Switch Manager...** on the left. The following window will be seen:

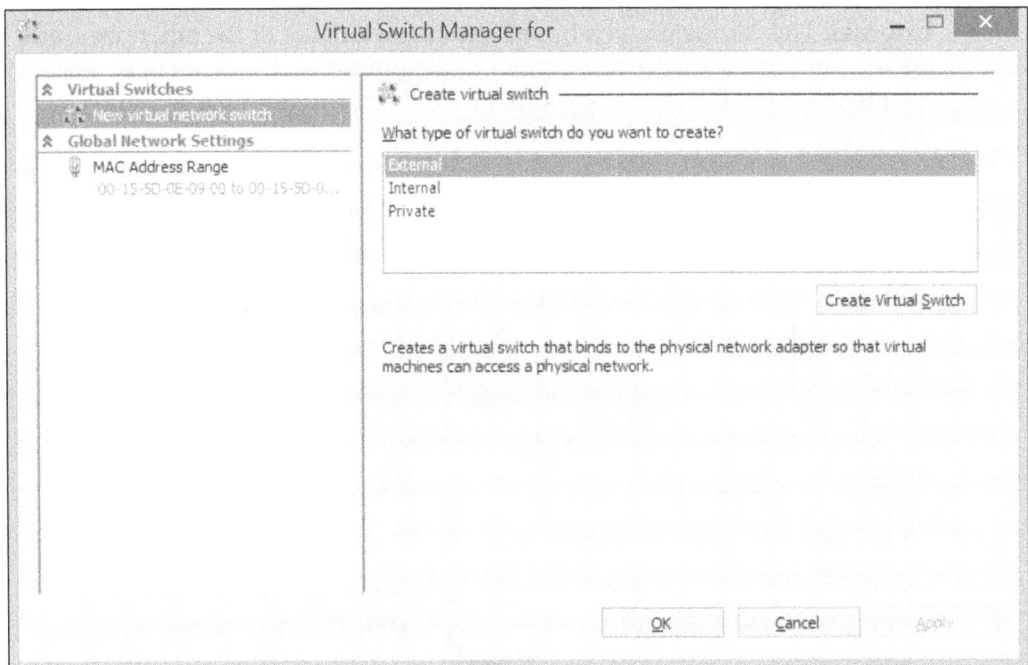

In the preceding screenshot, you can choose to create a Virtual Switch with the characteristics as seen earlier. You can always change the Virtual Switch type, but keep in mind that when changing to or from an External Virtual Switch, the host machine will lose connectivity temporarily, as the following message states:

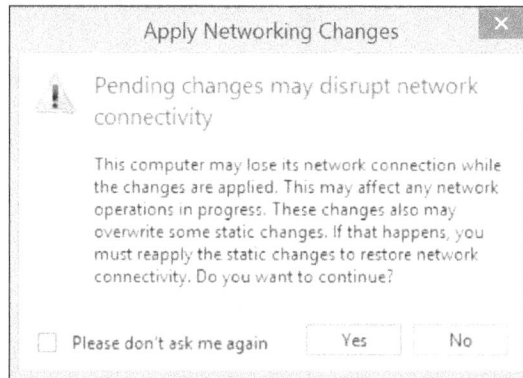

After selecting the appropriate Virtual Switch type and clicking **Create Virtual Switch**, you can see the details of the Virtual Switch. On the next screen, you can change the **Connection type** and the **VLAN ID** that will be used by the host OS for all network communication. You can edit VLAN for each VM later on the VM NIC. The VLAN ID is not available on Private Virtual Switch, as the host will not receive a virtual network in this case.

If you chose Private or Internal Virtual Switch, all you have to do is to fulfill the **Name:** and **Notes:** fields. In case you chose External Network field, you also have to choose which NIC you want this Virtual Switch to use as Uplink, as shown in the following screenshot:

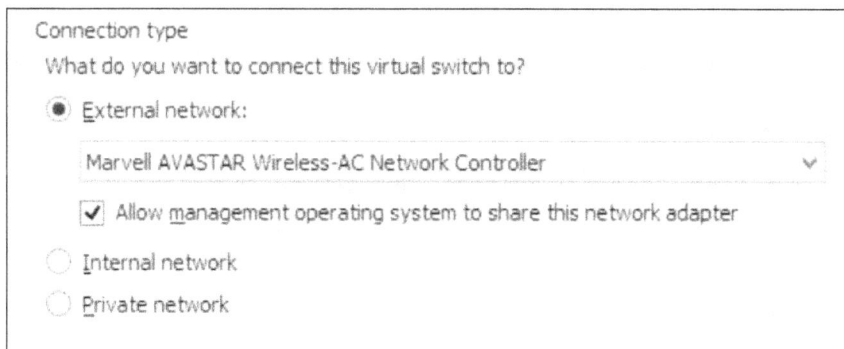

Besides NIC, you can choose to create a virtual network on the host OS in order to share this connection; this is done by selecting the option **Allow management operating system to share this network adapter**. If you clear this selection, the host won't be able to communicate with this Virtual Switch. If the option is marked, a new Virtual Network Interface will be created on the host for it to be able to communicate with this switch.

To delete a Virtual Switch, you can select the Virtual Switch you want to remove and click on the **Remove** button at the bottom. This will remove the Virtual Switch, and, in the case of an Internal or External Switch, it will remove the Virtual Network associated to the Virtual Switch.

After creating the Virtual Switch, you can connect the VMs to the Virtual Switch so that they can also share the connection. We will cover this topic soon, but first, let's see how to perform the same operations using PowerShell.

# Creating a Hyper-V Virtual Switch using PowerShell

The process to create the Virtual Switch is the same as on a GUI, but in PowerShell, you'll have to insert some additional information depending on the type of Virtual Switch you're creating. The PowerShell command (cmdlet) to create a Virtual Switch is New-VMSwitch. There are, though, multiple inputs for the command.

To create a Private Virtual Switch, you can use the following PowerShell command (cmdlet):

```
New-VMSwitch -Name "Private Switch" -SwitchType Private -
ComputerName Host01
```

The preceding command will create a new Private Virtual Switch on Host01. See that the -ComputerName option is not mandatory, but you have to use it when managing a server remotely. To create an Internal Virtual Switch, you can use the following command:

```
New-VMSwitch -Name "Internal Switch" -SwitchType Internal -
ComputerName Host01
```

The preceding command is the same as the one before, but now it will create an Internal Virtual Switch on `Host01`.

For the External Virtual Switch, the command is slightly different as now you have to identify which NIC to bind on the host. To do that, you'll use either `NetAdapterInterfaceDescription` or `NetAdapterName`. Since you're explicitly identifying the NIC on which the External Virtual Switch will bind, you don't have to use the input `-SwitchType`. See the following example:

```
New-VMSwitch -Name "External Switch" -NetAdapterName Ethernet -
AllowManagementOS $True -ComputerName Host01
```

The preceding command will create an External Virtual Switch binding it to the adapter `Wi-FI`, and will also create a Virtual Network on `Host01` that is connected to this Virtual Switch.

To delete a Virtual Switch, you can use the following command:

```
Remove-VMSwitch -Name "External Switch" -ComputerName Host01
```

This will delete the Virtual Switch `"External Switch"` on the host `Host01`.

# Connecting a VM to a Virtual Switch

Now that the Virtual Switch is created, we can connect the VM to it so that the VM can communicate with other VMs and with the network. The easiest and most common way to connect a VM to the Virtual Switch is when you're creating a new VM. The process of creating a new VM will be detailed in *Chapter 6, Virtual Machines and Virtual Machine Templates,* so for now, keep in mind that a part of the process of creating a new VM includes the connection to a Virtual Switch. If you're creating a new VM through the GUI, you can either specify to connect the virtual network of the VM to a Virtual Switch or keep the VM not connected to a Virtual Switch.

If the VM is already created, you'll have to open the VM **Settings...** on **Hyper-V Manager**, select the **Network Adapter** you want to configure, and choose the **Virtual switch** that the virtual network should be connected to, as shown in the following screenshot:

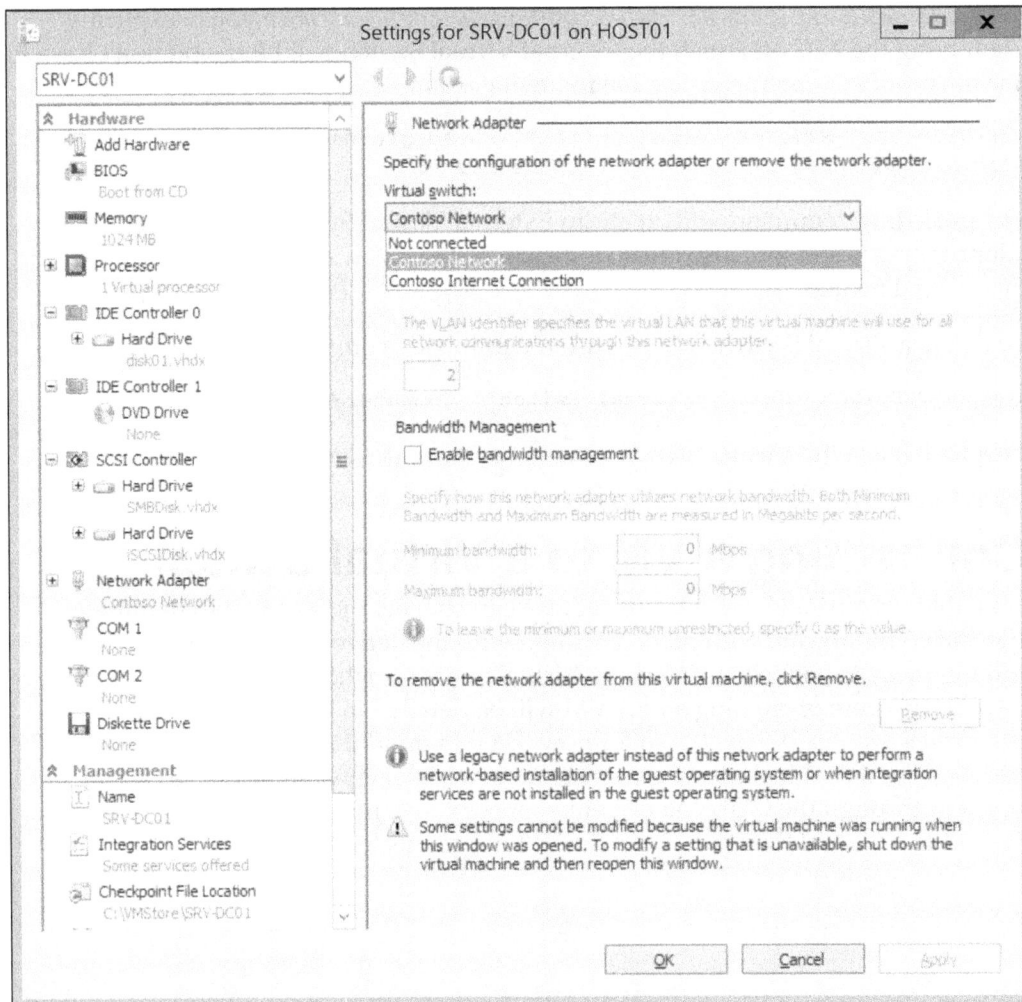

In PowerShell, you can use the following cmdlet to create a VM:

```
New-VM -NewVHDPath "C:\VMStore\Hard Disks" -NewVHDSizeBytes
17045651456 -ComputerName Host01 -Generation 1 -MemoryStartupBytes
536870912 -Name VM-01 -Path C:\VMStore -SwitchName "External
Network"
```

The preceding cmdlet will be detailed in the *Virtual machine management* section of *Chapter 6*, *Virtual Machines and Virtual Machine Templates*. For now, all you have to understand is that the input -SwitchName is responsible for connecting the VM to the Virtual Switch, in this case, the "External Network" Virtual Switch.

So far, you are able to understand and create a Virtual Switch on Hyper-V and connect the VMs to this Virtual Switch. However, this basic configuration is not really useful when it comes to large deployments of Hyper-V. It's time to see how it works at the Enterprise level.

# Advanced configuration for Hyper-V networking

When it comes to Enterprise, customers have some requirements for their environment. High Availability, Performance, and Security are examples of the features that customers are looking for, and which Hyper-V is able to deliver on Windows Server 2012 R2. From now on in this chapter, we will see how to evolve the concepts that you learned so far.

The first thing that will be covered is the design of the host networking. It is important because it will affect the design for VM networking. For example, when you're acquiring the hardware for your host server, firstly you have to plan with your vendor how many NICs the host will have. If you acquire a host with only one NIC, you'll be able to connect both—the host and the VMs to the network. The problem is that both—the host and the VMs may have different types of traffic and each traffic has its own requirement for bandwidth.

As an example, let's use the case of a Hyper-V Host working in a cluster of Hyper-V. Hyper-V Cluster; High Availability will be detailed in *Chapter 7*, *Implementing High Availability*, so, for now, we will focus on networking for a cluster.

A cluster node, which is one of the servers in the cluster, by default, has the following traffic:

- **Management**: For management purposes, such as backup, management agent, management console, and so on.
- **Cluster communication**: For communication between the cluster nodes and **Cluster Shared Volume** (**CSV**). CSV will be detailed in *Chapter 7*, *Implementing High Availability*.
- **Live Migration**: For moving a powered-on VM from one node to another.
- **Storage**: For accessing the storage, if using iSCSI or SMB3. Both iSCSI and SMB3 will be detailed in *Chapter 5*, *Managing Storage*.

One of the options you have is to run all this traffic on the same NIC. It is obviously not recommended, as you'll be creating a bottleneck. All communications from both—the host and the VM will struggle on the same NIC.

The other alternative, prior to Windows Server 2012 and 2012 R2, was to dedicate one NIC for each traffic—Management, Cluster, Live Migration, Storage and one more for the VMs to use. Today, a host with five NICs is not something out of this world. However, when planning a cluster node, you have to think about all the single points of failure. If you're using a dedicated NIC for the given traffic, and the NIC goes down, all the traffic on that NIC will be affected.

An alternative, not supported by Microsoft prior to Windows Server 2012 and 2012 R2, was to use NIC Teaming. With NIC Teaming, you can combine two NICs into one virtual NIC that will use the physical NICs with **Load Balancing and Failover (LBFO)**. On the other hand, you would need ten NICs per server to create this configuration. It would be something like the following diagram:

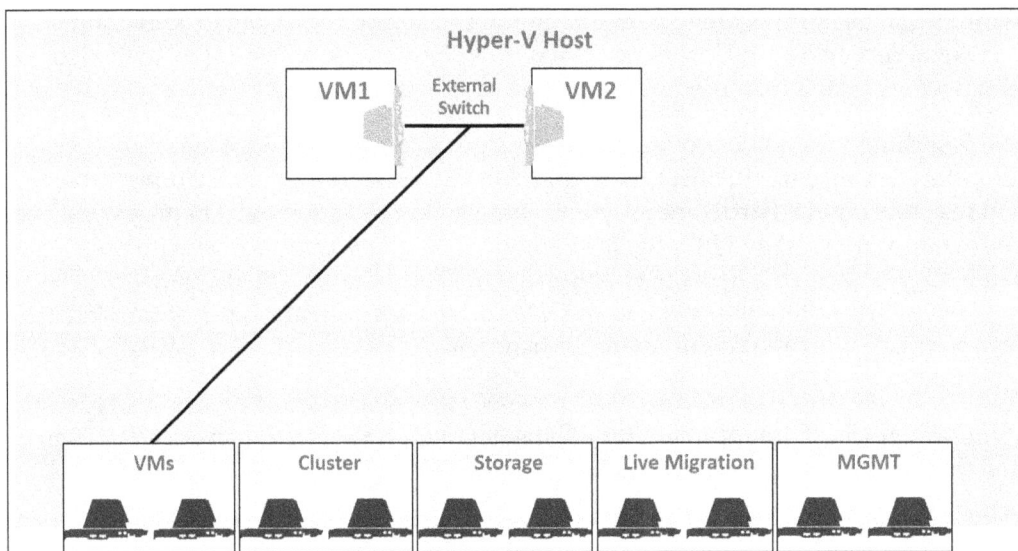

Needless to say, a host with ten NICs is not usual, even today; another problem is that all the support for NIC Teaming was provided by the hardware vendor. If you had any problem with Hyper-V caused by a malfunction of the NIC Teaming, Microsoft would not support you and you had to contact the hardware vendor. Not an easy position for an enterprise. However, in Windows Server 2012 and 2012 R2, all this changed.

# Converged Networking on Hyper-V

The concept of Converged Networking is very simple actually. However, it uses two new features that are only available in Windows Server 2012 and 2012 R2, which are NIC Teaming and Bandwidth Management (usually called QoS).

With Hyper-V in the Windows Server 2012 and 2012 R2, you can leverage these new features to enable a new scenario called Converged Networking. Let's take a look at the following diagram:

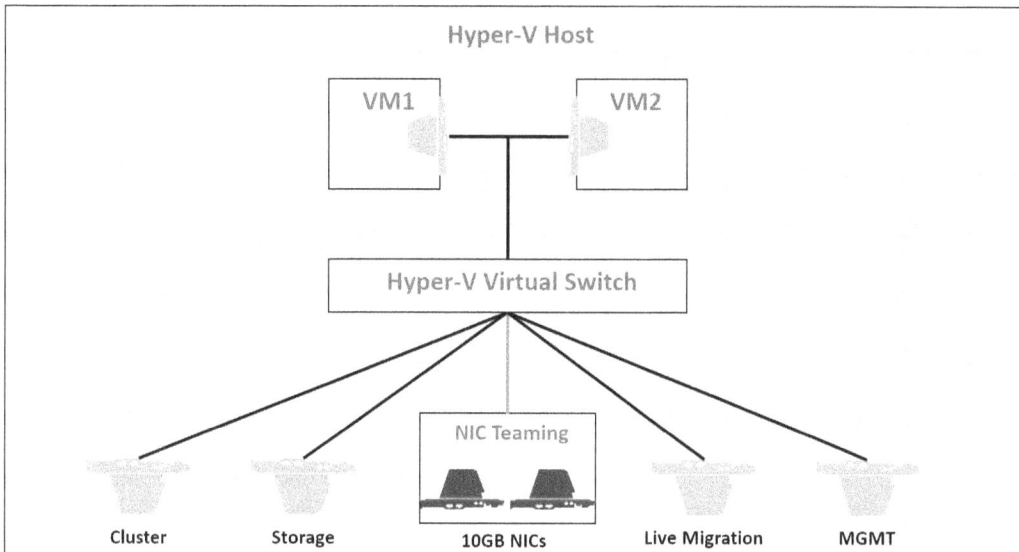

As you can see from the preceding diagram, the host has only two NICs. In this case, the NICs are 10 GB NICs. It is recommended that you use these NICs in this case, as all the traffic will flow through them. In case you don't have this kind of NIC, you can use 1 GB NIC, but it is also recommended to add more NICs, and to use load balance on NIC Teaming.

With the two NICs, you can create NIC Teaming. On top of the NIC Teaming, you will create a Virtual Switch. You can then connect the virtual networks, both from the host and the VMs, to the Virtual Switch. With that, the traffic is isolated on each virtual network. Right now, you might be thinking "What difference does it make, as the NICs and NIC Teaming are still a bottleneck?". Well, that's one of the reasons for using 10 GB NICs or multiple 1 GB NICs. The fact, actually, is that you can also apply Bandwidth Management on all virtual networks, including the ones from the host. Applying Bandwidth Management will ensure that each traffic has the bandwidth it needs to perform its operations. Let's see how to apply all of this.

# Creating NIC Teaming

To create NIC Teaming on Windows Server 2012, open **Server Manager** and click **Local Server** on the left-hand side. You can see the entire configuration for the given server on the right. On the **NIC Teaming** option, click the **Disabled** option. It will open the **NIC Teaming** wizard.

In the NIC Teaming Wizard, you can see the server you're working on, at the top. At the bottom left, you have the Teams, and on the bottom right, you have the available NICs. To create a new NIC Team, click **TASKS** on the bottom left and click **New Team**:

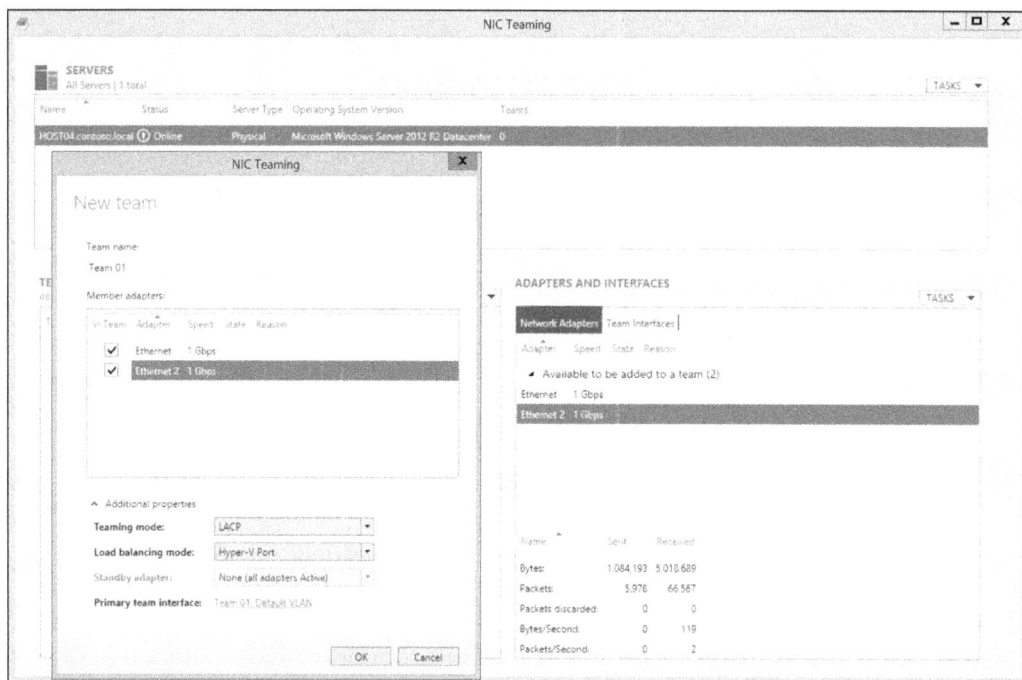

There are multiple options to configure in this step. The first one is to name your Team. Then you have to select which NICs will be part of the Team. You can select up to 32 NICs for the same Team.

Then you have to set Teaming mode. This option will basically configure how to handle the physical switch that the host NICs are connected to. The options are as follows:

- **Switch Independent**: The simplest option, determining that the physical switch is not aware of the NIC Team. This is used in cases where the physical switch is a simple switch and does not support management, or in cases where you want to connect one or more NICs to a different switch. The problem with the **Switch Independent** option is that it will load balance the outbound traffic but not the inbound one, since the physical switch will register the MAC address of the team on only one switch port.

- **Static Teaming**: A bit more efficient than **Switch Independent**, this option uses the 802.3ad Standard. The benefit of **Static Teaming** over **Switch Independent**, is that Static Teaming allows you to load balance the inbound traffic although, you have to configure the physical switch. On the other hand, it does not allow you to have connection to multiple switches. This standard is not common today, as many vendors used their own implementation of it and with the arrival of the **LACP**, even Cisco (Cisco is the vendor that has implemented it on most of its data center products) is now implementing it.

- **LACP**: An evolution of the Static Teaming protocol uses the 802.1AX standard and has the same benefits and problems of Static Teaming regarding inbound load balance and connecting multiple switches by default. However, this standard has the benefit of dealing with connection problems better than Static Teaming. Also, the new implementation of data center switches includes a management module which the managed switches connect to. With that, some implementations allow you to configure the managed switches to understand the NIC Team over multiple switches, providing high availability for the network in case a switch is down. As in Static Teaming, there is a configuration to be made on the switch side, which is not in the scope of this book.

> You should always consult your networking vendor to check which implementation your hardware supports.

With the NIC connected to the switch, and the correct Teaming mode in place, it is time to decide how the load balance will work on the NICs, so next you have to configure the Load balancing mode. Keep in mind that the Load balancing mode will configure the load balance for outbound traffic, since the Team Mode will configure the physical switch to work on the inbound traffic load balance.

One important aspect of the Load balancing mode is that the GUI will provide you with three options. In fact, there are five. However, they are only available if you use PowerShell to configure it. Let's understand what are the options:

- **Address Hash**: The concept of using a hash, in this case, is that when the traffic is sent to the NIC, Windows Server will create a hash from the components of the traffic and will assign all the traffic that meets that hash to that adapter. If configured through the GUI, Windows Server will try to use port hash, IP Address Hash, and MAC Hash, in that order. Via PowerShell, you can choose one of the options exclusively. This option is very useful for non-virtualized workloads.

- **Hyper-V Port**: The Hyper-V Port balancing mode is designed for virtual environments. This technique will assign a virtual network to a physical network, the team in this case, and balance the inbound traffic across the NICs on the host, as the physical switch will use the VM MAC address that is assigned to the Team. However, it will only be functional if a Virtual Switch stands on top of the NIC Team. Another consideration is that virtual networks will never use more bandwidth than a single NIC of the Team.

- **Dynamic**: This is new to Windows Server 2012 R2 and combines the benefits of hash and Hyper-V Port Load balancing modes. For the outbound traffic, a port or IP Address Hash will be used. For inbound, the traffic will be balanced by the Hyper-V Port mode.

Right now, I believe you are asking yourself "What are the implications of combining one option with another?" To understand that, let's have a look at the following table:

| Distribution mode → <br><br> Teaming mode ↓ | Address Hash | Hyper-V Port | Dynamic |
| --- | --- | --- | --- |
| **Switch Independent** | Outbound traffic will be better load balanced, but inbound will not be so. | Outbound traffic will be load balanced, but inbound will not. However, the VM inbound traffic will be directed to multiple NICs on the host. | Outbound traffic will be better load balanced, but inbound will not. However, the VM inbound traffic will be directed to multiple NICs on the host. |

| Distribution mode → Teaming mode ↓ | Address Hash | Hyper-V Port | Dynamic |
|---|---|---|---|
| **Switch Dependent (Static Team or LACP)** | Outbound traffic, as well as the inbound one will be better balanced. However, Dynamic mode uses the Hyper-V Port mode for inbound traffic which will benefit the VMs. | Outbound traffic, as well as the inbound traffic will be balanced However, Dynamic will better balance the outbound traffic using the Hash mode. | Outbound and inbound traffic will be balanced on the best possible option available for both, the host and the VMs. |

As you can see, there are multiple ways for configuring NIC Teaming on Windows Server 2012 R2. For more information on NIC Teaming options, you can check the official document at `http://www.microsoft.com/en-us/download/confirmation.aspx?id=40319`.

If you chose the **Switch Independent** Teaming mode, you can also choose which of the available NICs will be in Standby mode, or if you want all of them to be used, which is the default option. This is useful as you can specify one of the NICs available on the host to automatically replace an NIC that fails. It is only recommended in case you have at least three NICs on the Team.

After choosing the **Teaming mode, Load balancing mode,** and Standby mode, you can choose how to handle VLAN membership and click **Ok** to create the Team.

To perform this operation through PowerShell, you can use the following cmdlet:

```
New-NetLbfoTeam -Name "Team 01" -TeamMembers Ethernet, Ethernet2 -
LoadBalancingAlgorithm Dynamic -TeamingMode Lacp
```

The preceding cmdlet will create a Team named `Team 01` using the NICs Ethernet and Ethernet2 with the Dynamic Load balancing mode and LACP Teaming mode.

Moving on, after configuring the NIC Teaming, you can create a Virtual Switch on top of it, using the same process you learned earlier. After creating the Virtual Switch, you can connect the VMs to the Virtual Switch. There is, however, a missing piece—the Virtual NIC on the host.

# Creating a virtual NIC on the host

As you saw earlier, when you create an External Virtual Switch on Hyper-V, it will automatically create a virtual NIC on the host, so that the host OS can share the connection with the VMs. In the case of Converged Network, the concept is the same. The only difference is that now you have to manually create more virtual interfaces on the host. This process can only be made with PowerShell. To create a new virtual Network Adapter on the host, you can use the following cmdlet:

```
Add-VMNetworkAdapter -Name MGMT -SwitchName "vSwitch Team01" -
ManagementOS
```

The preceding cmdlet will create a new virtual network adapter on the host and connect it to the Virtual Switch `"vSwitch Team01"` that was created on top of the NIC Team. If you need to assign a VLAN to the virtual network adapter, you can use the following cmdlet:

```
Set-VMNetworkAdapterVlan -VMNetworkAdapter "MGMT" -Access -VlanId
2 -ManagementOS
```

Keep in mind that you'll need to run the preceding commands for each of the traffic you have on the host — Management, Cluster, Live Migration, and Storage.

To recap, what we did was to create an NIC Team on the host using two NICs. On top of it, we created a Virtual Switch, and then we created virtual network adapters binding the Virtual Switch. If you're paying attention, you're probably asking yourself "What's the point of all this if all the traffic is going to the physical NICs with no control?" You're right.

# Bandwidth Management on Hyper-V

Right now, the physical NIC is a bottleneck. That's because, regardless of the isolation of the traffic on multiple virtual NICs, all the traffic is going to the physical NIC, with no priority. A new Hyper-V feature on Windows Server 2012 and 2012 R2 is the Bandwidth Management per VM and per virtual NIC.

This means you can set which traffic should have more or less priority. Keep in mind that we are configuring it for Converged Network purposes, but you can define the bandwidth available for a given VM at any time, even if the VM is powered-on. To define the bandwidth available for a VM, you can open the VM **Settings...** in **Hyper-V Manager** and click the virtual **Network Adapter** that you want to configure.

Bandwidth Management

☑ Enable bandwidth management

Specify how this network adapter utilizes network bandwidth. Both Minimum Bandwidth and Maximum Bandwidth are measured in Megabits per second.

Minimum bandwidth:                    100   Mbps

Maximum bandwidth:                    300   Mbps

ⓘ  To leave the minimum or maximum unrestricted, specify 0 as the value.

On the GUI, you can specify the Minimum and Maximum Mbps available for that specific virtual NIC on that VM. However, in the Converged Network scenario, you cannot use the GUI.

To perform this operation on the virtual NICs of the Converged Network scenario, use the following cmdlet:

```
Set-VMNetworkAdapter -Name MGMT -MinimumBandwidthWeight 50 -
ManagementOS
```

As you can see, the preceding cmdlet will perform the same operation as the GUI. There is, however, a difference from the GUI option. The PowerShell cmdlet lets you configure a weight for the virtual NIC. This option is interesting as you can define a weight for the virtual NICs and Windows Server will manage the amount of bandwidth for each virtual NIC, depending on the traffic of the other virtual NICs. This number can be between 1 and 100 and the highest number has more priority.

> PowerShell still gives you the option to use **Minimum bandwidth** and **Maximum bandwidth**. You can use the -MaximumBandwidth and -MinimumBandwidthAbsolute inputs.

To avoid misconfigurations, you can define which of the options the Virtual Switch will use to define the virtual NIC bandwidth. If you're creating the Virtual Switch, this can be done through PowerShell using the following cmdlet:

```
New-VMSwitch -Name "vSwitch Switch Team01" -
NetAdapterInterfaceDescription Team01 -ComputerName Host01 -
MinimumBandwidthMode Weight
```

In this case, we are using the same cmdlet to create a new Virtual Switch, but now we used the `-MinimumBandwidthMode` input. In the preceding case, we used `Weight` which will use the weight configuration of the virtual NICs as the default bandwidth configuration. There are still the Absolute, Default, and None options. Absolute will use the minimum value of bits per second on the virtual NIC. If None is specified, all the configurations on the virtual NICs will be discarded.

The last one is Default, which in fact will use `Weight` as the configuration for Bandwidth Management, if the SR-IOV is not enabled. If SR-IOV is enabled, then the option None will be used. SR-IOV will be explained later in this chapter.

It is important to remember that all virtual NICs created in Converged Network scenarios, from both VMs and host, must be configured with bandwidth limits. Otherwise, the concept will not work in real life as the physical NICs will become a bottleneck.

> All the Converged Network configurations must be made through PowerShell if you're using Hyper-V. By using System Center Virtual Machine Manager 2012 SP1 and above, you can accomplish this configuration with a GUI. This process is not within the scope of this book.

Now that the Converged Network scenario is in place, let's recap what the options for your virtualization host, regarding networking, are:

- Using a single NIC with all the traffic flowing through it
- Using multiple NICs and segregating the traffic through the multiple NICs
- Using multiple NICs with NIC Teaming but still physically isolating the traffic
- Using multiple NICs with NIC Teaming without isolating the traffic
- Using multiple NICs with NIC Teaming and logically isolating the traffic using the Converged Network concept

There are still other hardware components and features to observe on the host, but we are going to explain it by presenting the VM features, so you can have a better idea of what is the impact of the feature on the VM itself.

# VM network features

If you're creating a new VM today, this VM will probably need to access the network. Even if isolated, most of the workloads need to access network resources to work properly. For that reason, when you create a VM in Hyper-V, it will have at least one virtual Network Adapter by default.

To start understanding how a virtual Network Adapter works on a Hyper-V VM, it is important to remember how any hardware is presented to a VM. As explained in *Chapter 1*, *Getting Started with Hyper-V Architecture and Components*, all hardware devices are presented to the VMs as synthetic devices. This is no different for the virtual Network Adapter. For a VM to be able to use the virtual Network Adapter, the Integration Components (IC) must be installed on the guest OS.

If the guest OS does not support IC, a Legacy Network Adapter can be presented to it. The Legacy Network Adapter, however, does not support any of the features that we are going to present later in this chapter; even worse, it works as a 10 Mbps NIC. The Legacy Network Adapter is useful when you have to boot the VM from the network. In this case, the standard Network Adapter is not going to work.

> Hyper-V in Windows Server 2012 R2 supports Generation 2 VMs. Gen 2 VMs support booting from the network using standard Network Adapter. This topic will be detailed in *Chapter 6*, *Virtual Machines and Virtual Machine Templates*.

Since the Legacy Network Adapter is rarely used on production environments, except for booting from the network, from now on, we will refer to the standard Network Adapter as vNIC.

We already know that a vNIC is added to a VM when the VM is created. Let's take a look at all its capabilities.

# Network Adapter features

To check the available features of a vNIC, open **Hyper-V Manager**, select the VM
you want to configure and open its settings. If the VM is turned off, the first thing
you'll note is that you can add a new vNIC to the VM, as well as the Legacy Network
Adapter. Furthermore, you can edit the vNIC properties by selecting the vNIC and
expanding the configuration, as shown in the following screenshot:

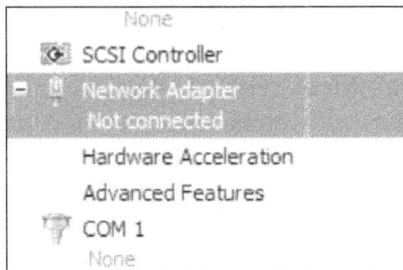

In the **Network Adapter** settings, you can connect the vNIC to a **Virtual Switch**,
as explained earlier. You can also specify the **VLAN ID** that the communication
of this vNIC must use. Also, you can specify the **Bandwidth Management** as seen
previously in this chapter.

> Bandwidth Management is usually misinterpreted as **Quality
> of Service (QoS)**. QoS is a standard for ensuring that a specific
> traffic is more or less prioritized in comparison with other types of
> traffic. This is done by protocol. Hyper-V Bandwidth Management
> does not prioritize a specific protocol; it only specifies how much
> bandwidth a virtual Network Adapter can use.

# Hardware Acceleration

On the **Hardware Acceleration** page, you have three options that will impact
the performance of the VM network. Before going into details, it is important to
remember that all of them require a physical NIC that supports these features. Check
with your hardware vendor if your virtualization host supports these features. If
you're planning the acquisition of a new virtualization host, see if these features will
influence your decision.

# Virtual Machine Queue

Looking back on what you learn about the network, you can see that the flow of the inbound traffic is: physical switch to physical network to Virtual Switch to VM vNIC. This is true in concept, but what happens when the inbound traffic arrives at the host NIC is that the parent OS has to examine the traffic to see the VM to which that packet belongs.

With **Virtual Machine Queue (VMQ)** the packet will be assigned, by hardware, to the VM queue. If a VM has VMQ enabled, and the physical NIC supports it, the VM will request a queue for it when it is turned on. In large deployments of Hyper-V that concentrates multiple VMs on a single, or a few NICs, VMQ can improve the inbound traffic performance.

Some hardware vendors have their own implementations of VMQ, and also each NIC will have a limited number of queues. The recommendation is to verify with the hardware vendor if your hardware supports it, and how many queues are available. You can choose to disable VMQ for VMs to prioritize VMs that are more important. To enable or disable VMQ with GUI, select the **Hardware Acceleration** option and check or clear the **Enable virtual machine queue** option.

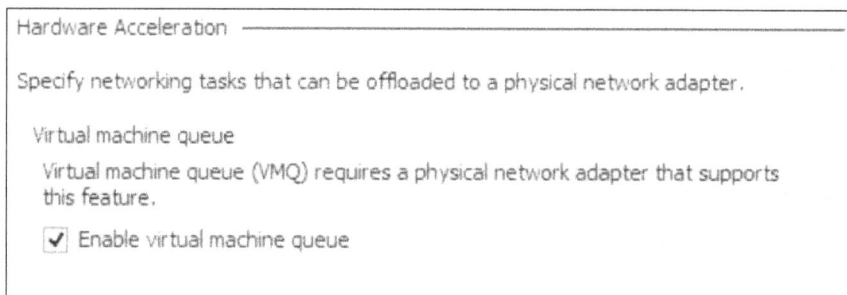

Hardware Acceleration ――――――――――――――――――――――――――――――――――

Specify networking tasks that can be offloaded to a physical network adapter.

Virtual machine queue

Virtual machine queue (VMQ) requires a physical network adapter that supports this feature.

✔ Enable virtual machine queue

To enable VMQ using PowerShell, use the following cmdlet:

```
Set-VMNetworkAdapter -VMName VM-01 -VmqWeight 0
```

As you can see, the VMQ configuration is not just enabled or disabled. You have to specify 0 for disabled or 100 for enabled.

The problem with the configuration of VMQ through PowerShell is that the preceding command will perform the operation on all vNICs of the VM on your running the command. If you want to specify the vNIC on which to perform the operation, you have to use the input -Name. However, all Network Adapters have the same name in Hyper-V. To identify the vNIC you want to run the operation on, run the following command:

```
Get-VM VM-01 | Get-VMNetworkAdapter | fl ID
```

The preceding command will show the IDs of the vNICs on the VM. At the end, to enable or disable VMQ for a specific vNIC, you have to run the `Get-VMNetworkAdapter` cmdlet, pipe it into the `Where-Object` cmdlet query and pipe it again in the `Set-VMNetworkAdapter`. Take a look at the following example:

```
Get-VMNetworkAdapter -VMName VM-01 | Where ID -eq
Microsoft:8B3BEF0D-18CB-4DA9-8614-FEB71485D9CD\1F3DBE46-7E2B-428D-
9A47-033556D27003 | Set-VMNetworkAdapter -VmqWeight 0
```

To enable VMQ, run the same cmdlet but with the value `100` for `-VmqWeight`:

```
Get-VMNetworkAdapter -VMName VM-01 | Where ID -eq
Microsoft:8B3BEF0D-18CB-4DA9-8614-FEB71485D9CD\1F3DBE46-7E2B-428D-
9A47-033556D27003 | Set-VMNetworkAdapter -VmqWeight 100
```

# IPsec task offloading

IPsec is a Windows feature that encrypts all the data that is sent to the network. By default, the processor is the component responsible for encryption and decryption of the packets. The IPsec concept, how it works, and how to implement it is not within the scope of this book. For now, keep in mind that a large amount of IPsec traffic can create a bottleneck on the processor as it will struggle to process all the packets.

To avoid this situation, some physical NICs support a feature called IPsec task offload. This feature transfers the responsibility of encryption and decryption of IPsec packets to the NIC, releasing the processor for other tasks.

To better configure IPsec task offload, it is important to consult your hardware vendor. On the GUI, you can specify if IPsec task offload will be enabled or not for that vNIC, and the maximum number of security associations (encryption and decryption) that the physical NIC will handle. If there are no more hardware resources, the security associations will be handled by the guest OS. Look at the following screenshot:

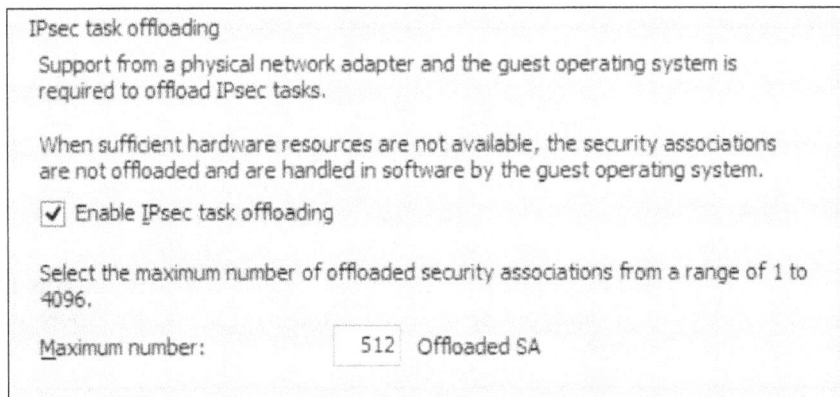

IPsec task offloading

Support from a physical network adapter and the guest operating system is required to offload IPsec tasks.

When sufficient hardware resources are not available, the security associations are not offloaded and are handled in software by the guest operating system.

☑ Enable IPsec task offloading

Select the maximum number of offloaded security associations from a range of 1 to 4096.

Maximum number:    512    Offloaded SA

To perform the operation via PowerShell, use the following cmdlet:

```
Set-VMNetworkAdapter -VMName VM-01 -
IPsecOffloadMaximumSecurityAssociation 512
```

As the PowerShell cmdlet to configure VMQ, the IPsec PowerShell cmdlet does not handle multiple vNICs very well. Use the same process to run the operation on multiple vNICs:

```
Get-VMNetworkAdapter -VMName VM-01 | Where ID -eq
Microsoft:8B3BEF0D-18CB-4DA9-8614-FEB71485D9CD\1F3DBE46-7E2B-428D-
9A47-033556D27003 | Set-VMNetworkAdapter -
IPsecOffloadMaximumSecurityAssociation 512
```

To disable IPsec task offloading for a vNIC, change the value to 0, as in the following cmdlet:

```
Get-VMNetworkAdapter -VMName VM-01 | Where ID -eq
Microsoft:8B3BEF0D-18CB-4DA9-8614-FEB71485D9CD\1F3DBE46-7E2B-428D-
9A47-033556D27003 | Set-VMNetworkAdapter -
IPsecOffloadMaximumSecurityAssociation 0
```

# SR-IOV

As you've seen so far, one of the aspects of the vNIC is that it is a synthetic device for the guest OS. You don't have to, for example, install the network driver on the guest OS, as it is presented in the IC.

However, using a synthetic device has its drawbacks. In the case of a vNIC, the drawback is that you cannot make use of the specific features available on the physical NIC. The VM will just not see these available features.

The SR-IOV feature allows you to present the entire physical NIC to a VM. Needless to say that the physical NIC must support this feature, just like all other Hardware Acceleration features.

To enable the SR-IOV feature, mark the **Enable SR-IOV** checkbox as shown in the following screenshot:

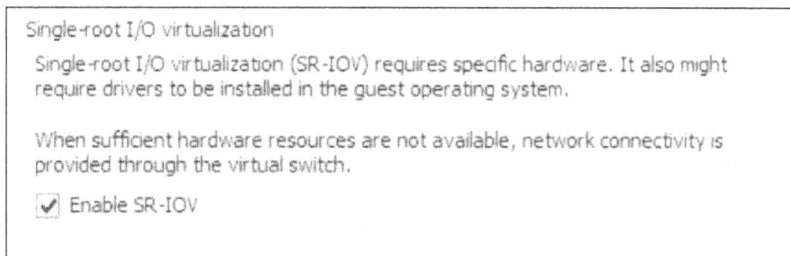

The benefit of using an SR-IOV enabled NIC and vNIC is that this feature reduces the CPU overhead for processing the network traffic. With that, the VM will benefit from more throughput and lower network latency in mission-critical applications.

Keep in mind that you'll need to install the Network Adapter device driver on the guest VM for the vNIC to work.

One of the differences of the SR-IOV implementation in Hyper-V is that it will not prevent you to Live Migrate the SR-IOV enabled VM to another host, as long as the other host has an SR-IOV capable NIC. Otherwise, the vNIC will connect to a Virtual Switch.

# Advanced Features

Besides the features in the preceding section, there are additional features available on Hyper-V that do not depend on the physical hardware. These features include special security configurations that are extremely useful in a virtual environment. Let's take a look.

## MAC address

As with any Ethernet Network Adapter on any computing system, the vNIC needs a MAC address to work. As this is a virtual Network Adapter, Hyper-V can dynamically configure the vNIC MAC address. To configure the vNIC MAC address, you can select one of the following options:

MAC address

⦿ Dynamic

◯ Static

    00 - 15 - 5D - 0E - 09 - 01

MAC address spoofing allows virtual machines to change the source MAC address in outgoing packets to one that is not assigned to them.

☐ Enable MAC address spoofing

If you select Dynamic, Hyper-V will generate a MAC address based on the MAC address range. You can check the MAC address range by opening the **Virtual Switch Manager...** in **Hyper-V Manager**, and selecting **MAC Address Range**.

The **Static** option allows you to define a fixed MAC address. This option is usually used in Physical to Virtual (P2V) conversions, where you want to keep the MAC address of the physical server.

The **Enable MAC address spoofing** option will allow another MAC address to pass on the port configured to the vNIC MAC address. By default, this is not allowed, but, in some cases, such as **Network Load Balance** (**NLB**), it is necessary.

## DHCP guard and Router guard

Imagine you're the administrator of a company responsible of operating multiple customers, a **hoster** by definition. Usually in these cases, you do not have administrative privileges on the VM. If someone installs a DHCP Server or a Router Application on the guest OS and you can't access it, you won't be able to prevent this VM to deliver IPs for the network or to advertise routing information to other router devices. To avoid this, you can use DHCP guard and Router guard.

DHCP guard helps you prevent this situation by blocking all DHCP Server communication on the VM. It will not prevent the VM to acquire an IP from a DHCP Server.

Router guard will work in the same way as DHCP guard, but, in this case, it will block routing advertising from the VM.

## Protected network

This option is a tentative one to prevent the VM from being disconnected because of hardware failures. If this option is enabled and a network disconnection occurs on this vNIC, Hyper-V will attempt to move the VM to another host. Keep in mind that this option will only work on Hyper-V Cluster, but, as in Windows Server 2012 and 2012 R2, you can move a VM from a standalone host to a cluster, and this option is checked by default.

## Port mirroring

This option is important for cases where you want to check the traffic flowing to a VM and, for any given reason, you cannot install Network Inspection software inside the VM.

The Port mirroring option allows to mirror all packets sent to a VM vNIC to another vNIC. To configure this option, you have to set the VM vNIC you want to listen as the **Source** and another VM vNIC, usually on another VM on the same host, as the **Destination**. See the following screenshot:

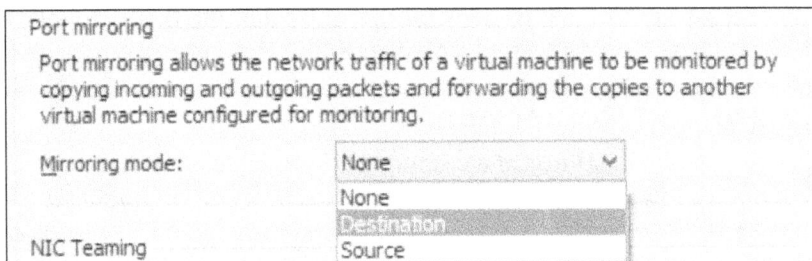

## NIC Teaming

Although you can configure NIC Teaming on the host, an alternative is to configure NIC Teaming directly on the VM. The concept is the same as you saw earlier in this chapter.

The issue here is that Hyper-V will prevent the traffic from one vNIC to failover to another vNIC, by default. Since this is the regular behavior of the NIC Teaming on the failover operation, you have to instruct Hyper-V to not drop the packets.

To do that, mark the **Enable this network adapter to be part of a team in the guest operating system** checkbox.

# Other network implications

So far, you have been able to have a pretty good look at the Hyper-V network configuration and usability. We have checked all the available configurations on the GUI. There are, however, some network items related to Hyper-V, and virtualization in general that are not so obvious. This section will walk you through these concepts. As these items are not focused on virtualization, we will cover just the basic concepts. Deployment, management, and the customization of these items are not within the scope of this book, although I would highly recommend you to study these concepts.

# Policy-based QoS

As explained earlier in this chapter, Hyper-V does not have a QoS configuration, but a Bandwidth Management system. However, Windows Server has a QoS policy configuration. This QoS policy is extremely comprehensive as it can prioritize specific network traffics, such as Voice over IP (VoIP), or deprioritize other network traffics like Peer-to-Peer (P2P) protocol.

To learn more about Policy-based QoS on Windows Server, see the official article at `http://technet.microsoft.com/en-us/library/jj159288.aspx`.

# Data Center Bridging

**Data Center Bridging** (**DCB**) is a standard that works over the standard Ethernet protocol to handle the loss of packets due to queue overflow, or lossless Ethernet. One of the main goals of DCB is to handle traffic so that protocols such as **Fibre Channel over Ethernet** (**FCoE**), which are highly sensitive to packet loss, can be prioritized.

Windows Server 2012 and 2012 R2 support DCB and can work along with DCB enabled devices. To learn more about DCB and how Windows Server 2012 and 2012 R2 support it, see the official article at `http://technet.microsoft.com/en-us/library/hh849179.aspx`.

# Remote Direct Memory Access

**Remote Direct Memory Access** (**RDMA**) is a hardware technology that allows access to the memory on the destination server without involving the destination operating system. There are multiple benefits from using RDMA on virtualization with Hyper-V, including Live Migration, SMB-Direct, and others.

RDMA application on Live Migration will be covered in *Chapter 8, Implementing Live Migration and Replica*. To learn more about RDMA, see the SMB-Direct official article at `http://technet.microsoft.com/en-us/library/jj134210.aspx`.

# Jumbo Frame

When an information is sent across the network from one machine to another, all the information is divided into multiple tiny packets. This behavior is implemented for scenarios where, when a packet is lost, a new packet can be sent. Since the packet is very small, there is not much processing needed for sending the packet again. This is the ideal scenario for WAN networks or over the Internet.

The drawback here is that the processor has to break the multiple information packets, occupying multiple cycles, and degrading the host performance. For Datacenter networks, it makes no sense to divide all the traffic in multiple tiny packets as these are reliable networks.

Jumbo Frame is a solution for Datacenter networks where the packets are divided on large frames, and sent to the destination. As the packets are larger, the process to divide the frames will use less cycles of the host processor, benefiting the overall performance.

By default, the payload size of an Ethernet packet, which is the size of the packet discarding source and destination MAC address, is 1500 bytes. The size of a Jumbo Frame (or Jumbo Packet) may vary but is usually between 9000 and 9216 bytes.

Keep in mind that all the devices on which the packet will flow, that is, switches, routers and, other servers, must support the Jumbo Frame size.

To learn more about Jumbo Frames, see the article at `http://en.wikipedia.org/wiki/Jumbo_frame`.

# Windows Firewall

Windows Firewall is usually the cause of access problems in multiple environments, generally caused by the administrators' lack of knowledge about opening or closing the correct ports on the servers.

The good news is that the Windows Firewall comes with multiple rules already created, but not enabled. If you need a particular program, traffic, or component to be allowed, go to the Start screen on Windows Server 2012 and 2012 R2 and type `Firewall`. Open the **Windows Firewall** with **Advance Security**.

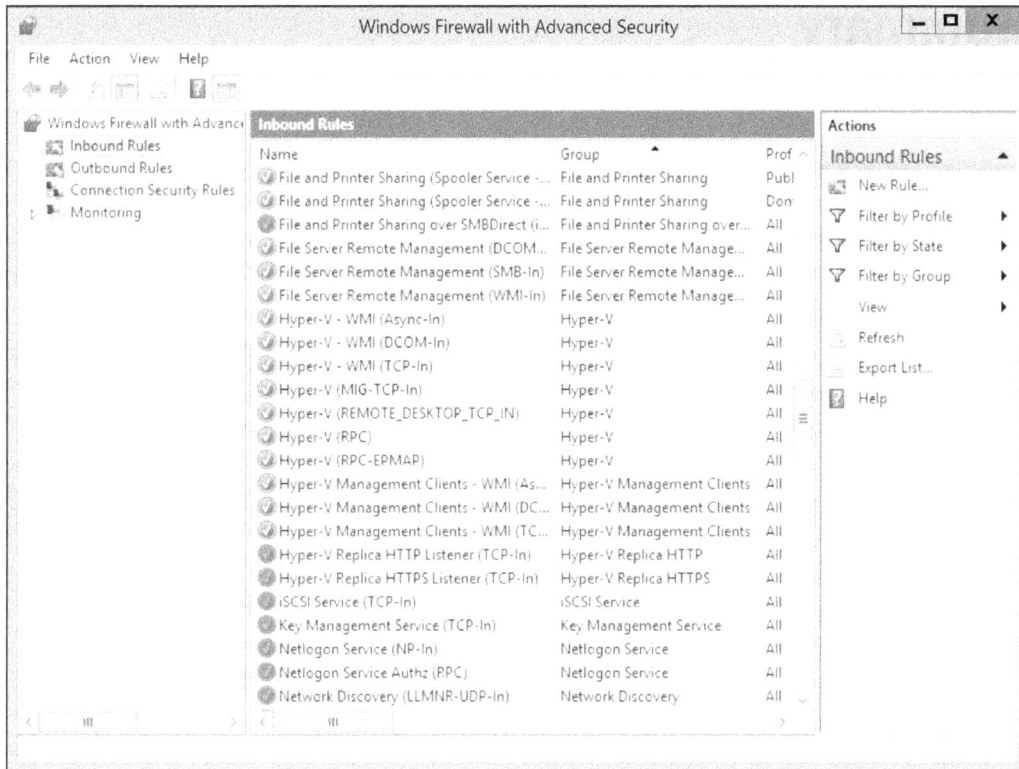

To enable a Rule, simply select the Rule, right-click it and select **Enable Rule**. You can also create new Rules by selecting **New Rule...** at the top right corner.

# Hyper-V Extensible Switch

Besides all the configurations you've seen so far, you can still find that there is something missing. In fact, Microsoft believes that partners are an important part of the stack. With that said, in Windows Server 2012, Microsoft opened the Hyper-V Virtual Switch to partners to build new solutions on top of it.

These solutions include Network Inspection, Antivirus, Firewall, Packet Forwarding, and many others.

To see the new features of the Hyper-V Extensible Switch, check the official blog post from the networking product team at `http://blogs.technet.com/b/networking/archive/2013/07/31/hyper-v-extensible-switch-enhancements-in-windows-server-2012-r2.aspx`.

# Summary

In this chapter, you were able to have a comprehensive understanding of the Hyper-V networking capabilities. You saw how the Hyper-V Virtual Switch works, how the Private, Internal and External configurations work, and how to connect a VM to the Virtual Switch.

We covered advanced aspects of networking on the host machine with NIC Teaming and multiple ways of implementing it. Then, we changed gear to understand how the VM is impacted with network features.

To finish, we provided some additional content to be aware of when administrating a Hyper-V environment. In the next chapter, we will focus on storage and networking, its impact on the performance and features for the host and VMs.

# 5
# Managing Storage

In the previous chapter, we started by mentioning that network and storage are the two components that can heavily influence the host and the VM performance. Both, network and storage, must be carefully planned. Otherwise, as mentioned in the previous chapter, changing the hardware configuration on the fly can be painful. From the storage perspective, today we have some techniques that minimize the impact of changing the underlying hardware for the VM.

In fact, throughout this chapter, you will be able to understand that there are multiple options for configuring both the host and the VM storage. You have the disk options that can be a spinning disk or a solid state drive. Then you choose how to connect your host to your Storage Fabric, which can be a Storage Area Network (SAN) or a Network Attached Storage (NAS); you can even choose to use a local storage or a Direct Attached Storage (DAS). The VM storage is another multiple option plan: Physical or Virtual Disk? VHD or VHDX? Shared VHDX or Dedicated VHDX?

In this chapter, we will cover the options and the pros and cons of each of them. It is important to plan for an option that will better fit your environment, but make sure to plan and avoid configuration mistakes, since this can involve not only an extra cost, but also VM and application downtime.

In this chapter, we will cover the following topics:

- Host storage
- Disk types
- Storage fabric interconnection
- Windows Server as a storage option
- VM storage
- Virtual Disk types
- Advanced Virtual Disk configuration

# Host storage

Let's start the chapter by understanding the implications of the host storage, as this will probably be your starting point when planning your virtualization host storage. Before we go into details of each component, it is important to deconstruct a storage device, in this case, imagining that you're using an external storage device and not the local disks.

A Storage Device is basically a set of Connectivity Adapters, Controllers, and physical disks. The Connectivity Adapters are the communication channel between your host and the Storage Device. They can be an iSCSI, Fibre Channel (FC), Fibre Channel over Ethernet (FCoE), Network File System (NFS), or even a Server Message Block (SMB). Each one comes its own implementation, protocol and sometimes even different hardware, despite the fact that most of them run on Ethernet.

Another component is the Controller, which is responsible for the intelligence of the underlying disks. It is usually an x86 CPU with RAM memory, like a regular server. This component is responsible for providing features such as Thin Provisioning, Data Deduplication, Data Tiering, and many other features.

Furthermore, a Storage Device has the physical disks, which can be spinning disks or SSDs. There is a huge performance difference between them, as well as a huge difference in the price range.

The reason we are going through this is that choosing a storage device is extremely important, as this device will influence the performance of the VM. There is a direct relationship between performance and the cost of implementation, so it is important that you understand the applications running on the VMs and plan accordingly. A standard application that does not require much storage performance can run on a cheaper storage device, and in some cases, even on local storage. A mission critical application will probably require a more complex storage device: in some cases because of the uptime SLA, in some because of the performance itself, and in others, both.

# Hard Disk Drive (HDD) or Solid State Drive (SSD)?

Regardless of the options of using local storage or an external storage device, one point is unanimous: the underlying physical disk. Today we have two available technologies, the traditional Hard Disk Drive (HDD) and the Solid State Drive (SSD). The differences between them are huge. Performance, reliability, cost, are just a few of those.

An HDD is probably the most common technology and you probably have or had a computer, desktop or server, with this type of disk. The HDD is composed of a magnetic disk on which the data is written, using sectors where the blocks of data are recorded. A magnetic arm that moves over the magnetic disk is used to read and write the information. As the disk rotates, the arm can go over all sectors of the disk. The faster the rotation, the more read/write operations the HDD is capable of performing. There are, however, several obvious physical limitations for using this type of disk.

A top performance enterprise grade HDD can have up to 15.000 RPM (rotations per minute), which allows a 1 Gbit/s transfer rate, depending on the host interface. Still, this mechanical, motor-powered process is subject to several hardware problems and malfunctions, and, of course, physical limitations. An alternative to the traditional HDD is the SSD.

An SSD has no mechanical moving parts. Instead, it uses integrated flash memory circuits that store the data persistently. Since it does not use mechanical techniques to read/write data, SSD has a lower penalty performance, is less noisy, is more reliable, and can achieve up to 6 Gbit/s of transfer rate, depending on the interface.

The technical aspects of each technology are not within the scope of this book, but it is important for you to understand the limitations and benefits of each technology. In virtualization, the practical guide for choosing between these technologies is the performance needs of the application inside the VM. The cost of an SSD, however, is the most prohibitive for a number of companies. For small to medium companies, a good architecture of HDD will probably achieve the needs of the company's applications.

There is a painful point on which both technologies lie on. Both technologies are subject to hardware failure. If given data is allocated on an HDD or an SSD, and this disk/drive fails, the application that requires this data can go down, or won't be able to perform the operation. To avoid this situation, we have the RAID technology.

# RAID recommendations for virtualization

There are multiple options for preventing the data from a server to be inaccessible because of the disk/drive failure. The term RAID stands for Redundant Array of Independent Disks, and is basically a combination of disks that use a particular technique to avoid failures. Today, we have several options of RAID configuration, like RAID 0, 1, 5, 6, 10, 50 and 60.

> Although SSD is more reliable, it is still subject to hardware failure. The problem of using RAID technology with SSD drives is that the cost of using multiple SSD drives can be extremely high. On the other hand, it can leverage the RAID benefit of expending the total size of the drive, since an SSD tends to be smaller than an HDD.

To understand these options, let's take a look at the most common options available:

- **RAID 0**: The simplest implementation of RAID, this uses only the stripe technique. This means absolutely no prevention for hardware failure. Instead, it will sum the size of each disk and the total available size will be the sum of all disks.

- **RAID 1**: The opposite of RAID 0, RAID 1 will use the mirror technique to avoid data loss in case a disk is down. The drawback of RAID 1 is that it will have only the available size of the mirror. Additional disks will not add more space.

- **RAID 5**: RAID 5 is maybe the most common implementation of RAID. It uses parity between, at least, three disks to provide fault tolerance, as well as providing more available space as you add more disks. If one disk fails, parity is used to calculate the data on the remaining disks, which reduces performance, but still maintains the application.

- **RAID 6**: RAID 6 uses the same technique as RAID 5, but in this case, it uses double parity. Double parity allows fault tolerance for up to two disks. It has the same drawback as RAID 5, in which performance is reduced in case a disk fails. Also, RAID 6 requires at least four disks.

- **RAID 10**: RAID 10 is basically a nested RAID, implementing RAID 1 +0. In this case, the physical disks are mirrored and then striped. This allows for a fault tolerance system while keeping up the performance with striped disks.

- **RAID 50 and 60**: These are not so common. They have the same principle as RAID 10, but use RAID 5 or 6 on the physical disks. A stripe is used to gain performance on top of RAID 5 or 6, and will still have more efficiency on the available space over RAID 10.

With some of the many available options, you might be asking yourself "What is the practical guidance for RAID on virtualization?". It will depend, of course, on your budget. RAID 10 and above provide better performance and reliability, but, on the other hand, may be expensive. For some small to a mid-size company, most of the applications will run perfectly on RAID 5. Some large enterprises, however, might require a complex implementation of RAID 10. A few critical, high performance applications will require RAID 50 or 60, but these are not so common and a few vendors will implement it on their high-end storage devices.

# Local storage or Local disks

The simplest option for running a VM is obviously the local disk of the virtualization host. However, in production environments, it is not usual, neither recommended. Unless you are running a development or a test environment, using the local disks usually has more problems than using an external storage device.

This is because the local disk does not usually have a storage controller that provides all the options as the controller on the external storage device. RAID options, failure detection, and even throughput, are some of the features that the local disk will probably not rely on. Even if it does, using the local disk will make it impossible to provide High Availability (HA), as HA will require a shared storage.

Still, for small companies using applications that do not require all these features, it is a good and cheaper option. Some Hyper-V features on Windows Server 2012 and 2012 R2 also provide ways for moving the VM storage without interrupting the VM. This feature will be explained later in this chapter. Any additional requirement will require an external storage device.

When you add a new disk to the server on Windows Server 2012 and 2012 R2, you can use the Server Manager to manage the disk and the volume. Open **Server Manager** and click **File and Storage Services**:

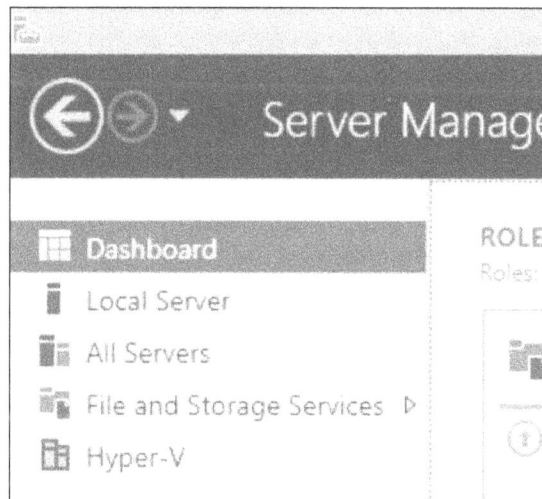

In the **File and Storage Services** menu, click **Disks**. If the added disk is not available in the list, you can click **TASKS** on the top-right corner and click **Refresh**. Select the disk you want to use, right-click it and select **Bring Online** as shown in the following screenshot:

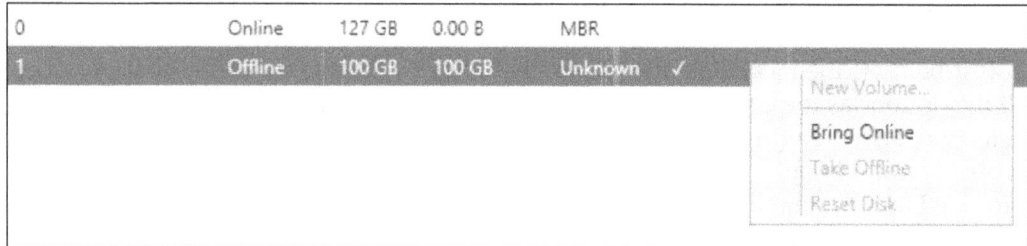

Click **Yes** on the warning. Rick-click the disk again and select **Initialize**. This will put the disk in a state ready to be formatted. Right-click the disk and select **New Volume...**. In the wizard, click **Next >**. Check if the selected disk is listed and click **Next >**. Choose the volume size and click **Next >**. Select the **Drive letter** and click **Next >**. On **File System Settings**, check if the **File system** is **NTFS**, as Hyper-V only supports NTFS volumes.

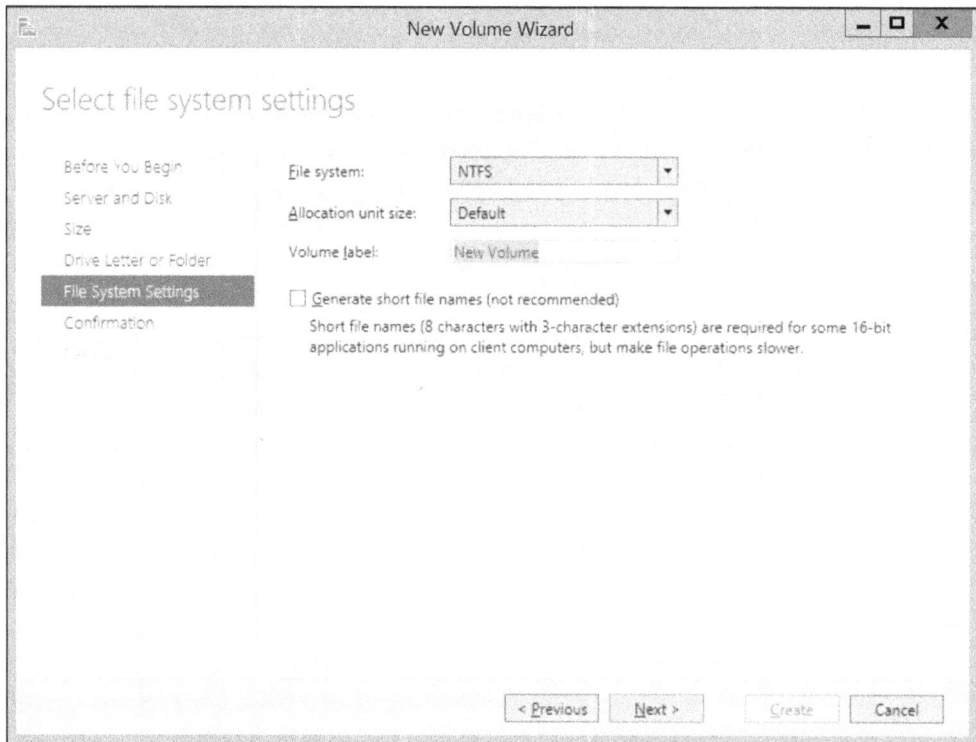

On **Volume label**, provide a label to identify the volume and click **Next >**. Check if all the configuration is correct and click **Create**. After finishing, you'll be able to use the disk as a regular volume.

To perform the same operation using PowerShell, use the following cmdlets.

To list the disks:

```
Get-Disk
```

To bring the disk online:

```
Set-Disk -Number 1 -IsOffline $false
```

The preceding command will mark disk number 1 as online. To initialize the disk, use the following cmdlet:

```
Initialize-Disk -Number 1
```

To create a partition and format the volume, use the following cmdlet:

```
New-Partition -DiskNumber 1 -UseMaximumSize -AssignDriveLetter |
Format-Volume
```

# Direct Attached Storage (DAS)

The definition of a DAS system is that it is, as the name states, directly attached to the host or, depending on the DAS device, hosts. The main difference between this and the other Network Attached Storage (NAS) and Storage Area Network (SAN) storage devices is that DAS does not have an actual network between the device and the host(s).

A DAS device is usually connected through a Fibre Channel or Small Computer Systems Interface (SCSI). Depending on the DAS device, it can connect to one or more servers depending on the number of ports available. This makes DAS devices a good choice for small and medium companies that require High Availability (HA) for their applications. As an HA cluster will require shared storage, DAS devices are a good fit for this scenario.

There are, however, some limitations to this type of system. The first one is that it will probably not scale, given the port limitations. The other problem is that most of the DAS devices do not support storage replication to another DAS device, making the DAS device a single point of failure.

Each vendor will have its own process to implement the DAS device hardware properly. However, once the hardware is implemented, you'll be able to use the associated disks like a local disk in the previous section.

# Storage Area Network (SAN)

SAN storage devices differ from DAS devices as they have the ability to connect the storage device to the hosts using a network. This network can be either a dedicated or a shared network, although it is highly recommended that you dedicate the network for storage communication only. The most common implementations of SAN are Fibre Channel (FC) and iSCSI.

## Fibre Channel (FC)

Fibre Channel is the most common choice for enterprise grade applications in mid to high-end companies. FC uses a dedicated Host Bus Adapter (HBA) to handle all storage traffic. Additionally, FC uses a pair of fiber optic cables. The edge of each pair of cable has a transmitter and a receptor. The transmitter sends a light signal to the receptor.

As the pair of cables are isolated, and the loss of light is almost inexistent, the only limitations for information exchange on FC are the transmitter and the receptor. Unlike other implementations, FC uses its own protocol called **Fibre Channel Protocol** (**FCP**).

Another benefit of FC is that, since it has minimal loss during transmission, the FCP protocol works in lossless mode, which means that all information from a transmission is reliable data.

The drawback of FC is its cost of implementation. An FC system will require a storage device with an FC port, a fibre switch and an HBA on each host. Additionally, scaling requires more investment to have more HBA, and to license each port of the device. Still, FC is the number one choice for high performance applications.

Each vendor will have its own process to implement the FC device hardware properly. However, once the hardware is implemented, you'll be able to use the associated disks like a local disk in the previous section.

## iSCSI

An alternative for high costs on FC, iSCSI uses the standard SCSI protocol over the regular Ethernet communication. Since it uses the regular Ethernet standard, it is, by default, always cheaper than FC. Of course, it is less efficient, too.

As the opposite of FCP, which is a lossless protocol, Ethernet accepts packet loss. In fact, TCP was designed to deal with packet loss. In addition to this, the processing for Ethernet is made by the processor, which can easily affect performance on a virtualization host.

However, the Ethernet hardware has evolved, and today there are specific iSCSI controllers. Even regular NICs offload processing which removes the burden of processing from the processor, and makes iSCSI an excellent choice for mid-load performance applications.

The iSCSI system is composed of a target server, which is the storage device presenting the disks, and the initiator, which is the host connecting to the target server. The target server can be a Storage Device provided by a vendor or a Windows Server with the iSCSI target server role installed. In this book, we will not cover all possibilities for the target server side. However, unlike FC, Windows Server has a native client for iSCSI. To use it, open the Start screen and type iSCSI, as shown in the following screenshot:

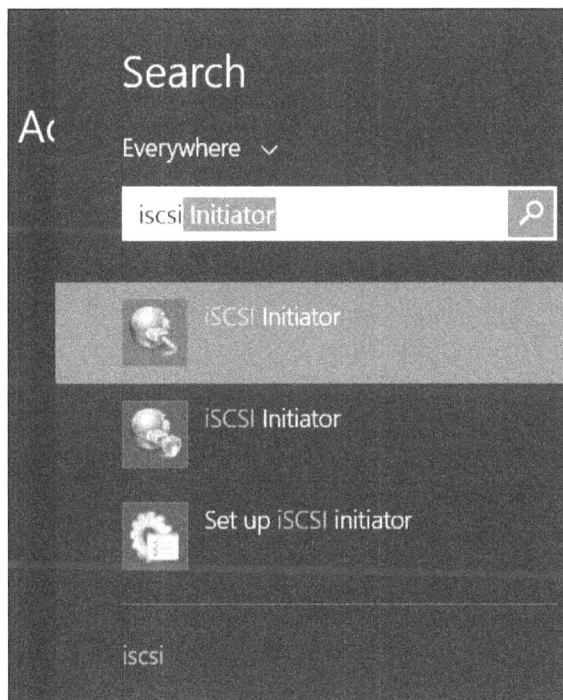

When you open the **iSCSI Initiator** for the first time, you are presented with the following warning:

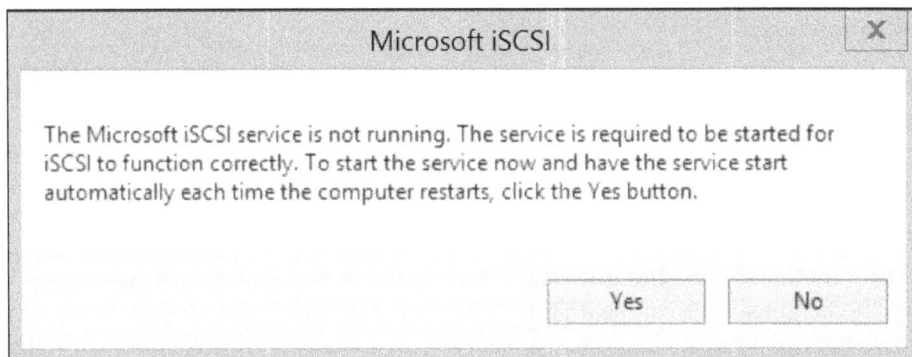

```
┌─────────────────────────────────────────────────────────────────┐
│                      Microsoft iSCSI                       │  X  │
├─────────────────────────────────────────────────────────────────┤
│                                                                   │
│  The Microsoft iSCSI service is not running. The service is       │
│  required to be started for iSCSI to function correctly. To start │
│  the service now and have the service start automatically each    │
│  time the computer restarts, click the Yes button.                │
│                                                                   │
│                              ┌──────────┐    ┌──────────┐         │
│                              │   Yes    │    │   No     │         │
│                              └──────────┘    └──────────┘         │
└─────────────────────────────────────────────────────────────────┘
```

It is important to understand the reason for this message. By default, the iSCSI Initiator service is configured on Windows Server as **Manual**. Whenever you open the iSCSI Initiator, it will start the service. The problem is that when you, for any reason, restart your server, the service will not be initiated and the host will not connect to the disks. That's the reason for this message. This message is asking you to change the default configuration of the service from **Manual** to **Automatic**. When on **Automatic**, the iSCSI Initiator service will start along with the OS and connect to the disks right after the OS boots up. If you did not set **Yes** the first time, you'll have to open the Services MMC and change the configuration manually, as this warning will not be shown again.

On the iSCSI Initiator screen, you have multiple options to connect to your iSCSI Target Server. The easiest way to perform this operation is to insert the target server IP in the Target textbox of **Fully Qualified Domain Name (FQDN)** on the first tab— **Targets**, and click **Quick Connect...,** as shown in the following screenshot:

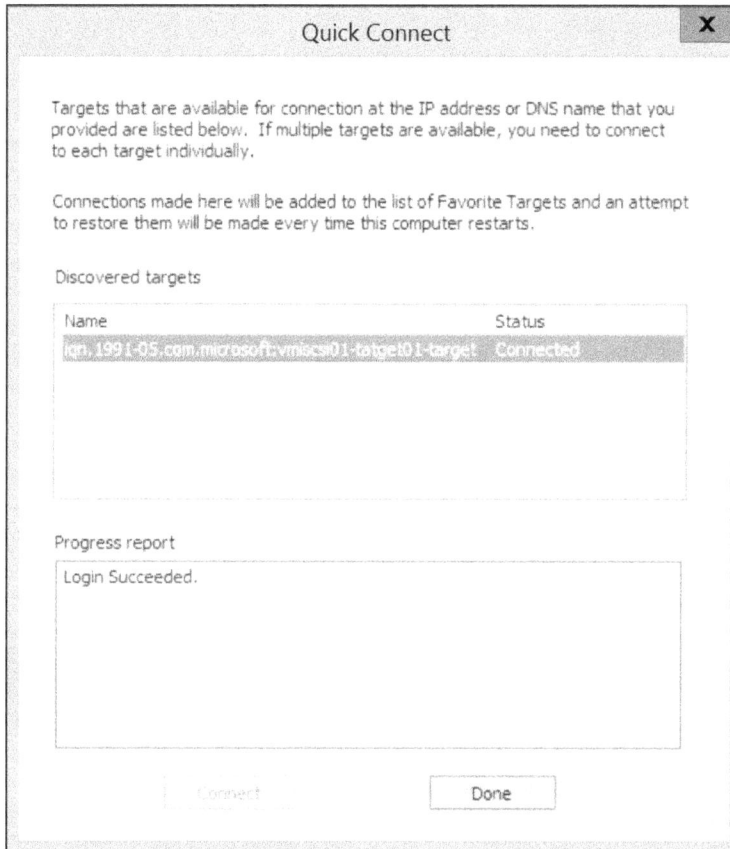

Click **Done** to confirm the connection. If everything is okay, you'll see the target server listed in the **Discovered targets** list.

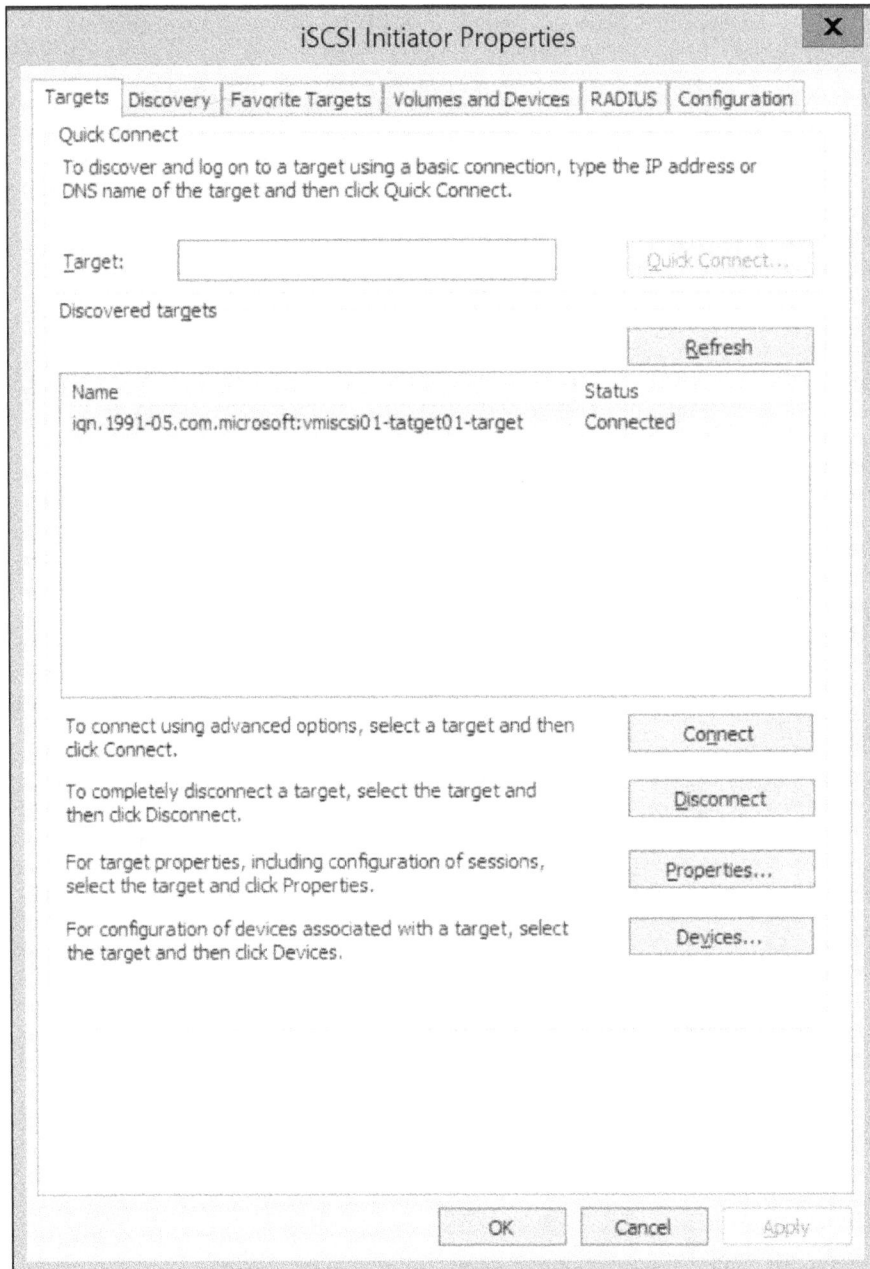

| iSCSI Initiator Properties | X |
| --- | --- |

Targets | Discovery | Favorite Targets | Volumes and Devices | RADIUS | Configuration

Quick Connect

To discover and log on to a target using a basic connection, type the IP address or DNS name of the target and then click Quick Connect.

Target: [                    ]    Quick Connect...

Discovered targets

Refresh

| Name | Status |
| --- | --- |
| iqn.1991-05.com.microsoft:vmiscsi01-tatget01-target | Connected |

To connect using advanced options, select a target and then click Connect.    Connect

To completely disconnect a target, select the target and then click Disconnect.    Disconnect

For target properties, including configuration of sessions, select the target and click Properties.    Properties...

For configuration of devices associated with a target, select the target and then click Devices.    Devices...

OK    Cancel    Apply

Once the initiator successfully connects to the target, the disks will be listed the same way as the local disks in the previous section. However, it is possible to identify an iSCSI Disk as shown in the following screenshot:

# Network Attached Storage (NAS)

Both DAS and SAN devices have one characteristic in common. Both will present the disk to the OS to which it was connected. This means that the entire disk presented will be assigned to the OS, and this OS is responsible for formatting the disk and using it like a regular local disk. An NAS storage, on the other hand, will present a network area on which the host can write application data. It is usually represented by accessing \\SANStorageServer\SharedFolder\.

NAS is usually implemented using **Network File System** (**NFS**) or **Server Message Block** (**SMB**). Both were not supported on Hyper-V in Windows Server 2008 and 2008 R2. In Windows Server 2012 and 2012 R2, Microsoft invested on the SMB protocol for it to support applications like Hyper-V and SQL Server. Hyper-V on Windows Server 2012 and 2012 R2 now supports SMB3, which is present in Windows Server 2012 and 2012 R2. Some Storage Device hardware vendors are also implementing SMB3 on their devices, so it is possible that it might become more popular with time.

> Other virtualization vendors also support NAS with NFS. However, they introduce several feature limitations for using NFS. Microsoft is committed to make every Hyper-V feature available on SMB3 as well as any other storage option. NFS is not supported on Hyper-V.

# Server Message Block 3 (SMB3)

Server Message Block is a protocol created for sharing access to files and folders, as well as printers and other network resources. Over time, Microsoft has made several contributions and changes to the protocol, culminating in Windows Server 2012 and 2012 R2 (in 2012 R2 the protocol was updated to 3.02).

The idea behind SMB3 is to provide a robust protocol for supporting applications, such as Hyper-V. To provide such support, new features were added to the protocol such as:

- **SMB Direct**: SMB Direct uses the available resources of Remote Direct Memory Access (RDMA) enabled NICs to offload the processing from the CPU, providing more performance on throughput and low latency. For more information on SMB Direct, check the official article at `http://technet.microsoft.com/en-us/library/jj134210.aspx`.

- **SMB Multichannel**: As the name suggests, Multichannel enables multiple connection paths for the same connection between the client and the server. This allows for higher throughput, and network fault tolerance. This feature is enabled by default, and automatically discovers the available path between the client and the server. For information, check the official article at `http://technet.microsoft.com/en-us/library/dn610980.aspx`.

Accessing an SMB3 is extremely simple. All you have to do is provide the Uniform Naming Convention (UNC) path when creating a VM or a disk. The process for creating a VM will be detailed in *Chapter 6, Virtual Machines and Virtual Machine Templates*, but in the following screenshot you can see how to provide the UNC path for creating a VM on an SMB3 Storage Device:

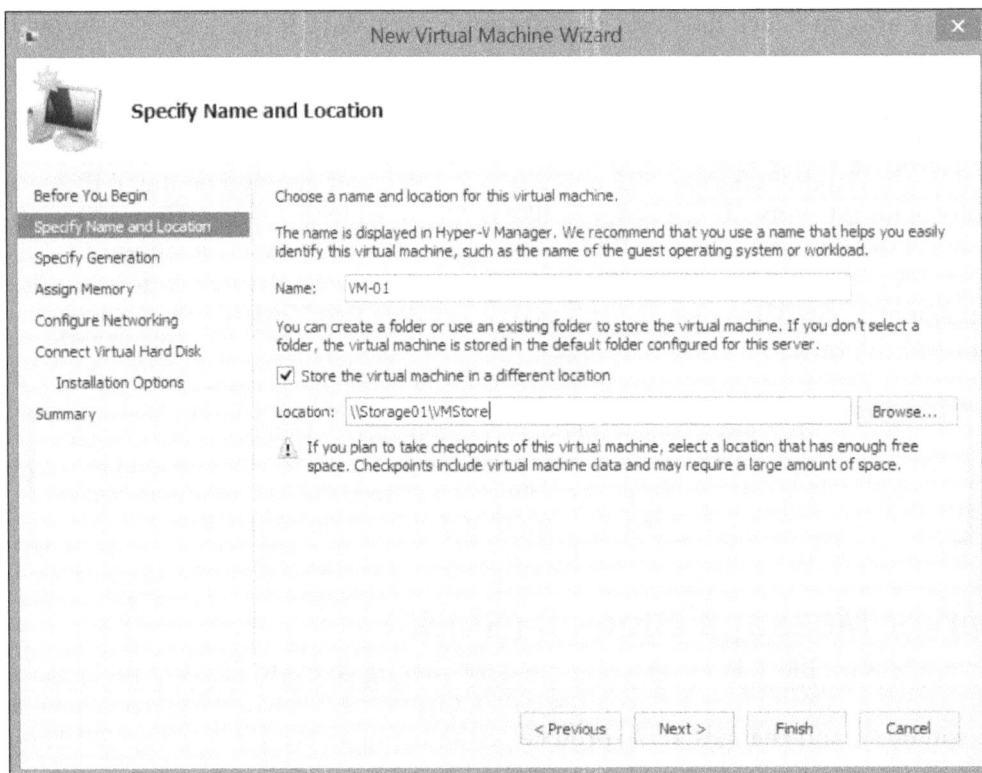

SMB3 is an excellent protocol for Hyper-V in Windows Server 2012 and 2012 R2. You must keep in mind, however, that it still uses the standard Ethernet communication protocol. This means that it has the same drawbacks as any other regular TCP protocol.

To avoid these drawbacks, the recommendations for SMB3 storage implementations are much like on iSCSI. Using a dedicated RDMA enabled 10 Gb NIC will allow for great performance. Using NIC teamed with LACP enabled is another great option to boost performance.

Because of these new features of the SMB3, even some high performance applications can benefit from it. However, there are some applications with intensive storage I/O utilization that will better benefit from a lossless protocol, such as FCP. Still, SMB3 is gaining more and more space, even in enterprise grade applications, as it is cheaper, yet reliable and has great performance as compared to FC. Another important benefit of SMB3 is scale. You can add more servers accessing the SMB3 server anytime with no impact to the environment.

A question that you might have is "Which vendors are providing SMB3 enabled storage devices?". In fact, some vendors announced that their new storage devices are going to support it, and some are already available in the market. However, there is an important configuration available to you, and maybe you haven't noticed. You can build your own storage device. Think about it — you have the x86 hardware, the brain of the controller (which is Windows Server 2012 R2), and the disks.

# Windows Server as a storage option

So far, you've learned about the regular options for storage on a virtualization host: local disk, DAS and SAN devices. Now, you can understand the pros and cons of each option. One option that is gaining visibility is to use a Windows Server Host attached to a Storage Device, or with the local disks, to provide a centralized shared storage. The great benefit of using this option is that you can take advantage of the features of a Windows Server File Server and provide enterprise class storage in an environment where it was not possible before, because of the costs for implementing such a solution.

There are two common options for using a Windows Server as a Storage Device, depending on the investment your company is able to make. The main difference between these options is the single point of failure of the storage itself.

Another interesting point is that Windows Server today can provide access through either iSCSI or SMB3. It is up to you to decide which protocol to use, depending on the infrastructure or investment that your company is planning. However, independent from the access protocol, Windows Server is able to provide some interesting features for File Services. Let's take a look at these features.

# Windows Storage Spaces

The first feature to discuss, is the foundation of a storage controller. In Windows Server, this feature is called Storage Spaces. Storage Spaces allows a Windows Server to manage the disks like a storage device would manage. To better understand how it works, let's start by implementing it. Open **Server Manager**, click **Manage** and then **Add Roles and Features**. Click **Next >** in the wizard, check the **Role-based or feature-based installation** option and click **Next >**. Confirm if the desired server is selected and click **Next >**. Expand **File and Storage Services** and select the options for enabling a File Server and iSCSI and SMB3, as shown in the following screenshot:

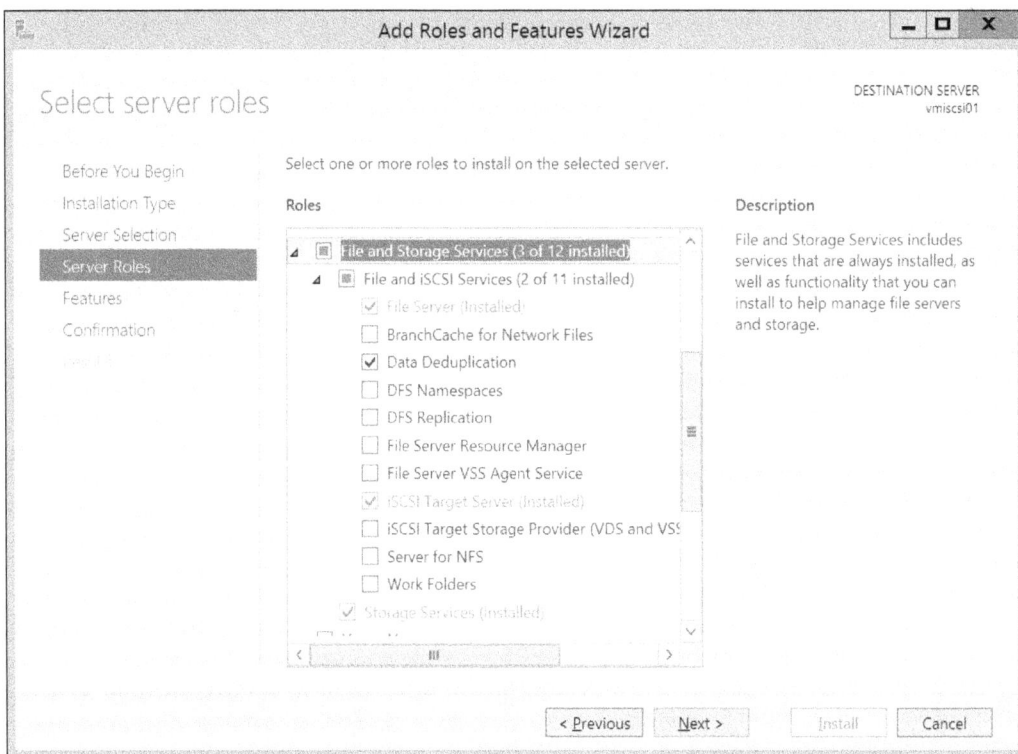

Click **Next >**. Click **Next >** again on **Features** and on the **Confirmation** screen, click **Install**.

To install these roles through PowerShell, use the following cmdlets:

```
$features = ('FS-FileServer', 'FS-Data-Deduplication', 'FS-
iSCSITarget-Server')
foreach ($feature in $features) {Install-WindowsFeature -name
$feature}
```

The preceding cmdlets declare the features that should be installed and store it on `$features`. The next cmdlet runs the `Install-WindowsFeature` cmdlet for each of the features declared previously.

To perform the File Server operations in Windows Server 2012 R2, on **Server Manager**, click **File and Storage Services** on the left. All the following available options will be shown:

In our demonstration, we will use four 100 GB disks. To start the configuration of the disks, click **Storage Pools**.

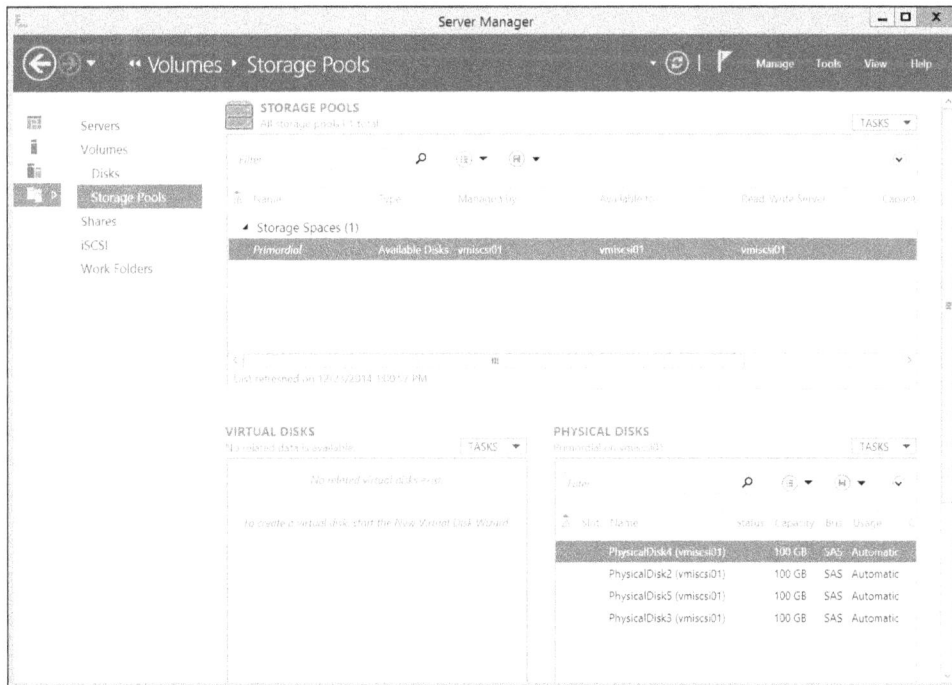

As you can see at the bottom-left, this screen shows all offline disks; in this case the four 100 GB disks.

With Storage Spaces, you can create a pool of disks to use them as a logical unit. To create a Storage Pool, select the disks you want to add to the Pool and click **TASKS** and **New Storage Pool...**.

In the wizard, click **Next >**. Name your Pool by typing the Pool name and click **Next >**. On the next screen, you can check which disks you want to add. The selected disks will be shown as added.

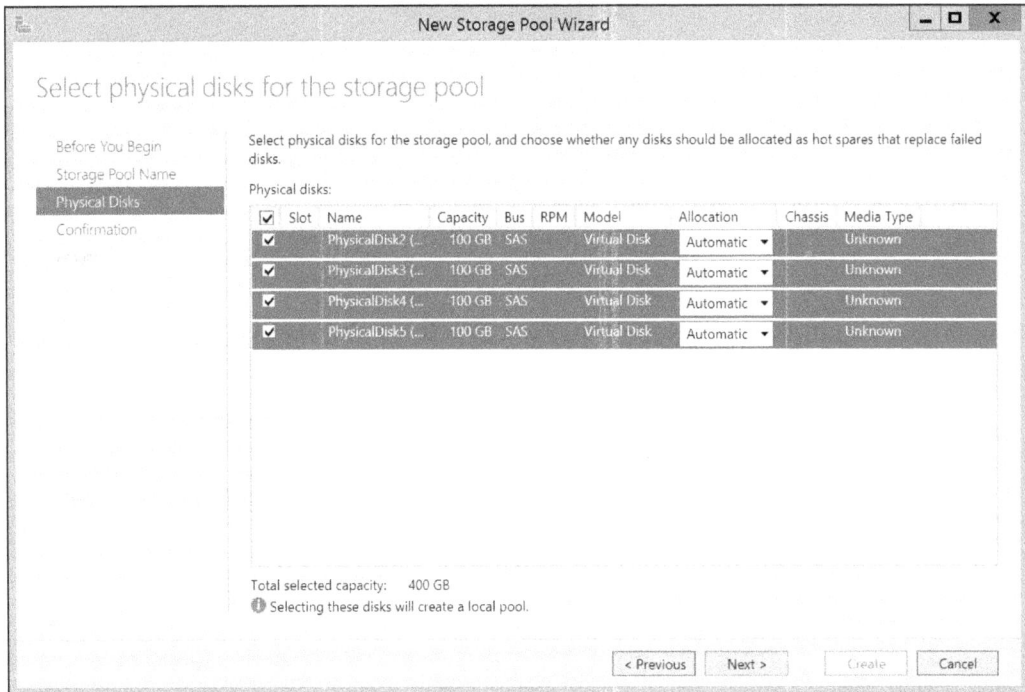

On **Allocation**, you can change the usage of the disk to be a **Hot Spare**. In this case, the disk will be added to the Pool but will only be used in case another disk fails; the Hot Spare disk will be used to replace the failed disk. Click **Next >**. On the **Confirmation** screen, click **Create**.

After creating the Pool, you can create a Virtual Disk on top of the Pool. In this context, the Virtual Disk is a logical unit to be presented to the host as a disk on which the volume will be created. To create a Virtual Disk, you can check the **Create a virtual disk when this wizard closes** before clicking **Close**.

On the New Virtual Disk Wizard, click **Next >**. Confirm that the Pool created in the previous step is selected and click **Next >**. Type the Virtual Disk name. In this screen, you can also check the **Create storage tiers on this virtual disk**, in case you have a mix of HDD and SSD disks and drives. This option is important, as Windows Server will move the hot data (the data that is being constantly accessed), to an SSD drive for better performance. Click **Next >**.

In **Storage Layout**, you can choose from **Simple**(which is basic), a RAID 0, **Mirror**, which is a RAID 1, and **Parity**, which is a RAID 5. Select the best option for your environment and click **Next >**.

Next you can choose from **Thin** or **Fixed** provisioning. **Thin** will allow you to create a volume smaller than the actual total size available and add more space as needed. Another great benefit of **Thin** is that you can add a new disk later and expand the volume to the new disk. **Fixed**, on the other hand will fix the volume size to the size specified. Select the option that meets your need and click **Next >**.

If you specified **Fixed**, you can choose the volume size, up to the total size, or the total size available. If you specified **Thin**, you have to specify the size of the volume. After specifying the volume size, click **Next >**, and on the **Confirmation** screen, click **Create**. When the wizard finishes, confirm that the **Create a volume when this wizard closes** checkbox is marked and click **Close**.

On the **New Volume Wizard**, follow the regular process to create a new NTFS volume on the Virtual Disk. On the **Data Deduplication** screen, you can choose to enable Data Dedup for the volume. Keep in mind that Hyper-V will not benefit from it, unless you're using a Virtual Desktop Infrastructure (VDI).

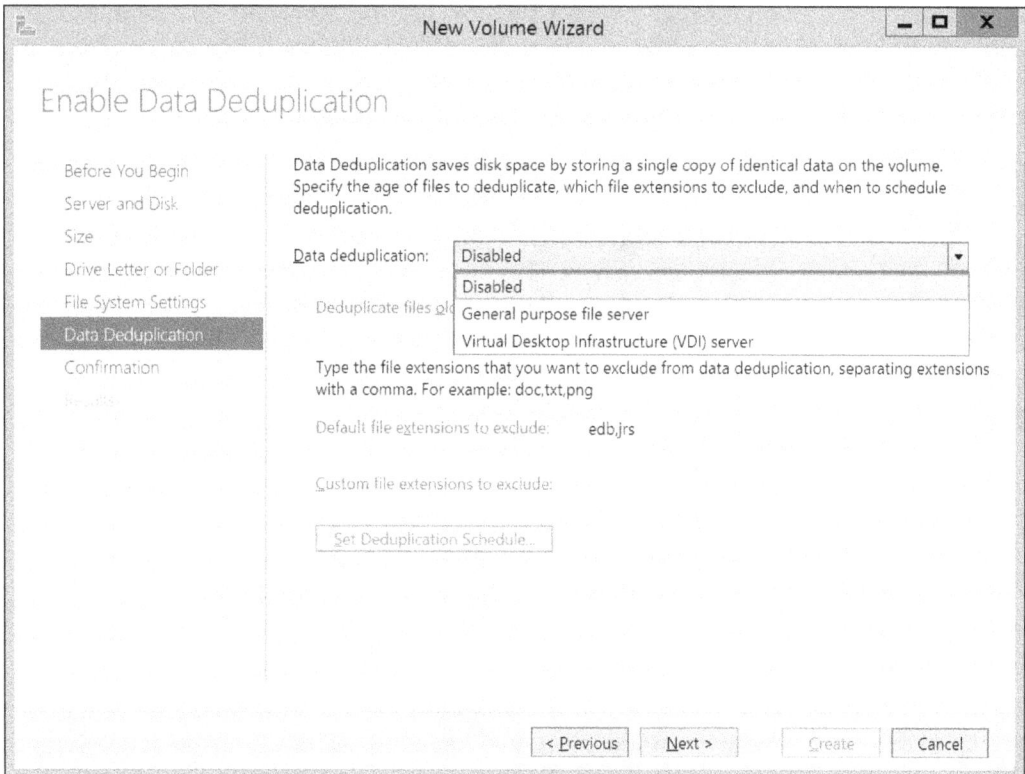

After creating the volume, you can start provisioning the VMs on the disks. To do that, you have to present this volume through iSCSI or SMB3.

# Installing a Windows Server iSCSI Target Server

In the previous step, the iSCSI Target Server Role was installed on the Windows Server. Now we can manage the iSCSI access to the clients, or initiators. To begin, open **Server Manager** and click **File and Storage Services**. Select **iSCSI**. Click on **To create an iSCSI virtual disk, start the New iSCSI Virtual Disk Wizard.** link in the **iSCSI VIRTUAL DISKS** section. In the wizard, select a volume letter or specify the path for creating a Virtual Disk to be presented as an iSCSI disk.

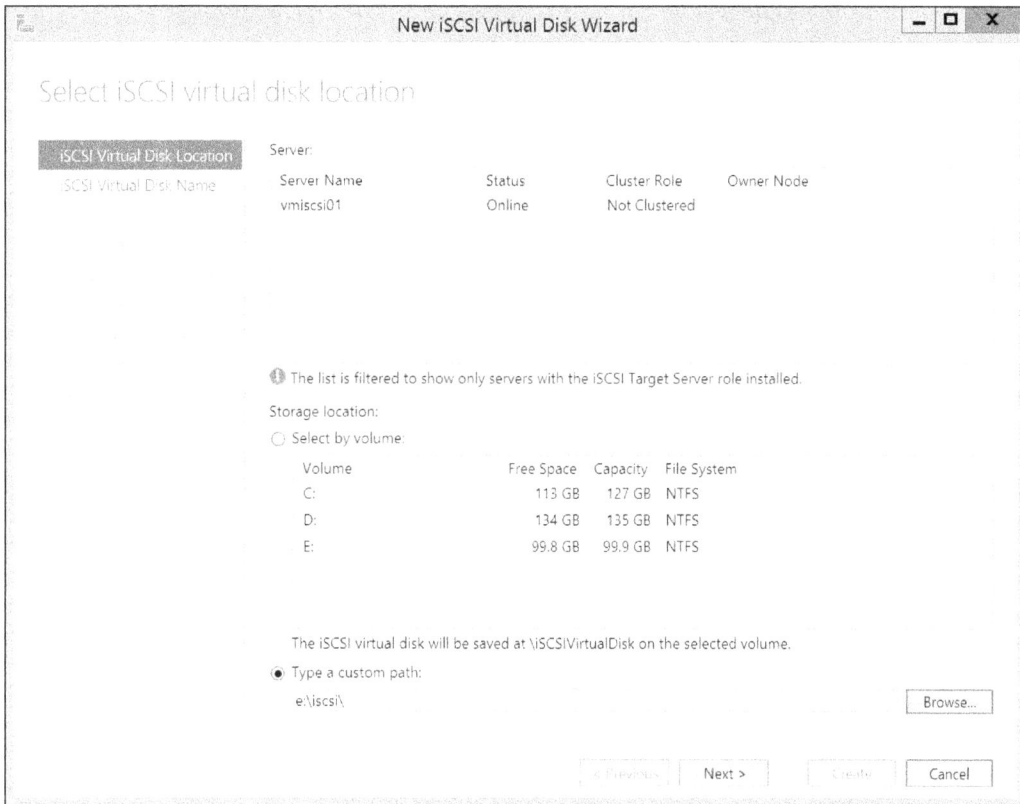

Click **Next >** after specifying the disk or local path. Type the **Name** of the iSCSI Virtual Disk and click **Next >**. Note that a virtual disk will be created on the specified path. Click **Next >**.

At the **iSCSI Virtual Disk Size**, you have to specify the **Size** of the iSCSI disk that the hosts will use. Also, since this is a Virtual Disk, you can choose from **Fixed Size**, **Dynamically expanding,** and **Differencing** disks. These options will be detailed later in this chapter. Click **Next >**.

Next, you have to create a new **iSCSI Target,** as you don't have any created. An iSCSI Target is the identification of the initiators that are connecting to the target server and the disks that should be presented to these initiators. Click **Next >**. Type the iSCSI Target name and click **Next**. On the **Access Servers** screen, click **Add...**.

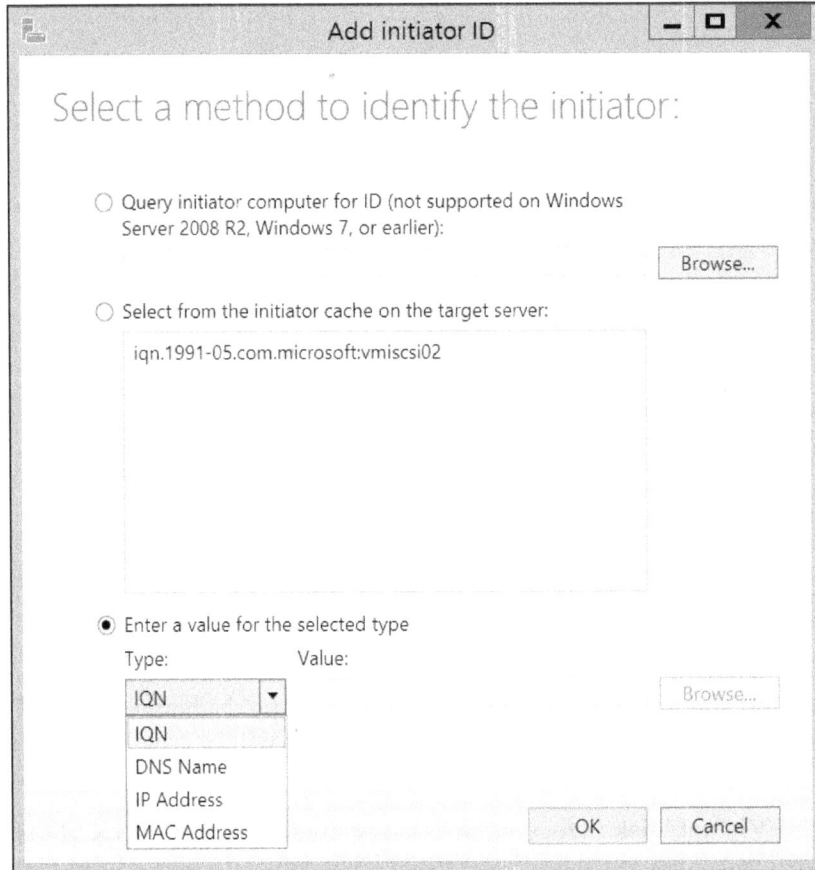

As you can see in the preceding screenshot, there are several ways to identify the initiator and the servers connecting to the target. The recommended one is by using the **iSCSI Qualified Name (IQN)**. The IQN is composed of: IQN, data on which the authority took ownership of the IQN domain (YYYY-MM), authority reserved domain, optional colon ( : ), and storage target name. To ensure that you enter the correct IQN, you can query the IQN of the initiator that you want to list as an initiator accessing this target by clicking **Browse...**. You can also specify the **DNS Name**, **IP Address,** or **Mac Address**.

After specifying the initiator that will connect to the target, click **OK** and click **Next >**. On the next screen, you can provide a CHAP or reverse CHAP authentication. Click **Next >** and click **Create** on the **Confirmation** page. Now you can connect the initiator, as shown earlier in this chapter.

# Installing a Windows Server SMB3 Server

Since SMB3 is a native Windows Server protocol, there is no need to install any additional role. By simply sharing a folder, Windows Server will configure all the prerequisites. To enable a shared folder to support an application, go to **Server Manager**, click **File and Storage Services**, and click **Shares**. In the Shares Section, click **TASKS** and click **New Share....** In the **New Share Wizard**, you can choose from the multiple share options.

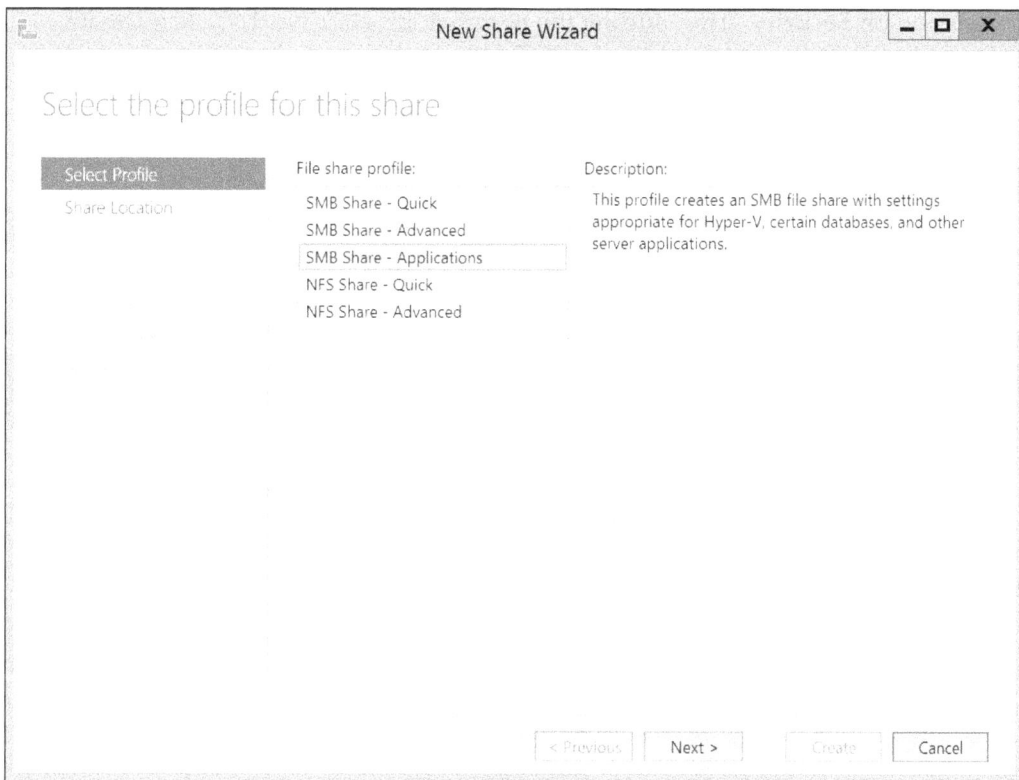

The option that is configured to support applications, such as Hyper-V, is **SMB Share - Applications**. This options brings the default configuration on SMB3 to support Hyper-V, and some of the configuration can be changed in the successive steps. Make sure that you select **SMB Share - Applications** and click **Next >**.

On the next screen, you have to specify a volume or a local path to create the folder to be shared. Specify the path and click **Next >**. On the **Share Name** page, confirm the name of the folder to be shared and the **Share name**. Click **Next >**. If the folder does not exist, a warning will be shown. Click **OK**.

In the **share settings**, you cannot use **Enable access-based enumeration** and **Allow caching of share**, since you selected **SMB Share - Applications** earlier. The only available option is **Encrypt data access**. This option will encrypt all the communication between the server and the client. If you have an isolated network and all the clients of the server sharing the SMB Share are virtualization hosts, and you also keep track of what is going on in your Datacenter, this is probably a feature you don't want to use. This is because enabling encryption on an SMB Share can lower the performance on the SMB Server. After reviewing the option, click **Next >**. On the **Permissions** page, make sure all computer accounts have at least the **Modify** permission on **Security**. After adding the permissions, click **Next >**. Click **Create** to create the SMB Share. Now that the SMB Share has been created, you can start provisioning the VMs on the SMB3 share, as shown earlier in this chapter.

# Clustered iSCSI Target and SMB3

A final option for larger companies is to cluster two or more servers to provide HA for the storage. The caveat here is that Windows Server, by itself, does not replicate local storage to another server. In this case, you have to connect two or more Windows Server computers to a shared storage, as shown in following diagram:

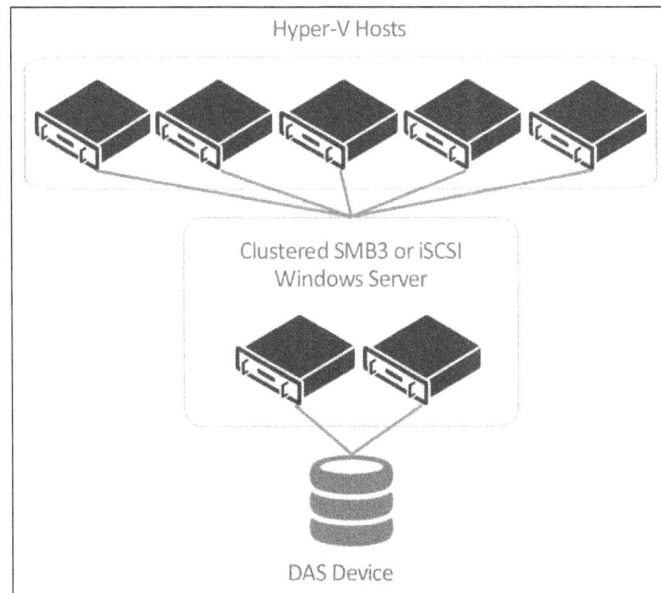

From the preceding diagram, you can quickly imagine what is the problem with this implementation. The Storage Device itself now becomes the single point of failure. To avoid that, you can use a replicated Storage Device. However, this will probably indicate that the application has higher uptime SLA and performance requirements. The benefit of the preceding implementation is that with new hardware and new storage technologies, it is very uncommon for a Storage Device to be totally offline. Plus, adding more servers to both layers, storage cluster, or Hyper-V Hosts, is extremely simple and has no impact on the environment.

> At the time that this book is being written, Microsoft announced a Technical Preview for the next generation of Windows Server. In the release notes of this release, Microsoft indicates that **Storage replication** is one of the new features that will be available in the next release.

Still, if your company understands that having a single point of failure in the environment is not acceptable, you probably want a more complex implementation of a SAN device.

As the implementation of iSCSI Cluster and SMB3 Cluster, also known as **Scale-Out File Server** (**SOFS**), are far more complex, and out of the scope of this book; for more information on their implementation, you can check the official articles at `http://technet.microsoft.com/en-us/library/dn305893.aspx` and `http://technet.microsoft.com/en-us/library/hh831349.aspx`.

# Other host storage implications

Up unitl now in this chapter, we've covered pretty much everything regarding host storage for a virtualization host. There are, however, other implications that you should be aware of, as they can influence performance and may impact your storage planning.

## Virtual SAN Manager and virtual Fibre Channel adapter

In a Fibre Channel environment, you'll have to install an HBA on the host for it to access the disks on the SAN. In some cases, you might want the VMs to access these SAN disks. Prior to Windows Server 2012, the only available option was to present the disk to the host and allocate it to the VM as a pass-through disk (this option will be explained later in this chapter).

Windows Server 2012 added a new feature for Hyper-V which is the ability to virtualize the HBA to the VM. This will create a virtual Fibre Channel adapter on the VM that uses the underlying HBA to access the SAN with the HBA **World Wide Names (WWN)** and its own **World Wide Port (WWP)**.

This feature is an excellent option for FC storage environment with a guest cluster, where the cluster is created at the VM level, and not at the host level.

Since the implementation of a virtual FC environment is very complex and will depend on the hardware vendor, you can check the official article for more information on how to implement it at `http://technet.microsoft.com/en-us/library/hh831413.aspx`.

# 4K disk

Traditional disks use sectors to write data with a size of 512 bytes. However, the storage industry is migrating to a 4096 bytes (4K or 4 KB) sectors that represents better performance for large amounts of data. The problem is that not all operating systems are prepared for this change. Windows 8 and Windows Server 2012 (8.1 and 2012 R2 as well) have native support for 4K disks. Additionally, the new VHDX format, which will be explained later in this chapter, also has native support for this format. For more information about Microsoft support on the 4K format, check the official KB at `http://support.microsoft.com/kb/2510009/en-us`.

# Multipath IO (MPIO)

MPIO is a software implementation on Windows Server to provide load balance and fault tolerance when accessing an FC or iSCSI Storage Device. Hyper-V supports MPIO for both implementations, and it is highly recommended on high performance environments. For more information on the MPIO implementation in Windows Server 2012 and 2012 R2, check the official documentation at `http://www.microsoft.com/en-us/download/details.aspx?id=30450`.

# VM storage

Now that we've covered the host storage, it is time to take a look at how to implement the VM storage. It may look simpler than the host storage, but there are, in fact, multiple choices and possibilities for different environments.

The VM storage can be placed on, basically, two options. A physical disk, also known as a pass-through disk, and a virtual disk. Until Hyper-V on Windows Server 2008 and 2008 R2, using a physical disk had some advantages over the virtual disk. First, the performance on the physical disk was better than using virtual disks. Plus, a virtual disk was able to grow up to 2 TB. If you needed more than 2 TB, it was mandatory to use a physical disk.

Nowadays, a virtual disk can achieve the same performance of a physical disk and can grow up to 64 TB per disk, so using a physical disk brings more drawbacks than benefits. The problem of using a physical disk today is that you don't have all the flexibility of using a virtual one.

Regardless of the disk type, the virtual controller type is another point of attention. A Hyper-V VM can have two types of virtual controller for the disks—it can be a virtual Integrated Drive Electronics (IDE) virtual controller or an SCSI virtual controller. The difference between them looks simple: SCSI virtual controller requires Integration Components (IC), so for operating systems that do not support IC, it is only possible to use IDE virtual controllers.

SCSI virtual controllers, on the other hand, offer additional benefits. The first one is that IDE virtual controllers support two devices per controller, and you can have only two IDE virtual controllers, with a total of four devices. SCSI virtual controllers support 64 disks per controller and you can have up to 4 SCSI virtual controllers per VM. This gives you a total of 256 disks per VM. In addition, SCSI virtual controllers allow you to add or remove disks with the VM powered on, while in the case of IDE virtual controller, you have to power off the VM to add or remove any disk.

[ CD and DVD drives can only be placed on IDE virtual controllers. ]

As mentioned earlier, the complete process of creating and managing a VM will be shown in *Chapter 6, Virtual Machines and Virtual Machine Templates*. For now, we will focus on how to manage disks and virtual controllers on the VMs. To manage the virtual controllers of the VM, open **Hyper-V Manager**, right click a VM and click **Settings....** As you can see in the following screenshot, a VM is already created with both, IDE and SCSI virtual controllers.

Note, however, that the two IDE virtual controllers are already created, and on the first position of the second IDE virtual controller, a DVD drive is allocated. Moreover, on the first position of the first IDE virtual controller, a disk is allocated. This is necessary in this VM type as the boot disk must be an IDE controlled disk.

> In *Chapter 6, Virtual Machines and Virtual Machine Templates*, we will cover Generation 2 VMs on which the boot disk can be on an SCSI virtual controller.

If you want to add another SCSI virtual controller, on this same screen, select **Add Hardware** at the top-left corner and select **SCSI Controller**. Click **Add** to add the second SCSI controller. To confirm the operation, click **Apply**. Keep in mind that while you can add disks to an SCSI virtual controller on the fly, adding another SCSI virtual controller requires the VM to be powered off.

To add the SCSI virtual controller through PowerShell, use the following cmdlet:

```
Add-VMScsiController -VMName VM-01
```

After configuring the virtual controller, it's time to configure the disks. Let's take a look at how to use a physical and a virtual disk, so you can decide for yourself which one to use.

# Physical disk or pass-through disk

A physical disk, also known as a pass-through disk, has the ability to deliver an entire disk to the VM. When delivering an entire disk to the VM, there are some prerequisites to perform this action. To better understand that, let's take a look at what it looks like:

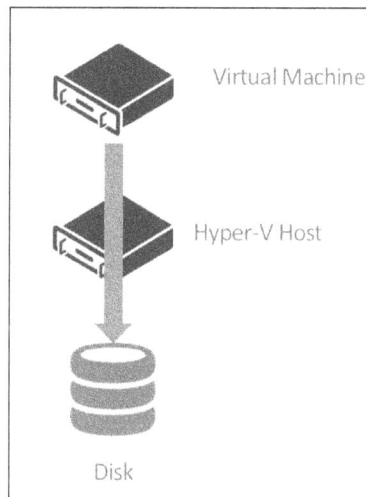

As shown in the preceding diagram, the VM will access the disk that is actually allocated on the host machine. With that said, the first imposition is that the physical disk must be offline on the host machine. That means that the host machine is able to *see* the physical disk, but it must not be available for the host.

With the disk offline on the host, do the following to allocate the disk for the VM: in the VM **Settings...**, select the virtual controller to add the disk, select **Hard Drive** on the option to add, and click **Add**.

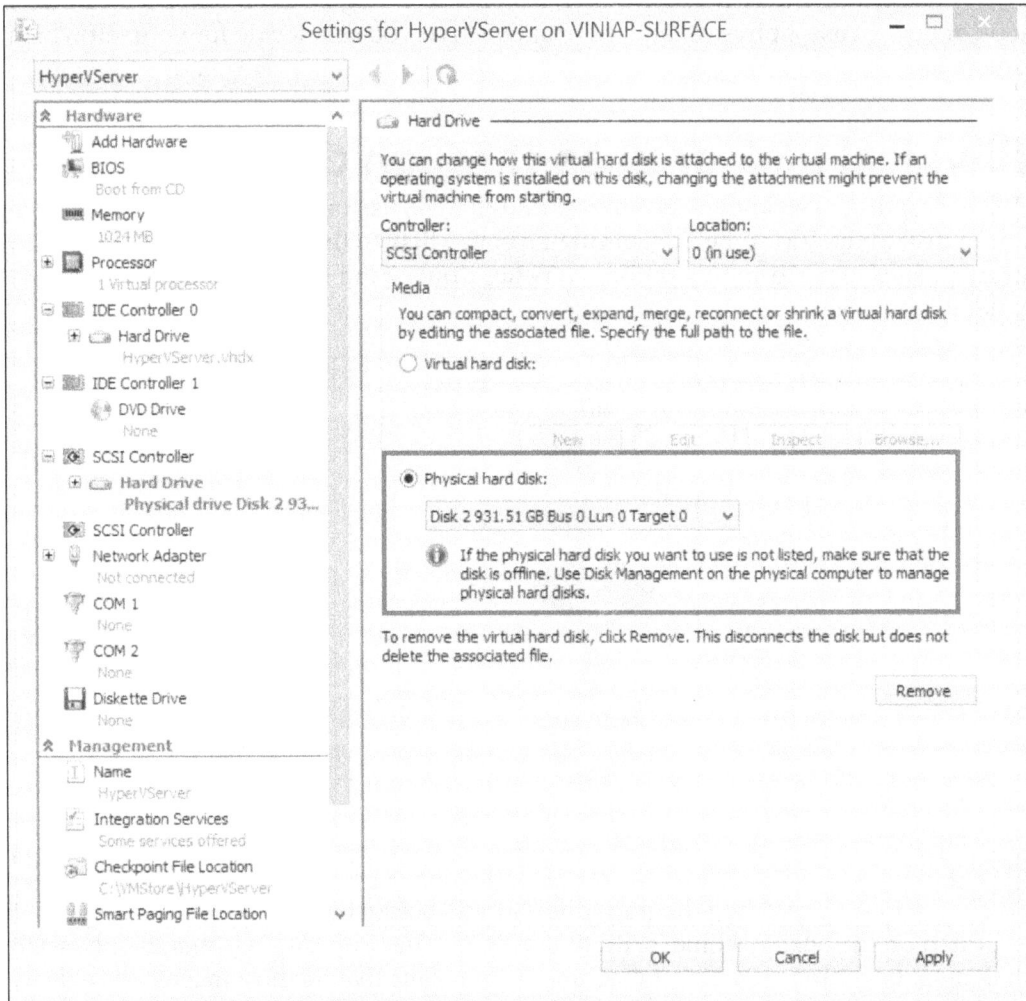

As shown in the preceding screenshot, the physical disks are listed under **Physical hard disk**. If the disk you want to add is not listed, make sure that it is offline on the host. To perform the same operation using PowerShell, use the following cmdlet:

```
Add-VMHardDiskDrive -VMName VM-01 -ControllerNumber 0 -
ControllerType SCSI -DiskNumber 2 -Passthru
```

The preceding command will add the disk number 2 as a pass-through disk on the VM-01. To identify the disk number, run the following cmdlet on the host:

```
Get-disk
```

After performing this process, the disk will be available on the VM. You'll need to bring the disk online, and if there are no volumes, you'll need to format the disk and create a new volume on it, as shown earlier in this chapter.

# Virtual Hard Disk (VHD)

While the physical disk option delivers the entire disk to the VM, the VHD option uses a file on top of the actual physical disk and its volume to deliver the so-called virtual disk to the VM. A virtual disk is, actually, nothing more than a file. However, since Windows Server 2008 and 2008 R2, Microsoft evolved its mechanism to provide a better performance. Today, on Windows Server 2012 and 2012 R2, a VHD/VHDX file have the same performance as its underlying disk. Let's take a look at how it differs from a physical disk:

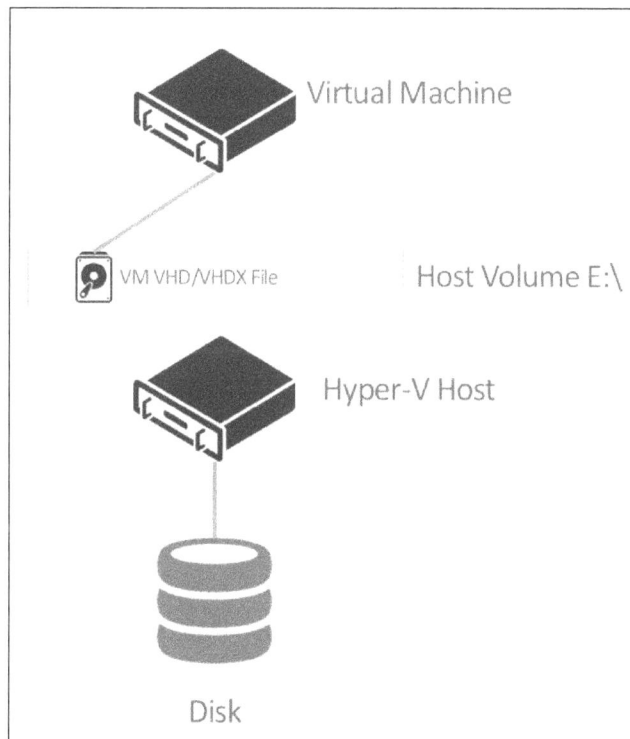

Since this is a virtual disk, which is actually a file, there are several benefits of using it. One caveat of using virtual disks is that it allows you to host multiple virtual disks on the same physical disk. This will reduce the performance as the physical disk may have concurrent requests. To better understand this, we will cover all the aspects of the virtual disk for the VM.

# VHD or VHDX?

From Windows Server 2008 R2 to Windows Server 2012, Microsoft introduced a new virtual disk type. Before Windows Server 2012, a virtual disk was the VHD traditional file. This file type, however, had the following limitations:

- A VHD file can grow up to 2 TB. Because of its structure, if a VHD file achieves more than 2 TB, it can slow down the performance and even be corrupted.
- The VHD file does not provide a transaction log. If the host power goes down, and the file is open because a VM was using it, the file is easily corrupted.
- The VHD file does not support new 4K disk type. Instead, it would emulate 512e, which emulates a 512-byte sector on a 4K disk, reducing performance.

The new VHDX format addresses all of the above. The new VHDX format has the following characteristics:

- Grows up to 64 TB, because of its new structure and format type.
- VHDX provides an internal transaction log. In case the host power goes down, the transaction log may be lost but the file is preserved.
- VHDX format supports 4K disks, leveraging all of its performance.

As you can see, there are multiple reasons to use the new VHDX format. Just keep in mind that in case you need to move a disk to a Hyper-V in Windows Server 2008 or 2008 R2, you'll have to change the disk type, as 2008 and 2008 R2 does not support VHDX. Also, remember that when you create a VM on Hyper-V in Windows Server 2012 and 2012 R2, the VM native disk will be a VHDX disk.

In case you need to convert a VHDX file into a VHD file, or vice-versa, you can use the following cmdlet:

```
Convert-VHD -DestinationPath E:\destinationdisk.vhd -Path
E:\originaldisk.vhdx
```

The preceding command will convert the original file into a VHD file. See that the original file will be kept. Also, this is an offline process and the virtual disk must not be attached at the moment when you run the conversion process.

# Creating a virtual disk and associating it with a VM

Although you can add the virtual disk directly to the VM just like a pass-through disk, there is a wizard to manage disks on the Hyper-V Manager.

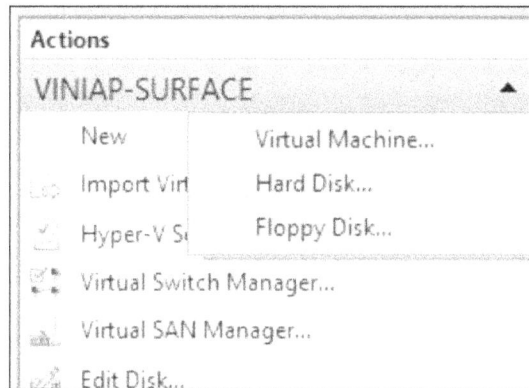

The wizard is the same when you add a new virtual disk to an IDE or SCSI virtual controller.

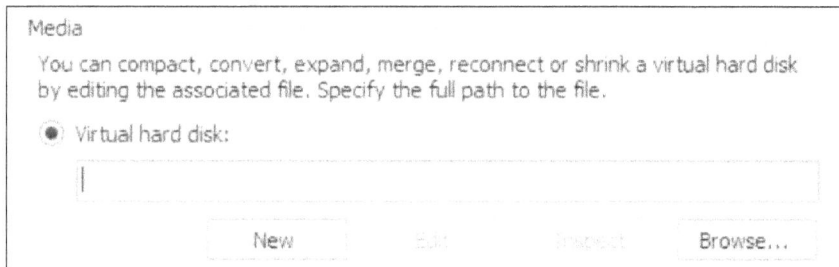

In the **New Virtual Hard Disk Wizard**, click **Next >**. The first information you have to provide is to set a new **VHD** or **VHDX** virtual disk. Select the option you want to use and click **Next >**. The next screen asks you to create a **Fixed size**, **Dynamically expanding** or **Differencing** disk. To better explain each option, take a look at the following:

- **Fixed size**: This will create a VHD or VHDX file with the same size as that indicated on the next screen. If you are creating a 100 GB virtual disk, the file will have the same 100 GB allocated to the underlying disk, even if the VM does not allocate the total size.

- **Dynamically expanding**: This type of disk will create a VHD or VHDX file with only the minimal information and metadata for the file itself. The file will only grow when the VM writes any data on it. See that the file will not shrink automatically when data is deleted. This type of disk will not present a significant difference in performance from a Fixed size disk. However, over time, this type of disk can have the performance degraded because of fragmentation on the host. Moving the virtual disk from one disk to another (When you run Live Migration or Storage Live Migration), or by running the defragmentation process on the host, can solve this problem. Still, it is not recommended for production environment.

- **Differencing**: This is an option for testing and development purposes. A differencing disk is a disk that has all the data that differs from the parent disk. You can install the guest OS on a virtual disk, fixed or dynamic, and create VMs with differencing disks from the parent disks. The benefit of using a differencing disk is that the total space allocated for them is minimal. However, performance is a real problem in this implementation. Differencing disks will be explained in detail in *Chapter 6, Virtual Machines and Virtual Machine Templates*, where we will cover VM templates.

After selecting **Fixed size** or **Dynamically expanding**, click **Next >**. On the next page, you can specify the virtual disk **Name** and **Location**. After doing so, click **Next >**.

At **Configure Disk**, you can choose one of the following options:

- **Create a new blank virtual hard disk**: To do so, specify the size of the virtual disk, and this will create a new blank virtual disk.

- **Copy the contents of the specified physical disk**: This will create a new virtual disk with the content of the specified physical disk. The new virtual disk will have the same size as that of the physical disk.

- **Copy the contents of the specified virtual hard disk**: This will create a new virtual disk with the content of the specified virtual disk. The new virtual disk will have the same size as that of the original virtual disk.

After selecting the option for your environment, click **Next >** and click **Finish** to create the virtual disk.

If you used the wizard from inside the VM, the new virtual disk will be allocated to the VM, so you just have to click **Apply** to confirm. If you used the wizard from Hyper-V Manager, you have to open the VM at the same point as the last screenshot and click **Browse...** to allocate the virtual disk that already exists.

To create a virtual disk through PowerShell, use the following cmdlet:

```
New-VHD -Path "E:\VMStore\VM-01\Virtual Hard Disks\Disk02.vhdx" -
SizeBytes 150GB
```

The preceding command will create a **Dynamically expanding** virtual disk, as this is the default, on the specified path, with a total of 150GB. To create a fixed virtual disk, use the input -Fixed.

To associate the virtual disk created to a VM, use the following cmdlet:

```
Add-VMHardDiskDrive -VMName VM-01 -ControllerType SCSI -
ControllerNumber 0 -Path "E:\VMStore\VM-01\Virtual Hard
Disks\Disk02.vhdx"
```

The preceding command will associate the virtual disk created in the previous cmdlet to the VM-01 on the SCSI -ControllerNumber 0, which is the first SCSI virtual controller created (SCSI virtual controllers are numbered from 0 to 3).

# Online VHDX Resize

Another reason for using a pass-through disk prior to Hyper-V on Windows Server 2012 R2, was to be able to resize the VM disk without shutting down the VM. Hyper-V on Windows Server 2012 R2 has a new feature to resize the VHDX file, without interrupting the VM. This operation will only work on SCSI virtual controllers and VHDX files. IDE controllers or VHD files will require the VM to be powered off.

To resize a virtual disk while the VM is running, open **Hyper-V Manager**, right-click the powered on VM and click **Settings....** Select the VHDX on the SCSI virtual controller and click **Edit**. In the **Edit Virtual Hard Disk Wizard**, click **Next >**. Since the disk is already selected, click **Next >**.

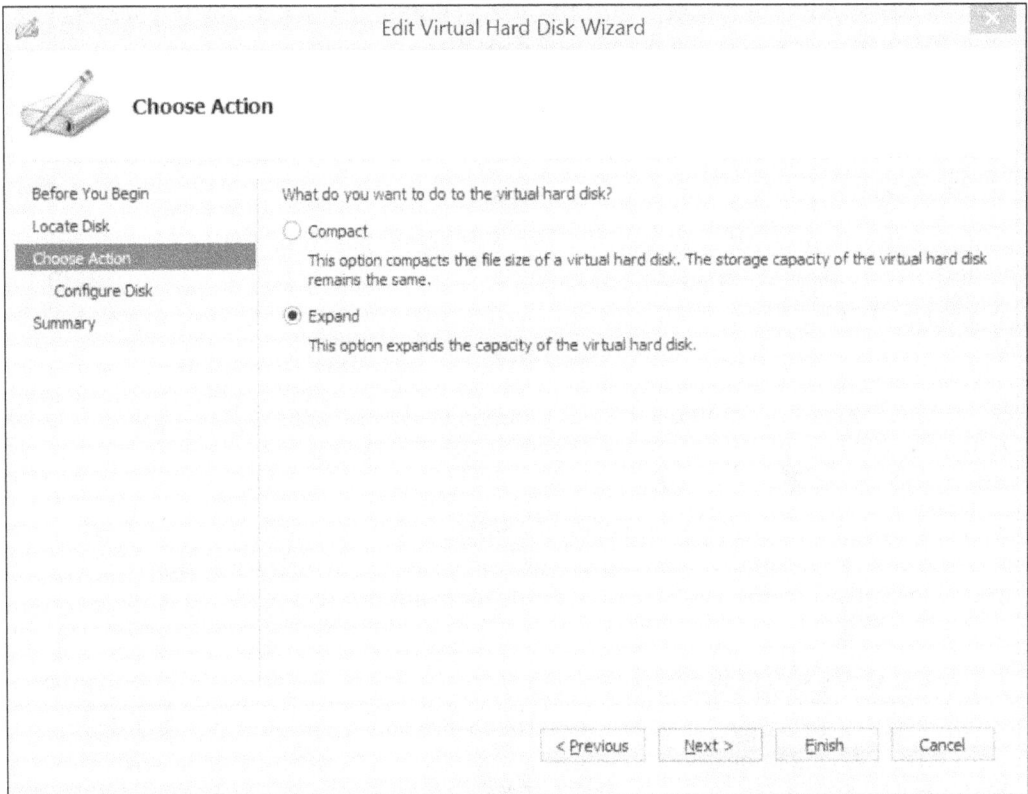

The **Compact** option will compact a Dynamically expanding virtual disk to the space allocated by the VM, reclaiming the unnecessary space allocated for the file on the host. This process pushes CPU performance and requires additional space to be allocated during the process. The **Expand** option will inflate the virtual disk and provide unallocated space on the disk inside the guest OS. To expand the VHDX size, select **Expand** and click **Next >**.

On the next screen you can specify the new size of the virtual disk. Specify the necessary value and click **Next >**. Click **Finish** to start the process.

After expanding the virtual disk, you can choose to shrink the virtual disk back to the original size or a value between the actual size and the initial size. Run the wizard again and the **Shrink** option will be available.

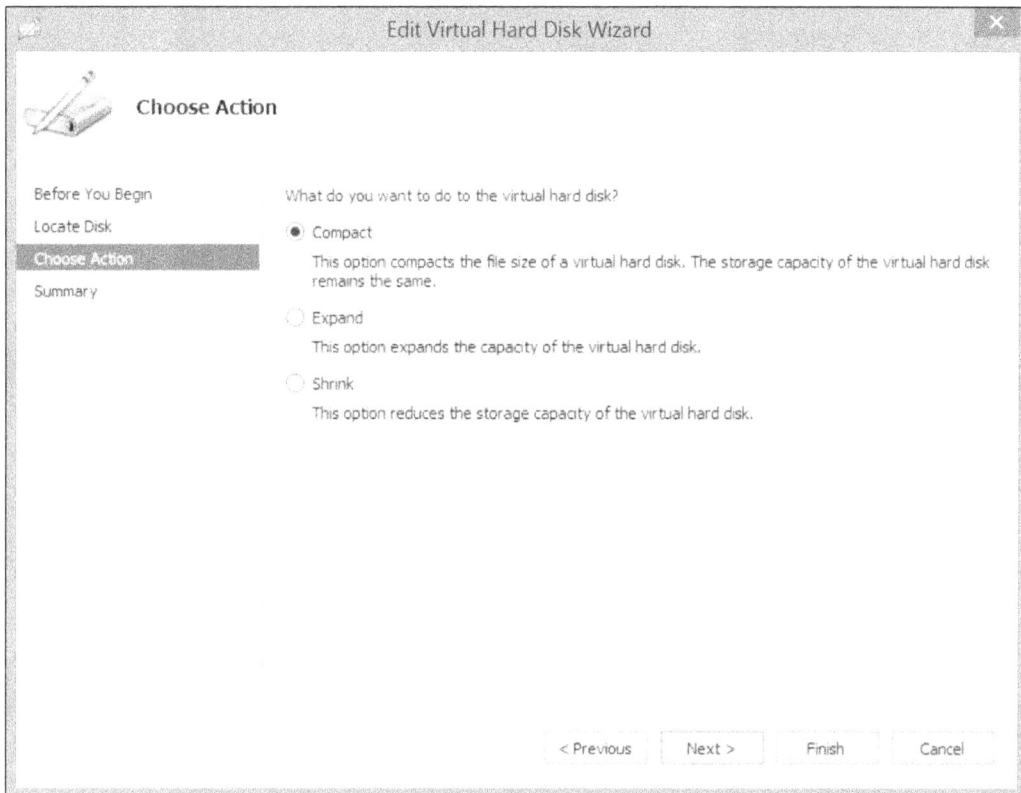

To perform the **Expand** operation via PowerShell, use the following cmdlet:

```
Resize-VHD -Path "E:\VMStore\VM-01\Virtual Hard Disks\Disk01.vhdx"
-SizeBytes 150GB
```

You can also use PowerShell to specify a value to shrink the virtual disk, or revert it to its minimum size, as follows:

```
Resize-VHD -Path "E:\VMStore\VM-01\Virtual Hard Disks\Disk01.vhdx"
-ToMinimumSize
```

The preceding cmdlet will revert the VHD to the original size. Keep in mind that the reclaimed space must be unallocated on the VM.

# Virtual disk Quality of Service (QoS)

Another new Hyper-V feature in Windows Server 2012 R2 is the ability to specify Storage QoS. This is a great feature for scenarios where multiple virtual disks are hosted on the same physical disk and you want to prioritize a specific disk, either because it is in a VM that requires more performance, or because a customer is paying for more performance. To enable Storage QoS on a virtual disk, open the VM **Settings...** on **Hyper-V Manager** and select the disk you want to configure. Expand the disk information and click **Advanced Features** as shown in the following screenshot:

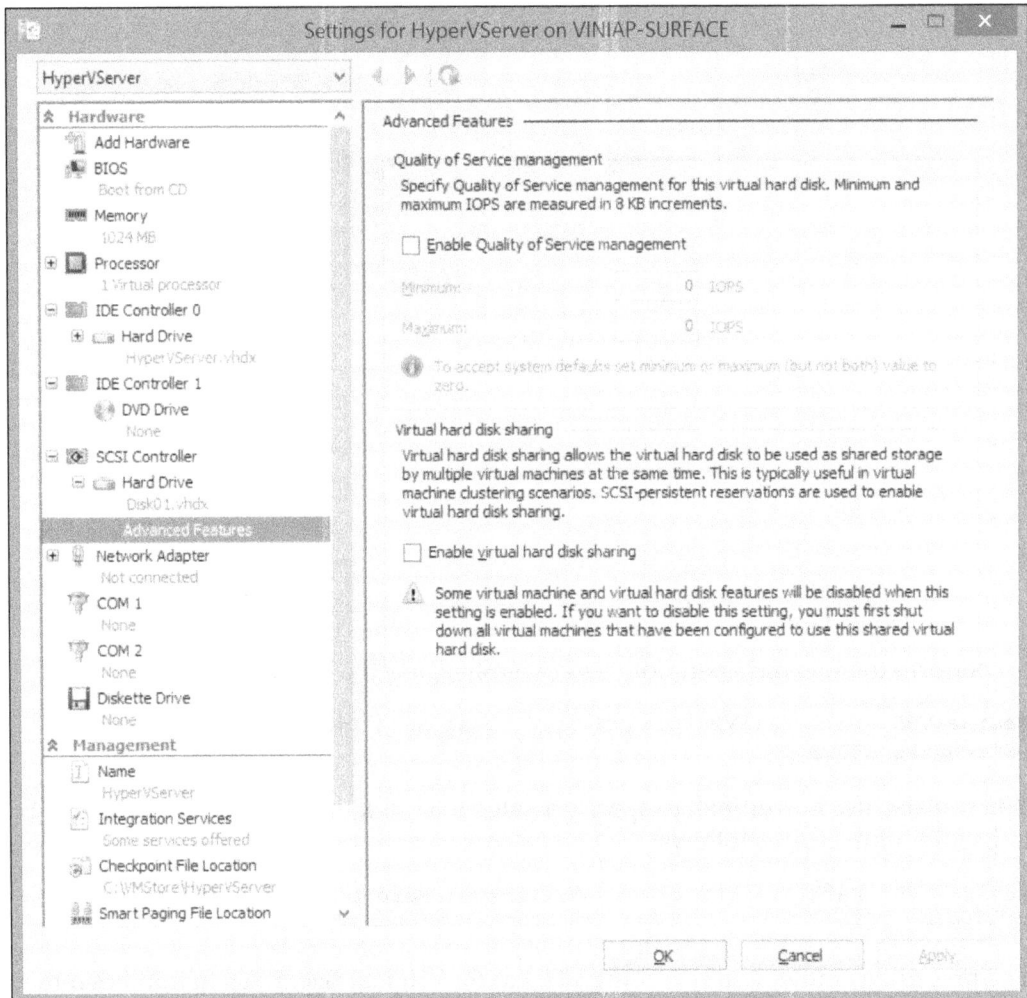

The Storage QoS is specified at **Input/Output Operations Per Second (IOPS)**, and you can specify the Minimum and Maximum IOPS for the virtual disk. Hyper-V will generate an event-based alert on the host OS if the minimum IOPS specified is not met on a VM.

To set Storage QoS via PowerShell, use the following cmdlet:

```
Set-VMHardDiskDrive -VMName VM-01 -ControllerNumber 0 -
ControllerType SCSI -DiskNumber 0 -MaximumIOPS 100 -MinimumIOPS 50
```

The preceding command will set the first disk (`DiskNumber 0`) on the first SCSI virtual controller (`ControllerNumber 0`) to a Minimum of 50 IOPS and a Maximum of 100 IOPS.

Setting Minimum and Maximum IOPS is not as simple as it looks in the preceding process. Before setting the desired values, you should have mapped the application needs for IOPS. However, the majority of software vendors do not specify the application needed for IOPS. For that reason, Microsoft introduced a performance counter that indicates the Read Operations/Sec, which will give you an idea of how much IOPS your application is consuming. You can use the performance counter by using the **Performance Monitor** on the host and adding the **Hyper-V Virtual Storage Device - Read Operations/Sec** counter on the virtual disks that you want to analyze.

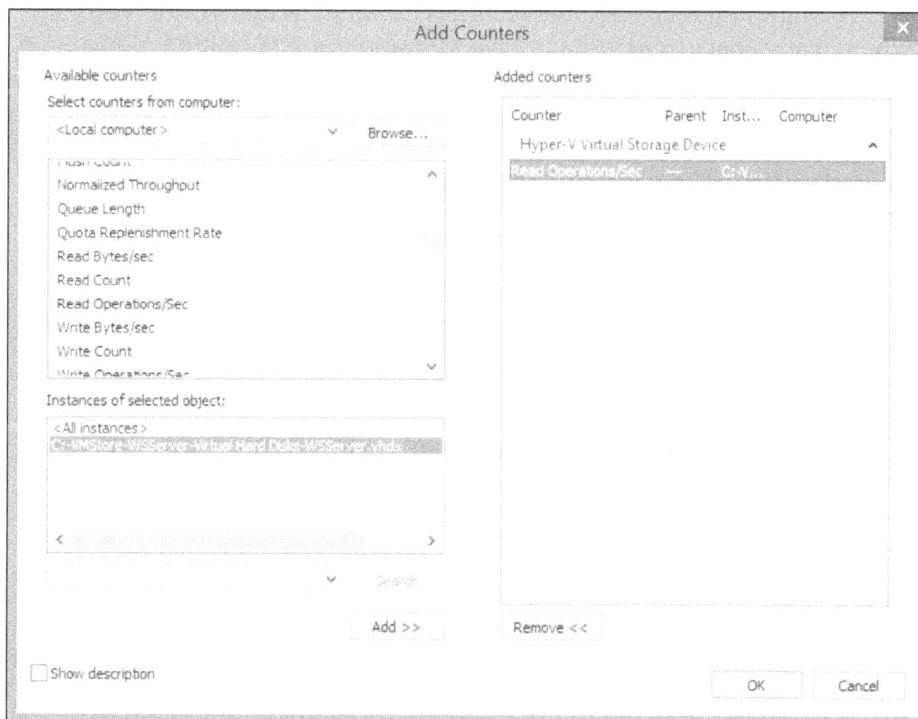

Still, it is not recommended that you set the Storage QoS without being absolutely sure of the values that you should specify. Working with the application owner is a good approach to avoid application disruption.

# Storage Live Migration

After all the information which you've absorbed so far, you probably have all the knowledge to plan and implement a good storage environment capable of supporting all type of applications, from a simple and low-performance one, to an enterprise class high performance application.

Still, in some cases, with everything running, you may realize that your VM storage is not okay. It might be a performance issue, or a disk that is running out of space, or any other reason, you may have a situation where the VM is running and still you have to move the VM virtual disk to another location.

If you're using a pass-through disk, there's nothing to do, other than using the regular tools to operate a physical disk. Now, if you're using a virtual disk, Windows Server 2012 introduced a new feature for Hyper-V called Storage Live Migration. This feature allows you to move the VM virtual disk from one location to another without interrupting the VM or even the applications using the virtual disk.

Storage Live Migration is enabled by default (you can't disable it), and you can specify how many concurrent Storage Live Migrations are permitted on the host. To do that, open **Hyper-V Manager** and click **Hyper-V Settings...** on the menu on the left. On the Hyper-V Settings menu, click **Storage Migrations**. In this page, you can specify how many **Simultaneous storage migrations** are allowed. Since this is not an usual operation, it is not recommended to change this property, unless you have a technical reason to do so.

To perform the Storage Live Migration on a VM virtual disk, right-click the VM you want to perform the operation on and click **Move...**. In the Move Wizard, click **Next >**. On the next page, select **Move the virtual machine's storage** and click **Next >**. Now you have to choose from the following options, as shown in the following screenshot:

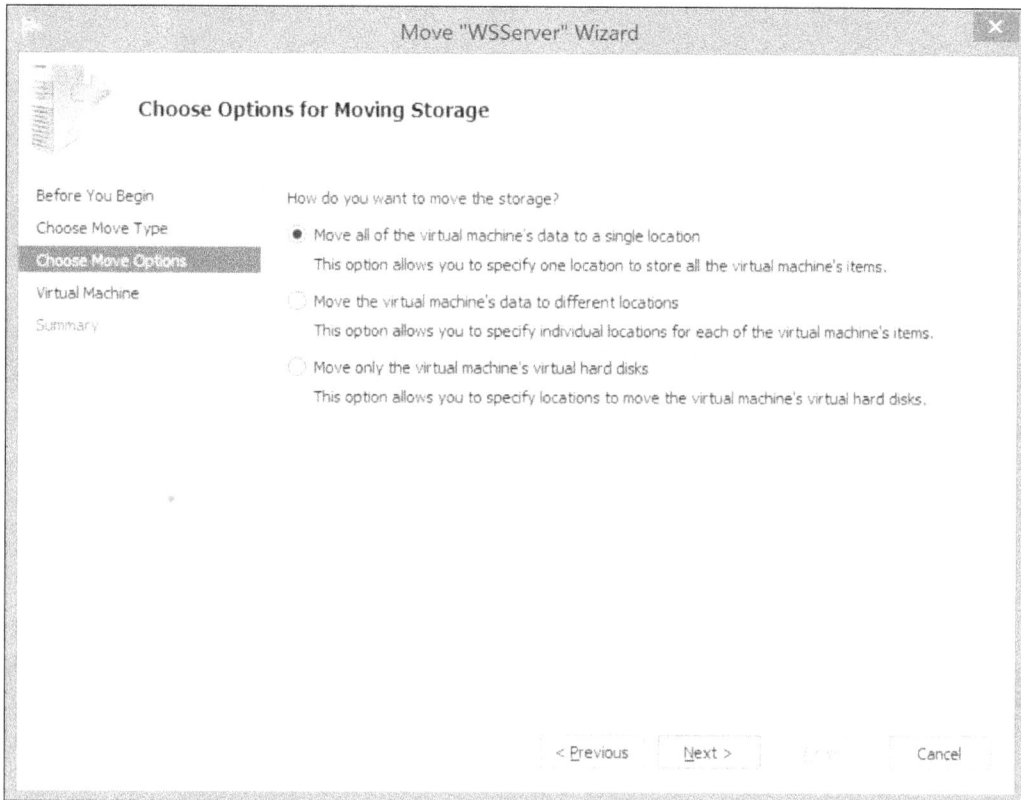

The first option will move all the VM data, including all disks and VM files, to the same location. The second option will let you choose where to store each item. The final option will move only the virtual disks to another location, keeping the VM files on the original location. In this case, we will move VM data to another location. Select the first option and and click **Next >**. Now you can specify the **New location** for the VM data.

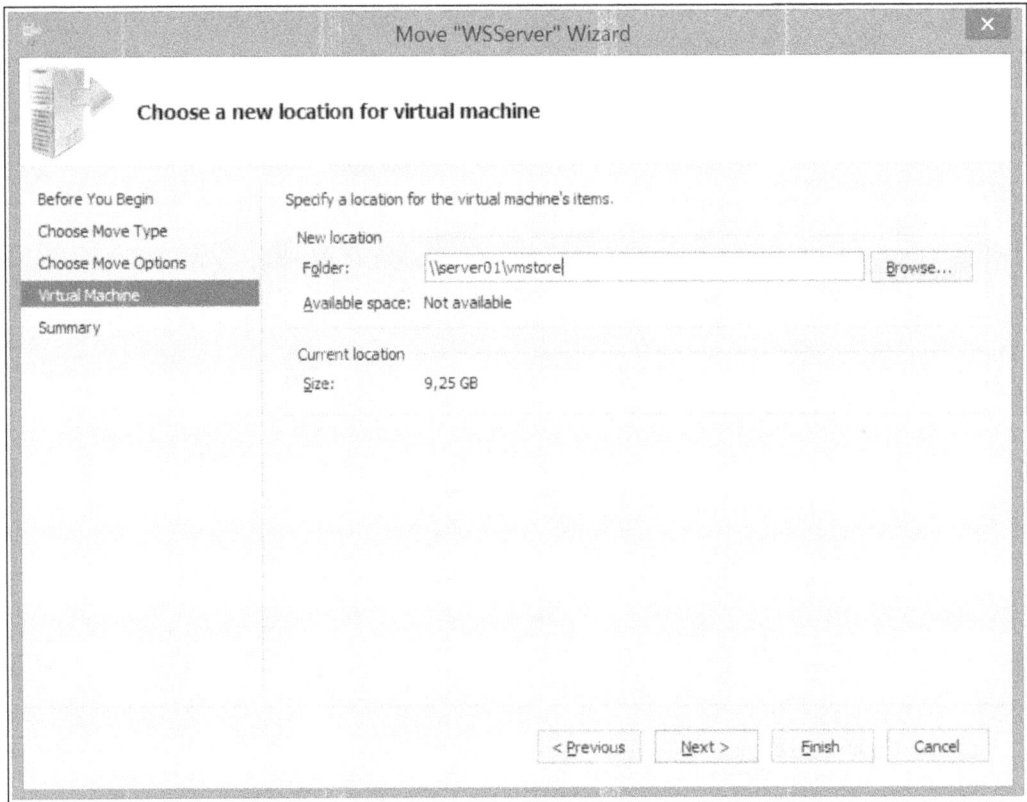

After specifying the final location, click **Next >** and on the completing page, click **Finish** to start the move.

To perform the operation using PowerShell, use the following cmdlet:

```
Move-VMStorage -DestinationStoragePath \\server01\vmstore -VMName
VM-01
```

# Summary

In this chapter, we covered multiple options for planning and implementing a storage solution for Hyper-V. We covered host storage using local disks, DAS and SAN devices, with FC and iSCSI communication. We also covered NAS with SMB3 and how a Windows Server host can be a Storage Device implementing several storage features, such as Storage Spaces and Pool, Data Deduplication and Storage Tiering. The disk configuration and RAID options were covered with details and indications for a virtualization environment.

Then, we came to the VM storage and all the possibilities for using physical or virtual disks. Now you know the difference between the virtual disk formats, and how to configure the VM storage correctly. Throughout the chapter, you might have noted that we did not cover Shared VHDX. This is because this topic will be covered in *Chapter 7*, *Implementing High Availability*, along with other High Availability options.

In the next chapter, we will cover how to manage a VM and the daily tasks of a virtualization admin.

# 6
# Virtual Machines and Virtual Machine Templates

So far, we have seen many concepts and components of Hyper-V: Hyper-V architecture, host deployment, Hyper-V Licensing as well as components such as processor, memory, network, and storage. Now, it is time to see how to perform day-to-day tasks on Hyper-V for managing VMs.

It is true, however, that in large Hyper-V deployments, administrators make use of other management tools, such as Microsoft System Center, especially the System Center Virtual Machine Manager (SCVMM), which is the component focused on virtualization environments. The SCVMM is a management component that uses Hyper-V Hosts, or even VMware ESXi or Citrix XenServer Hosts, to deliver a private cloud solution. Among other features, SCVMM is also capable of managing VMs and hosts, applying policies to hosts and VMs, and managing the VM templates.

Using a management tool is important in making day-to-day tasks easier to accomplish. However, understanding how all of this works is important, so that you are able to troubleshoot better, and even perform these tasks in an environment without these tools, like a small or a medium deployment.

Throughout the chapter, you will see tips for performing the most common tasks, as well as some advanced tasks using Hyper-V and the Windows Server components. Keep in mind that if your company has already made an investment on a management tool, you should leverage this investment by using those tools, but understanding the concepts here is equally important.

In this chapter, we will cover the following topics:

- VM Generations 1 and 2
- VM management
- Checkpoints
- VM templates
- Differencing disks
- PowerShell Desired State Configuration (DSC)

# Virtual machine management

Managing a VM day-to-day can look like an easy task, but when something goes wrong, it is time to use all the expertise to find the cause of the problem and solve it. Understanding how to perform these tasks is the key to troubleshooting your environment.

With all that you have read so far, you probably have a general idea of what a VM is composed of, and so the process of creating a VM is nothing more than putting all the components together. However, in Hyper-V on Windows Server 2012 R2, Microsoft introduced a new type of VM, the Generation 2 VM (Gen 2 VM). If you are familiar with the VMware technology, you probably have seen multiple VM hardware types that allow you to have more features depending on the hardware type. Gen 2 VMs in Hyper-V works in, essentially, the same way. However, the goal for Gen 2 VMs is to prepare the underlying VM hardware for the future.

## Generation 1 and 2 VMs

Since the first release of Hyper-V on Windows Server 2008, up to Hyper-V on Windows Server 2012, the VM hardware works the same way. You can find the same limitations in every release, such as booting only from the IDE disk, network booting from the Legacy Network Adapter only, and so on. To overcome these limitations, Microsoft has made some changes to the VM hardware in order to provide it with new features. The changes include the following:

- **New Firmware**: Instead of the traditional 16-bit BIOS, Microsoft introduced a Class-3 64-bit UEFI firmware. This means that not all OS' will work in this VM Generation.

- **Devices**: All emulated hardware was removed from the Gen 2 VM: Legacy Network Adapter, IDE virtual controller, virtual Floppy Disk Drive, and serial controller. In addition, a new DVD drive has been introduced to work on the SCSI virtual controller.

- **Boot Devices**: Since there is no IDE virtual controller or Legacy Network Adapter, the UEFI firmware was configured to support software-based devices, like the VMBus, allowing the SCSI virtual controllers, Network Adapters and DVD devices to boot.

- **Secure Boot**: The implementation of UEFI comes with the addition of the Secure Boot, which is a validation of the signature on the OS loader. This mechanism validates that only approved signatures are allowed to boot up.

- **Other minor hardware changes**: There are other minor hardware removals, such as PS/2 mouse, S3 video, and other changes. For a complete list of the changes in Gen 2 VMs, check the official article at `http://technet.microsoft.com/en-us/library/dn282285.aspx`.

With all these changes, not all OS' are supported on the Gen 2 VMs. The supported Windows OS' are listed as follows:

- Windows Server 2012

- Windows Server 2012 R2

- Windows 8

- Windows 8.1

- Some Linux distributions (check official link at `http://technet.microsoft.com/en-us/library/dn531030.aspx`)

The general guidance on the Gen 2 VMs is to check whether you'll need support for the old devices on the VM, and if the guest OS is supported. If you are not using old devices and your guest OS is supported, you probably want to go with the Gen 2 VM. This is because, as said before, the Gen 2 VMs are a preparation for the future. It is possible that in future versions of Hyper-V, new features will be available for the Gen 2 VMs, instead of Gen 1.

The process of creating and managing a Gen 2 VM will be shown in the next section, along with Generation 1.

# Creating and modifying a VM

Maybe the most basic task you will face on a day-to-day basis is creating a VM. Let's start by creating a VM on the GUI. In **Hyper-V Manager**, click **New**, and then click **Virtual Machine...**.

In the **New Virtual Machine Wizard,** click **Next >**.

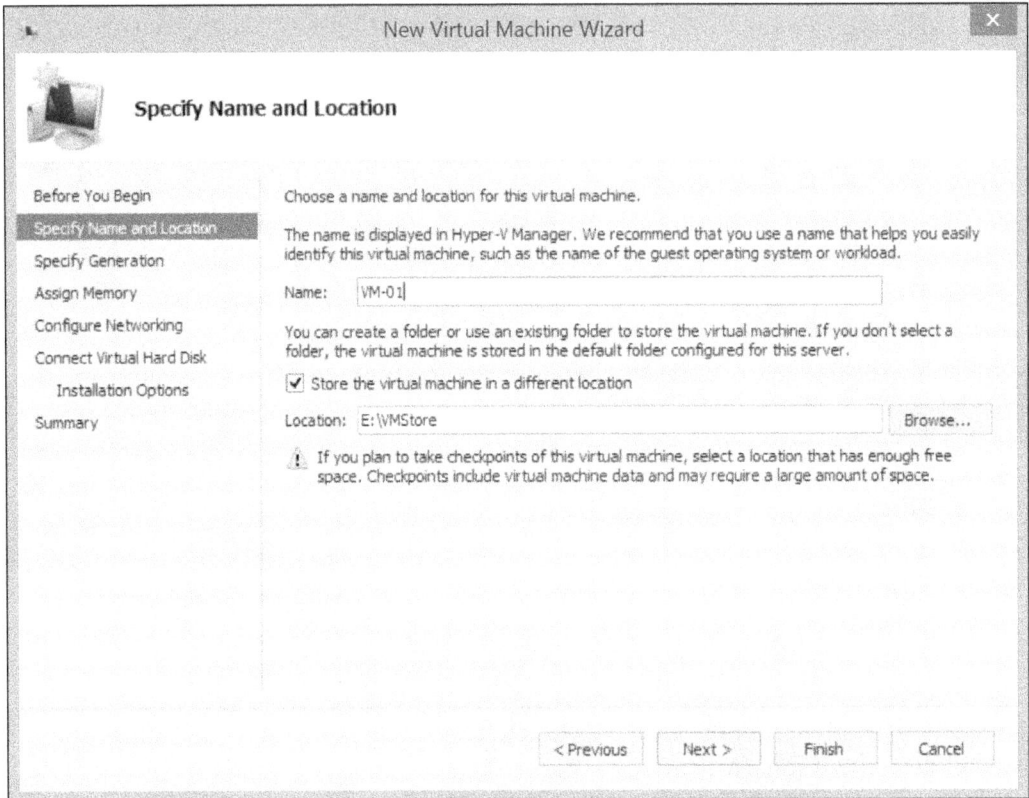

In the preceding screenshot, you can name the VM. Keep in mind that the name you are inserting here is the VM **Name** in Hyper-V; it will be used for management purpose only. Also, you can specify the **Location** to store the VM files. If you do not provide a location, the default location will be used. One interesting point is that a folder structure with the VM **Name** will be created at the specified location, or the default one. You can change the VM **Name** later, but this will not change the folder structure and folder name. After providing the VM Name and **Location**, click **Next >**.

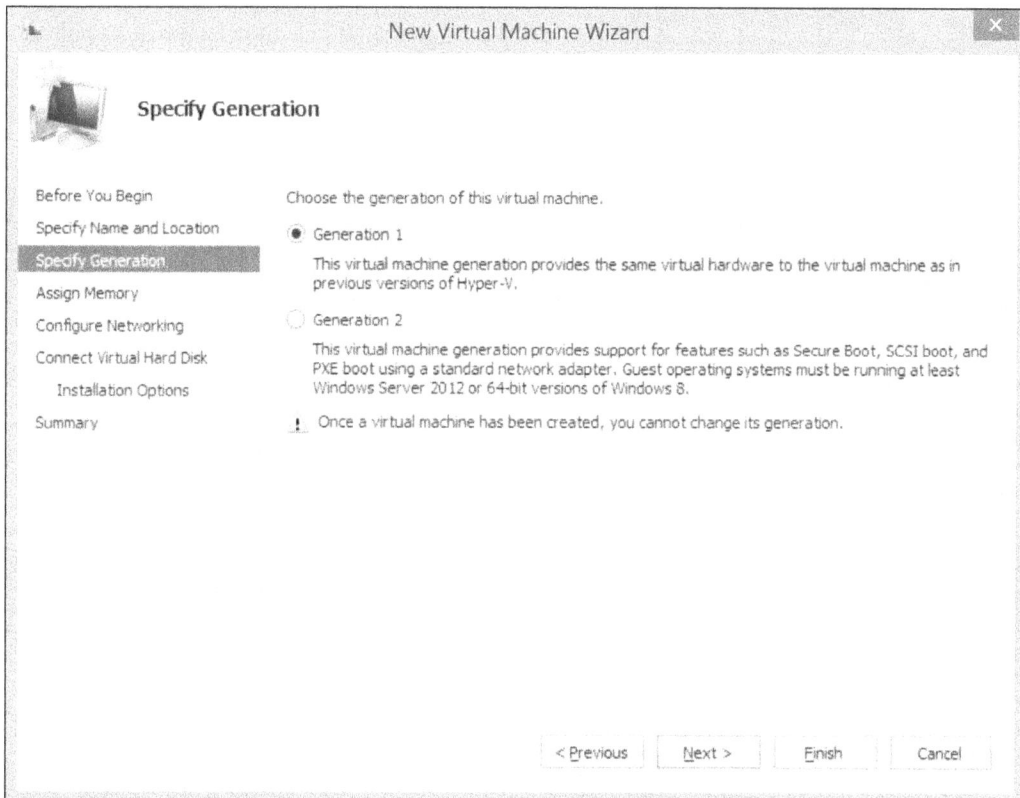

In the preceding screenshot, you can choose from the two generations — **Generation 1** and **Generation 2**. For now, there are small differences for choosing between one or the other, which will be shown later in this section. Select one of the options, and click **Next >**.

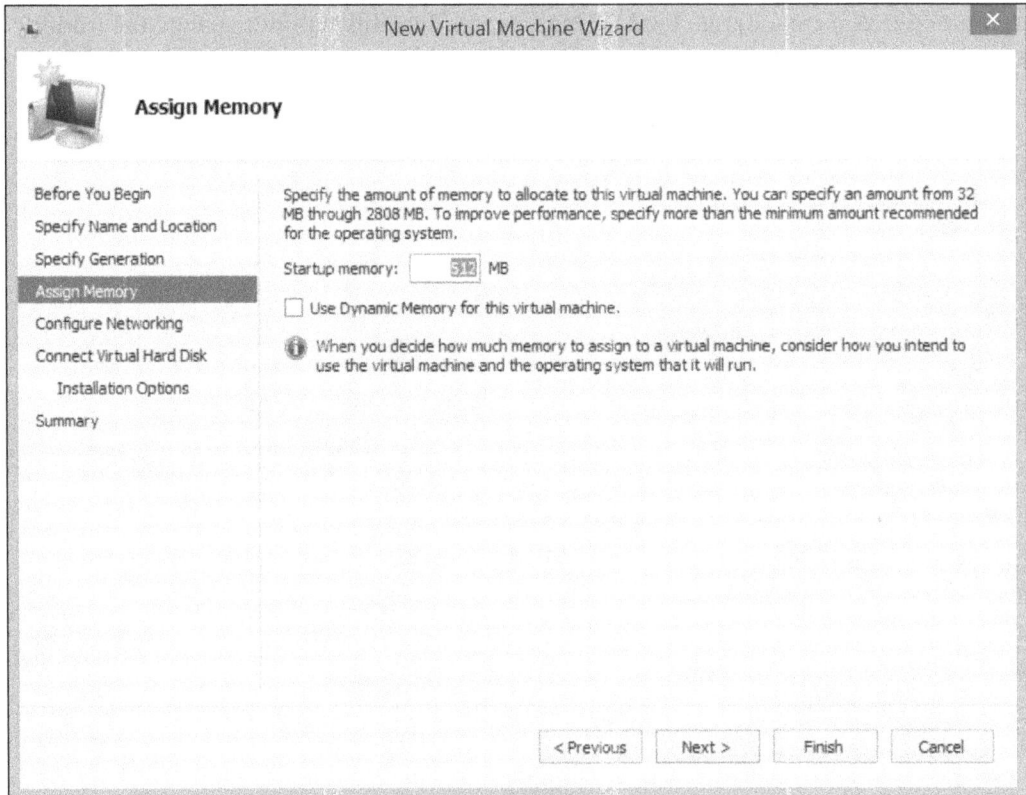

New Virtual Machine Wizard

**Assign Memory**

Before You Begin
Specify Name and Location
Specify Generation
Assign Memory
Configure Networking
Connect Virtual Hard Disk
Installation Options
Summary

Specify the amount of memory to allocate to this virtual machine. You can specify an amount from 32 MB through 2808 MB. To improve performance, specify more than the minimum amount recommended for the operating system.

Startup memory:  512  MB

☐ Use Dynamic Memory for this virtual machine.

ℹ When you decide how much memory to assign to a virtual machine, consider how you intend to use the virtual machine and the operating system that it will run.

< Previous    Next >    Finish    Cancel

Now you can specify the VM **Startup memory**. As explained in *Chapter 1, Getting Started with Hyper-V Architecture and Components*, Hyper-V allows you to use Dynamic memory. You can set the VM to use Dynamic memory at the time of VM creation. See, however, that you cannot specify the Minimum and Maximum values for RAM for Dynamic memory in this screen. If you want to specify these values, you will have to open the VM **Settings...** after creating it; otherwise, the Minimum RAM will be equal to the Startup RAM and the Maximum will be the Maximum RAM that a VM can have—1 TB. After specifying **Startup memory** and Dynamic memory, click **Next >**.

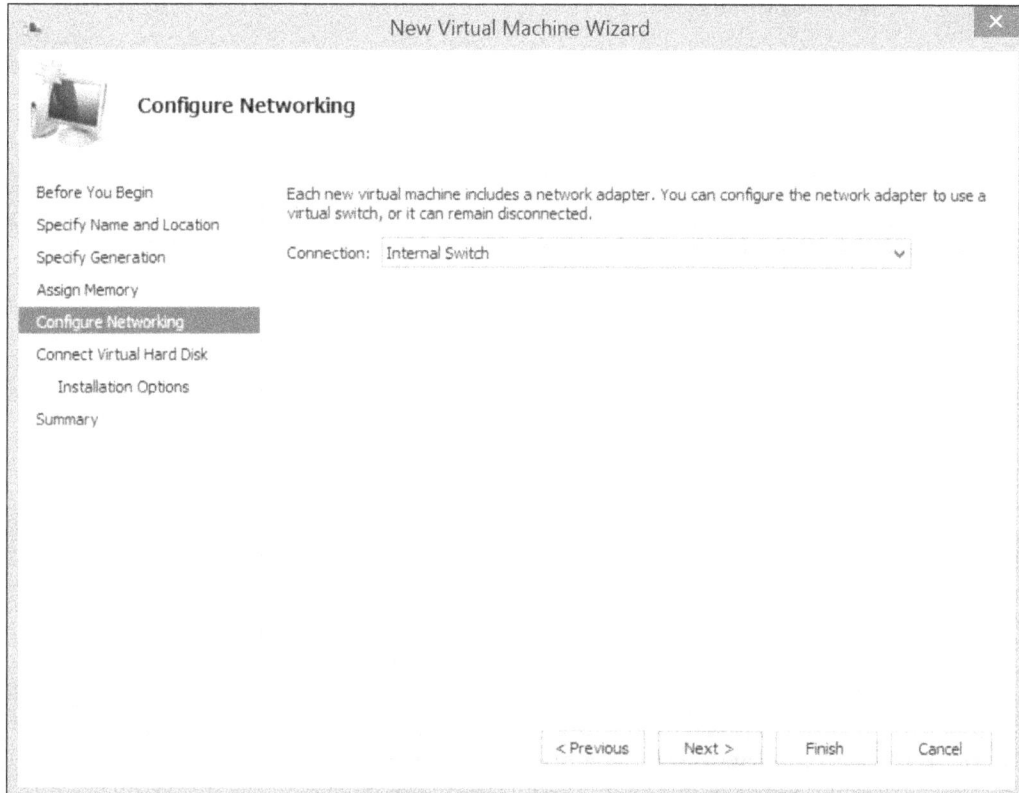

In the preceding screenshot, you can specify the Virtual Switch that the VM will be connected to. When the VM is created, it will be created with only one virtual NIC. You can add more NICs later by opening the VM **Settings...** and adding a new hardware. The default NIC can be connected to a Virtual Switch, or you can choose to connect it later. Click **Next >**.

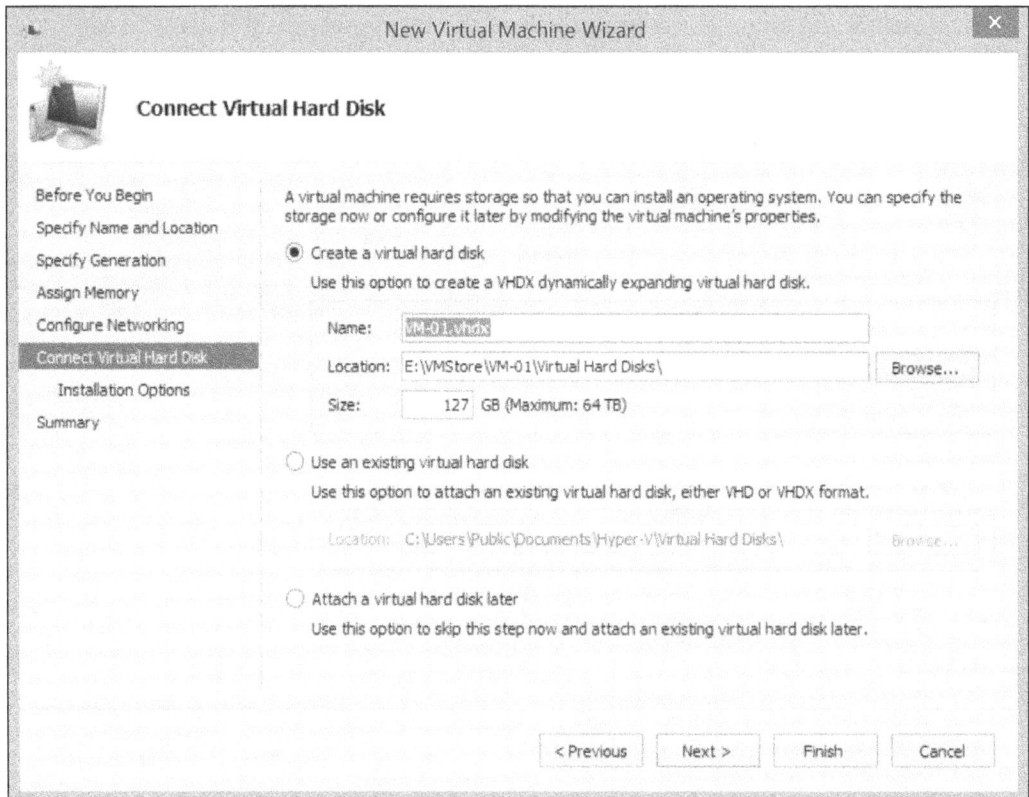

In the preceding screenshot, you have the disk options. There are three options for the VM disk in the Wizard. Let's see what each one means:

- **Create a virtual hard disk**: This option will create a Virtual Hard Disk (VHDX) file to be used as the VM virtual disk. This will be a dynamic VHDX file. You can also specify the file name, file location, and total size of the VHDX for the VM.

- **Use an existing virtual hard disk**: You can use an existing virtual disk. This is used, usually, when you are restoring a VM, but you only have the virtual disk of the given VM. This virtual disk can be a dynamic, fixed, or differencing disk, and can be either a VHD or VHDX file.

- **Attach a virtual hard disk later**: In this case, the VM will be created without a disk, and you will have to create or attach a new disk later by using the VM **Settings...**.

If you choose the first option, there is still a step to complete. As the new virtual disk is a blank disk, the Wizard will provide some options for installing the guest OS. However, after clicking **Next >**, the screen will be different for the Generation 1 and 2 VMs. Let's see the screen for the Gen 1 VM:

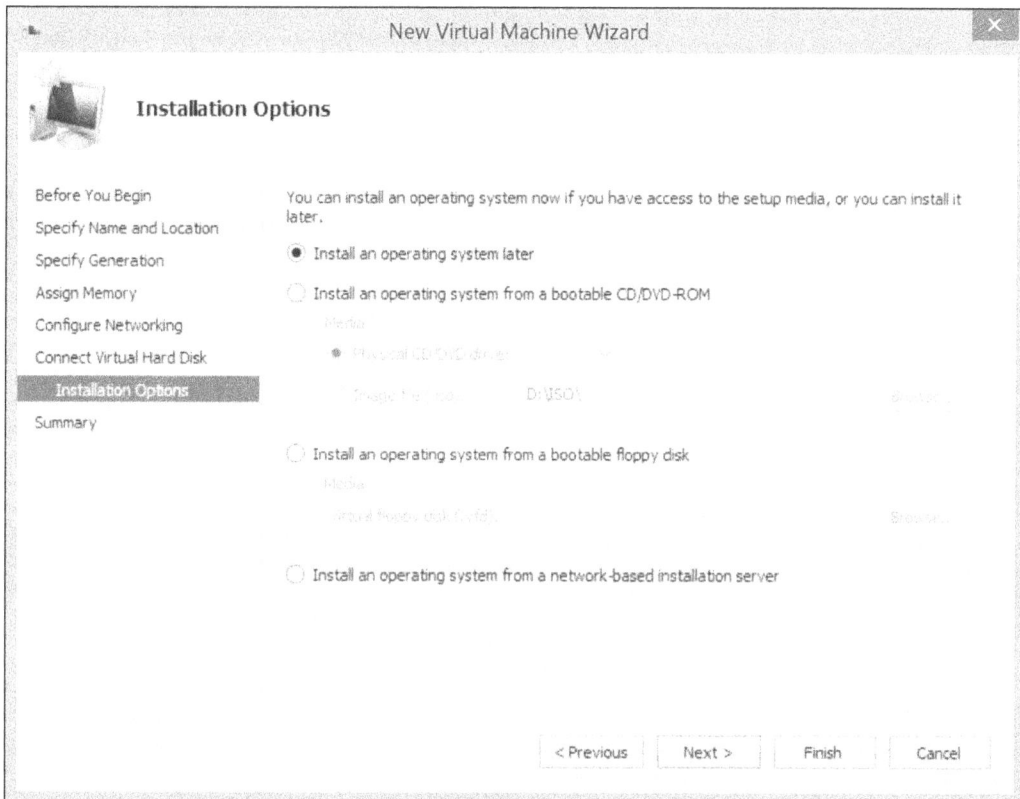

In the Gen 1 VM option, you have the following options:

- **Install an operating system later**: This option will simply skip the guest OS installation. You will have to perform the installation later.

- **Install an operating system from a bootable CD/DVD-ROM**: You can provide media for the VM to boot from. This can be physical media, allocating the host CD/DVD drive, or an ISO file.

- **Install an operating system from a bootable floppy disk**: This is a backward compatibility option for the guest OS that needs to boot up from a floppy disk. You have to create a virtual floppy disk (VFD) file to point it here.

- **Install an operating system from a network-based installation server**: This option is only available if you connected the virtual Network Adapter to a Virtual Switch in the previous step. In this case, the VM will boot from the network. The process for booting from the network in a VM is the same as any other machine, and a PXE server must be available.

If the VM you are creating is a Gen 2 VM, then the screen will look as shown in the following screenshot:

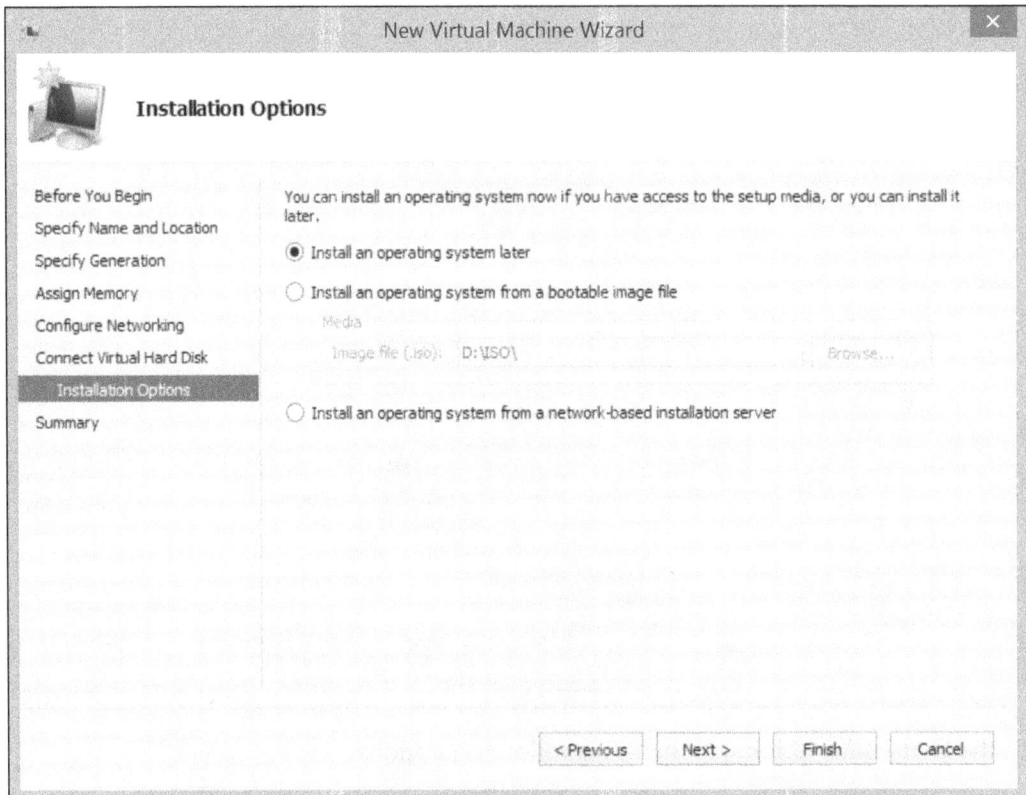

As you can see, there is no option for booting from a VFD. This is expected, as we explained the Gen 2 VM hardware earlier. After selecting the appropriate option, click **Next >** and click **Finish** to create the VM.

After creating the VM, you can see the VM **Settings...** in **Hyper-V Manager** by right-clicking the VM and selecting **Settings...**. Again, the Gen 1 and 2 VMs have different available options. This is the screenshot for the Gen 1 VM:

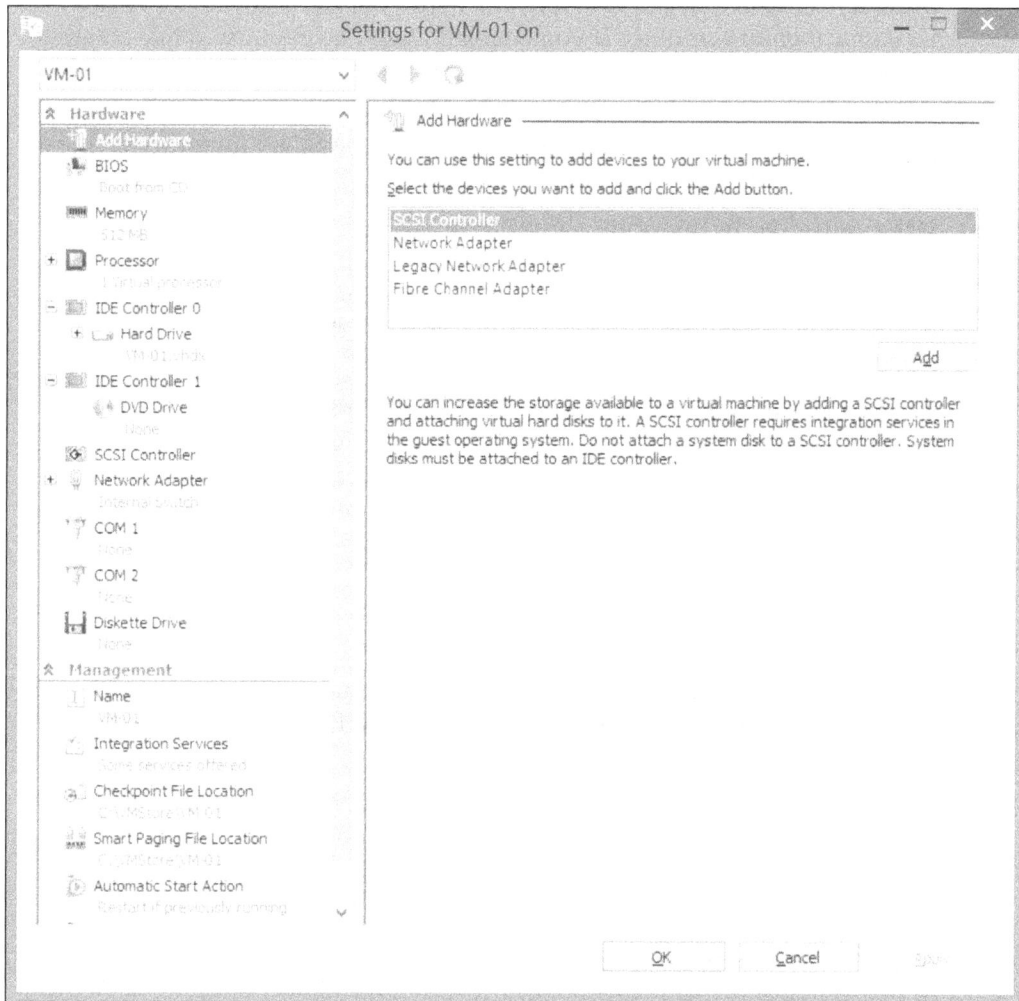

As you can see, all the options for managing the Gen 1 VM are shown in the preceding screenshot. The options are explained in detail, as follows:

- **Add Hardware**: The **Add Hardware** option lets you add new hardware to the VM. These options are only available if the VM is powered-off. You can add an **SCSI Controller**, a **Network Adapter**, a **Legacy Network Adapter**, and a **Fibre Channel Adapter**.

- **BIOS**: Since this is a Gen 1 VM, the **BIOS** option lets you configure the order of the boot devices. The default option is: **CD, IDE, Legacy Network Adapter,** and **Floppy** as the last option.

- **Memory**: The **Memory** option let's you configure the Static memory or Dynamic memory options. If you enabled Dynamic memory while creating the VM, you will have to open this to finish the configuration.

- **Processor**: The processor option lets you configure the number of virtual processors on the VM and the **Resource Control**, which will limit the VM processor as indicated. This will be explained in detail later in this chapter.

- **IDE Controller**: In this option, you can add virtual disks or DVD drives to the IDE virtual controller. The default configuration is one virtual disk on the position 0 of the **IDE Controller 0** and one **DVD Drive** on the position 0 of the **IDE Controller 1**. You can add one more device per IDE virtual controller.

- **SCSI Controller**: This option allows you to add additional virtual disks to the SCSI virtual controller on the VM. You can have up to four SCSI virtual controllers per VM. Each SCSI virtual controller can have up to 64 virtual disks, with a total of 256 disks per VM. The VM must be powered-off to add a new SCSI virtual controller, but can be powered-on to add new disks to the controller.

- **Network Adapter**: The **Network Adapter** option allows you to configure the virtual NIC of the VM. Even with the VM powered-on, you can still change most of the available options for networking, like **Virtual switch** connection, **Bandwidth Management,** and some **Hardware Acceleration** and **Advanced Features**.

- **COM ports**: The COM port option is a virtual COM port that uses a **named pipe address** to access the resource. For more information on how to use virtual COM ports, see the official article at `http://technet.microsoft.com/en-us/library/ee449417(v=WS.10).aspx`.

- **Diskette Drive**: This option will allocate a Diskette Drive to the VM. As explained earlier, you should create a virtual floppy disk(fd) file before associating it to the VM.

- **Name**: You can change the VM name. This will neither change the guest OS name nor the folder structure, which will be explained later in this chapter.

- **Integration Services**: The **Integration Services** (IS) option allows you to enable or disable some of the available services for the VM. Keep in mind that IS must be installed on the guest OS. The available options are as follows:

    - **Operating system shutdown**: This option allows you to gracefully shutdown the guest OS. A **Windows Management Instrumentation (WMI)** command is sent to the VM and the guest OS initiates the regular shutdown.

    - **Time synchronization**: This option will synchronize the guest OS clock with the host OS clock. This option can be a problem in Active Directory environments when the host is hosting a Domain Controller (DC) VM, or in case the host is not a member of the Active Directory but the VMs are. This will be explained in *Chapter 9, Virtualizing Active Directory Domain Controllers*.

    - **Data Exchange**: This option allows the guest OS and host OS to exchange information about the guest OS, so that the host can retrieve data for management purposes. Some examples are guest OS version, **Fully Qualified Domain Name (FQDN)**, and others.

    - **Heartbeat**: This option allows the parent OS to send regular heartbeat requests and checks if the guest OS has become unresponsive.

    - **Backup (volume checkpoint)**: This option can be used with guest OS' that support **Volume Shadow Copy Service (VSS)**. The VSS Requestor Service allows the parent partition to request the synchronization of the guest OS, when using Backup tools on the parent partition to backup the host and/or VMs.

    - **Guest services**: This option allows you to copy files from the host OS to the guest OS by using WMI APIs or the `Copy-VMFile` cmdlet. This is the only option that comes disabled by default.

- **Checkpoint File Location**: By default, Checkpoint (Snapshots) files are created at the same location as virtual disks. This option allows you to specify an alternative location for Checkpoint files. This is important in case the actual physical disk does not have free space, or you need a disk with a different performance level.

- **Smart Paging File Location**: As explained in *Chapter 1, Getting Started with Hyper-V Architecture and Components*, in a few cases, Dynamic memory will need a temporary location to store the page file for a VM that is restarting. This is, by default, the VM folder location. You can change it if necessary. It might be necessary in case the default location does not have free space, or you want to use a disk with different performance.

- **Automatic Start Action**: This option will specify what to do with the VM when the host starts. The options include doing **Nothing, Automatically start if it was running when the service stopped,** and **Always start this virtual machine automatically**. You can also set a delay for the VM to start. This is important in case the VM depends on another VM to start correctly, like an SQL Server depends on the DC to be online.

- **Automatic Stop Action**: The **Automatic Stop Action** allows you to set what to do with the VM when the host is shutting down. Keep in mind that if the host is abruptly powered-off, the VMs will be abruptly powered-off as well. This option is used for the regular shutdown of the host. The options include **Save the virtual machine state**, that will save the memory information in the VM disk and save the VM State for the VM to come back at the same stage when powered-on again. Also, you can set **Turn off the virtual machine**, which will abruptly power off the VM, and **Shut down the guest operating system**, which will gracefully shutdown the guest OS, but requires IS to be installed. The options can only be changed if the VM is powered-off.

The Gen 2 VM is a bit different, as you can expect:

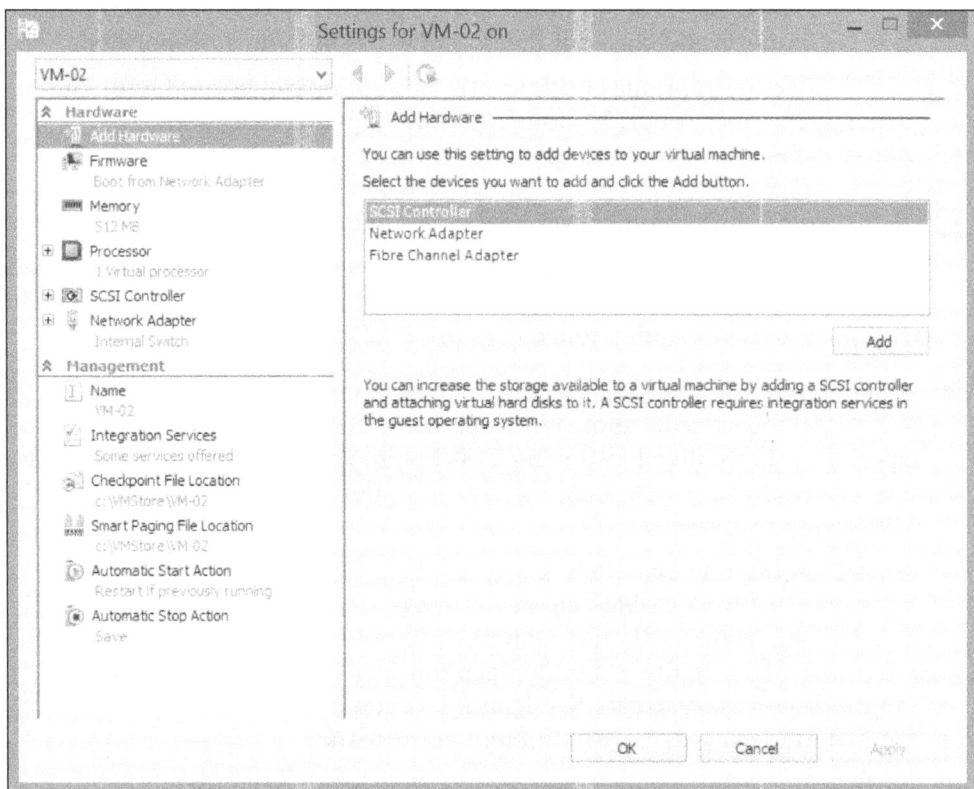

As you can see, there are fewer hardware options in the Gen 2 VM. On the **Add Hardware**, you do not have the Legacy Network Adapter. Instead of BIOS, you have the **Firmware** option, which presents other options as well:

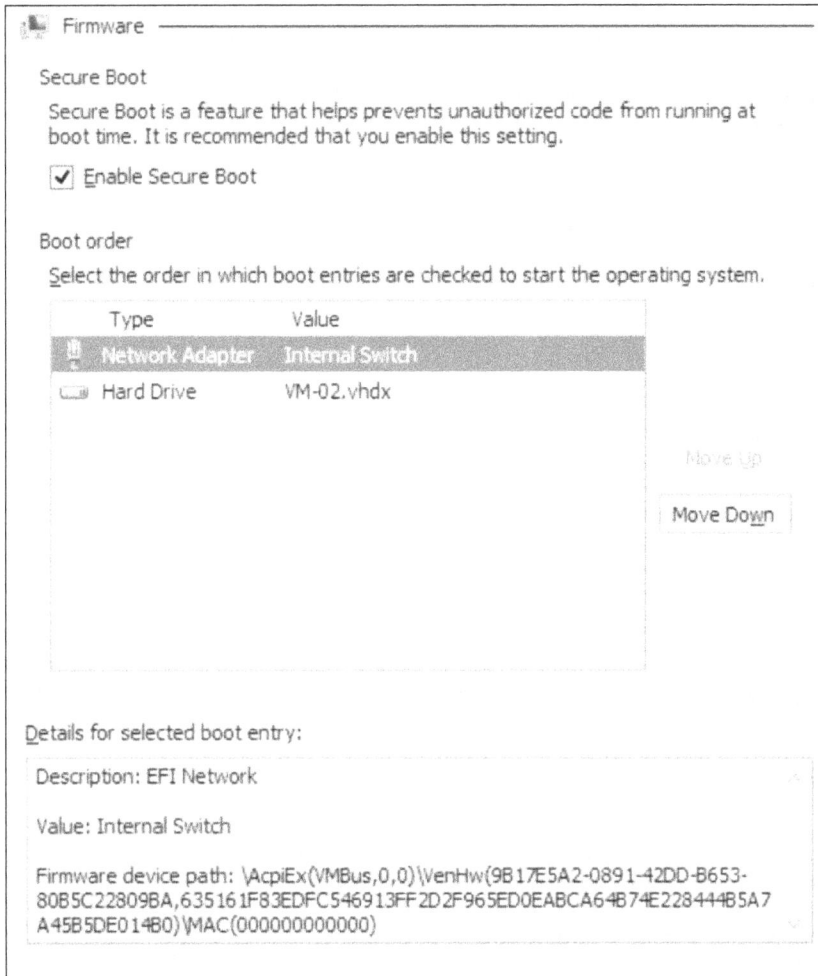

The **Firmware** option allows you to enable or disable Secure Boot, which will prevent any unauthorized software from running. In addition, you can set the boot order based on the available devices. You can also check the device details to make sure you are using the correct device to boot. All other options are the same as the Gen 1 VM.

To create a VM using PowerShell, you can use the New-VM cmdlet. The following are some options for using it:

```
New-VM -MemoryStartupBytes 512MB -Name VM-01
```

The preceding command will create a VM on the localhost named VM-01 with 512 MB of RAM. All other options will use the default configuration and there will be no VHD or VHDX attached to the VM. Let's take a look at the following cmdlet:

```
New-VM -ComputerName Host01 -Generation 2 -MemoryStartupBytes 2GB
-Name VM-01 -Path E:\VMStore\VM-01 -SwitchName "Internal Switch"
```

The option in the preceding cmdlet has more explicit information for the command. In this case, the VM-01 VM will be created on Host01 at the location E:\VMStore\VM-01. This will be a Gen 2 VM with 2 GB of RAM connected to the Internal Switch Virtual Switch. However, the VM will have no VHD or VHDX attached to it. Let's take a look at the following cmdlet:

```
New-VM -NewVHDPath E:\VHDStore\VM-01.vhdx -NewVHDSizeBytes 40GB -
ComputerName Host01 -Generation 2 -MemoryStartupBytes 1GB -Name
VM-01 -Path E:\VMStore\VM-01 -SwitchName "Internal Switch"
```

The preceding command is the same as the one before it, but this will create a VHDX file as the VM virtual disk with a total of 40GB of total size. This will be a dynamic virtual disk. Let's take a look at the following cmdlet:

```
New-VM -VHDPath E:\VHDStore\ExistingVHD.vhdx -ComputerName Host01
-Generation 2 -MemoryStartupBytes 1GB -Name VM-01 -Path
E:\VMStore\VM-01 -SwitchName "Internal Switch"
```

The preceding command will create a VM as well, but with an existing virtual disk. The benefit of this last option is that it can be a fixed size virtual disk, or any other type of disk, even with a guest OS already installed.

Another option is to have a reusable cmdlet saved as a PS1 file, to be used in the future. The following is an example of a simple reusable cmdlet:

```
$VMName = Read-Host
```

```
New-VM -MemoryStartupBytes 512MB -Name $VMName
```

The preceding command will ask you to provide the value of the variable $VMName before executing the cmdlet.

You can also manage the VM via PowerShell. The command to manage VMs is Set-VM. This command has multiple inputs and you can manage all the VM related configurations with it. Let's see some examples:

```
Set-VM -Name VM-01 -MemoryStartupBytes 4GB
```

The preceding command changes the VM memory from the actual value to 4 GB. Let's take a look at the following command:

```
Set-VM -Name VM-01 -SnapshotFileLocation E:\VHDStore\Snapshots
```

The preceding command changes the default Checkpoint location to the one indicated in the cmdlet. Let's take a look at the following command:

```
Set-VM -Name VM-01 -DynamicMemory -MemoryMaximumBytes 4GB -
MemoryMinimumBytes 512MB -MemoryStartupBytes 1GB
```

The preceding command will enable Dynamic memory on the VM and set the specified values as Minimum, Maximum, and Startup RAM.

For a complete list of options for the `Set-VM` command, check the official article at `http://technet.microsoft.com/en-us/library/hh848575.aspx`.

After checking the article you will probably see that some operations are not present. For example, managing network and storage. This is because these operations have a specific cmdlet. Here are some examples of cmdlets to manage network and storage.

```
Connect-VMNetworkAdapter -SwitchName "Internal Switch" -VMName VM-
02
```

The preceding command will connect the `VM-02` virtual network to the `Internal Switch`. Let's take a look at the following cmdlet:

```
New-VHD -Fixed -Path E:\VHDStore\Disk01.vhdx -SizeBytes 50GB
```

```
Add-VMHardDiskDrive -VMName VM-01 -ControllerNumber 0 -
ControllerType SCSI -DiskNumber 1 -Path E:\VHDStore\Disk01.vhdx
```

The preceding command will first create a 50 GB fixed size virtual disk and then attach it to the `VM-01` VM.

There many other cmdlets to manage VMs with Hyper-V. In fact, you can manage absolutely everything through PowerShell, if you want. A complete list of PowerShell cmdlets to manage Hyper-V is available in the official documentation at `http://technet.microsoft.com/en-us/library/hh848559.aspx`.

# Checkpoints

Before going any further, it is important to explain that Checkpoints are the well known Snapshots. If you are familiar with any other virtualization tool, this is probably the name you are familiar with. The name Snapshot was the name of this feature in Hyper-V until Windows Server 2012. In Windows Server 2012 R2, Microsoft decided to change the name of the feature to reflect the feature name on the System Center Virtual Machine Manager. However, the feature continues to work in, basically, the same way.

Additionally, more important than the name of the feature, is to understand that it is not, under any circumstance, a backup or disaster recovery solution. It is simply a solution for recovering from accidental misconfiguration or an error occurred during OS or application updates. Moreover, Checkpoints cannot be used in replicated database environments, as the database must always be synchronized with its replica. If you apply a Checkpoint to a VM that has a database replicated to another instance, like Active Directory, Exchange, or SQL Server, the database version on the VM is authoritative for that information, but the information is actually outdated.

To better understand this, let's see how the Checkpoint currently works, so that you can have an idea of why it should only be used in special cases.

So far, you have learned that all the information that a VM needs to write or retrieve is written or retrieved from the virtual disk. Since Checkpoints cannot be used with pass-through disks, we are ignoring it for now. When the guest OS or an application on the VM writes information, this information is written on the virtual disk. If the information is deleted, the information is deleted from the virtual disk. On a fixed size virtual disk, it will not influence the size of the virtual disk, but on a dynamic virtual disk, you can even reclaim this unused space as we have seen in *Chapter 5, Managing Storage*.

When you create a Checkpoint, the VM stops using the virtual disk for any operation other than reading. Any write or delete operation is made to a temporary disk with the AVHD or AVHDX extension. All the information is stored in this temporary disk because if you decide to go back to the moment when the Checkpoint was created, Hyper-V can use this disk to retrieve the VM state at the exact time that the Checkpoint was created.

In order to do that, this temporary disk does not work as a regular virtual disk. Instead, it only writes operations, working like a log of activities. For example, after creating a Checkpoint, you can create a new file on the VM. This operation will be written on the Checkpoint temporary virtual disk and it will need to grow in size. If you delete the file, a log of the operation will be written. The file will grow again. A Checkpoint temporary virtual disk has no limits for growing, and it is possible that it will use all the available disk space. If this happens, the VM will enter into a pause state until there is space available for the virtual disks.

Let's see how it works in real life. Before creating the Checkpoint, let's see the folder structure where the disk resides:

| Name | Date modified | Type | ▼ Size |
|------|--------------|------|--------|
| ☐ VM-01.vhdx | 13/01/2015 10:25 | Hard Disk Image File | 4.096 KB |

As you can see, the VM is using only one virtual disk. To create a Checkpoint, open **Hyper-V Manager** and right-click the VM where you want to create the Checkpoint, and select **Checkpoint**. After creating the Checkpoint, you will be able to see it on Hyper-V Manager by selecting the VM on the **Checkpoints** panel, as seen in the following screenshot:

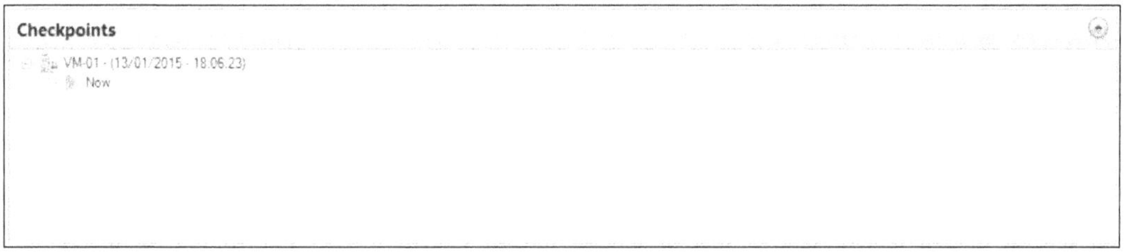

**Checkpoints**
- VM-01 - (13/01/2015 - 18.06.23)
  - Now

The folder structure will be reflect the Checkpoint created.

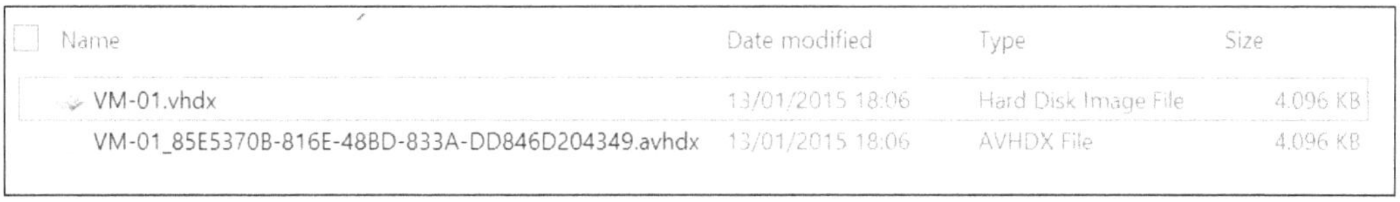

| Name | Date modified | Type | Size |
|------|--------------|------|------|
| ☐ VM-01.vhdx | 13/01/2015 18:06 | Hard Disk Image File | 4.096 KB |
| VM-01_85E5370B-816E-48BD-833A-DD846D204349.avhdx | 13/01/2015 18:06 | AVHDX File | 4.096 KB |

It is recommended that you rename the Snapshot using a conventional name to identify the reason of the Checkpoint. To do that, right- click the **Checkpoint** and click **Rename...**.

To avoid problems with Checkpoints, it is recommended that you create a new Checkpoint if you are going to execute an operation on the VM that can result in problems on the guest OS, such as Windows Update, Application Updates, and other tasks that you think can cause errors to the VM. Delete it right after you confirm that the operation succeeded. In case something goes wrong, you can revert the VM to the moment when the Checkpoint was taken. To revert the VM to the moment of a Checkpoint, right-click the Checkpoint and select **Apply...**, as shown in the following screenshot.

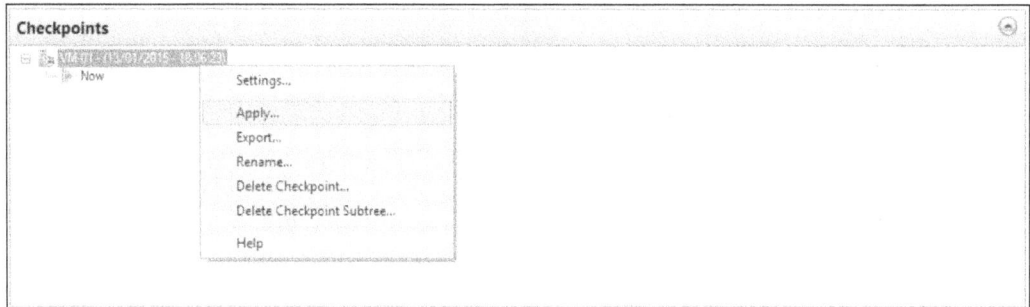

You'll be able to see the progress of the process on Hyper-V Manager under the status information. If the Checkpoint was taken with the VM powered-on, the VM will be placed in a pause state and you can start the VM after the process finishes. If the Checkpoint was taken with the VM powered-off, the VM will return to the powered-off state after the execution.

However, if you keep the Checkpoint even after finishing the process that you were running on the VM, the VM will continue to use the Checkpoint temporary virtual disk. As explained earlier, this file will only grow and can cause the VM to pause if the disk space ends. To avoid this situation, it is highly recommended that you delete the Checkpoint right after you verify that it is not necessary.

When you delete a Checkpoint, Hyper-V will merge the log of the Checkpoint temporary virtual disk to the original VM disk, and the VM will remain in the same state as it is, powered-on or off. To delete the Checkpoint, right-click the Checkpoint and click **Delete Checkpoint...**.

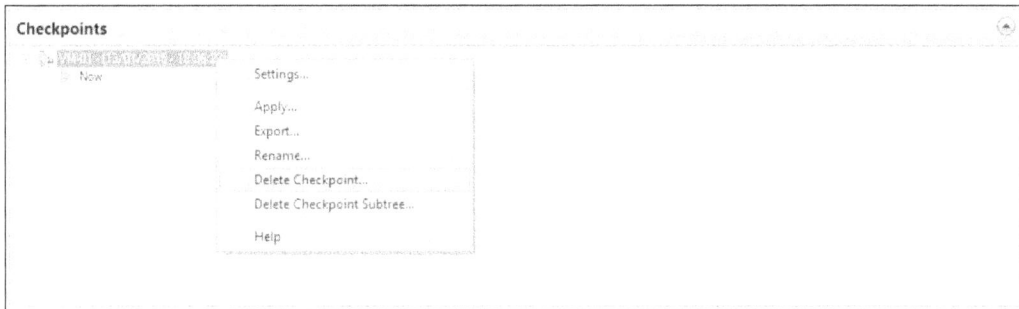

Until Windows Server 2012, if you deleted the Checkpoint (Snapshot in this case), the Checkpoint temporary virtual disk continued to be used by the VM until you had shutdown the VM. When you had shutdown the VM the file was merged to the original virtual disk. In Windows Server 2012 and 2012 R2, the merge occurs right way, even with the VM powered-on. After the merge process ends, the Checkpoint temporary virtual disk is deleted.

> Under any circumstance, you should manually delete the AVHD or AVHDX file. If you do so, Hyper-V will not be able to recover the VM to the original state and you will have to point the original virtual disk manually, losing all the information on the checkpoint.

To perform these operations through PowerShell, you can use the following commands:

```
Checkpoint-VM -Name VM-02
```

The preceding command will create a new Checkpoint for VM-02.

```
Get-VMSnapshot -VMName vm-02
```

The preceding command will show all available Checkpoints for VM-02

```
Rename-VMSnapshot -Name "VM-02 - (13/01/2015 - 18:34:04)" -NewName
Checkpoint01 -VMName VM-02
```

The preceding command will rename the Snapshot for Checkpoint01 on VM-02.

```
Get-VMSnapshot -VMName vm-02 -Name Checkpoint01 | Restore-
VMSnapshot –Confirm
```

The preceding command lists the Checkpoint Checkpoint01 and restores it on the VM-02.

Using Checkpoints is very useful in the day-to-day tasks and can help prevent problems on the VMs. However, not every application can work with Checkpoints. To exemplify an application that is not ready for Checkpoints, let's use the following example:

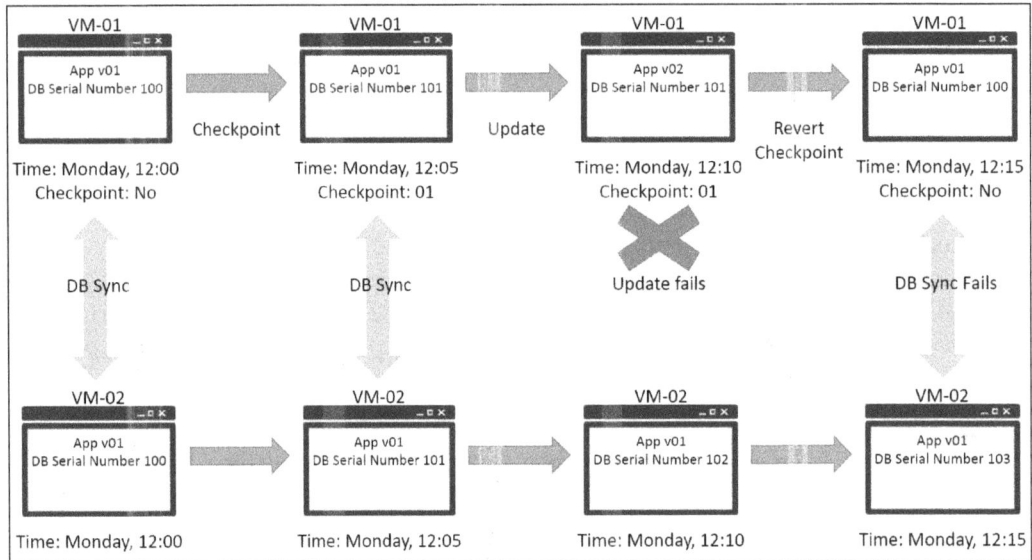

In the preceding diagram, two VMs are hosting the same application. Like most of the databases, the data is synchronized between the VMs. The synchronization happens when one of the databases has a new serial number indicating that this database has a new registry that needs to be updated on the other end. The end with a higher serial number is called authoritative and the other end accepts the synchronization as the non-authoritative end.

Following the diagram, you create a Checkpoint to ensure that you can rollback the actions in case a scheduled update fails. When applying the update, you find out that the update fails. To restore the VM, you revert to the Checkpoint. The VM starts to work. However, this database has different serial numbers on the VMs, and both are authoritative. The database synchronization will fail from this moment on.

This error occurs in every type of multimaster database environment, such as Active Directory, Exchange, and others. For Active Directory, Microsoft solved the problem in Windows Server 2012. This will be explained in detail in *Chapter 9*, *Virtualizing Active Directory Domain Controllers*. For all other solutions, the Checkpoint feature cannot be used, otherwise you can cause an application failure.

So far, you have seen some options for managing Hyper-V VMs, such as VM creation, modification, and Snapshots. Now it's time to see how to manage VM templates to make the day-to-day tasks easier.

# Virtual machine templates

If you think about it, it is a repetitive task every time you create a VM. After creating the VM, you have to boot from a CD or DVD, or even from the network to start the guest OS installation. The time you have to wait for the installation to finish is another pain. How do management tools make this task easier? They do so by using VM templates.

A template is nothing more than a collection of disk images, VM profiles, and configurations on the VM that will be used to configure VM with minimum interaction and administrative effort. As said before, System Center Virtual Machine Manager has this management out-of-the-box. Now, you will learn how to create your own VM template using all the native tools of Hyper-V and Windows Server.

# Sysprepped VMs

It all starts by creating an OS template. What we need is a configuration of a Windows Server as the base for our template. This consists of installing a regular Windows Server, applying the updates, installing the applications, and, after finishing the entire configuration, cleaning all the information related to that OS, such as Hostname, Windows Activation, and so on. Windows Server and Windows (client) have a native tool to clean up the OS information. This tool is called **Sysprep**.

To create a VM template, you will create a new VM and run all the steps we just listed, that is, install Windows Server, configure it, and so on. This VM will be your base VM for the template. After installing and configuring the VM, press Win+*R* on the keyboard and type `sysprep`. This will open Windows Explorer in the `C:\Windows\ System32\Sysprep` folder. In this folder, you will find the `sysprep.exe` tool. To start cleaning the guest OS unique information, execute the `sysprep.exe` executable.

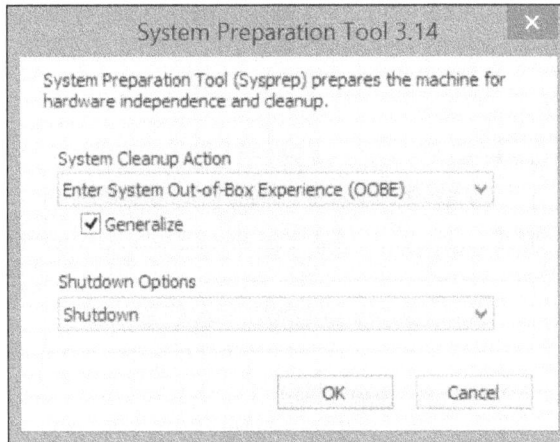

The Sysprep tool has different options for using, which are not in the scope of this book. To create a VM template, at **System Cleanup Action**, select **Enter System Out-of-box Experience (OOBE)**. This will configure the OS to request the necessary information to work properly, as and when you finish the installation.

Mark the option **Generalize**, as this will generalize the device drivers on the OS to use a different hardware. At **Shutdown Options**, select **Shutdown** as you don't need to perform any other action and you don't want to compromise your base image.

After executing the tool, the system will shutdown automatically and the VM will be powered-off. All you need from this VM is the virtual disk, as this is the base image of your template, so you can delete the VM and copy the virtual disk file to an appropriate location. When you need a new VM based on this image, all you have to do is to create a VM without a disk and attach a copy of the base virtual disk to it. In this case, performing it through PowerShell is much easier than using the GUI. You can use the following cmdlet to create a VM based on the base:

```
New-VM -MemoryStartupBytes 1GB -Name VM-01 -NoVHD -Path
E:\VMStore\VM-01 -SwitchName Internal Switch

Copy-Item -path E:\VHDStore\Template-2012R2.vhdx -Destination
E:\VMStore\VM-01
```

```
Rename-Item -NewName VM-01.vhdx -Path E:\VMStore\VM-01\Template-
2012R2.vhdx
```

```
Add-VMHardDiskDrive -VMName VM-01 -ControllerType IDE -
ControllerNumber 0 -Path E:\VMStore\VM-01\VM-01.vhdx
```

Let's understand what is being done here. The first cmdlet will create the VM with no virtual disk. The second command will copy the template virtual disk to the folder of the VM. The copied file will be the actual virtual disk of the VM, but since it keeps the original name of the template file, the next command changes the name of the file to match the VM name. The final cmdlet attaches the virtual disk file to the VM using the IDE controller.

When you initiate the VM, the result will look as seen in the following screenshot:

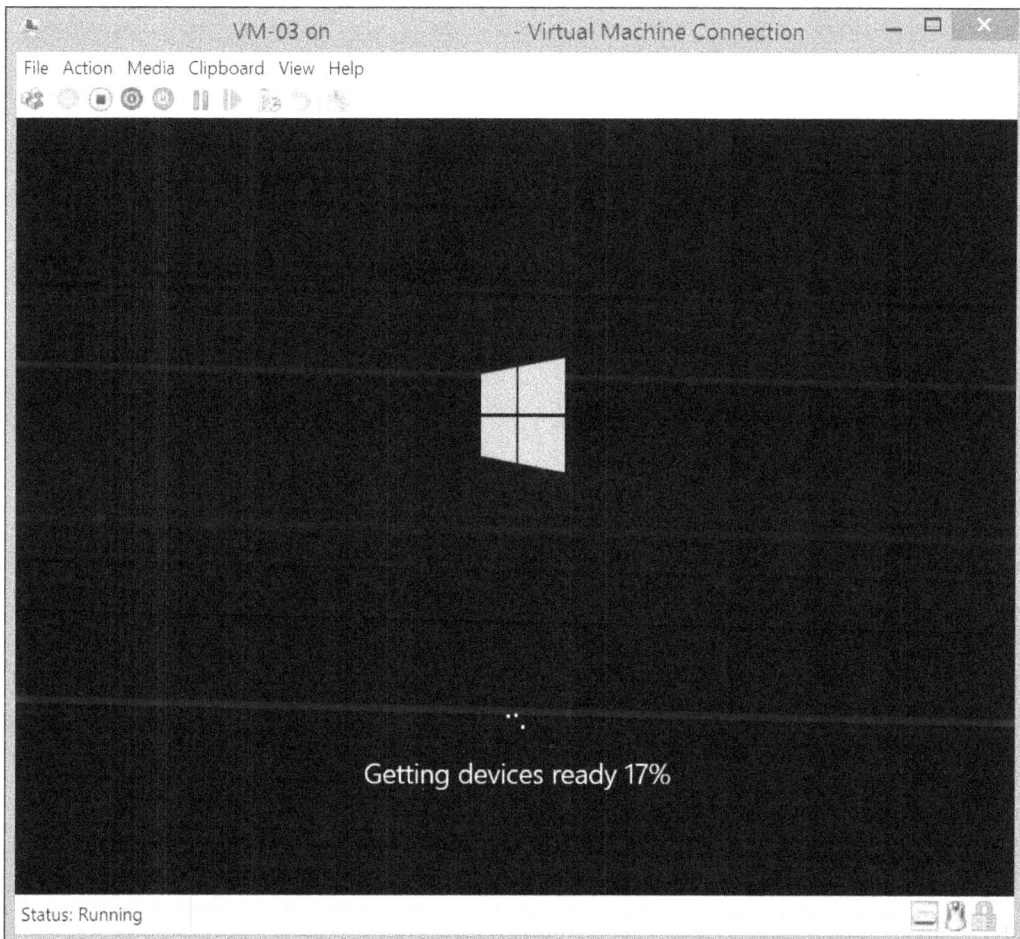

This process will take a few seconds to finish and after that, you will have to configure the basic settings for the guest OS to work, such as language and keyboard, accept the licensing terms, and input the admin password. After that, the VM is ready for use, with all the necessary applications and configurations done. You will still need to configure the IP address, domain membership and Windows Server activation. You can also use PowerShell to accomplish these tasks. However, these configurations are not in the scope of this book.

# Differencing disks

The process that we used in the previous section uses a copied file for use as the virtual disk on the VM. This is recommended in production environments. However, for testing and lab purposes, having multiple files for multiple VMs will require a considerable disk space. To minimize the disk size impact in testing environments, you can use Differencing disks.

A Differencing disk is a virtual disk that uses a parent disk as a base disk and writes all new information on the child disk. The benefit of Differencing disks is that you can have a single parent disk for multiple child disks attached to the VMs. This requires less disk space as the space used for the OS for all VMs will reside on a single virtual disk. The drawback of the Differencing disk is that it will reflect in a lower performance as multiple VMs are using the same virtual disk. Another problem is that if the parent virtual disk becomes unavailable, or if it crashes for any reason, all VMs will fail. That's why you should only use Differencing disks in testing environments.

To create a Differencing disk, open **Hyper-V Manager** and click on **New** on the top-left side of the console, and click **Hard Disk....** in the **New Virtual Hard Disk Wizard**, then click **Next >**. Choose the virtual disk format and click **Next >**. Select **Differencing** and click **Next >**.

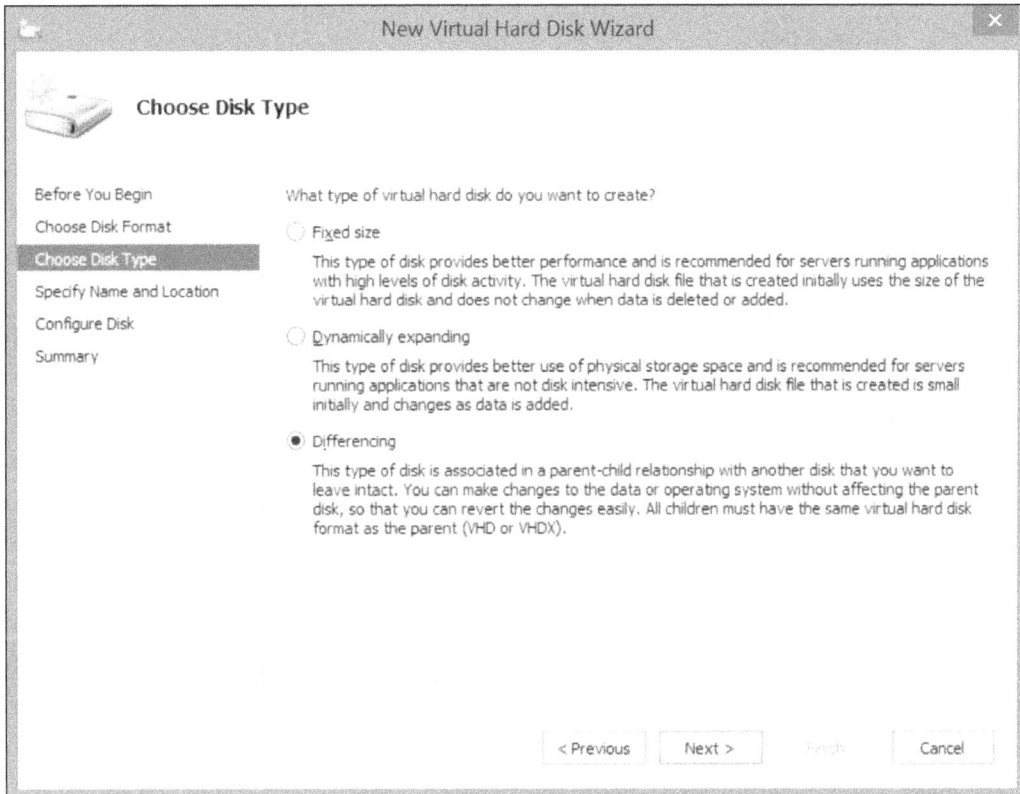

In the **Name** textbox, type the virtual disk name and in **Location**, type the location for the child virtual disk. Click **Next >**. On **Configure Disk**, select the parent virtual disk.

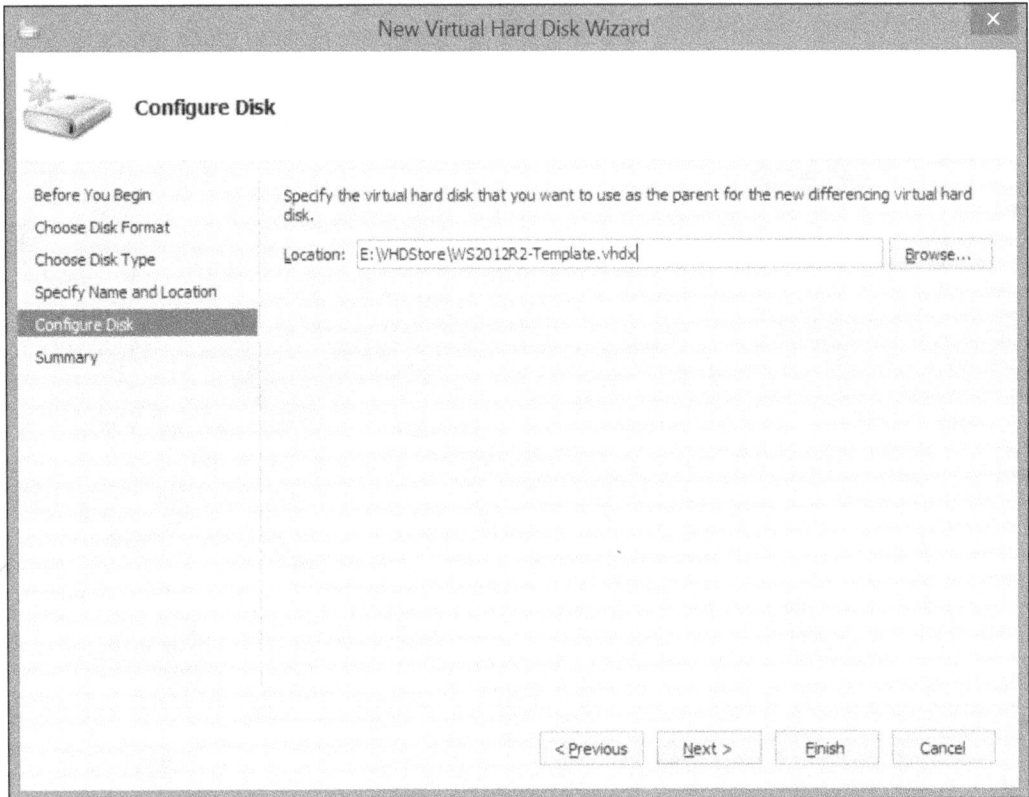

Click **Next >** and click **Finish** to create the Differencing disk. Now you can attach this child virtual disk to the VM. The outcome will be the same as shown in the previous section.

To create a Differencing disk via PowerShell, use the following cmdlet:

```
New-VHD -Differencing -ParentPath E:\VHDStore\Template-2012R2.vhdx
-Path E:\VMStore\VM-01 -SizeBytes 100GB
```

The preceding command will create a Differencing disk using the indicated parent. After creating the Differencing disk, you can attach it to the VM.

# PowerShell Desired State Configuration (DSC)

With the configurations that you've just learnt, you are able to manage a VM template that can be used to facilitate the process of creating new VMs with Hyper-V. You can actually create a single PowerShell file that can create the VM with all the configurations for it to start, that is, the VM will be ready to use right after creation.

However, besides the fact that it is a VM, the guest OS has the same management requirements as that of a regular OS. Using PowerShell can help you in the day-to-day tasks as it will facilitate the operations which you have to perform.

PowerShell DSC is not exclusive for virtualization, but since you are creating a VM template to reduce the administrative tasks, this feature can be extremely helpful.

PowerShell DSC works by running a PowerShell script that executes all the configurations that must be applied to the target server. It uses a script file that has a set of configurations, such as roles and/or features installation, registry management, file and directory management, process and services management, and many others.

DSC can be used in two modes:

- **Push**: This mode is the default option in which you will manually push a configuration file to a server, and the file will be used to configure the server as specified in the script file
- **Pull**: This mode uses a centralized server to apply the configuration files to the nodes, which are the servers you want to apply the DSC configuration to

PowerShell DSC has multiple applications and is an extensive topic, which will not be covered in detail in this book. To learn how to use PowerShell DSC, check the official article at `http://technet.microsoft.com/en-us/library/dn249912.aspx`.

# Summary

Using a management tool to perform day-to-day tasks is important as these tools usually facilitate our job. Understanding how these tools work and how to perform these tasks without these tools, on the other hand, will differentiate you from others in the market.

In this chapter, you were able to understand how the process for creating a VM works, how to customize it, and how to modify the VM settings. You can now differentiate between a Generation 1 and 2 VM and are familiar with the specifications of each option.

You saw how to use Checkpoints and how they works in the background, as well as the implications of the Checkpoint on the applications and databases in the VM.

You can now create a VM template using the native tools on Windows Server and Hyper-V, such as Sysprep, differencing disks, and PowerShell DSC.

In the next chapter, we will go through an important topic, which is High Availability to provide failover capabilities for important VMs in Hyper-V.

# 7
# Implementing High Availability

The term High Availability (HA) is a bit controversial and in many cases causes some confusion for inexperienced professionals on Hyper-V. The term HA for Microsoft represents the use of hardware and software technologies for providing an acceptable uptime and Service Level Agreement (SLA) for a given application. Since you have multiple components, such as networking, storage, electric, server hardware, OS, and even the application itself, there are multiple points to observe. Implementing an HA solution requires that you consider all of this to avoid application interruptions.

Microsoft implements HA to Hyper-V on the host OS level by leveraging the well-known failover cluster solution. Failover cluster is a Windows Server feature that, by definition, has no relation to Hyper-V. However, Hyper-V and failover cluster evolved together over the years to support virtualized application and today there are new failover cluster features that were implemented to support Hyper-V, such as VM Monitoring. Other features on failover cluster were removed to leverage Hyper-V capabilities, such as Print Services on failover clusters.

Another important aspect of failover cluster on Windows Server is that it provides HA, which means that all efforts to avoid application interruption will be in place. That doesn't mean fault tolerance. The objective of HA is that, in the case of a hardware failure in a server, also called a node in failover clusters, the application will failover to another host with minimal interruption, but there will still be an interruption. On Hyper-V, that means that the VM will fail along with the host, but will failover to another host as soon as possible.

In this chapter we will cover the following topics:

- Failover cluster overview
- Hyper-V cluster implementation
- Cluster Shared Volumes (CSV)
- Highly available VMs administration
- Shared VHDX

# Microsoft failover cluster and Hyper-V overview

As explained before, the failover cluster in Windows Server is a feature that you can enable to support the application on which you want to ensure HA. In order to enable and configure failover cluster, you have to attend to some prerequisites. Let's first understand how failover cluster works, to see how these prerequisites are important.

On a regular standalone virtualization host, as you've seen so far, a VM is placed entirely on the host. Checkpoints, disks, configuration, and so on, everything is in the host disk. If this host fails, the VM will fail too. What failover tries to create is a mechanism to fail over the VM to a healthy host. To understand that, look at the following diagram:

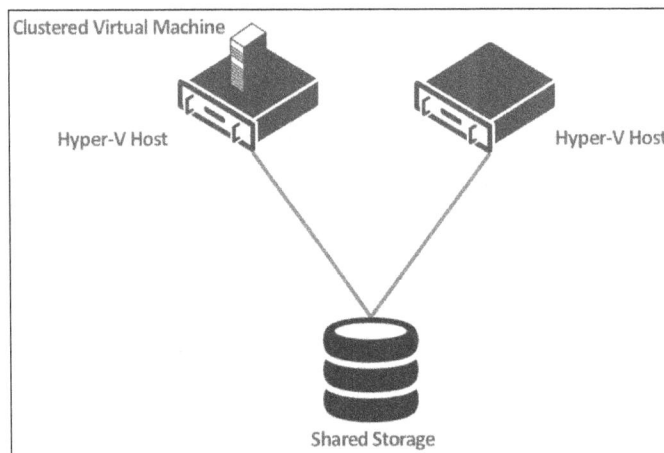

On a failover cluster, Hyper-V will host VM execution, just like a standalone host. However, all the VM files will be placed on a shared storage location. If the host fails, the cluster services notify the next available host and, as the host is able to access the VM files on the shared storage, the VM is automatically started on the next host.

By the preceding definition, it's obvious that for a failover cluster to properly work you must have at least two hosts and shared storage.

There are, however, other requirements for failover clusters to not only to work properly, but for Microsoft to support the failover cluster environment. To check that all the requirements are met before you create the failover cluster, the wizard will prompt you to run a validation test. This validation test will verify multiple configurations and settings on your environment in order to make sure that it has all the required settings in place. Prior to Windows Server 2012, this validation test checked for general settings on the hosts. On Windows Server 2012, Microsoft included a new validation to check if all the Hyper-V settings are configured correctly on all hosts. This validation is triggered if one of the hosts you want to check has the Hyper-V role installed. This validation will be discussed in detail later in this chapter.

# Failover cluster installation and configuration

To install failover cluster on a Hyper-V Host, open **Server Manager**, click **Manage** and select **Add Roles and Features**. On the Wizard, click **Next >** Select **Role-based or feature-based installation** and click **Next >**. Select the server you want to install the failover cluster feature on and click **Next >**. Click **Next >** on **Server Roles**. On the **Features** screen, select **Failover Clustering** and click **Add Features** if you want to install the Management Tools:

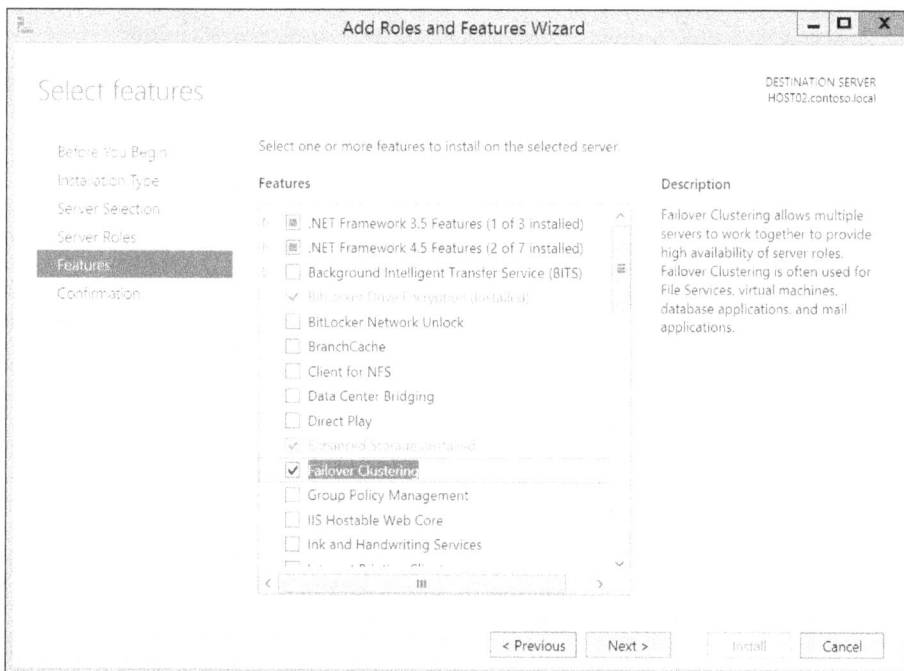

Click **Next >** and **Install** to install the failover cluster feature on the host. You need to repeat the operation on the hosts that you want to add to the failover cluster.

To perform the operation via PowerShell, use the following cmdlet:

```
Install-WindowsFeature -ComputerName Host01 -Name Failover-
Clustering -IncludeManagementTools
```

The preceding command will install the failover fluster feature and the necessary management tools on Host01.

Installing the failover cluster feature is the first step in creating your cluster. After installing the feature, you will have to create the cluster itself. However, when creating the cluster, the wizard will prompt you to run the validation wizard. To get started, open **Failover Cluster Manager**. Click **Create Cluster...** in the top right corner. Click **Next >** on the **Create Cluster Wizard**. On **Selected servers**, enter the host name of the servers that you want to add to the cluster:

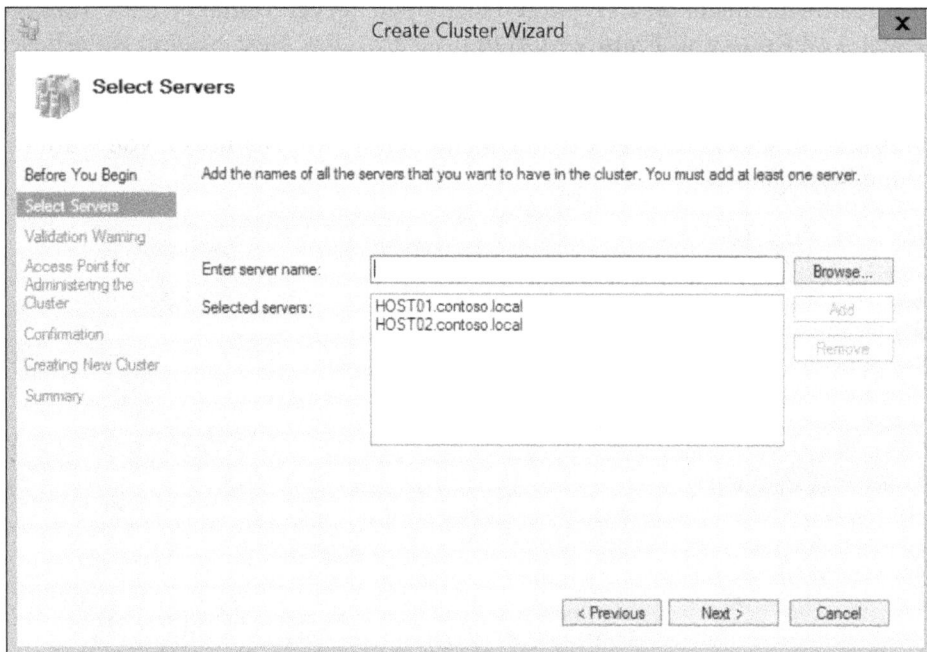

When you add the servers, the wizard will check if the failover cluster feature is installed. If the features are not installed, the wizard will ask you to do so prior to continuing. Click **Next >**. Now, you will be asked to run the Validation wizard.

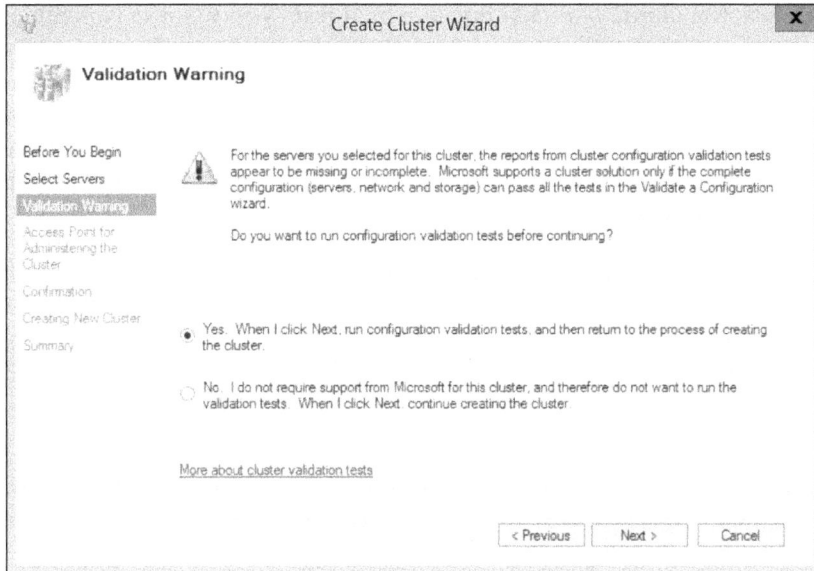

As you can see, you can skip the Validation wizard. This is only recommended on test environments or for when you are sure about the configuration and will run the Validation wizard later. Keep in mind that Microsoft will not support an environment on which the Validation wizard report is not available. Click **Next >** to run the Validation wizard. A new wizard will be launched. Click **Next >** on the Validation wizard:

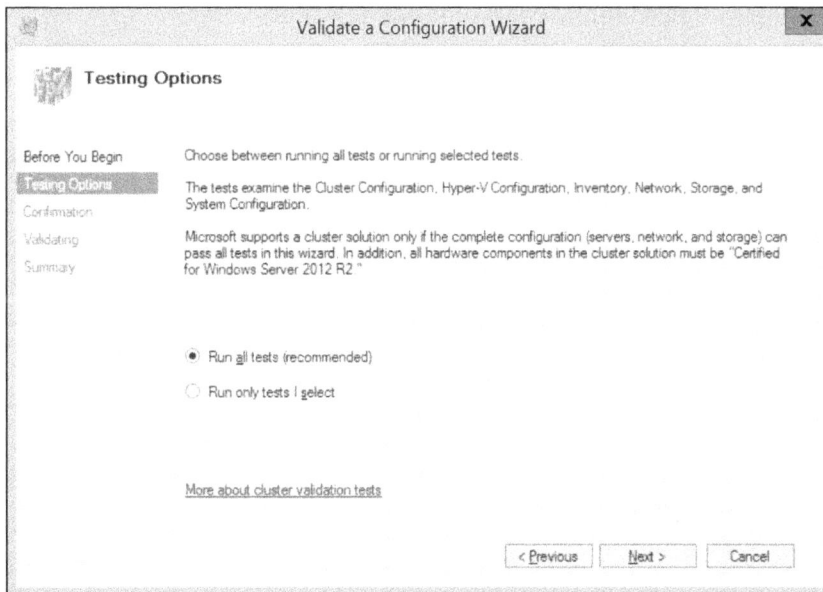

On the Validation wizard, you can choose which tests you want to run. Since you are creating a new cluster, it is recommended you run all tests. The **Run only tests I select** option is recommended for cases in which the cluster is already created, you changed a configuration, and now you want to test whether the configuration is okay. In fact, the Validation wizard must be executed every time you make a change on the cluster. Select **Run all tests (recommended)** and click **Next >**. A list of all tests is displayed. The tests are:

- **Hyper-V Configuration**: In this test, the Validation wizard will check Hyper-V compatibility, such as processor and memory compatibility, Virtual Switch consistency, and many other Hyper-V configurations. The most common mistake here is to have different Virtual Switches on each host. On a cluster environment, Virtual Switches must have the same naming convention, including upper and lower case letters in the Virtual Switch name.

- **Inventory**: In this test, the Validation wizard will list the system information. In this test, no errors will be presented but the information collected will be used in the following tests.

- **Network**: In this test, the Validation wizard will check for network configuration issues. Common issues include using a single communication route between the hosts and not setting at least one default gateway.

- **Storage**: The Validation wizard will try to find a shared storage. If a given storage disk that can be accessed by all nodes is found, the validation will check if the disk can be failed over the nodes. Also, common issues include using disks that do not support **SCSI-3 Persistent Reservation**, which is available on most of the recent storage solutions.

- **System Configuration**: This test validates the general settings of the nodes. In this test, the Validation wizard will check OS and even hardware configuration, such as service pack and update information, processor architecture, and others.

Running all these tests is important to make sure the cluster will work properly. Keep in mind that, if you need any assistance from Microsoft on your cluster environment, you will need to provide the report that is generated at the end of the wizard. Click **Next >** to start the test.

At the end of the validation, there are three possible situations:

- **Validation test reports Success**: In this case, all the configuration is OK and you can continue creating the cluster.

- **Validation test reports Warning**: In this case, you have the minimal configuration for creating a cluster environment. However, some issues are present on your environment. Since these issues will not prevent you from creating the cluster, you can continue with cluster creation. Keep in mind that it is recommended you solve all issues, regardless of being able to continue. Additionally, you will not be able to request support from Microsoft if the validation is not presenting **Success**.

- **Validation test reports Failed**: In this case, you will have to review the report to understand which configuration is presenting as **Failed** and correct the issues presented on the report. After correcting them, you must run the Validation wizard again.

In the following screenshot, you will see a summary of the tests carried out:

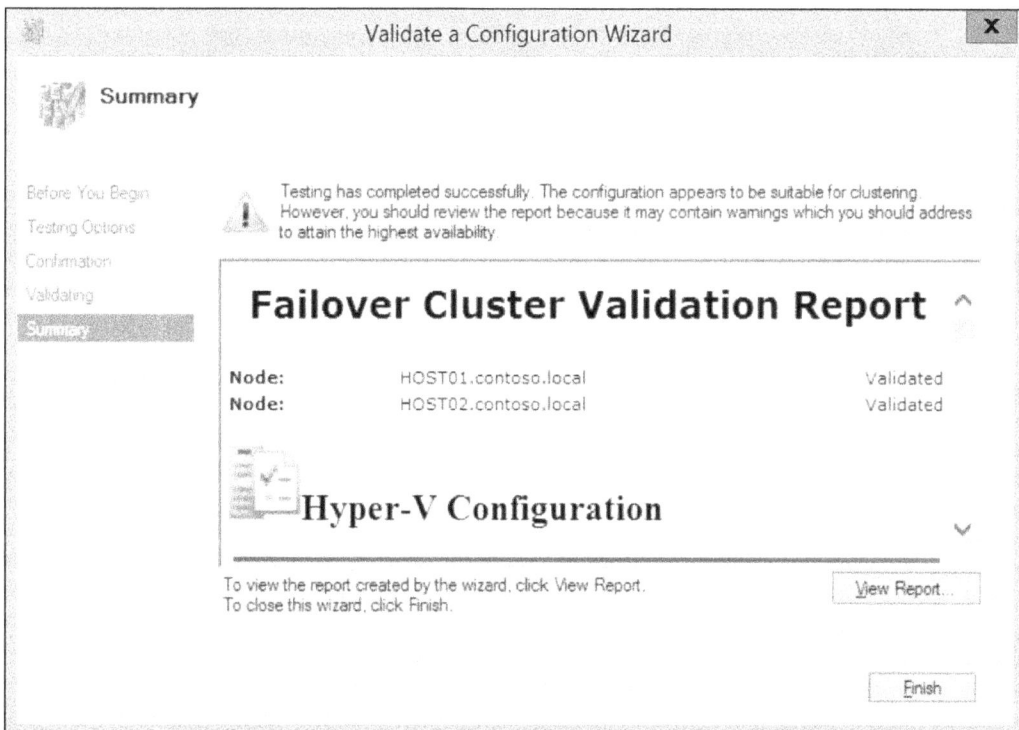

On the Validation wizard **Summary** screen, you can click **View Report...** to review the outcomes:

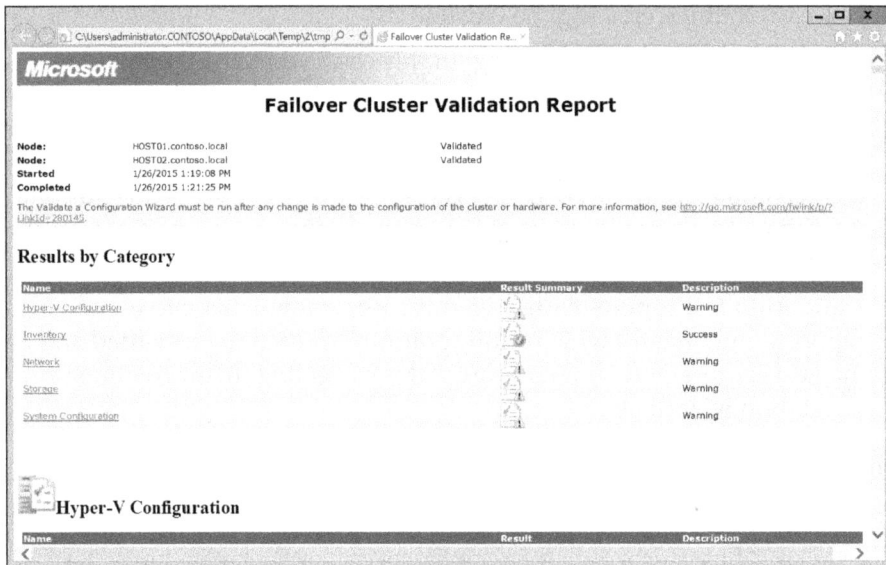

Navigate through the report to check which configuration on each section presented a **Failure** or a **Warning**. You can find more information about the Validation wizard in the official article at `http://go.microsoft.com/fwlink/p/?LinkId=280145`. Close the report and click **Finish**. If the validation reported **Success** or **Warning**, cluster creation will continue. Now, you have to provide the **Cluster Name**:

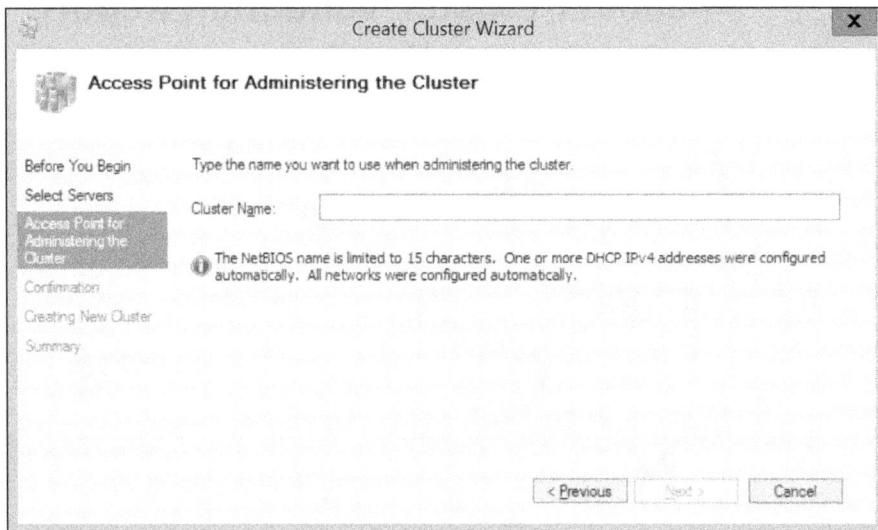

The **Cluster Name** is an important cluster resource, although in virtualization it is rarely used. The **Cluster Name** will be used to create a computer account on Active Directory and a DNS name will be assigned on the FQDN. Plus, an IP address must be assigned. In the preceding screenshot, you can see that a DHCP IPv4 address has been assigned. You can change the IP address later, if you want to change to a fixed IP address.

> On other types of cluster, such as File Servers, the **Cluster Name** will be used to map the cluster resources. On a File Server cluster, for example, you access the file shares by accessing `\\ClusterName\Share`.

Insert the **Cluster Name** and click **Next >**. On the review page, you can confirm the information and select whether or not to add the eligible storage to the cluster. Checking the **Add all eligible storage to the cluster** option will associate the shared storage found on the Validation wizard to the cluster. If you're not sure about the storage association, you can clear the checkbox and change the storage configuration later. Click **Next >** to create the cluster. Wait for the wizard to finish. If any error is presented at this time, especially network latency, the wizard won't be able to create the cluster. When the process finishes, the following screen is presented:

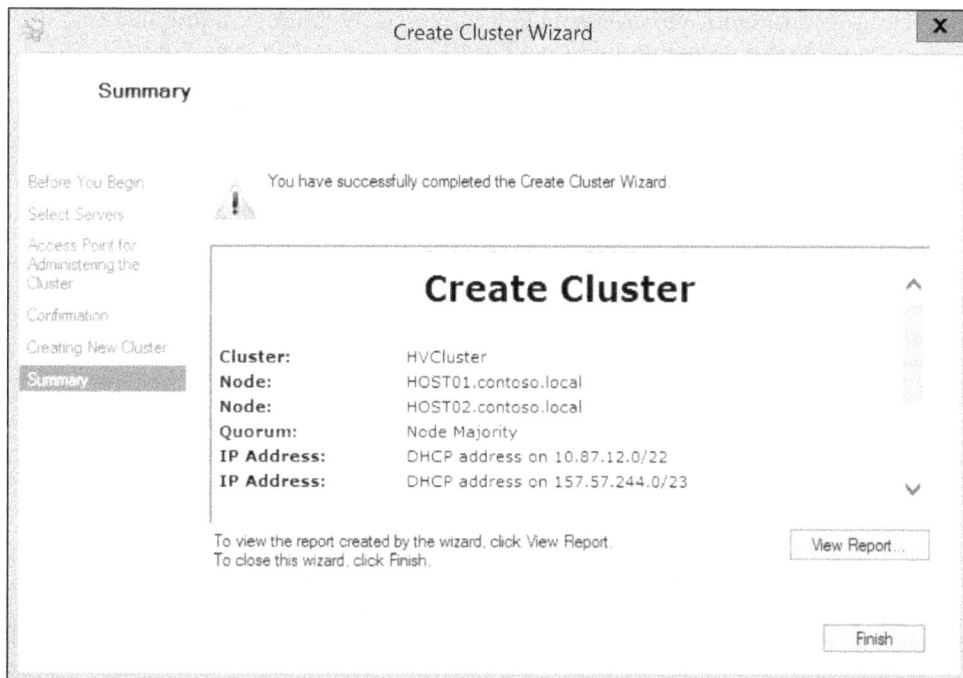

If a disk was presented, the cluster creation process will assign the disk as a disk witness in a Quorum, which will be explained later. If not, the wizard will present a warning, as in the preceding screenshot, showing that the Quorum is configured as **Node Majority** and that you should configure a Quorum. Quorum options will be explained later. Click **Finish** to go back to the **Failover Cluster Manager**.

To create the cluster using PowerShell, you can use multiple cmdlets. Let's have a look at some of them:

```
Test-Cluster -List
```

The preceding command will only list the available validation tests. To effectively run the validation test, using all the available tests, run the following command:

```
Test-Cluster -Node Host01, Host02 -ReportName
c:\ClusterReport\Report01.mht
```

The preceding cmdlet will run all the tests on the validation test against Host01 and Host02 and store the results on the indicated file. You can review the file, just as you did on the GUI. To create the cluster, run the following cmdlet:

```
New-Cluster -Name HVCluster -Node Host01, Host02 -StaticAddress
192.168.100.200 -NoStorage
```

The preceding command will create a cluster named HVCluster using Host01 and Host02 as cluster nodes and will set the IP address as 192.168.100.200. Additionally, the cluster will be created without any storage attached.

After creating the cluster, you can check the configuration by opening **Failover Cluster Manager**:

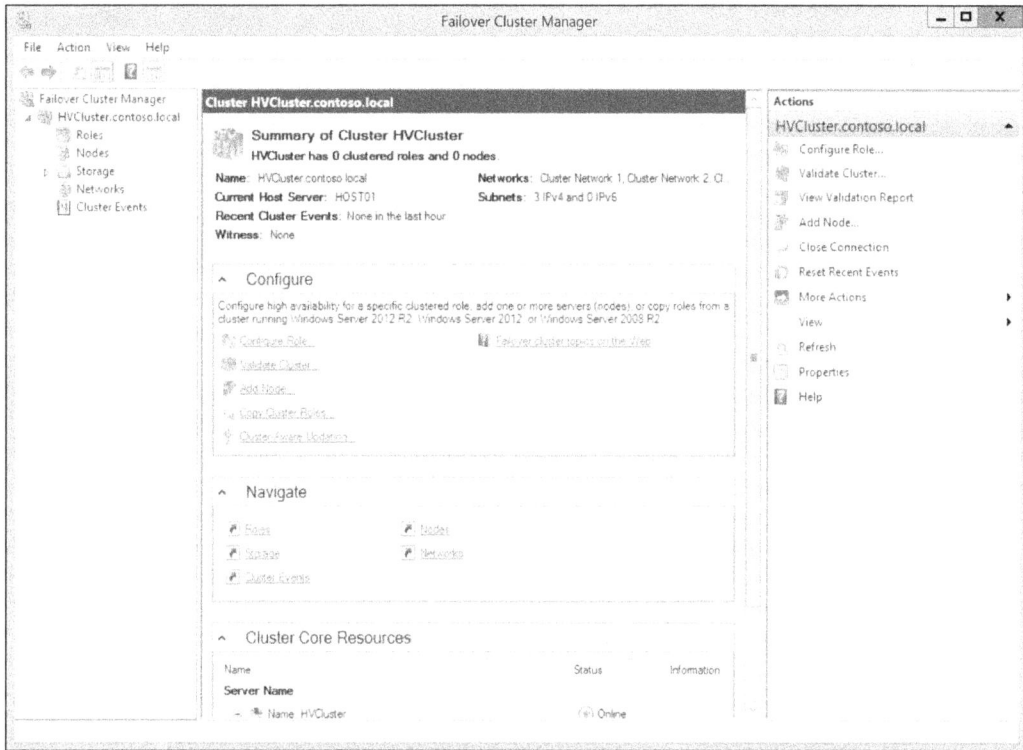

To manage the cluster using PowerShell, there are multiple cmdlets available. We will use some of them throughout the chapter.

# Quorum and Node Majority

In all the previous examples, you've seen the creation of the cluster by using two nodes, or servers. As explained, the goal of the HA solution is to provide a failover system in case a node fails. This is true, but there are some scenarios when a more robust validation needs to occur. To better understand that, let's imagine another scenario:

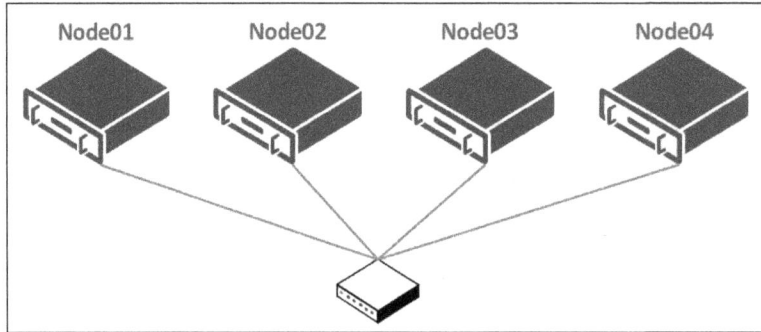

In the preceding diagram, a cluster is formed by four nodes. In a regular operation, if Node01 fails, all the VMs are failed over to the other nodes. Imagine, however, that Node01 has a communication problem with the switch. In this case, the node itself knows that it is online. However, the other hosts have no information about whether Node01 is experiencing a hardware problem, a network problem, or if it experiencing a general failure. Since the other nodes can't contact Node01, they need a mechanism to validate that they have the authority to declare Node01 as offline. Additionally, Node01 itself must be able to understand that the VMs running on it are being failed over to the other nodes and it must be taken offline. The mechanism to accomplish that is Quorum and Node Majority.

Quorum and Node Majority are a voting mechanism in which voters will define who has the majority of votes. In the above scenario, each node has a vote. Since Node01 is isolated from the other nodes, it will have only one vote. The other nodes together have three votes. With that, Node01 will be automatically placed as offline and the other nodes will assume the VMs that were running on Node01.

Now imagine the following: A network problem isolates Node01 and Node02 from Node03 and Node04. In this case, we have two votes for each side and the nodes cannot decide who must assume the VMs. If this happens, all nodes will fail and the cluster will be completely offline. To avoid this situation, the Quorum and Node Majority feature uses another vote. The vote is from a disk, hosted on a Storage Device, or file share, hosted on any host that is not part of the cluster. This disk (the disk witness in Quorum) and the file share (the file share witness) are cluster resources and will be online in one of the nodes.

> The file share witness option is usually recommended to GeoCluster where nodes reside on multiple sites, since this option requires the Quorum to be on a different site. However, a file share witness can be used on a regular cluster, as well.

The result will be something like this:

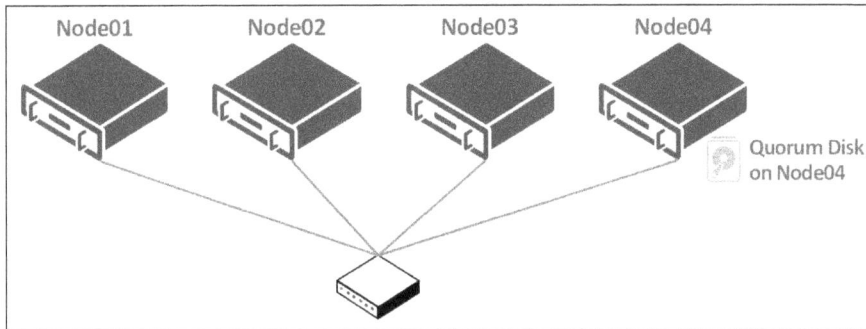

With the disk witness online on Node04, if a communication error isolates Node01 and Node02 from Node03 and Node04, Node01 and Node02 will have a total of two votes and Node03 and Node04 will have three votes. With that, Node01 and Node02 will be placed offline and Node03 and Node04 will assume the VMs from Node01 and Node02.

Right now, you might be thinking "What if I have 3 nodes?" This question is totally valid. Actually, a Quorum is only needed in scenarios where you have an even number of nodes. In a scenario with an even number of nodes, you can have an equal number of votes, as explained. With an odd number of nodes, you will never find this scenario.

However, imagine a scenario with five nodes. In this case, you do not need a Quorum. If a host fails, however, you have four nodes and a possible scenario resembling the one described earlier. In this case, you will need a Quorum.

To solve the problem of adding and removing a Quorum manually when needed, Microsoft created a feature on Windows Server 2012 called **Dynamic Quorum**. Dynamic Quorum is a configuration where the cluster service will check the number of nodes and automatically enable or disable the Quorum if needed. If the failover cluster has an odd number of nodes, the cluster service will disable the Quorum vote. If an even number of nodes is detected, the cluster service will enable it automatically.

When you create the cluster, if an available disk is found and the validation test detects that the disk is able to failover to all nodes, this disk will be assigned as the disk witness. If a disk is not presented, you can add a shared disk to the cluster. Since the scope of this book is not to explain Microsoft failover cluster in detail, we will assume the disk is already added to the cluster.

To manage the Quorum configuration, right click the cluster name on **Failover Cluster Manager**, select **More Actions** and click **Configure Cluster Quorum Settings...**, as shown in the following screenshot:

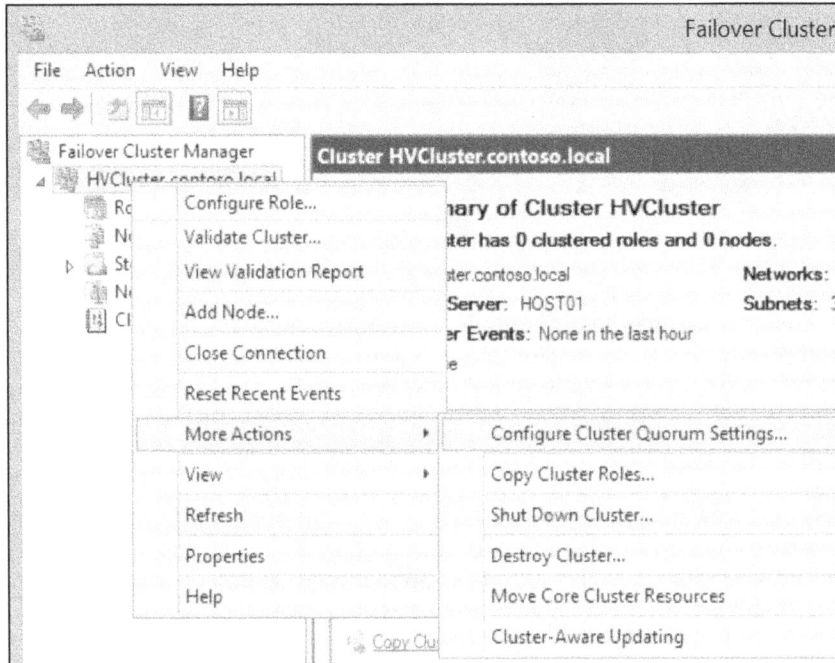

Click **Next >** on the **Configure Cluster Quorum Wizard**. On the first step, you have three available options:

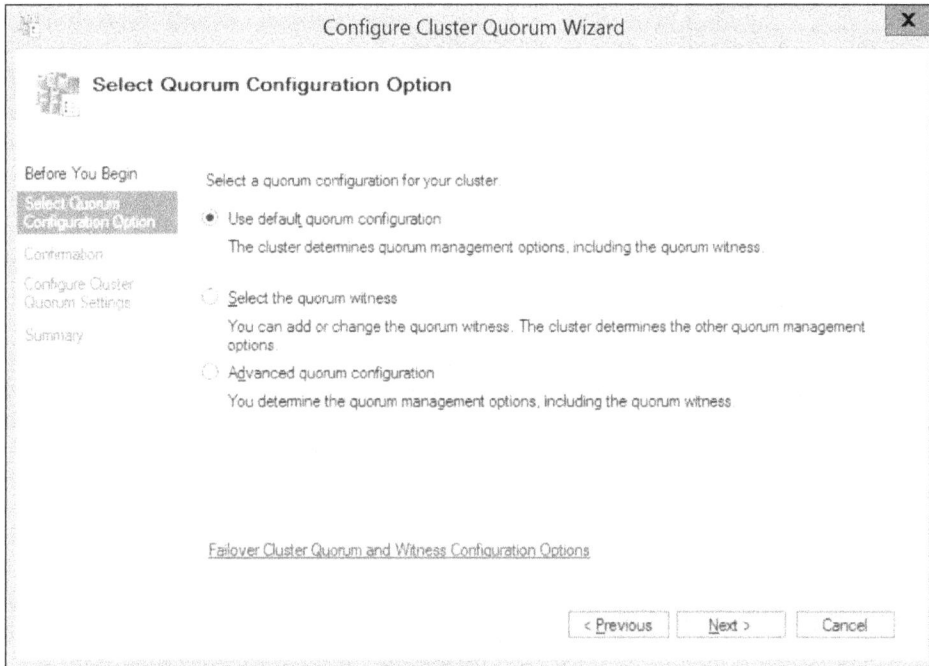

Let's understand these options:

- **Use default quorum configuration**: This option will run a validation test on storage and will automatically define the best possible option for the available configuration.

- **Select the quorum witness**: In this option you will be able to provide a disk witness or file share witness. You will not be able, though, to change node votes.

- **Advanced quorum configuration**: This option let's you change the entire Quorum and vote configuration for the cluster.

In this case, we will choose the **Advanced quorum configuration** option and click **Next >**. Keep in mind that, by following this path, you can incorrectly configure the Quorum settings, so be sure about the best configuration for your environment is. Using **Select Voting Configuration**, you can select which nodes will have a vote:

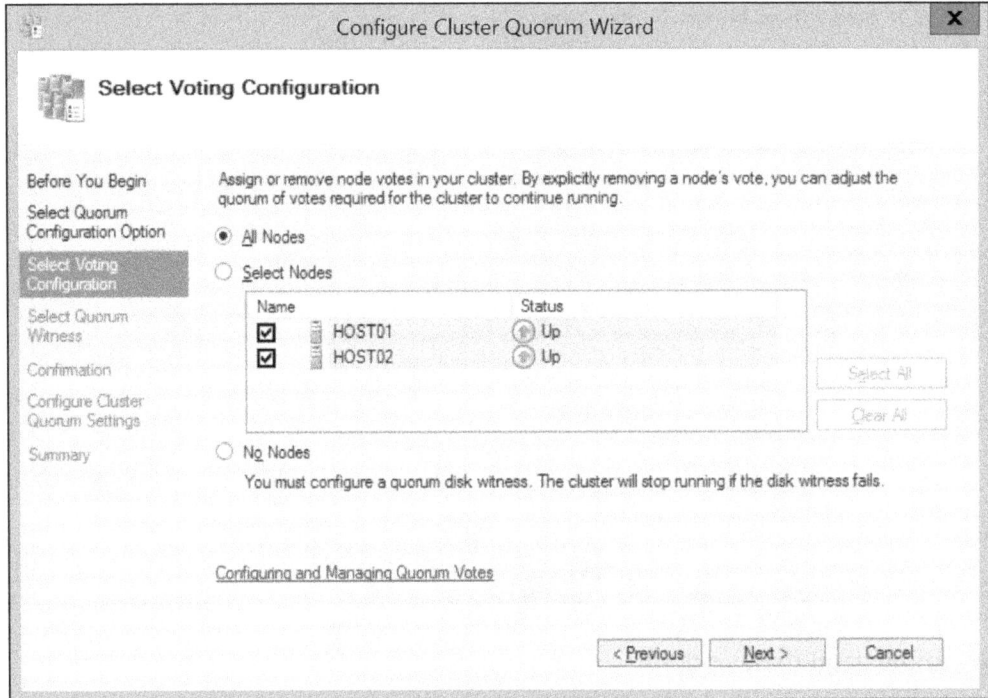

The options will vary in this case:

- **All Nodes**: All nodes will have a vote. This option is the most common choice. Keep in mind that if you're not adding a Quorum and you have an even number of nodes, you will put your cluster at risk.

- **Select Nodes**: you can select which nodes will have a vote on the cluster. With that, you avoid the problem above of an even number of nodes and no Quorum.

- **No Nodes**: This option is used when you want the Quorum to be the only voter. This can be a problem when your Quorum is offline. Other than that, it is a suitable option for environments in which you don't want to deal with manual configurations.

After choosing the best option for your environment, click **Next >**. Now, you have the Quorum settings:

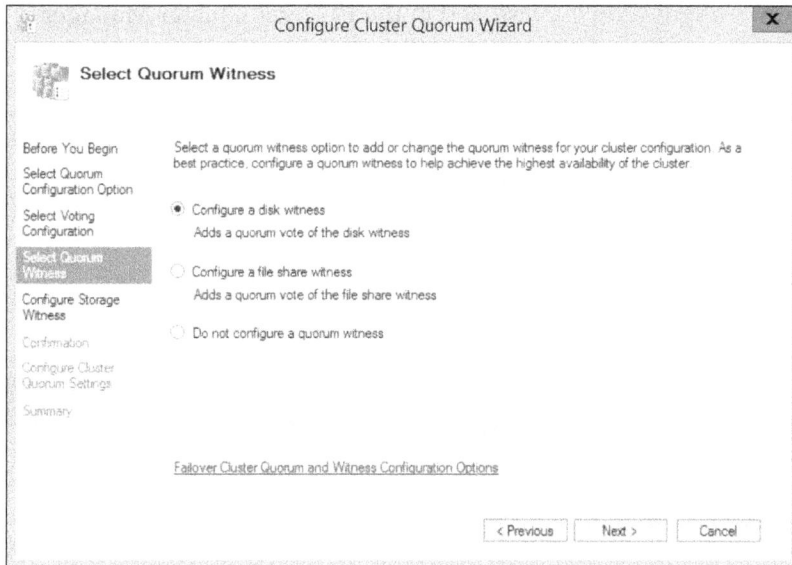

Here, you can choose a disk witness, file share witness, or even no Quorum. In this case, we will choose the **Configure a disk witness** option and click **Next >**. Since the disk is already associated to the cluster, the disk is displayed as available storage and can be used as a Quorum witness:

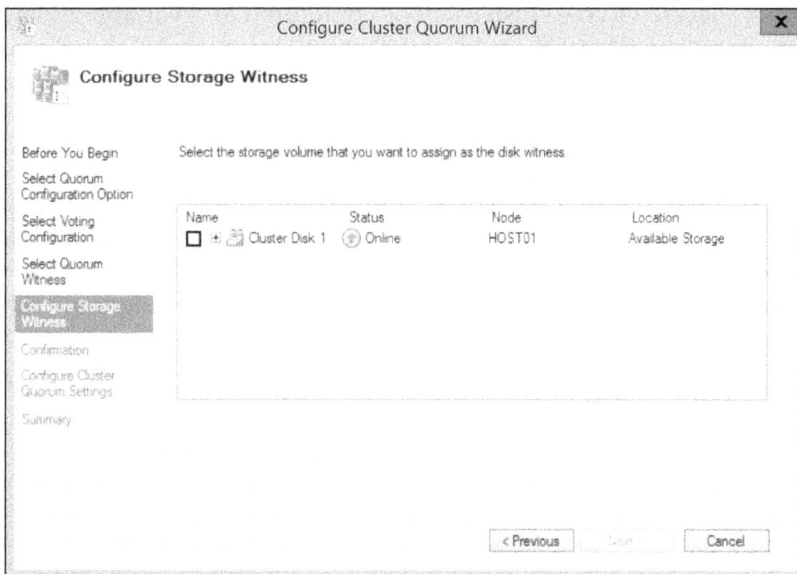

Select the disk you want to configure as disk witness and click **Next >**. After reviewing the configuration, click **Next >** and **Finish**.

The Quorum configuration is presented in the **Failover Cluster Manager** summary information:

> If you're using a disk witness, the cluster will create a configuration file on the disk. Since the file is extremely small, any disk size bigger than 1 GB is enough. However, many administrators tend to use the same configuration they are used to since Windows NT failover cluster, which is a 5 GB disk allocated on the Q drive letter.

# Configuring storage for Hyper-V cluster

As explained earlier, one of the prerequisites for a failover cluster environment is shared storage. Shared storage is the location where the VM will be hosted in order for all the nodes to be able to read/write the VM files.

A regular disk allocated to the cluster will be configured as **Available Storage**. There is a problem, though, with NTFS and virtualization. A regular NTFS volume does not allow more than one host at a time to access the volume. If multiple hosts try to access the volume at the same time, the volume will crash and all the information on it will be lost.

One of the features of Hyper-V, which we will explain how to use later in this chapter, is Live Migration. Live Migration is a feature where you can migrate the VM from one host to another while the VM is up and running. During the process of migrating the VM, both hosts will need to access the VM files. Since the NTFS system will not allow it, a Live Migration cannot be accomplished using a regular NTFS volume. On Windows Server 2008 R2, Microsoft introduced a new technology called Cluster Shared Volume (CSV).

CSV is an option for disks allocated to the cluster on which multiple nodes can access the same NTFS volume at the same time. This is possible because CSV orchestrates the read/write operations on the volume by using a SMB and a coordinator node. The coordinator node is responsible for managing the access to the volume and ensures it maintains a healthy state. Behind the scenes, CSV will coordinate the access to the volume to ensure that the nodes are not accessing the same block at the same time. Since access to blocks on the storage is faster, you have the feeling that all nodes are accessing the same information at the same time, which, in fact, they are.

CSV enables a Hyper-V cluster to use the Live Migration because all nodes are now able to access the VM files during the migration operation. To enable CSV on a disk associated to the cluster, open **Failover Cluster Manager,** expand **Storage,** and click **Disks**.

On the top right side, click **Add Disk**. On the wizard select the desired disk and click **OK**:

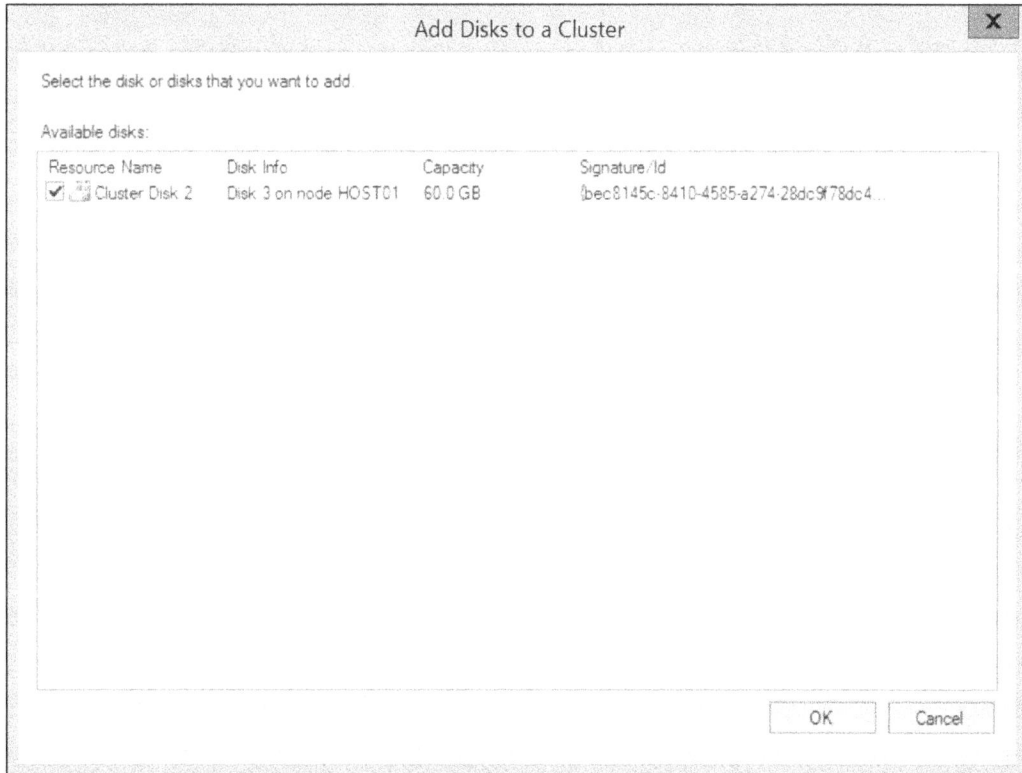

Add Disks to a Cluster

Select the disk or disks that you want to add

Available disks:

| Resource Name | Disk Info | Capacity | Signature/Id |
|---|---|---|---|
| ☑ Cluster Disk 2 | Disk 3 on node HOST01 | 60.0 GB | {bec8145c-8410-4585-a274-28dc9f78dc4... |

OK    Cancel

Now that the disk is associated to the cluster, you can enable CSV on the disk. Before doing that, note the disk is configured as an **Available Storage**, has a drive letter associated to it, and is **Online** on a single host:

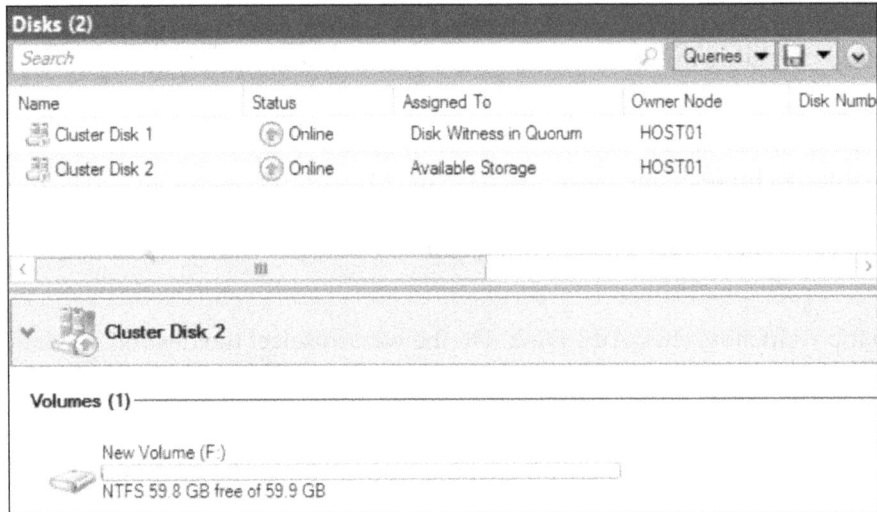

To enable CSV, right click the disk and select **Add to Cluster Shared** Volume. The result will be this:

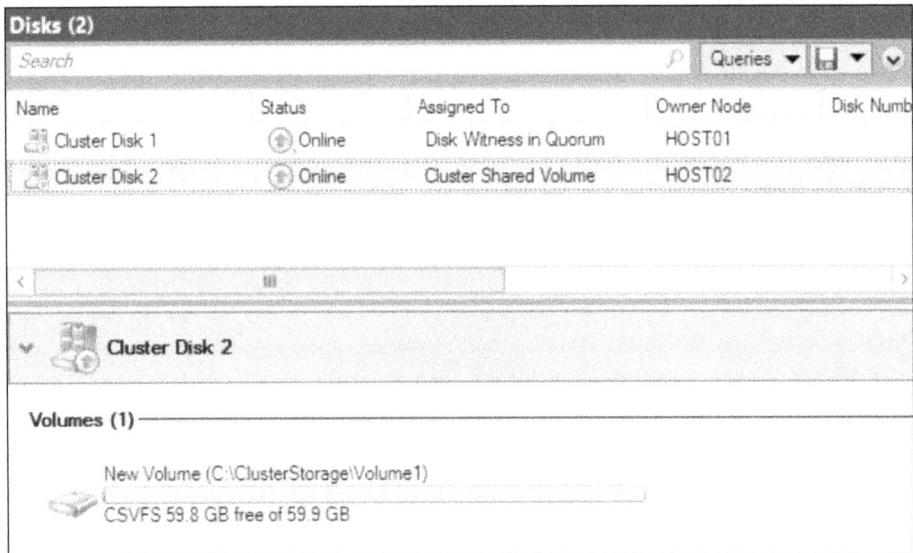

As you can see, a CSV disk does not have a drive letter associated. Instead, it uses a mounting point. You can now open Windows Explorer on all nodes and see the mounting point:

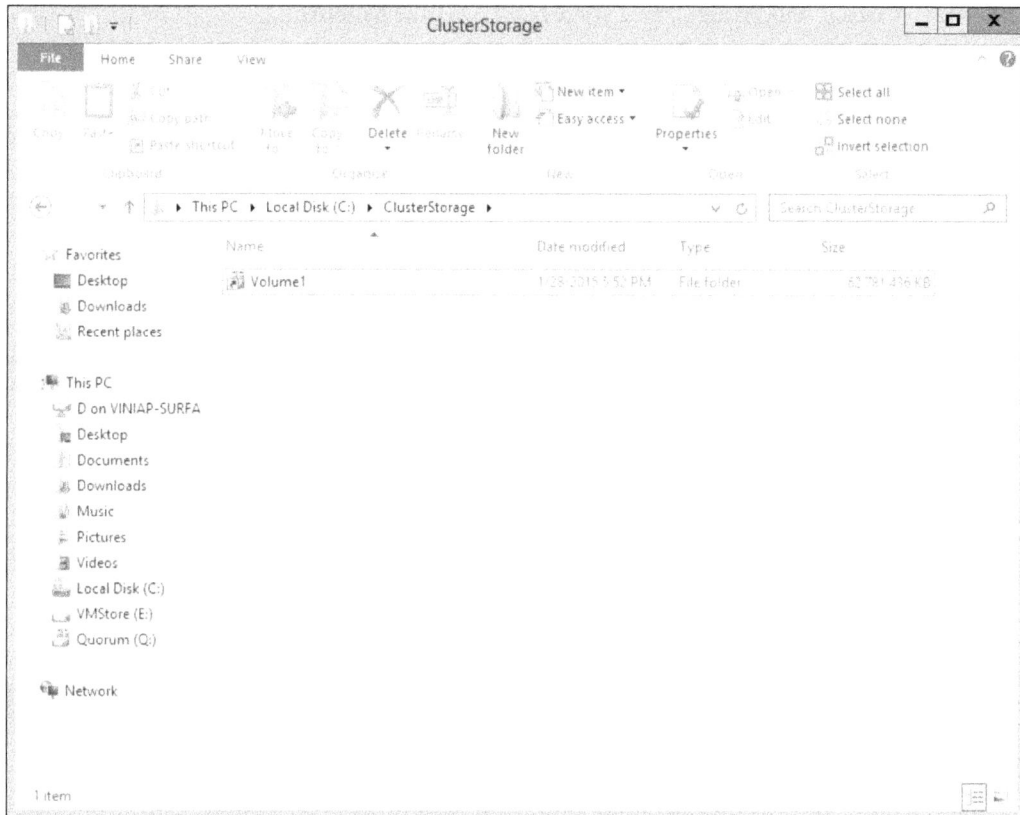

From now on, all the VMs must be created at the location: `C:\ClusterStorage\Volume1`. Keep in mind that `Volume1` represents this disk. The next disk attached will `Volume2`, and so on.

To add a CSV disk via PowerShell, use the following cmdlet:

```
Get-ClusterAvailableDisk | Add-ClusterDisk
```

The preceding command will list the disks available to the cluster and add them. Let's take a look at the following cmdlet:

```
Add-ClusterSharedVolume -Name "Cluster Disk 2"
```

The preceding command will add `Cluster Disk 2` to CSV.

# Creating a highly available VM

Now that the storage is correctly configured, you can create a VM on the cluster. To do that, open **Failover Cluster Manager**, expand the cluster name, right click **Roles** and select **Virtual Machines...** and then **New Virtual Machine...**.

Before the **New Virtual Machine** wizard pops up, you have to select the node you want to create the VM on:

| New Virtual Machine | x |
|---|---|

Select the target cluster node for Virtual Machine creation.

Look for:

| Search | Clear |
|---|---|

Cluster nodes:

| Name | Status |
|---|---|
| HOST01 | Up |
| HOST02 | Up |

| OK | Cancel |
|---|---|

After selecting the node, click **OK**. The **New Virtual Machine wizard** will start. By now, you must be familiar with this wizard, as it is the same as the **New Virtual Machine Wizard** on **Hyper-V Manager**. The only important point that you have to be careful about is that you need to store the VM on the shared storage; thus, in **Location**, point to the mounting point of the shared storage:

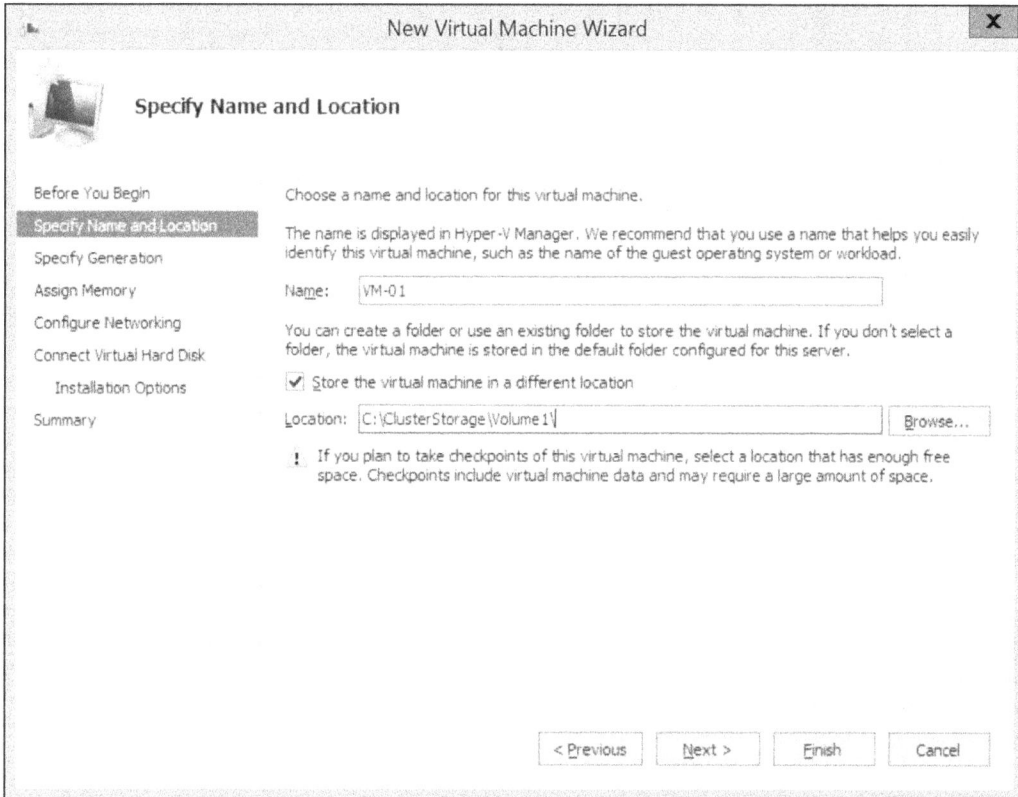

You can go through the Wizard and configure the other options of the VM, just like for Hyper-V Manager. At the end of the process, after finishing the VM configuration, another wizard will pop up and confirm that High Availability has been configured for the VM:

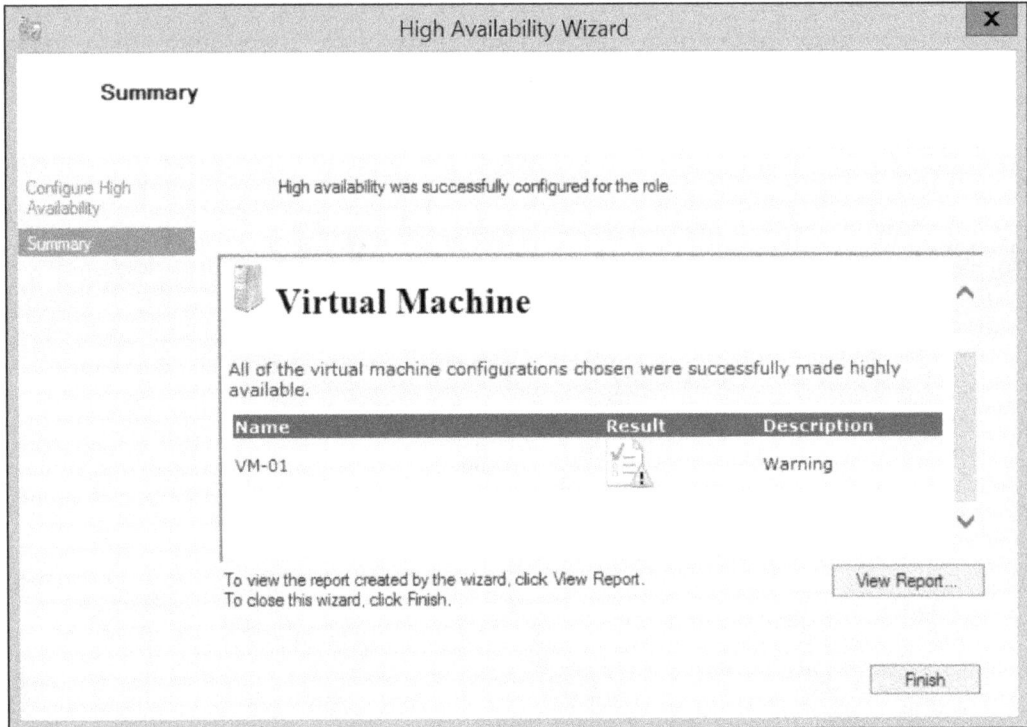

Click **Finish** to close the wizard.

> A warning may be presented if, during the VM creation, you pointed an ISO file that is only present on one of the nodes. Since this ISO file is not present on all nodes, the VM cannot be failed over to another node. The alternative is to host the ISO file on a shared location or simply ignore the warning. Just remember to remove the ISO from the VM after installing the guest OS.

To create a VM using PowerShell, you will have to use two cmdlets:

```
New-VM -NewVHDPath c:\clusterstorage\volume1\VM-02\disk01.vhdx -
NewVHDSizeBytes 127GB -ComputerName hvcluster -Generation 1 -
MemoryStartupBytes 1GB -Name VM-02 -Path
c:\clusterstorage\volume1\VM-02
```

The preceding command is the regular `New-VM` cmdlet already explained. The only difference is that in this case the `ComputerName` is the name of the cluster and the location of the VM and VM disk is the shared storage. However, the VM created is not configured for HA. To do so, use the following cmdlet:

```
Add-ClusterVirtualMachineRole -Cluster hvcluster -Name VM-02 -
VirtualMachine VM-02
```

This preceding command will configure HA for `VM-02` and will also name the cluster resource (the VM itself) as `VM-02`.

Now the VMs are created, you can manage them by using the **Failover Cluster Manager** on the **Roles** pane:

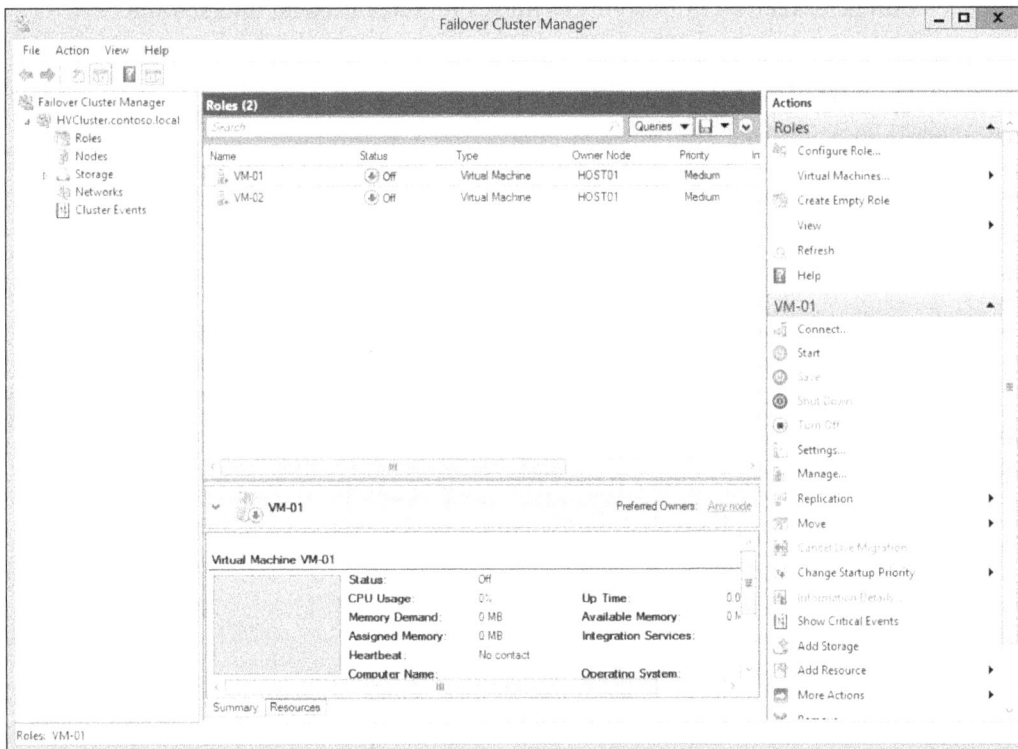

At this point, if you open **Hyper-V Manager** you will see the VM there, too. On Windows Server 2012, a VM created on Failover Cluster Manager should only be managed by the Failover Cluster Manager snap-in. If you change any settings on the VM by Hyper-V, the change will not be replicated to Failover Cluster Manager and you will have execution problems. On Windows Server 2012 R2 this issue has been removed and now you can manage the highly available VM from both snap-ins.

From now on, you will probably deal with day by day activities already explained in *Chapter 6, Virtual Machines and Virtual Machine Templates*. However, a highly available VM can require some additional configurations.

# Managing a highly available VM

A highly available VM is, in fact, just like a regular VM. However, because this VM is hosted by a cluster, it will have some additional attributes that you can configure in order to make sure the VM is running as expected. In this section, we will show some of these configurations. As the scope of this book is to show you how to manage Hyper-V, we will focus on virtualization-related tasks on the failover cluster. Keep in mind, however, that the VM is much like a regular cluster resource and has important items to configure, such as **Preferred Owners**, **Prevent failback,** and so on.

## Setting Startup Priority

When managing a virtual environment, you will be dealing with a consolidation of workloads on a limited number of resources. It is not unusual for a VM hosting a given application to be more important than other VMs hosting other not so important applications. In a cluster environment, you will try to keep all nodes up and running so that all the VMs, both more and less important, continue to work.

However, if a node fails, you will have fewer resources to start your VMs. In fact, if a node fails, you will probably want to the more important VMs to be online as soon as possible. The failover cluster can set which VMs are the most important for your environment. This is the Startup Priority feature.

The name can lead you to believe that this feature will only be used when the VM is started up, but it is more than that. In fact, all operations made by the failover cluster will consider the Startup Priority information, such as turning the VM on, Live Migration priority, failover priority, and a few other.

To set the Startup Priority on a VM, open **Failover Cluster Manager**, expand the cluster name and select **Roles**. On the **Roles** pane, right-click a VM, select **Change Startup Priority,** and select the appropriate priority for the VM:

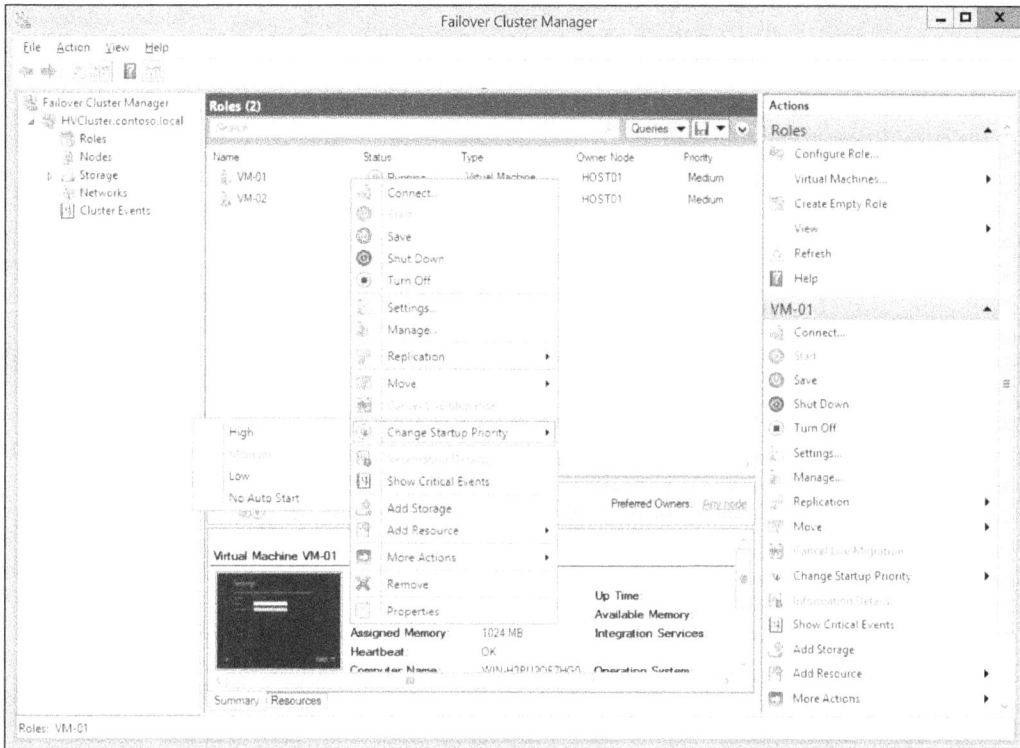

[ If the node experience any problems and a VM is configured as **No Auto Start**, this VM will remain powered off when the node is back online. You will have to turn the VM on manually. ]

To change the Startup Priority through PowerShell, use the following cmdlet:

```
(Get-ClusterGroup VM-01).priority=3000
```

The preceding command will configure VM-01 with a High Startup Priority. As you can see, configuring Startup Priority on PowerShell is accomplished by using a value. These values are as follows:

| Values | Startup Priority |
|--------|------------------|
| 3000   | High             |
| 2000s  | Medium           |
| 1000   | Low              |
| 0      | No Auto Start    |

The practical application on Startup Priority is to understand how your applications work. For example, let's say you have an environment with 5 VMs, one Active Directory Domain Controller, a File Server, a SQL Server, an application server, and an Exchange Server.

In this scenario, you probably want to configure the Active Directory VM as the **High** Startup Priority, as all other roles will need this VM up-and-running. After that, you should consider starting the backend of the applications. In this case, you probably want to set the SQL Server VM as **Medium**. The other VMs can now start as all the dependencies are up, so you can set the other VMs as **Low**.

> Through PowerShell you can set values different from the defaults (3000, 2000, 1000 and 0), such as 1500. Keep in mind that, although this can work, it is not supported.

## Live migrating a VM

By now, you are familiar with the failover process and the concept of High Availability. You now know that a failover is the process where, if one of the Nodes has a problem, the VM is then powered up on another node, resulting in minimal interruption, but, still, some interruption.

In some cases, you will find that you are aware of a node interruption, such as a scheduled maintenance for hardware repair. In these cases you don't have to go through the failover process, you can migrate the running VM to another node without interruptions. This is the Live Migration process that was mentioned earlier.

Before starting the Live Migration process, you have to make sure that you dedicate a network for this purpose. To configure which available network the Live Migration process must use, open the **Failover Cluster Manager**, expand the cluster name, and click **Networks**. On the right site under **Actions**, click **Live Migration Settings...**:

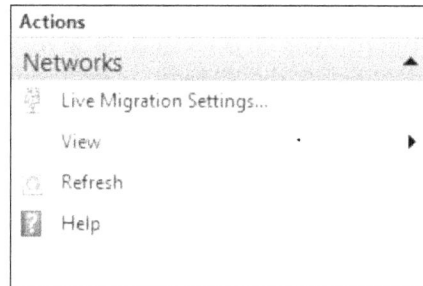

On **Live Migration Settings**, you can choose which network the Live Migration process will use. You can choose more than one network, and set which is the preferred network:

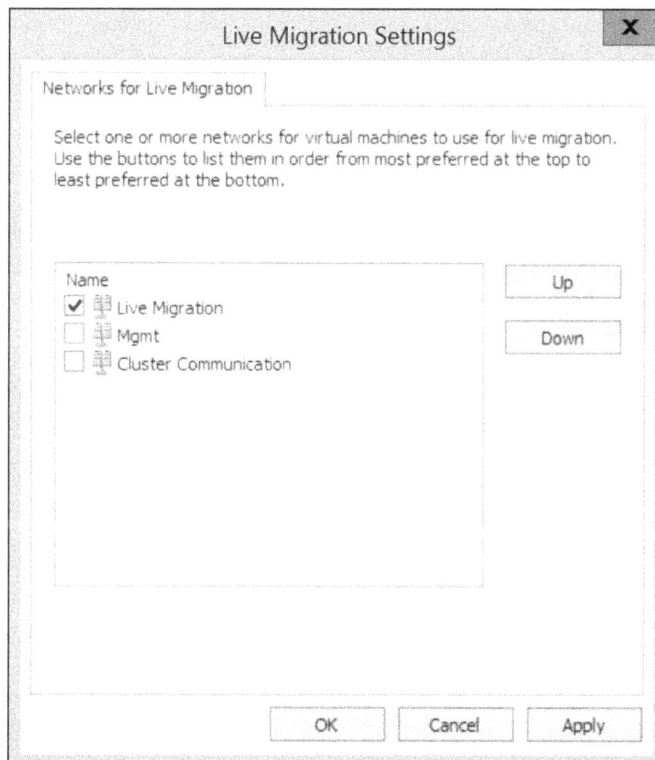

Configuring the preferred network for Live Migration via PowerShell is a bit confusing and, to leverage the knowledge from the Hyper-V product team, my recommendation is that you check the following article to learn how to do it at: `http://blogs.msdn.com/b/virtual_pc_guy/archive/2013/05/02/using-powershell-to-configure-live-migration-networks-in-a-hyper-v-cluster.aspx`.

To initiate the Live Migration process on a VM, on **Failover Cluster Manager** go to **Roles**. On the **Roles** pane, right click the VM you want to move and select **Move**:

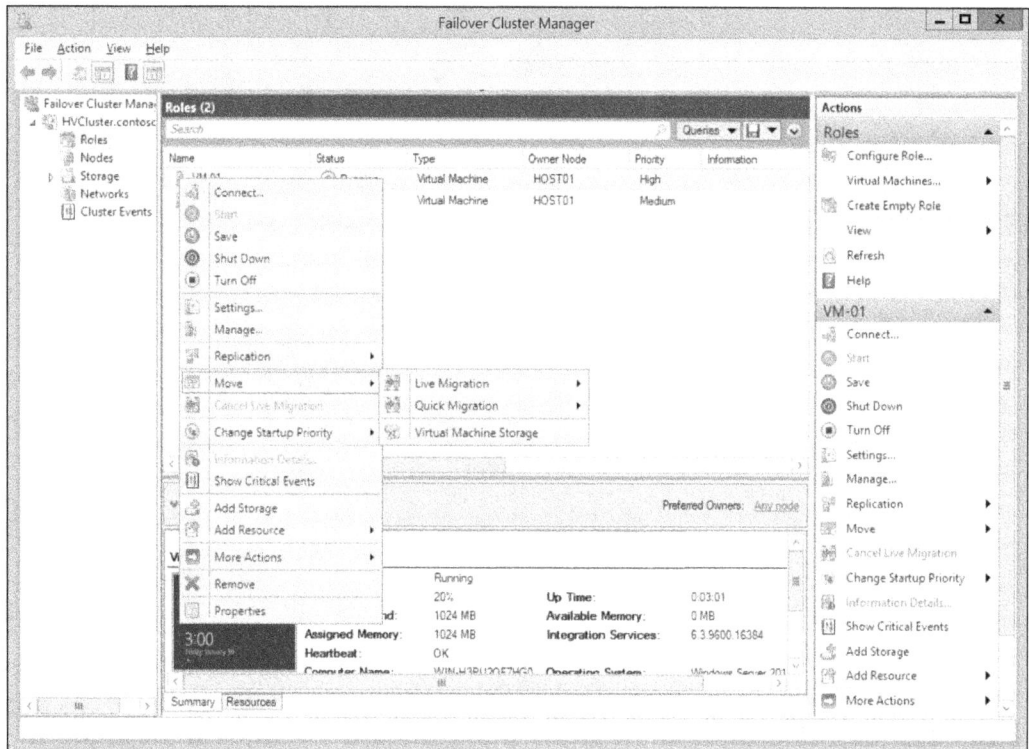

As you can see there are three types of Move:

- **Live Migration**: The process on which the VM is moved from one node to another while turned on.

- **Quick Migration**: In this process the memory content is written on the disk and the VM is moved to the other node on a saved state mode. Once the VM is moved, it returns to the same state. Although **Quick Migration** causes an interruption on the VM during the move process, it is usually quicker than **Live Migration**.

- **Virtual Machine Storage**: In this process the VM storage is moved to another location, but the VM will remain on the same node. Usually, this is used when the CSV disk is close to the size limit and you want to move the VM storage to another CSV disk that has more free space available.

To initiate the Live Migration process, select **Live Migration**:

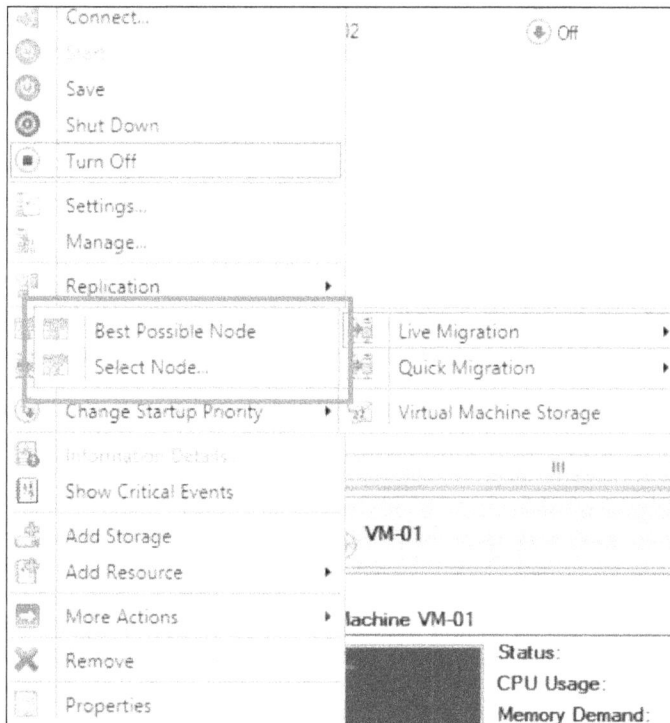

These two options were introduced on Windows Server 2012. By clicking **Select Node...**, you can choose the node you want to move your VM to. However, if you have too many nodes and you're not sure which one is the best to host your VM based on performance, you can choose **Best Possible Node**. With this option, Hyper-V will check host and VM performance, NUMA configuration, and many other metrics to select which is the best node to host the VM. Once you start the process, you can see the progress on the VM information:

| Roles (2) | | | | | |
|---|---|---|---|---|---|
| *Search* | | | | | Queries ▾ 🖫 ▾ ⌄ |
| Name | Status | Type | Owner Node | Priority | Information |
| VM-01 | Live Migrating | Virtual Machine | HOST01 | High | Live Migrating, 3% completed |
| VM-02 | Off | Virtual Machine | HOST01 | Medium | |

Once the operation finishes, you can confirm the **Owner Node** on the VM **Information**. You can also select multiple VMs and perform the Live Migration operation. If there is not enough bandwidth available, Hyper-V will queue the VMs with less priority and try to move the high priority VMs first.

To Live Migrate a VM using PowerShell, use the following cmdlet:

```
Move-ClusterVirtualMachineRole -Cluster hvcluster -MigrationType
Live -Name VM-01 -Node Host01
```

The preceding command will move the `VM-01` VM to `Host01` using the Live Migration operation. On the `-MigrationType` you can also use:

- `TurnOff`: This will turn off the VM before moving to the other node
- `Quick`: This will initiate the Quick Migration operation
- `Shutdown`: This will gracefully shutdown the guest OS before moving the VM to the other node
- `ShutdownForce`: This will initiate the shutdown operation and enforce closing any open applications

One important aspect of Live Migration is that it is, as you have already seen, moving the VM while it is powered on and the applications are running. It is important to understand how this process is accomplished to make better use of this feature.

When a VM is powered on, it will allocate some space in hardware memory. This memory allocation is made in memory blocks and the guest OS will read/write information while it is powered on. Many of the *blue screen of death* errors are caused by hardware or driver errors due to which the OS cannot access the memory information.

With that said, Live Migration has the huge responsibility of moving not only the VM configuration but also the memory blocks to the other node. The problem is that as the VM is turned on and the applications continue to run, simply moving the memory blocks is not enough. The process that is initiated when you start the Live Migration is a copy of the VM configuration to the other node. Then Hyper-V will keep both VMs, source and destination, running, but all access to the VM still directed to the source VM.

At this point, Hyper-V will start to read and copy all the memory blocks from the source VM to the destination VM. Since the VM is running, when Hyper-V finishes the reading and copying, some blocks are changed and Hyper-V has to go through it again. Hyper-V will perform this operation five times if necessary. At end of the fifth time, if the memory information is consistent on both source and destination VMs, Hyper-V will redirect all the client access to the destination VM and once the process finishes, Hyper-V will remove the source VM. There are some cases, however, when Hyper-V will be unable to move the VM:

- **Too many changes on the memory blocks**: A VM that runs a very memory-consuming application, especially if the application is being heavily used, can cause Hyper-V to not be able to read the memory blocks on the five tentative. The recommendation is to perform the Live Migration out of working hours, or using Quick Migration.

- **Network bandwidth limitations**: If you're performing a Live Migration operation on a low-performance, high-latency network, Hyper-V might not be able to move all the memory blocks in an acceptable timeframe and the Live Migration can be aborted. The recommendation is to use an exclusive network with at least 1 Gbps.

In either case, Hyper-V will not be able to finish the Live Migration operation. However, this will not cause any interruption to the application or the VM itself. Keep in mind that, as a high amount of memory is allocated to the VM, memory-consuming applications and poorly performing networks can cause the Live Migration to fail, so try to dedicate a network to it and run Live Migration after working hours.

# Configuring VM Monitoring

Another great feature that was introduced on Windows Server 2012 to the failover cluster feature is the ability to monitor VM applications. In fact, what the failover cluster service will do is watch for the service on the VM, and if it is in an unhealthy state, Hyper-V will perform an action to try to repair it.

To configure VM Monitoring, though, you have to deal with some prerequisites:

- The guest OS must be at least a Windows Server 2012 OS.
- The VM must be on the same Active Directory domain as the host or on a trusted domain.
- The user account used to configure VM Monitoring on the Failover Cluster Manager must be on the local Administrators group on the guest OS.
- The **Virtual Machine Monitoring** firewall rule must be enabled on the guest OS. You can do this by using the GUI or PowerShell:

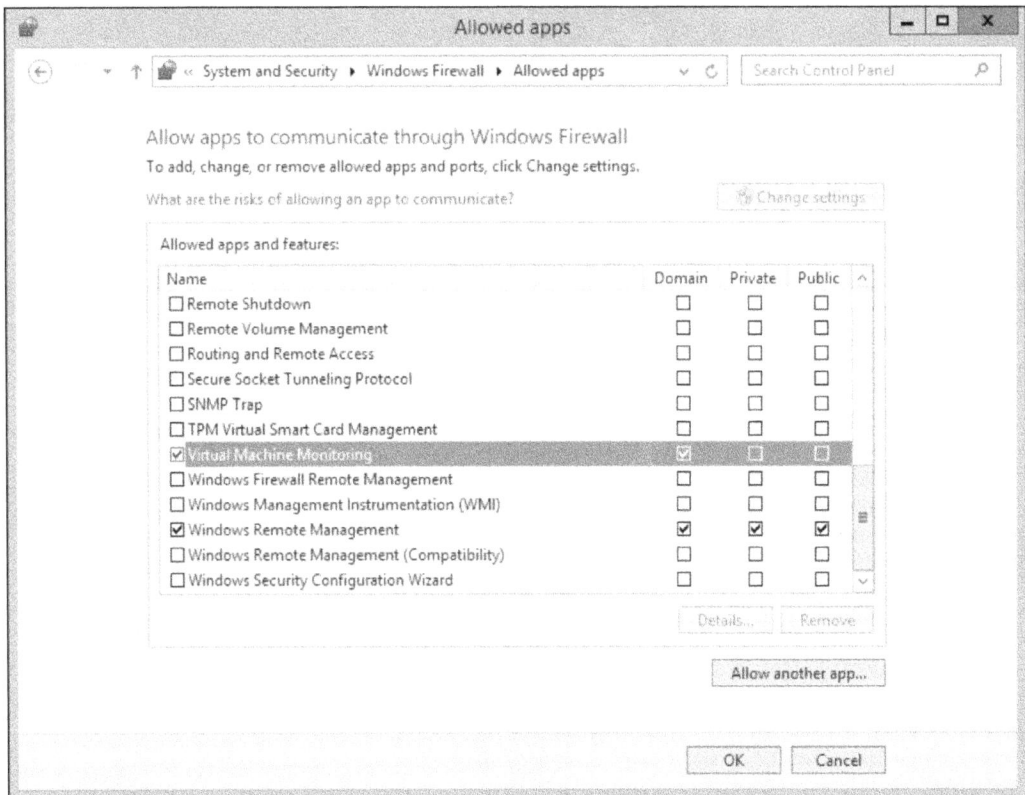

Enter the following command to configure the firewall using PowerShell:

```
Set-NetFirewallRule -DisplayGroup "Virtual Machine
Monitoring" -Enabled True
```

After ensuring all the prerequisites are configured, you can enable VM Monitoring. To do that, on the **Failover Cluster Manager**, right-click the VM you want to monitor, select **More Actions,** and click **Configure Monitoring...**:

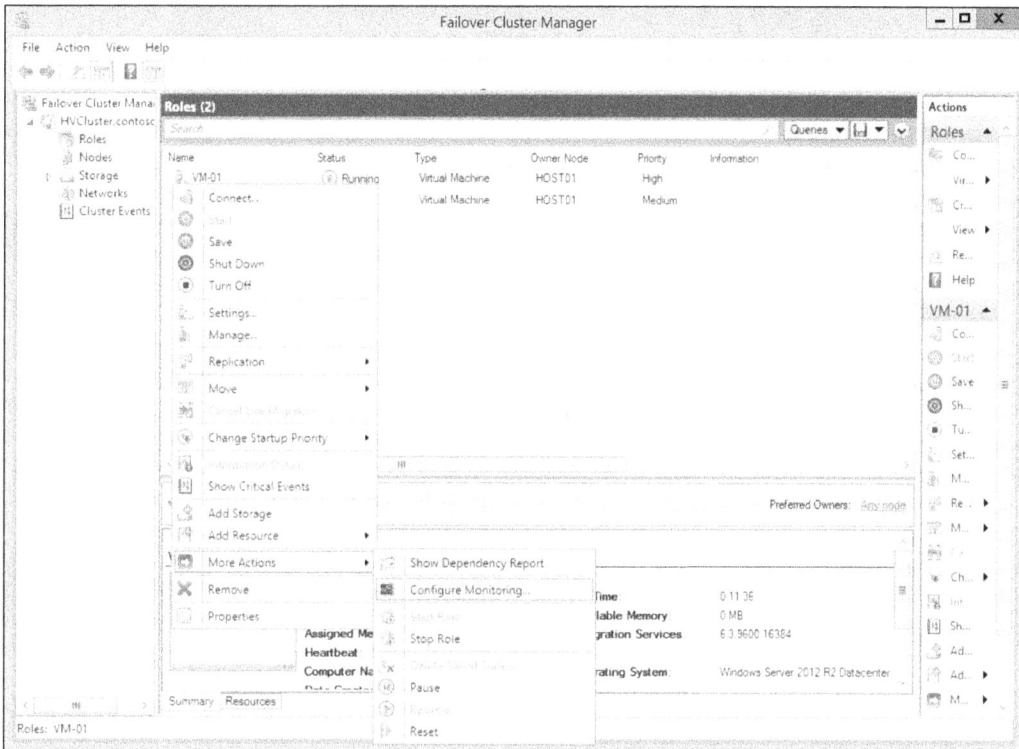

A list of services on the VM will be listed. In fact not all services are listed here. To make sure that the service you want to monitor is listed, on the guest OS, open `Services.msc` and open the properties of the service you want to monitor. On the **Recovery** tab, make sure that at least one of the actions is configured as **Take no Action**:

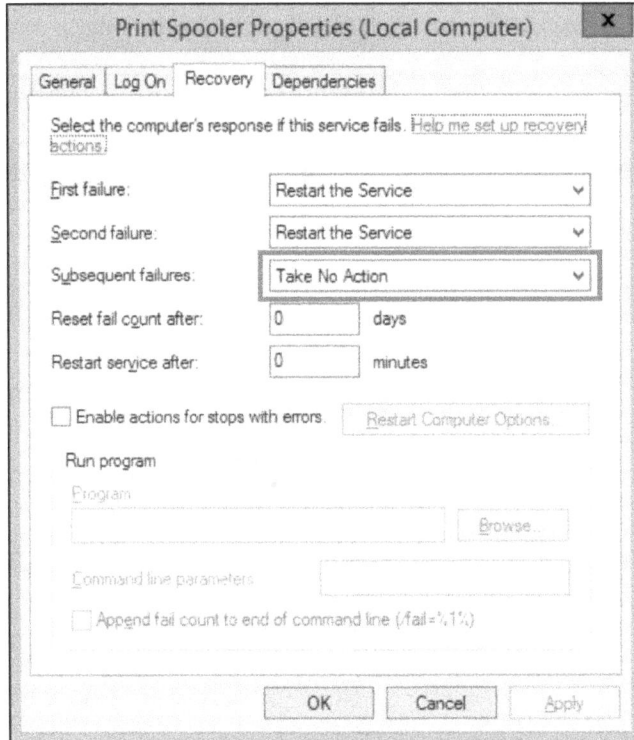

If the service is configured as indicated, it can be monitored by the cluster service:

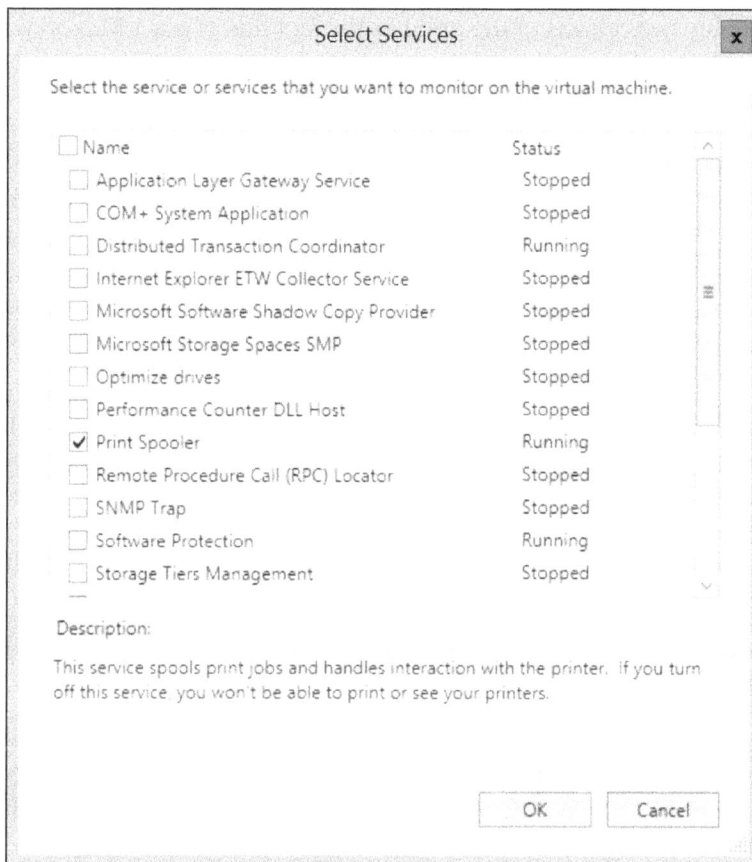

By checking the service in the preceding screenshot, you are allowing the cluster service to try to solve the problem with the application. In fact, if the service fails, the guest OS on the VM will try to perform the operations as stated in the service configuration. In the preceding example, only on the third failure will the cluster service be notified.

Once the cluster service detects that the **Status** service is **Stopped**, it will take the following actions:

- The first time the failover cluster service detects that the service is stopped, the VM will be restarted.

- If this does not solve the problem then on the second time the failover cluster service detects that the service is stopped, the VM is moved to another node. If that does not solve it, an event viewer entry will be created.

With these actions, it is probable that the application on the VM returns to work normally. If none of these actions work, that's because you have a major problem, which is probably not related to the node or the fact that it is a VM; you will have to investigate further.

# Shared VHDX

So far, we've talked about creating a failover cluster on the host to create a Hyper-V cluster. This configuration has the objective of providing HA to the VM itself. However, even with the VM Monitoring feature that was introduced on Windows Server 2012, keep in mind that the application running on the VM is not highly available. If the application crashes for any reason, the Hyper-V cluster will not be able to detect and/or take any action.

To solve this, some companies use a relatively new concept called **guest cluster**. A guest cluster is a regular cluster that is created inside the VM guest OS, not on the host level. Another option is to use both clusters, on the host/Hyper-V and on the guest OS. With that, you can achieve HA in the case of a hardware failure while, in the case of an application failure, maintaining the flexibility of the virtualization.

Using a model of guest clustering is relatively simple, but delivering a storage solution to this model can be a problem. The question is, "How to deliver a shared storage to two or more VMs?"

As we've seen in earlier chapters, you can deliver a storage solution to Hyper-V VMs using multiple methods: virtual or physical disks and any type of connection such as iSCSI, FC, or SMB3. On Windows Server 2012 R2, Microsoft introduced another method specifically for guest clusters. It is the Shared VHDX feature.

Shared VHDX works by presenting a data disk to two VMs. There are two possible ways to present a Shared VHDX to a guest cluster:

- If you deployed a Hyper-V cluster and the VMs are highly available VMs, you already have a shared location to host the VHDX file that will be shared by the VM, which is the CSV disk presented to the Hyper-V cluster. In this case, you can create the `.vhdx` file on the `C:\ClusterStorage\VolumeX`. On the VM that you want to add the disk to, open the VM **Settings...** and add a new VHDX file as a SCSI disk, the same way you learned in *Chapter 5, Managing Storage*. The result will be:

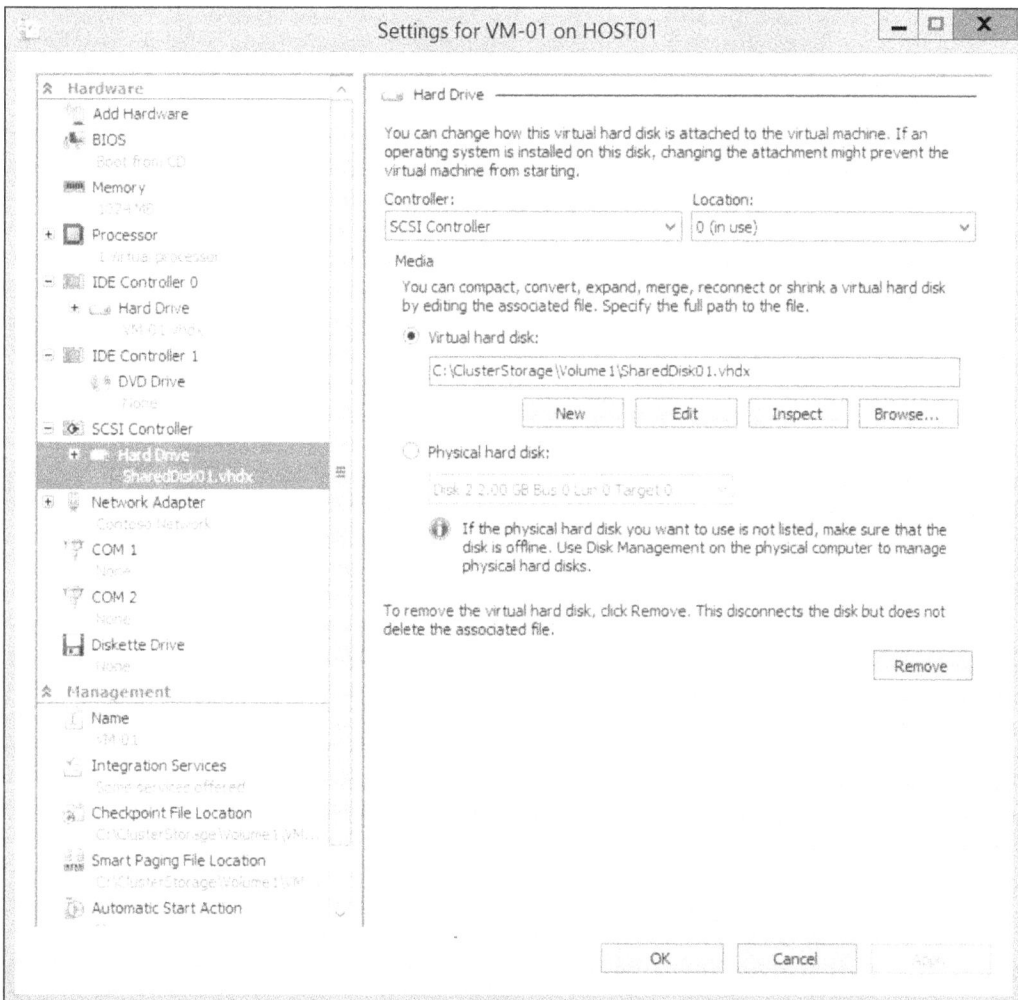

Now that the disk has been added to a location that all the VMs can access, you can enable the Shared VHDX feature. To do that, expand the hard disk configuration and select **Advanced Features**. Check the **Enable virtual hard disk sharing** option:

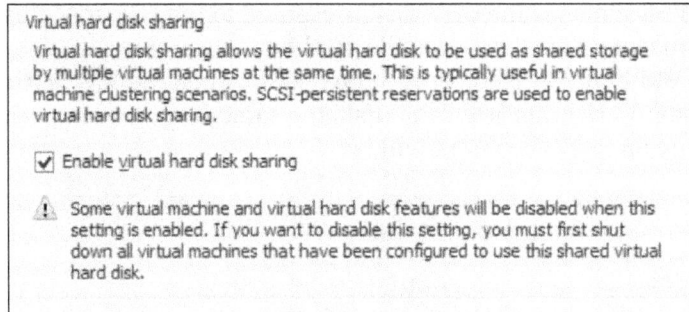

Virtual hard disk sharing

Virtual hard disk sharing allows the virtual hard disk to be used as shared storage by multiple virtual machines at the same time. This is typically useful in virtual machine clustering scenarios. SCSI-persistent reservations are used to enable virtual hard disk sharing.

☑ Enable virtual hard disk sharing

⚠ Some virtual machine and virtual hard disk features will be disabled when this setting is enabled. If you want to disable this setting, you must first shut down all virtual machines that have been configured to use this shared virtual hard disk.

* Another option is if the VMs are not part of a Hyper-V cluster. In this case, you need an SMB3 shared folder. The process to do this is the same as the previous one. The only difference is that the VHDX file will be hosted on a different location. It will be something like this:

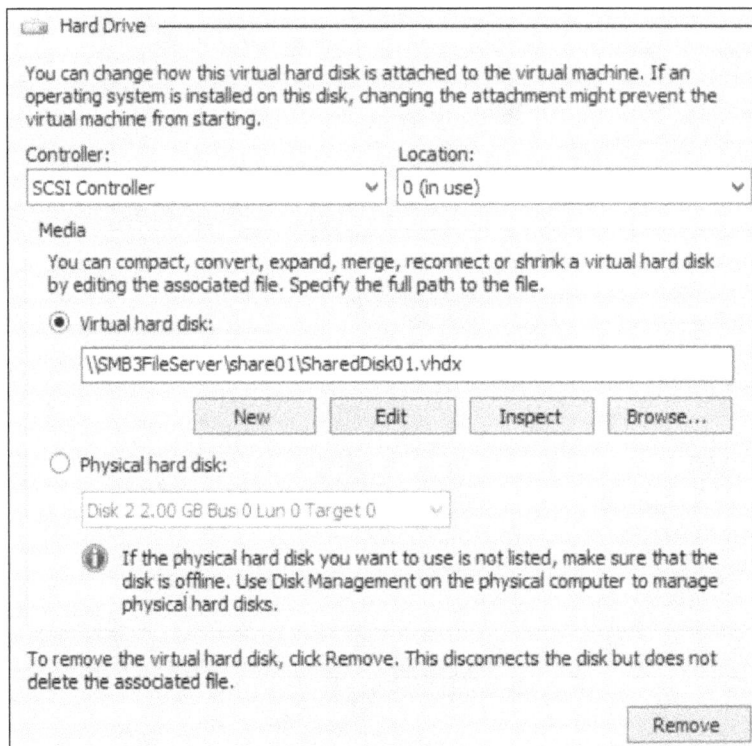

⌨ Hard Drive

You can change how this virtual hard disk is attached to the virtual machine. If an operating system is installed on this disk, changing the attachment might prevent the virtual machine from starting.

Controller:                                    Location:

SCSI Controller                           ∨    0 (in use)                              ∨

Media

You can compact, convert, expand, merge, reconnect or shrink a virtual hard disk by editing the associated file. Specify the full path to the file.

◉ Virtual hard disk:

\\SMB3FileServer\share01\SharedDisk01.vhdx

[ New ]      [ Edit ]      [ Inspect ]      [ Browse... ]

○ Physical hard disk:

Disk 2 2.00 GB Bus 0 Lun 0 Target 0    ∨

ℹ If the physical hard disk you want to use is not listed, make sure that the disk is offline. Use Disk Management on the physical computer to manage physical hard disks.

To remove the virtual hard disk, click Remove. This disconnects the disk but does not delete the associated file.

[ Remove ]

After configuring the first VM, you can simply add a new disk to the other VMs that will be part of the guest cluster and point to the recently created VHDX. Remember to also select the **Enable virtual hard disk sharing** option.

From now on, you can follow the regular process of creating a failover cluster inside the guest OS, which is beyond the scope of this book. When the cluster is created, you can bring the disk online on one of the VMs, create a new volume, and add the disk to the cluster. Additionally, you can enable this disk as a CSV disk.

# Summary

In this chapter, you learned the concept of a failover cluster, and what High Availability will provide to a virtualization environment. You saw how to implement a Microsoft failover cluster and configure a Quorum to make sure your environment continues to work even with the failure of a node, or when a communication error occurs between the nodes.

You've seen how to manage the Startup Priority in order to ensure that the applications start after their requirements are already up. Then we've seen how to leverage the benefits of Live Migration and how to avoid Live Migration problems. After that, you saw how the failover cluster service can monitor a VM application.

To finish, we introduced the Shared VHDX feature that allows for a guest cluster scenario. In the next chapter, you will see how to implement Live Migration without a failover cluster and how to implement Hyper-V Replica with and without a cluster.

# 8
# Implementing Live Migration and Replica

In *Chapter 7, Implementing High Availability*, we discussed how to implement an HA solution with the Microsoft failover cluster. You learned that with a failover cluster, you can create an environment on which if a node that is member of the cluster fails, the VM is automatically failed over to another host with minimal interruption. Additionally, you learned that you can manage other aspects of the VM on a cluster to ensure that it is running even in a situation in which you will need to stop a node for any reason, such as a predicted maintenance activity.

The pain point for some companies is that they will need to take into account all the prerequisites for a cluster. Not all companies are willing to provide the necessary resources for it. In these cases, there is not much to do regarding HA. There are, however, other features on Hyper-V that can be used. Two of them are very important and deserve a chapter for you to understand how to implement it and how to leverage these features in your environment.

The first is the Share Nothing Live Migration, which consists of a regular Live Migration, as you learned in the previous chapter, without the need of a failover cluster. The second is the Hyper-V Replica, which consists — as the name states — of a Replica of a VM on another host. This can be accomplished using a failover cluster or a regular standalone host.

In this chapter, we will cover the following topics:

- Share Nothing Live Migration
- Authentication methods
- Storage Live Migration

- Hyper-V Replica configuration
- Testing Hyper-V Replica
- Extended replication

# Share Nothing Live Migration

When Microsoft first launched Hyper-V on Windows Server 2008, the only available VM migration option was the already covered Quick Migration. At that time, the main pain point was that the regular NTFS filesystem did not support simultaneous read/write operations from multiple nodes. On Windows Server 2008 R2, Microsoft introduced the CSV filesystem, which works on top of NTFS, as explained in the previous chapter.

During the development phase of Windows Server 2012, one of the feedbacks from customers was that Live Migration was an excellent feature, but some of them wanted to be able to move VMs onto standalone nodes that were not using shared storage. At that time, it sounded like an impossible task to accomplish.

On Windows Server 2012, Microsoft introduced Share Nothing Live Migration. This feature allows you to move a running VM from one host to another host without a cluster and without shared storage. So, how does this work?

The Share Nothing Live Migration process is very similar to the regular Live Migration that was explained in the previous chapter. The main difference is that in this case, as there is no shared storage, the VM virtual disk must be copied to the new destination. This process is very much like the memory Blocks copy process.

In the storage copy process, storage blocks are copied from the source VM to the destination VM. Once all the blocks are copied, Hyper-V checks which blocks were changed during the copying process and copies those blocks. This process is repeated until the storage is consistent in both source and destination. After the process has verified that that memory, configuration, and storage are consistent, the destination VM starts receiving all the connections, and the source VM is deleted.

Additionally, the Share Nothing Live Migration feature is not configured by default on the hosts, just like the regular Live Migration on a cluster, so you will have to enable it. To enable Share Nothing Live Migration on the host, open **Hyper-V Manager** and click on **Hyper-V Settings...** on the left. In Hyper-V Settings, go to **Live Migrations** and check the **Enable incoming and outgoing live migrations** option, as shown in this screenshot:

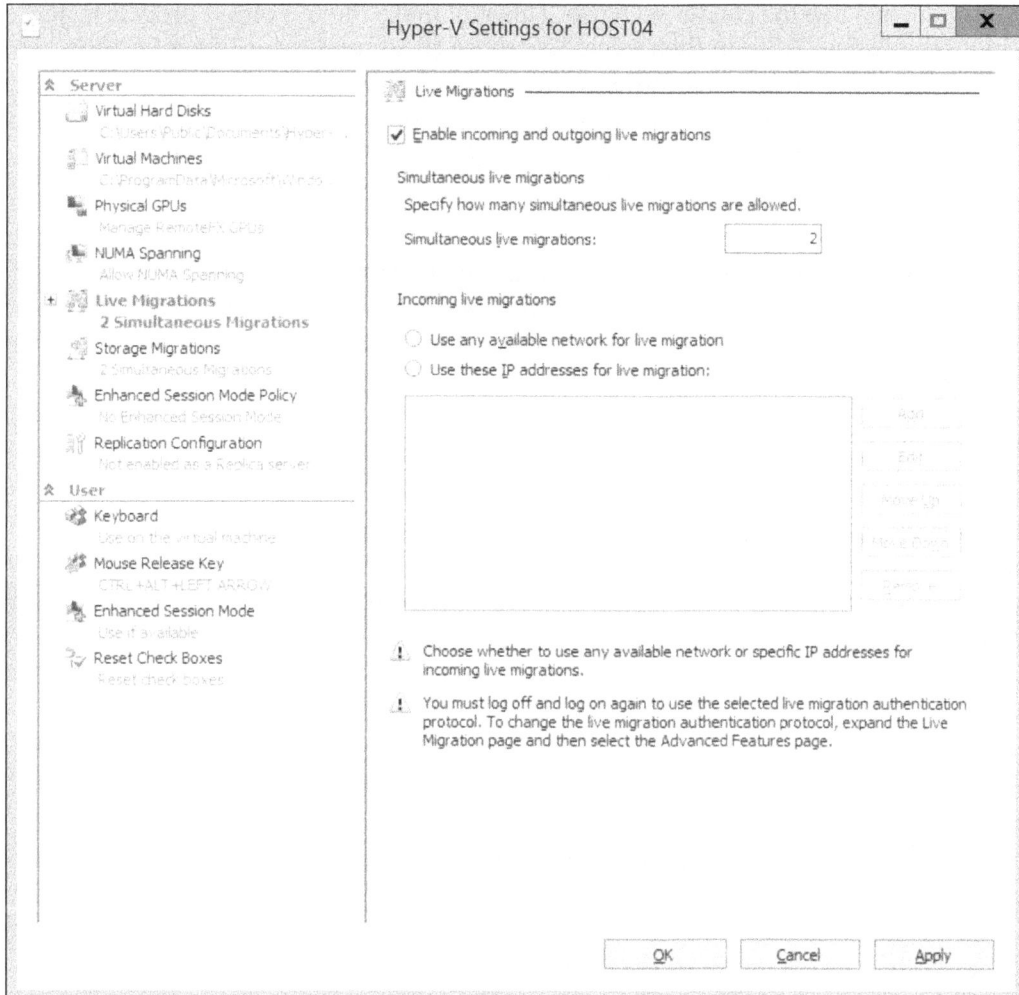

The first configuration involves setting number of **Simultaneous live migration** you want to allow. Keep in mind that Hyper-V will not limit you, but your available network will. Additionally, as you can see, there are two warnings at the bottom. The first is regarding the network configured for Live Migration.

In the **Incoming live migrations** section, you can choose the network to be used for the Live Migration process. The ideal configuration has a dedicated network for Live Migration, just like the cluster scenario. This will make the migration process faster and more reliable. You can then select **Use these IP addresses for live migration**, and configure the address or addresses that should be used as well as the preference of each network. You can also select **Use any available network for live migration**. In this case, the network with a better metric that can connect both hosts will be used. The metric is based on the advanced settings of the network configuration on Windows Server.

When you select one of the options to configure the network for Live Migration, the first warning will disappear. The second warning is related to the authentication method. The issue here is that in the failover cluster, the nodes are operating under an **Active Directory** (**AD**) account, that have the necessary rights for moving the VM. In a standalone environment, the hosts must be on the same AD forest, or in a trusted domain. However, the account used for authentication does not have, by default, the necessary rights for performing the operation.

To solve this issue, you have to indicate which authentication method you want to use. There are two options available, and you can configure it by expanding the **Live Migrations** configuration and selecting **Advanced Features**, as shown in the following screenshot:

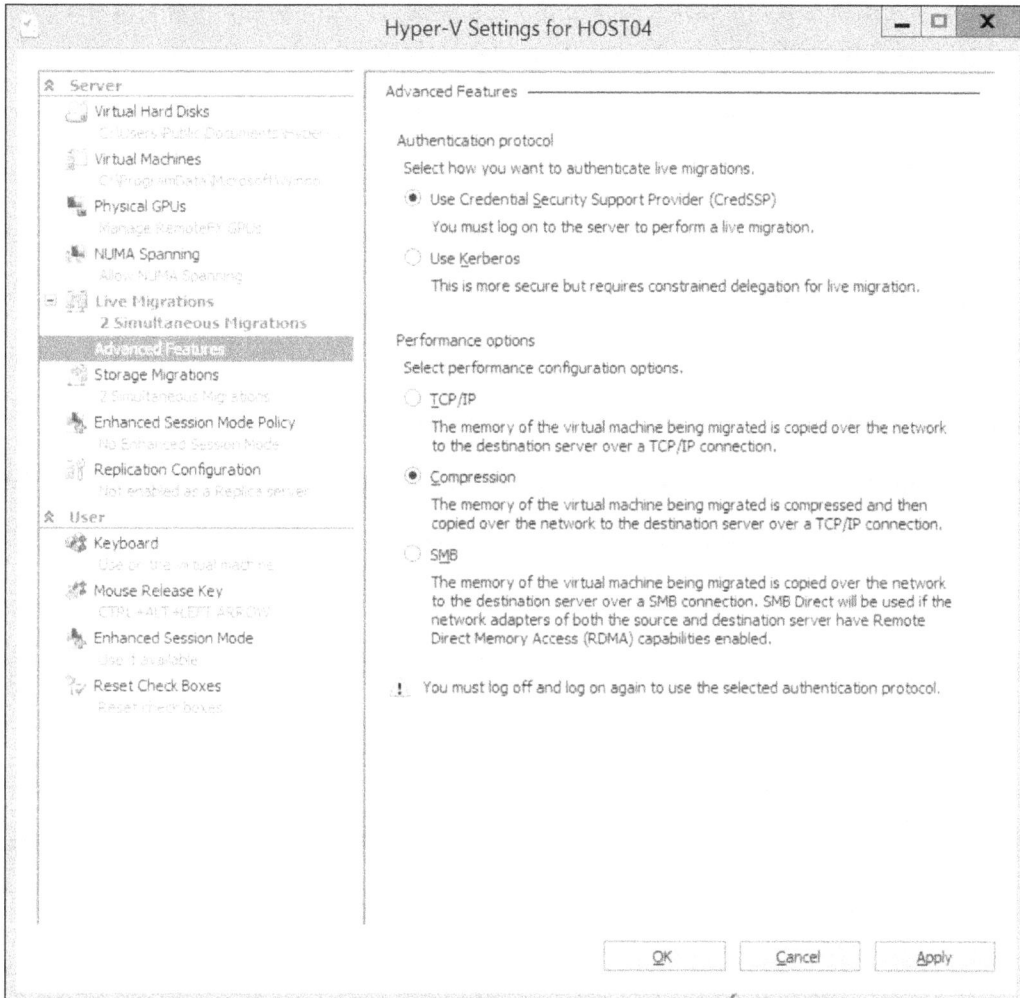

In the **Authentication protocol** section, you have the two options. Let's understand what are the implications of using each one:

- **Use Credential Security Support Provider (CredSSP)**: This option will use the logged user's credentials to authenticate on the destination server. This means that you must log in to the host to be able to perform the Live Migration. For example, if you've installed the Hyper-V Manager on a Windows 8.1 client and you are performing the operation remotely, you will not be able to migrate the VM.

- **Use Kerberos**: In this option, the Hyper-V service will check if the source host account on the AD has the appropriate delegation. Using Kerberos requires you to configure the AD account.

If you select the CredSSP option, you will have to log off and log in again for the user token to be regenerated with the appropriate information. Once you log in again, you can move the VMs. If you select the Kerberos option, you still have to configure the computer accounts on AD. After selecting the authentication method, you can configure **Performance options**. But first, let's see how to properly configure the Kerberos authentication.

# Configuring the Kerberos authentication for Live Migration

If you have selected the Kerberos authentication method, you need to configure the appropriate delegation on AD for the computer account. To do that, open **Active Directory Users and Computers** and then open the Organizational Unit (OU) that contains the computer accounts of the **Hyper-V Hosts** you want to configure, like this:

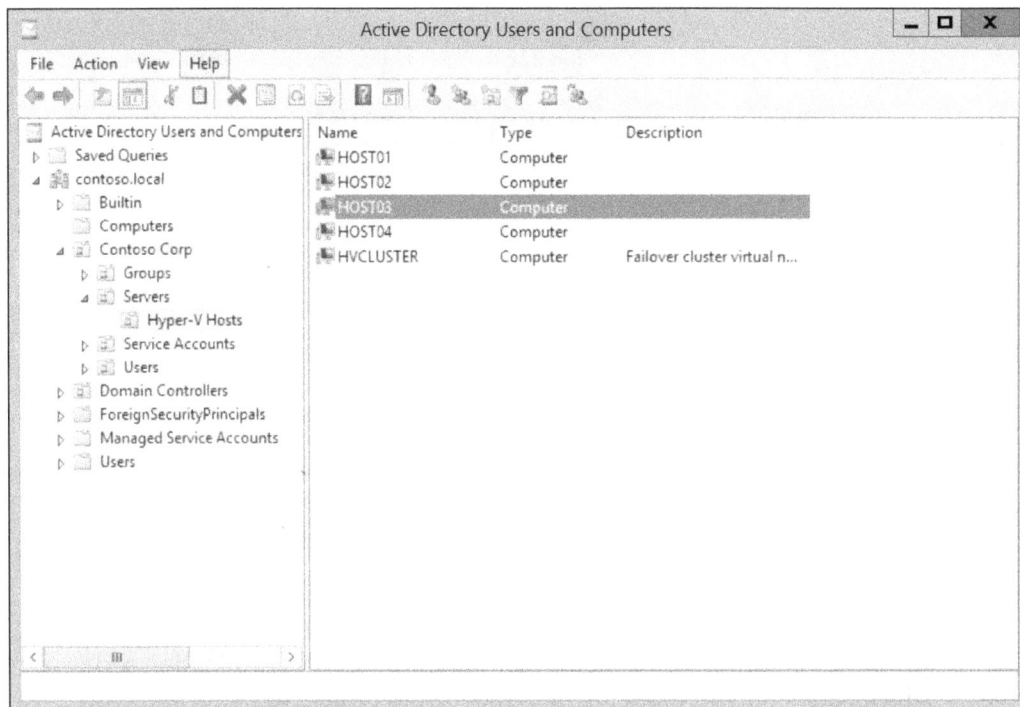

Since this is a delegation for trusting some Kerberos services that can be used in both ways (the source host can be the destination host in the case where you want to move the VM back to the host), you will have to configure all the hosts with the service for each possible host. For example, if you have **HOST01**, **HOST02**, **HOST03**, and **HOST04**, you will have to configure **HOST01** to delegate the Kerberos services for Live Migration for **HOST02**, **HOST03**, and **HOST04**. On **HOST02**, you will have to configure the delegation for **HOST01**, **HOST03**, and **HOST04**, and so on.

To configure the delegation for a host, right-click on the host, select **Properties**, and go the **Delegation** tab, as shown in this screenshot:

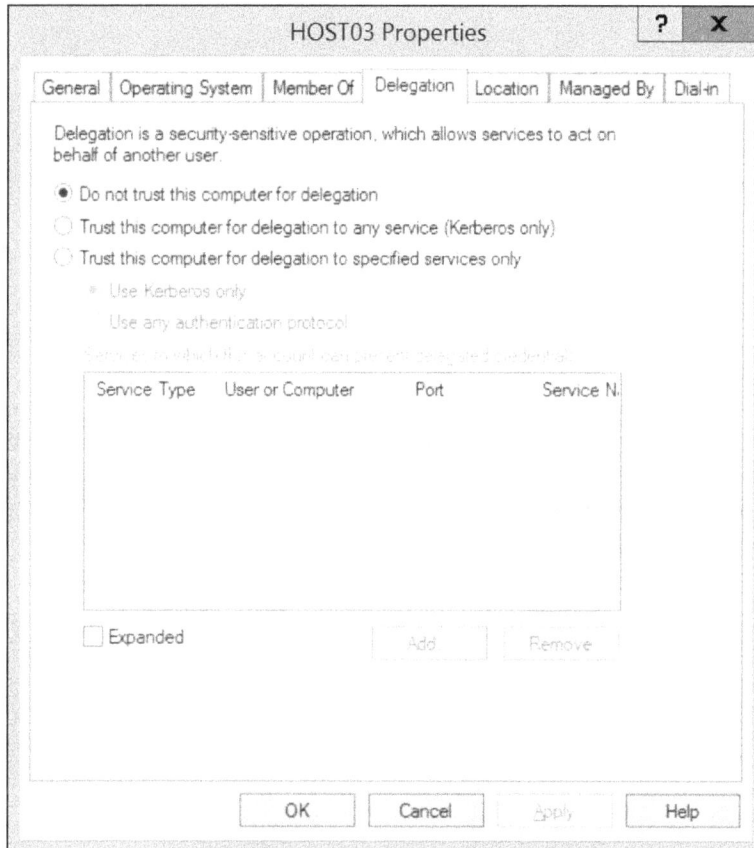

Select the **Trust this computer for delegation to specified services only** option and then **Use Kerberos only**. Click on **Add...** to add the appropriate services, as shown in the following screenshot:

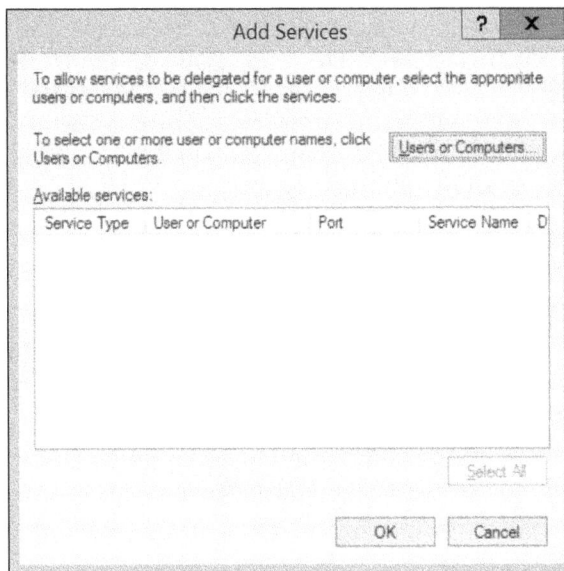

As you can see, there are no available services. Click on **Users or Computers....** Type the name of the host you want to delegate, and click on **OK**. In the **Add Services** window, beneath the **Available services** section, you will be presented with all the services available for delegation, as shown in this screenshot:

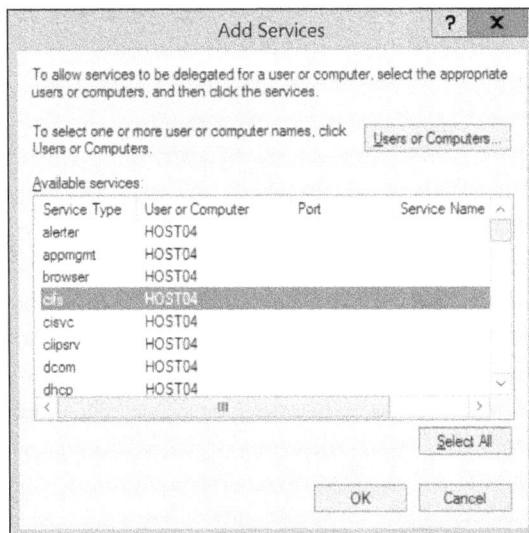

You will have to select the **cifs** service and the **Microsoft Virtual System Migration Service** service.

> The **cifs** service is necessary for moving the VM storage along with the VM, or when you select the Storage Live Migration option. **Microsoft Virtual System Migration Service** is the service meant for moving the VM itself.

When you're done, the services will be listed in the **Available services** section. Let's take a look at the following screenshot that illustrates various **Delegation** options for a host:

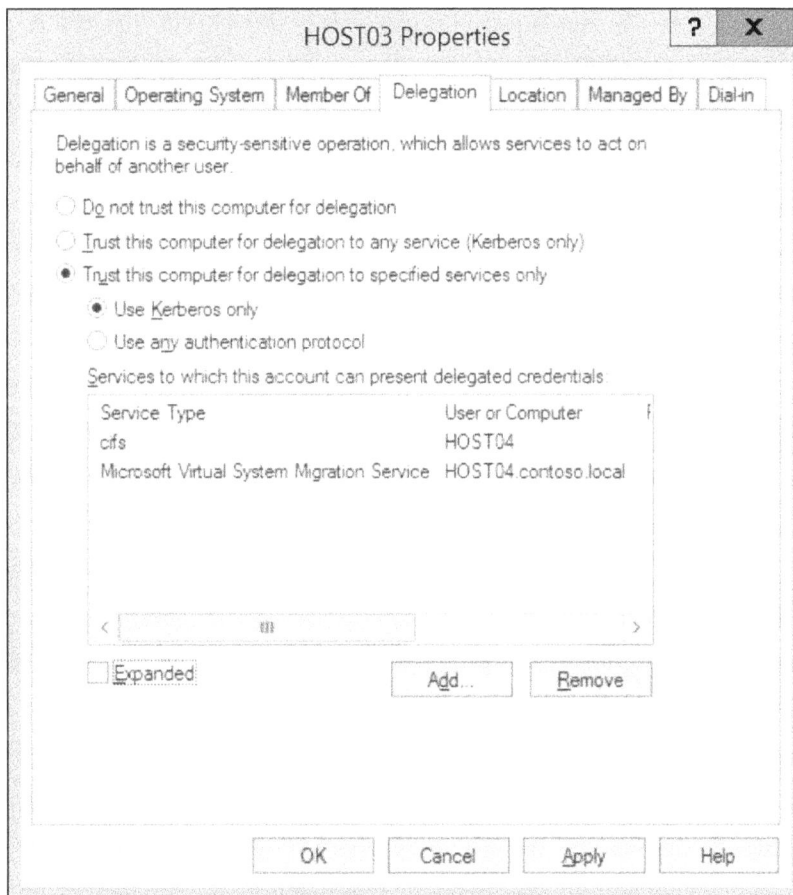

Repeat the process for the other hosts, as necessary. After configuring the Kerberos authentication, you can configure **Performance options** for Live Migration.

# Performance options for Live Migration

Back in the **Advanced Features** section under **Live Migration**, you have three options for configuring Performance, as shown in this screenshot:

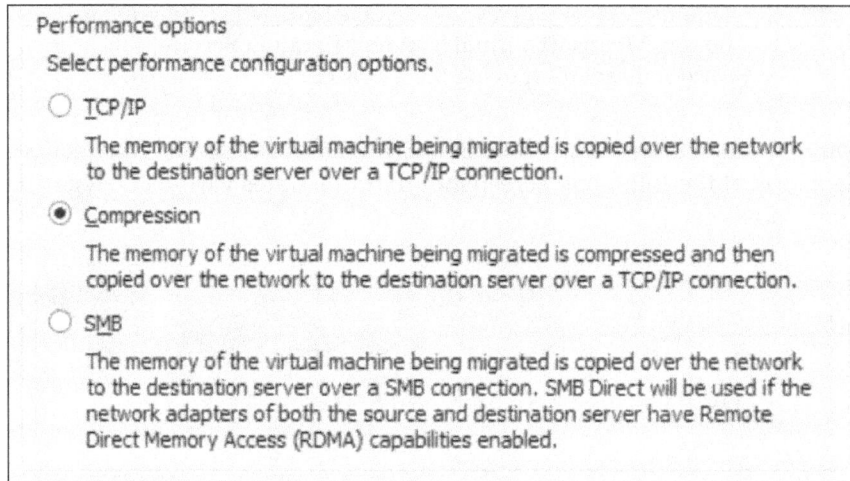

Performance options

Select performance configuration options.

○ TCP/IP

The memory of the virtual machine being migrated is copied over the network to the destination server over a TCP/IP connection.

◉ Compression

The memory of the virtual machine being migrated is compressed and then copied over the network to the destination server over a TCP/IP connection.

○ SMB

The memory of the virtual machine being migrated is copied over the network to the destination server over a SMB connection. SMB Direct will be used if the network adapters of both the source and destination server have Remote Direct Memory Access (RDMA) capabilities enabled.

To better understand the options mentioned in the preceding screenshot, let's take an in-depth look at them:

- **TCP/IP**: This was the regular option for Hyper-V until Windows Server 2012 R2. Before 2012 R2, Hyper-V simply transferred the memory content from one host to another. The advantage of this option is that there is minimal impact on the host processing. However, you need more network performance.

- **Compression**: New to Windows Server 2012 R2, this option compresses the memory information before transferring it to the other host. Its pros and cons are the opposite of the previous option. In this case, host processing can have some impact because of the process of compression. On the other hand, there is less impact on the network. This is the default option, but if you think it can impact the host processing, use the other options available.

- **SMB**: Also new to Windows Server 2012 R2, this option uses the hardware acceleration feature on RDMA-enabled NICs to offload the memory compression process. This is the best option, as it compresses the memory and uses less network. Also, the impact on Host processing is minimal. However, you need an RDMA-enabled NIC.

After selecting the appropriate option, click on **OK**. If you've configured the CredSSP authentication option, you will also need to log out and log in to complete the process.

# Configuring Share Nothing Live Migration with PowerShell

To enable Share Nothing Live Migration using PowerShell, you will have to use multiple cmdlets to accomplish it. To begin, use the following cmdlet:

```
Enable-VMMigration -ComputerName Host01
```

The preceding command will enable Share Nothing Live Migration on Host01. After running the command, you will receive the following warning:

```
WARNING: Live migrations of virtual machines cannot be sent to the
destination host because no migration networks are specified for
incoming live migrations. To specify networks, run the Add-
VMMigrationNetwork cmdlet on the destination host. To use any
available network for live migration, run the command Set-VMHost -
UseAnyNetworkForMigration $true on the destination host.
WARNING: You must log off and log on again to use the selected
virtual machine migration authentication type.
```

This is expected, as you will have to run other commands to finish the process. The next command you have to run is as follows:

```
Add-VMMigrationNetwork -Subnet 192.168.100.101 -ComputerName
Host01
```

This will configure the indicated subnet as the subnet to be used for Live Migrations. This also allows the host to receive VMs from Live Migration. To complete the process of configuration, use the following cmdlet:

```
Set-VMHost -VirtualMachineMigrationAuthenticationType Kerberos -
VirtualMachineMigrationPerformanceOption SMB
```

The preceding command will configure the authentication method as Kerberos. If you want to use CredSSP, you can change the Kerberos input to CredSSP. Also, the command will configure the performance option as SMB. The other options for input are TCP/IP and Compression.

With all the options configured, you can start migrating your VMs.

# Live migrating a VM

There are multiple options for moving a VM from one host to another. To better understand what all the options are, let's start the process and see what is available. To initiate the migration process, open **Hyper-V Manager**, right-click on a VM and select **Move**.

In the Move Wizard, click on **Next >**. On the next screen, you have to select the option that you want to use, as shown in this screenshot:

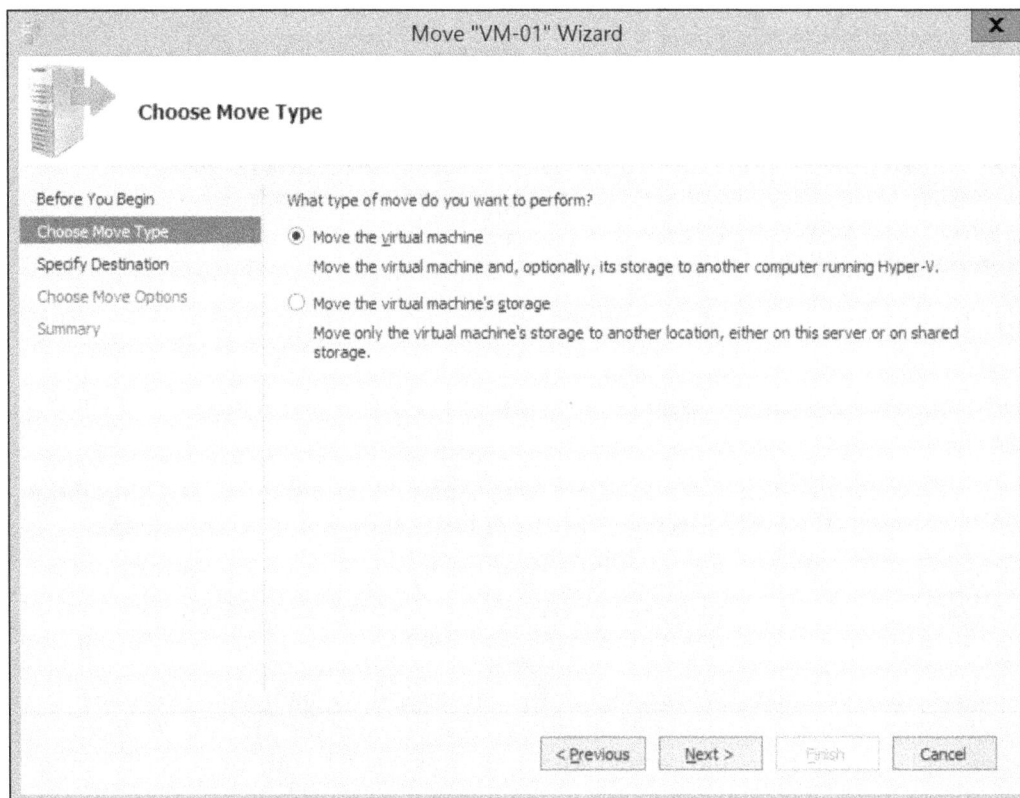

The first option will migrate the VM from one host to another. The second option will migrate the VM storage from one location to another without changing the VM host. Since there are multiple suboptions on each option here, we will divide this topic into two sections.

# Move the virtual machine

The first option, as explained, will move the VM from one host to another. After selecting this option, click on **Next >**, as shown in the following screenshot:

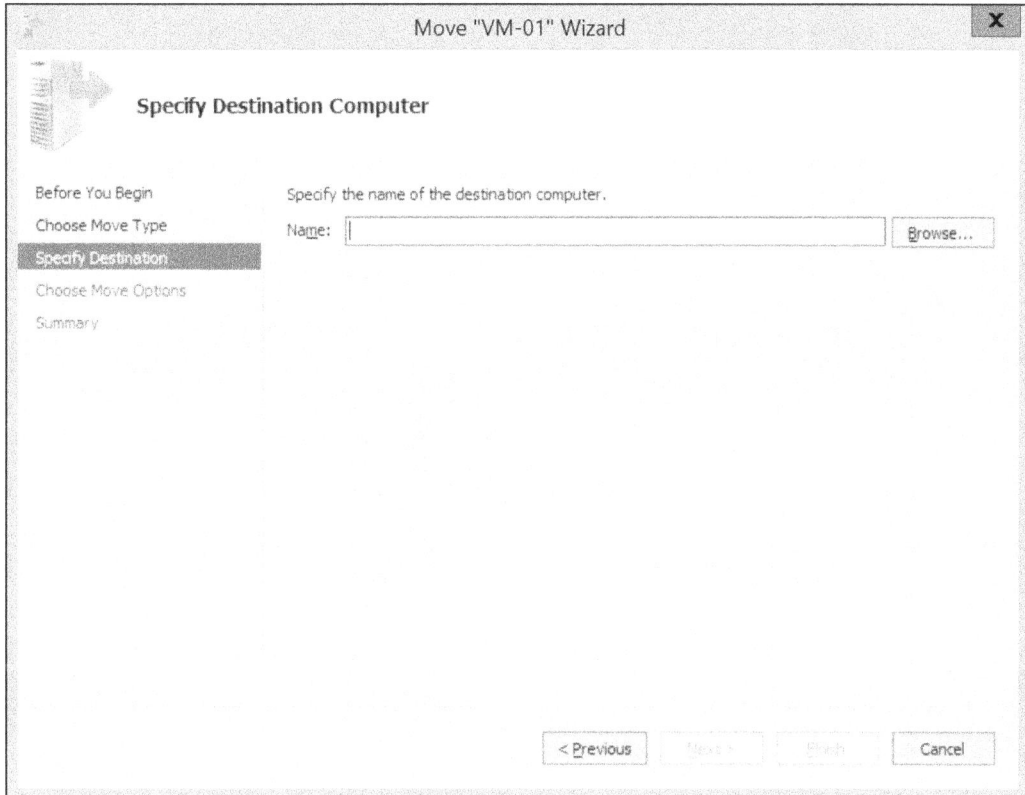

Type the name of the host you want to move your VM onto in the **Name** textbox, and click on **Next >**. In the next step, you will have three options for moving the VM, as shown here:

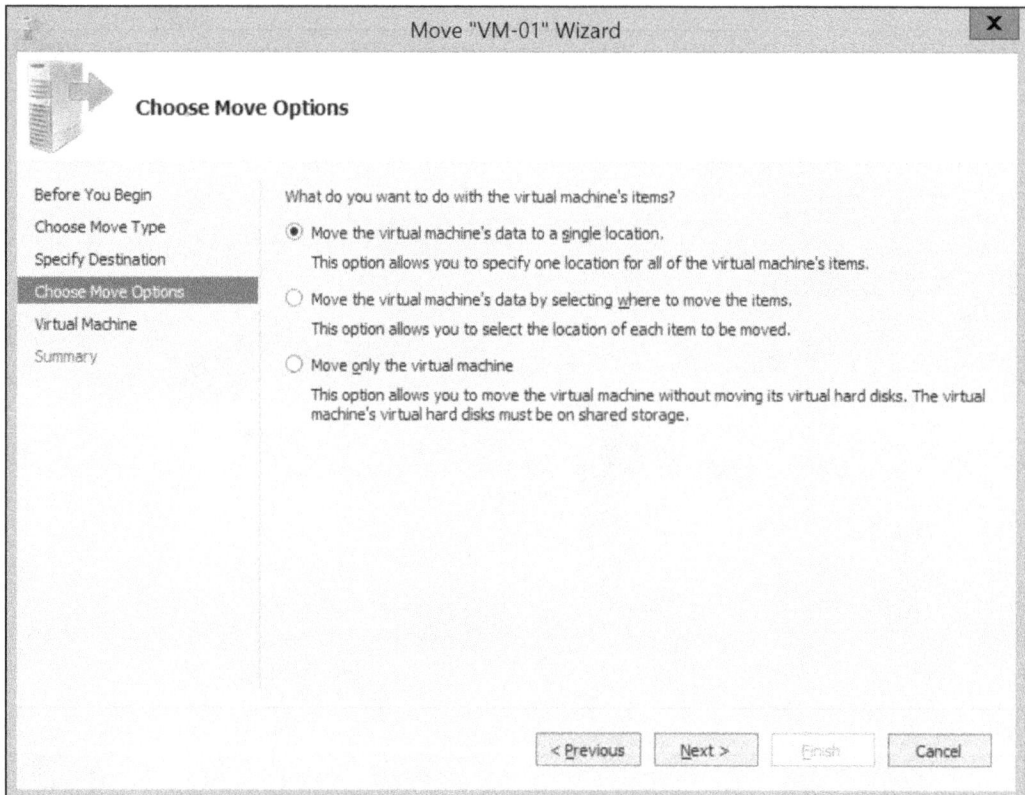

You've learned so far that a VM is made up of multiple components and files. The options in the preceding screenshot are important, as you can move the VM files to a different location or to a single location. Now, it's time to understand what each option is:

- **Move the virtual machine's data to a single location**: This option will move all of the VM data, or the VM files, to a single location. In this option, you will have to indicate a location in the destination host to accommodate all the VM files.

- **Move the virtual machine's data by selecting where to move the items**: This option will give three other suboptions to move the VM's data, as shown in this screenshot:

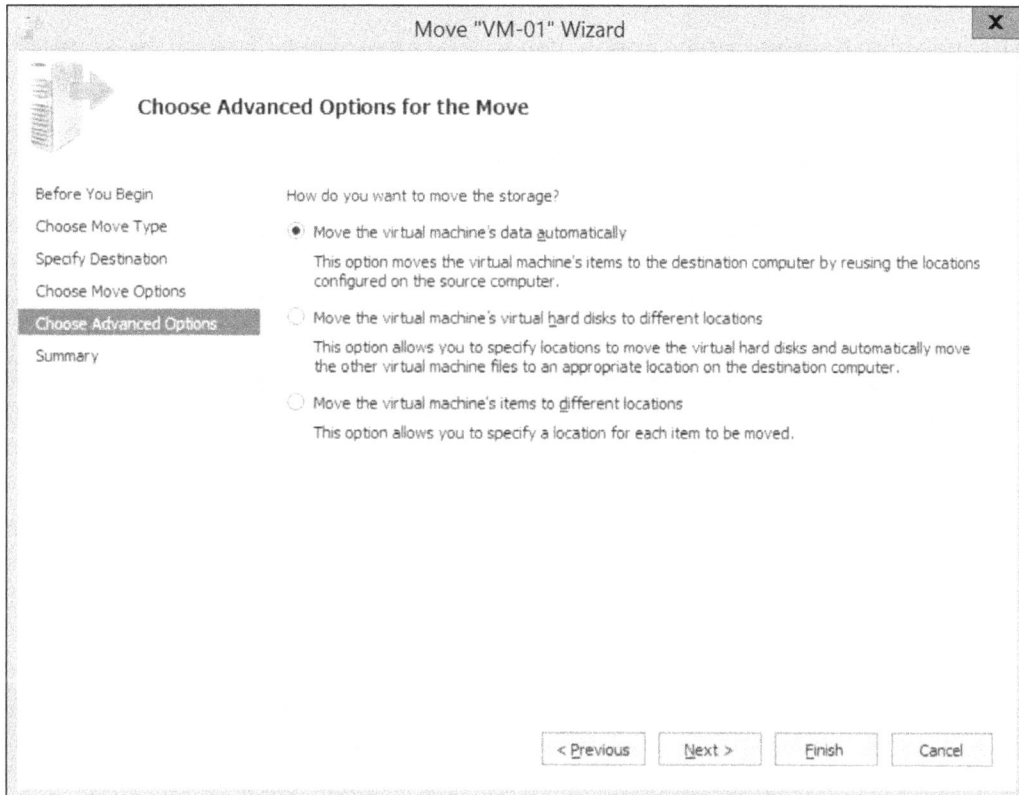

- **Move the virtual machine's data automatically**: This option will use the same location on the source host. For example, if the VM is hosted at `E:\VMStore` on the source, it will be placed at `E:\VMStore` on the destination host.

- **Move the virtual machine's virtual hard disks to different locations**: This option will let you select the disks of the VM and indicate a different location for each disk.

- **Move the virtual machine's items to different locations**: This option lets you select a different location not only for the disks but also for the VM files, such as **Current configuration**, **Checkpoints**, and **Smart Paging**.

- **Move only the Virtual Machine**: This option will move only the VM. This means that the VM disks will not be moved. Since the VM disks are not going to be moved, they must be on a shared location, which in this case is probably an SMB3 location, such as `\\servername\sharedfolder`.

After selecting the appropriate option, you will be prompted to indicate the location of the file you are going to move, as shown in the following screenshot:

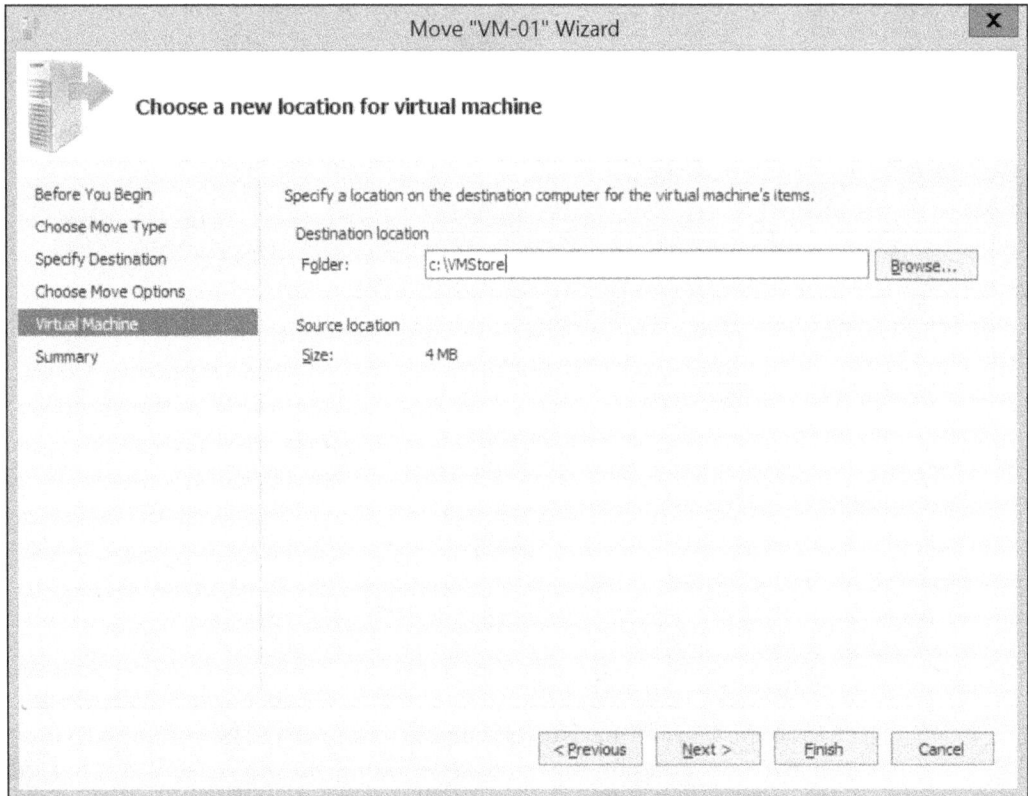

After indicating the folder on the destination host, you will get a summary of the movement in the **Summary** section, as shown in this screenshot:

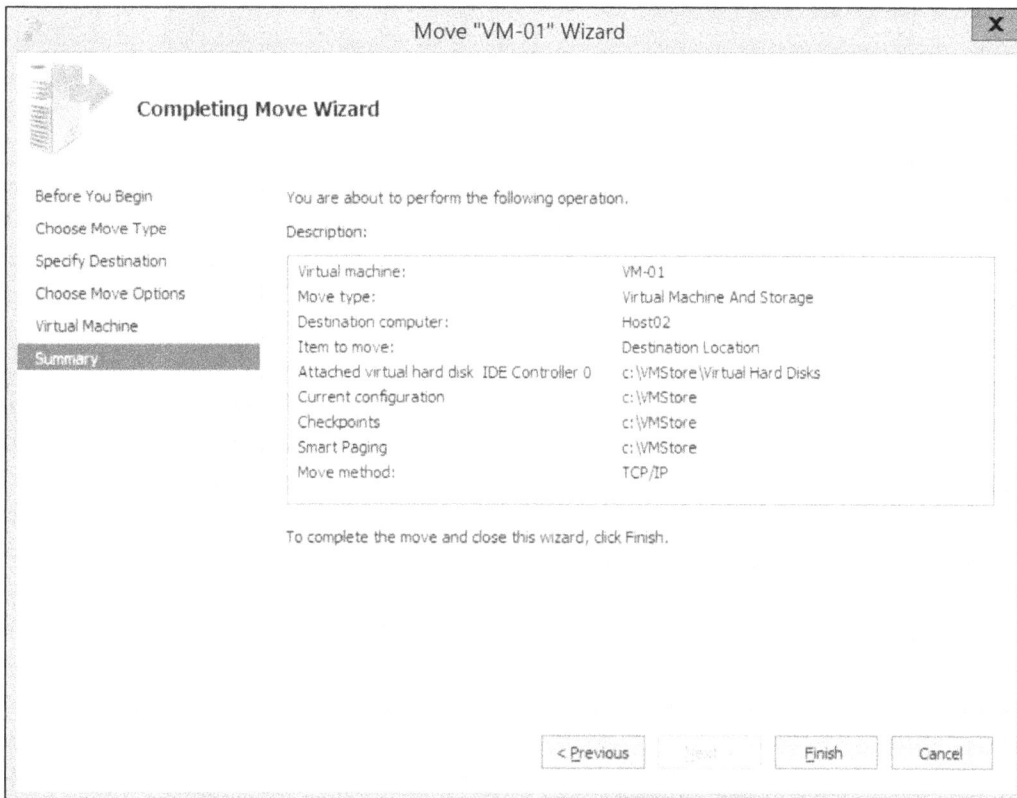

Clicking on **Finish** will start the move process. Wait for the process to complete, and then check the VM on the destination host to confirm that it was moved.

To move a VM using PowerShell, you will have to indicate all the parameters about the movement. The following examples illustrate the process of moving the VM using PowerShell:

```
Move-VM -DestinationHost Host02 -Name VM-01 -ComputerName Host01 -
DestinationStoragePath c:\VMStore –IncludeStorage
```

The preceding command will move all of the VM-01 data to single location, from Host01 to Host02. The -DestinationHost and –Name parameters are optional, and you can suppress them using the following command:

```
Move-VM VM-01 Host02 -ComputerName Host01 -DestinationStoragePath
c:\VMStore –IncludeStorage
```

This will execute the same operation, but is smaller than the one before it. Now look at the following command:

```
Move-VM VM-01 Host02
```

This command will move VM-01 to Host02, assuming that the VM storage is in an SMB3 shared location.

There are many other options for moving the VM using PowerShell. Check out the official article at https://technet.microsoft.com/en-us/library/hh848547.aspx to learn about them.

# Moving the VM storage

The previous options move the VM from one host to another. It the storage files may not be moved, but the VM will move from one host to another. Another alternative is to move only the VM storage and keep the VM on the host on which it is running.

This is an important option for scenarios where you host the VM storage in a location that is running out of space, and you need to move the VM storage to another location that has more free space. To perform this operation, select **Move the virtual machine's storage** as shown in the *Live migrating a VM* section in this chapter. After selecting this option, click on **Next >**. Let's take a look at the following screenshot that illustrates the options for moving the VM storage:

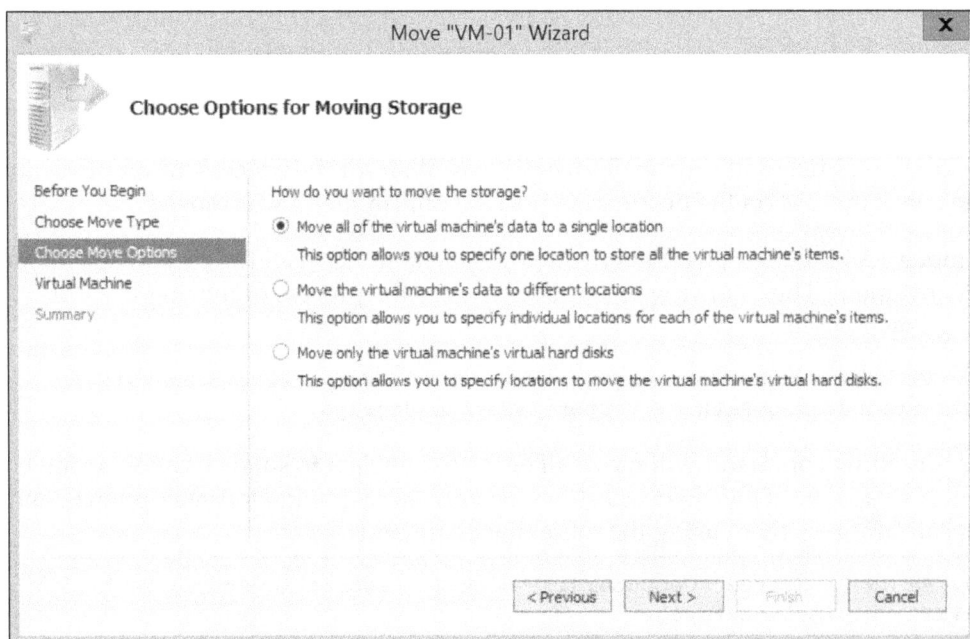

Just like options for moving the VM, there are three options for moving the VM storage, which will lead to many suboptions:

- **Move all of the virtual machine's data to a single location**: This option will move all of the VM data to a single location on the destination host. In the next step, you have to indicate the destination location, which can be on the same host or at a shared SMB3 location.

- **Move the virtual machine's data to different locations**: This option will give you the ability to select a new location for each file of the VMs, such as VM disks, **Current configuration**, **Checkpoints**, and **Smart Paging**.

- **Move only the virtual machine's virtual hard disks**: This option lets you select a different location for each VM disk.

After selecting the appropriate option, you will have to indicate the location of the destination of the files you are going to move, and you will be presented with a summary in the end, just as in the case of moving the VM.

Keep in mind that while moving the VM files from one location to another, these files can be moved to a different location on the same host, from `E:` to `F:` for example, or to a shared SMB3 location, such as `\\servername\sharedfolder`.

To move the VM storage using PowerShell, use the following cmdlet:

```
Move-VMStorage -DestinationStoragePath D:\VMStorage -VMName VM-01
-ComputerName Host01
```

This command will move all of the `VM-01` VM storage to a single location at `D:\VMStorage`.

Just like the VM moving commands, there are multiple options that can be used to move the VM storage. To see all the available options, check out the official article at `https://technet.microsoft.com/en-us/library/hh848599.aspx`.

# Hyper-V Replica

The features you saw in this chapter, Share Nothing Live Migration and Storage Live Migration, are features that help you when you need to evacuate a host, prevent a VM from stopping in case of low free space, and so on—but always to prevent a problem. None of these features will help you if a problem that has already occurred. In *Chapter 11*, *Protecting Your Virtualization Environment*, you will learn how to use some techniques to back up and restore VM and files in case of a problem with your environment.

Moreover, there is new feature on Windows Server 2012 that helps you in the event of a disaster. This is the Hyper-V Replica feature. When Microsoft first designed Hyper-V Replica on Windows Server 2012, it designed it imagining that customers were going to use it as a Replica site. This means that you can replicate a VM from one site to another. If, due to any disasters, you lose the primary site, you can power on the VM on the secondary site.

As you can probably imagine, there are many tools in the market that can be used to replicate one site to another. The difference between Hyper-V Replica and other tools is that Hyper-V Replica doesn't need a mechanism to replicate the storage. It is storage agnostic and replicates the storage content from the primary site to the secondary site on an asynchronous basis. What this means is that from time to time, Hyper-V will synchronize the storage content on both the sites. In Windows Server 2012, there was only a default configuration of 5 minutes for synchronization. You might notice that this has changed in Windows Server 2012 R2. To understand how Hyper-V Replica works, let's take a look at its architecture, as shown in the following diagram:

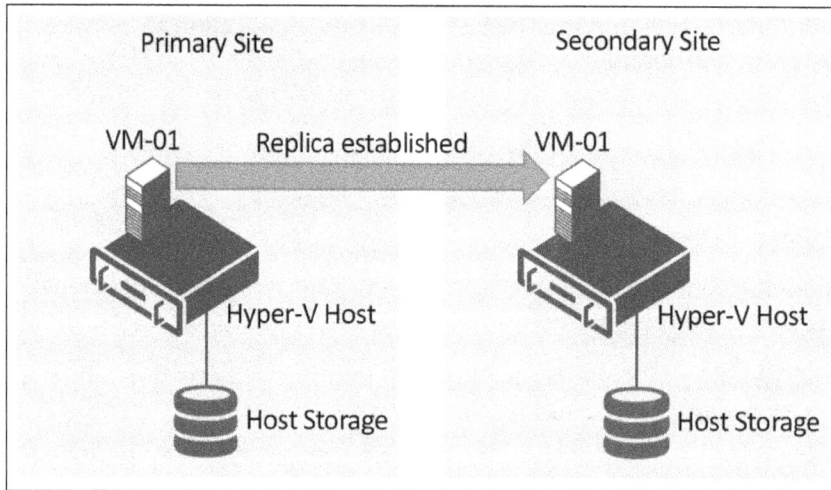

The idea is that Hyper-V Replica will, from time to time, replicate the configured VM from the host on the primary site to the host on the secondary site, each host using its own storage. Another important aspect of Hyper-V Replica is that it only needs a means of regular communication between the hosts, which can be a VPN tunnel, a point-to-point connection, or any other way to let the hosts communicate between the sites. To better understand how it works, let's see how to configure Hyper-V Replica.

# Configuring Hyper-V Replica

To initiate the Hyper-V Replica configuration, open **Hyper-V Manager** and click on
**Hyper-V Settings....** In Hyper-V Settings, click on **Replication Configuration**, as
shown in this screenshot:

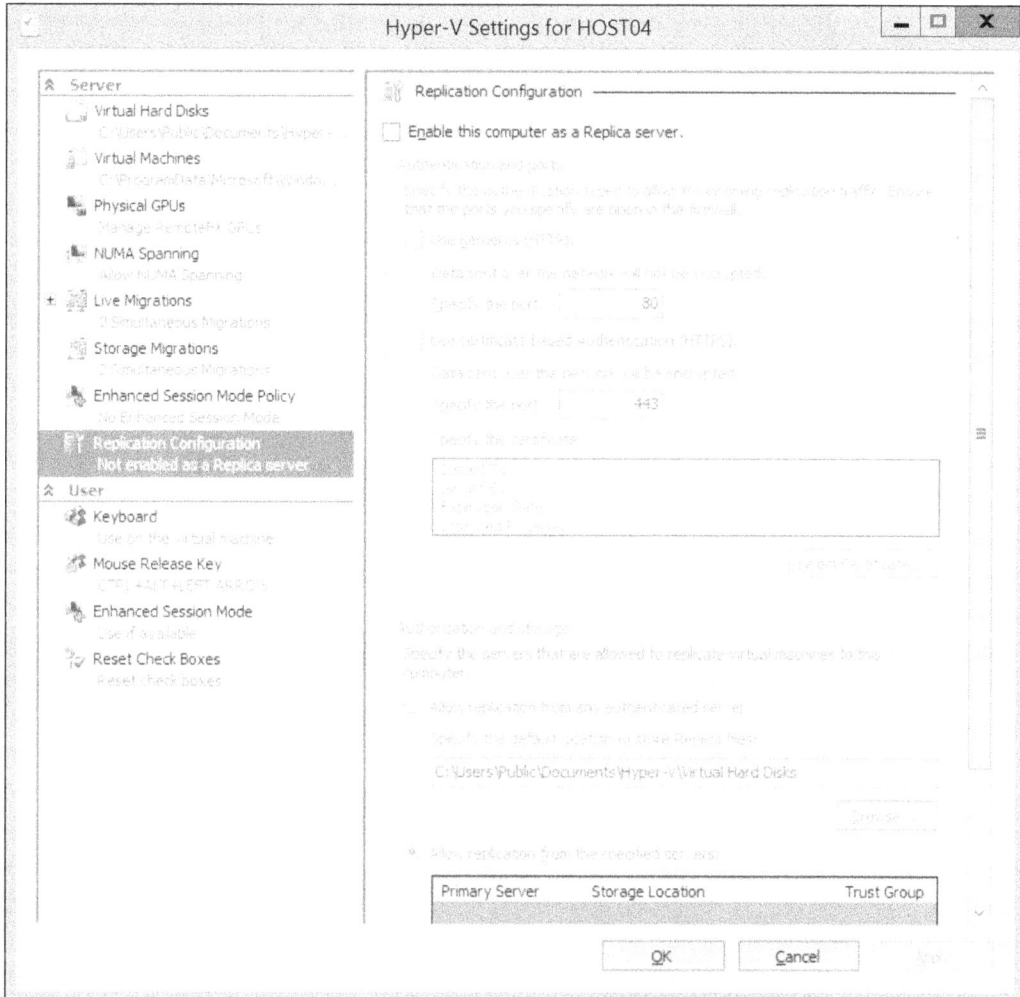

To enable Hyper-V in this host, click on **Enable this computer as a Replica server**.
This will enable this host to receive a replicated VM, so this procedure must be done
on the secondary site.

> If you want to be able to replicate the VM back to the original host, you will have to perform the same procedure on the host of the primary site.

After enabling the Hyper-V Replica feature, you will have to indicate the ports to be used. There are two protocols: HTTP and HTTPS. You can change the default ports of these protocols, which are `80` and `443` respectively.

For the HTTP, simply check the **Use Kerberos (HTTP)** option and, if necessary, change the default port. For the HTTPS option, you will also have to choose a certificate to authenticate the process, as shown in the following screenshot:

The general rule for choosing the protocol is to decide whether or not you trust the link between the hosts. After choosing the appropriate protocol, you will have to configure the **Authorization and storage** location, as shown in the following screenshot:

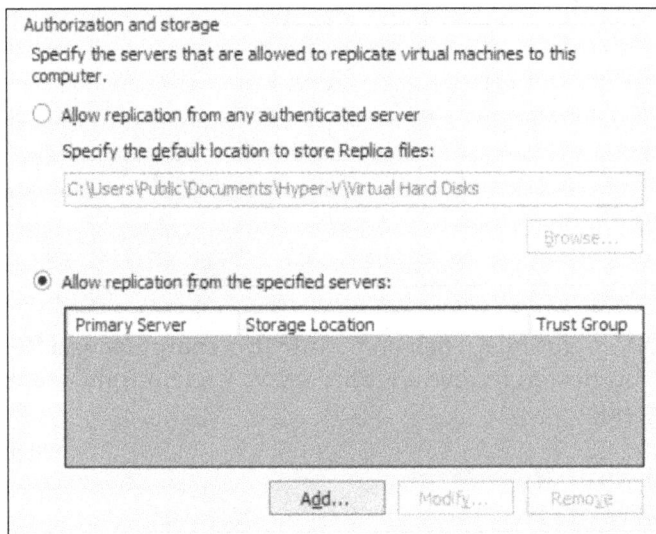

The first option will allow any host on the same AD domain, or a trusted domain, to replicate the VMs to this host, and will use a single location to store the VMs. In the second option, you can specify which servers are authorized to replicate the VMs, and a location for each authorized host. After selecting the appropriate option, click on **OK** or **Apply**. You will see the following warning:

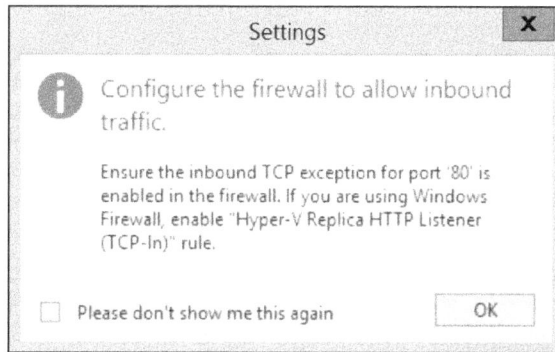

This warning appears because although the configuration on the Hyper-V Host is done, you still have to configure the firewall that is active on the host. If you are using a third-party firewall, check with the software vendor how to enable Hyper-V Replica. As the warning message states, if you are using the Windows Firewall, there is a rule required to enable it. To enable this rule, open **Windows Firewall with Advanced Security**, as shown in this screenshot:

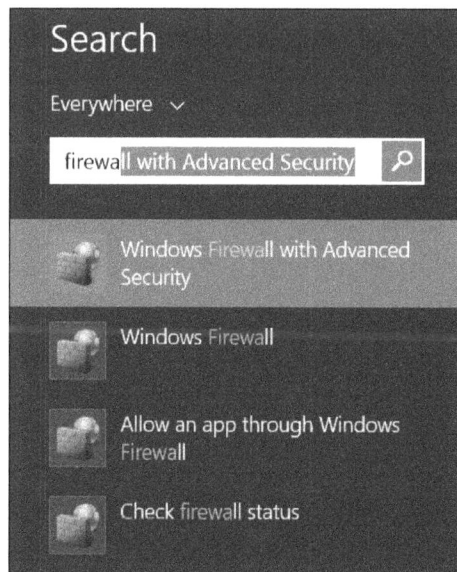

In **Windows Firewall with Advanced Security**, click on **Inbound Rules** on the left side and navigate to the Hyper-V Replica rules. There are two rules: one for HTTP and one for HTTPS. You have to enable the rule relative to the protocol you configured in the Hyper-V Replica configuration. To enable a rule, right-click on it and click on **Enable Rule**, as shown in the following screenshot:

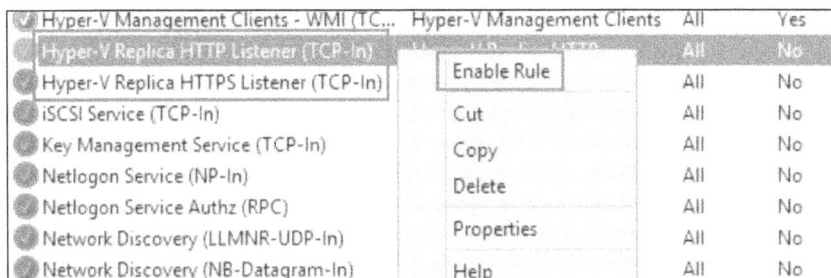

| | | | |
|---|---|---|---|
| Hyper-V Management Clients - WMI (TC... | Hyper-V Management Clients | All | Yes |
| Hyper-V Replica HTTP Listener (TCP-In) | | All | No |
| Hyper-V Replica HTTPS Listener (TCP-In) | Enable Rule | All | No |
| iSCSI Service (TCP-In) | Cut | All | No |
| Key Management Service (TCP-In) | Copy | All | No |
| Netlogon Service (NP-In) | Delete | All | No |
| Netlogon Service Authz (RPC) | | All | No |
| Network Discovery (LLMNR-UDP-In) | Properties | All | No |
| Network Discovery (NB-Datagram-In) | Help | All | No |

After you enable the Windows Firewall rule, the host is configured to receive the Replica VMs.

To enable Hyper-V Replica on a host using PowerShell, use the following cmdlet:

```
Set-VMReplicationServer -AllowedAuthenticationType Kerberos -
ComputerName Host04 -DefaultStorageLocation D:\ReplicaVM
```

The preceding command will configure Host04 as a Replica server using Kerberos authentication, and change the default storage location to D:\ReplicaVM.

There are other examples of configuring a Replica server using PowerShell, especially when using HTTPS. To better understand all of these options, check out the official article at https://technet.microsoft.com/en-us/library/hh848598.aspx.

# Replicating a VM

To replicate a VM, open **Hyper-V Manager**, right-click on the VM you want to create a Replica of, and click on **Enable Replication....** In the wizard, click on **Next >**, as shown in this screenshot:

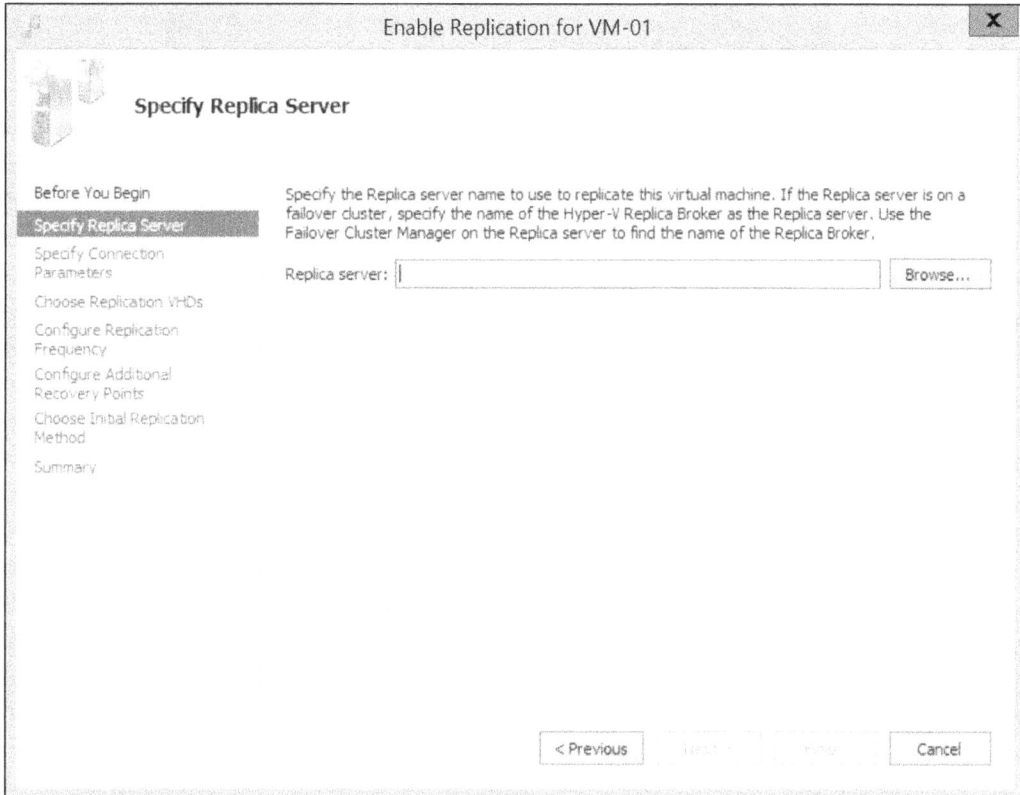

The first step is to indicate **Replica server**, or the server on which you want to create a Replica of the VM. After indicating **Replica server**, click on **Next >**, as shown in the following screenshot:

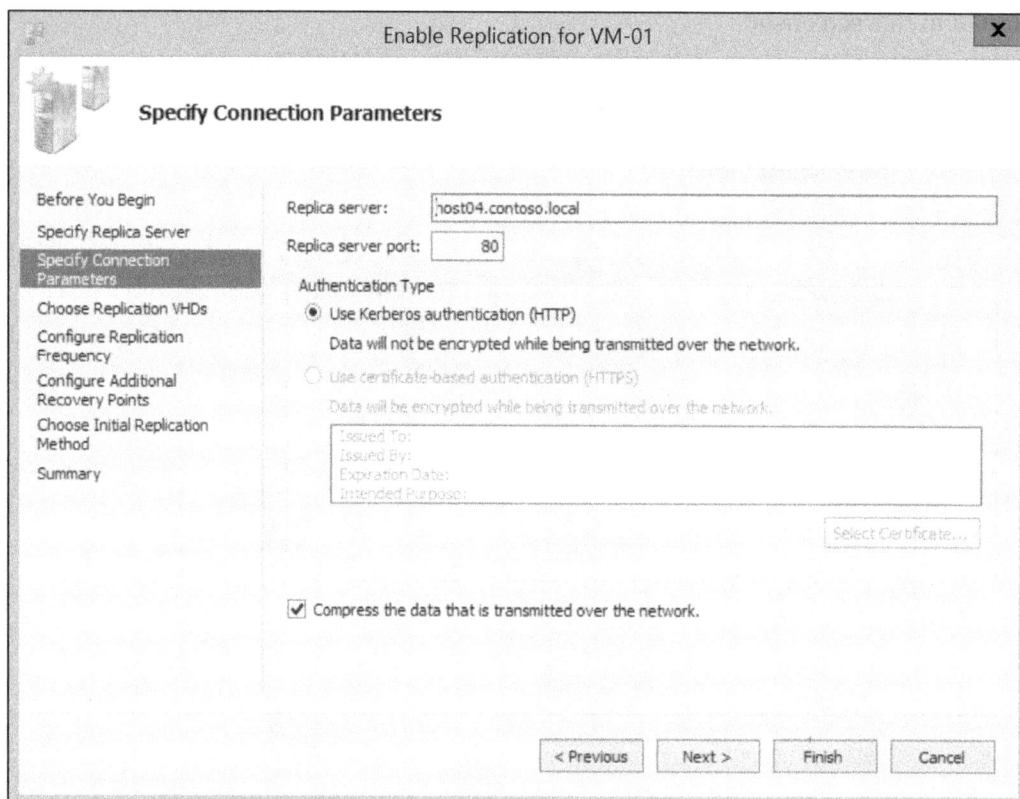

In **Specify Connection Parameters**, you can choose from the allowed protocols. Note that if one of the protocols was not enabled, you will not be able to choose it here. Also, you can use data compression by checking the **Compress the data that is transmitted over the network** option. Click on **Next >**. You will be taken to this screen:

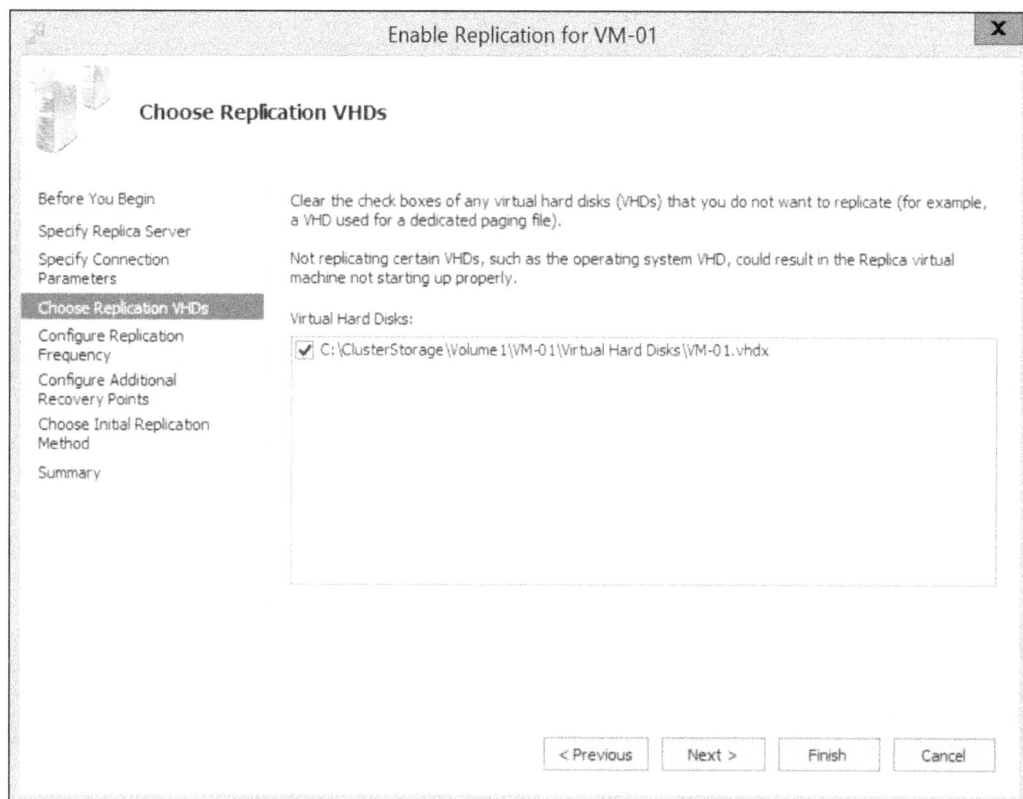

In this step, you can choose which disks on the VM you want to keep on the Replica VM. This is an important option because not all disks are important, and sometimes, if checked, the disks will be replicated using up network and processing time. After selecting the appropriate disks, click on **Next >**. Let's take a look at the following screenshot that shows the options for configuring the replication frequency:

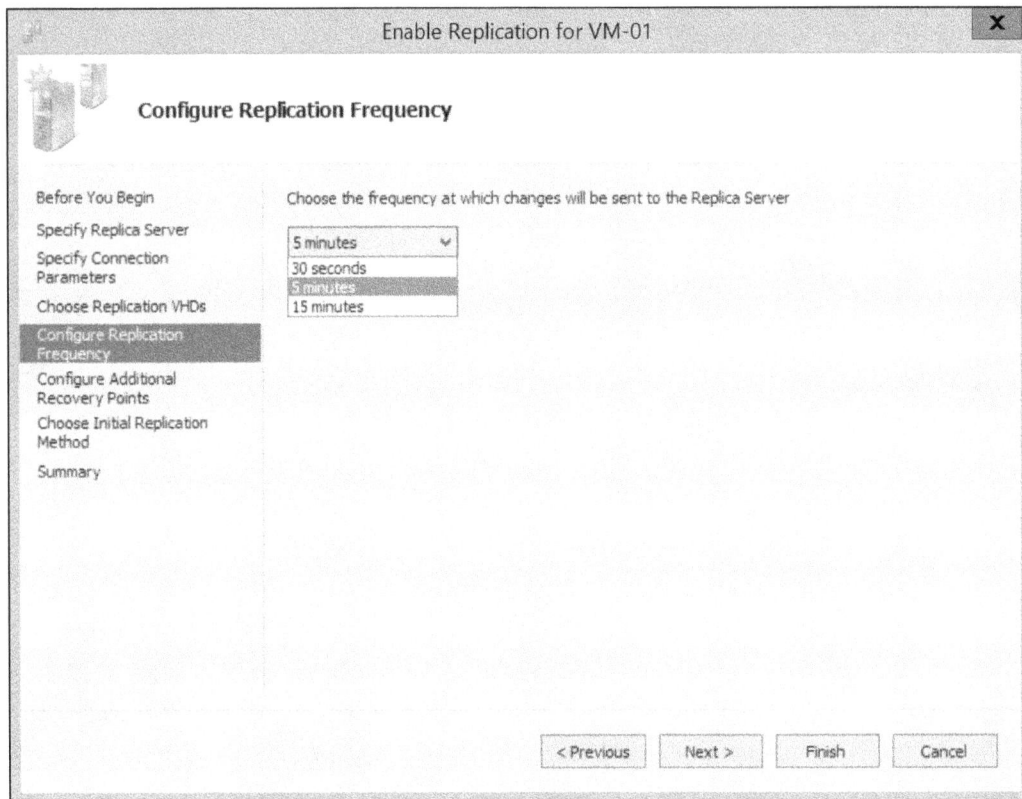

In **Configure Replication Frequency**, you can choose the time at which Hyper-V will synchronize the Replica VM. As explained earlier, in Windows Server 2012, the default was **5 minutes**, and this step was not actually exhibited. Before Microsoft launched Windows Server 2012 R2, many customers gave feedback stating two new scenarios for Hyper-V Replica:

- The first is having both hosts—source and destination—on the same site with a very high performance network between them

- The second scenario is in which the source and destination hosts are so far away from each other and the network performance is so poor that **5 minutes** is not enough to replicate the VM changes

With this in mind, Microsoft introduced two new options for replication frequency: **30 seconds**, which is recommended for the first scenario, and **15 minutes**, which is recommended for the second scenario. Any other regular implementation should use the default **5 minutes**. After selecting the appropriate option, click on **Next >**.

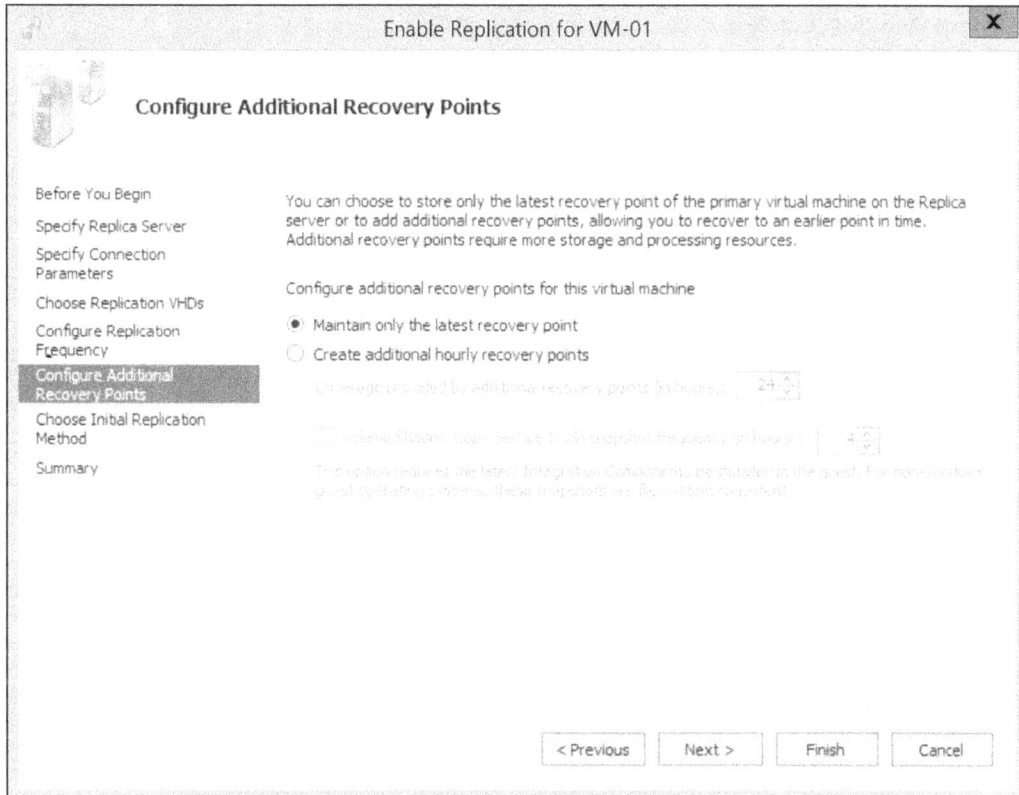

Another interesting aspect of Hyper-V Replica is that it can keep multiple **Recovery Points** of a VM. A recovery point is a snapshot of the VM in a point in time, so you can recover the VM for that state. It is important for scenarios in which you know that the last Replica of the VM is actually a VM that already failed, and recovering it will not achieve the goal of recovering the VM. When you select **Create additional hourly recovery points**, you can select the number of recovery points you want to keep. Each recovery point will need extra space in the Replica storage. The maximum value for this option is 24.

It is important to understand that a recovery point will be created every hour, but the Replica server will receive the VM modifications at the time you established on the previous step.

Additionally, you can configure the **Volume Shadow Copy Service (VSS)** to take application-consistent snapshots of the guest OS. Although this can facilitate the recovery process, keep in mind that it will have an impact on the guest OS at the moment the VSS needs to run. After configuring the appropriate settings, click on **Next >**. Let's take a look at the following screenshot which illustrates various options that you can choose for the initial replication of your VM:

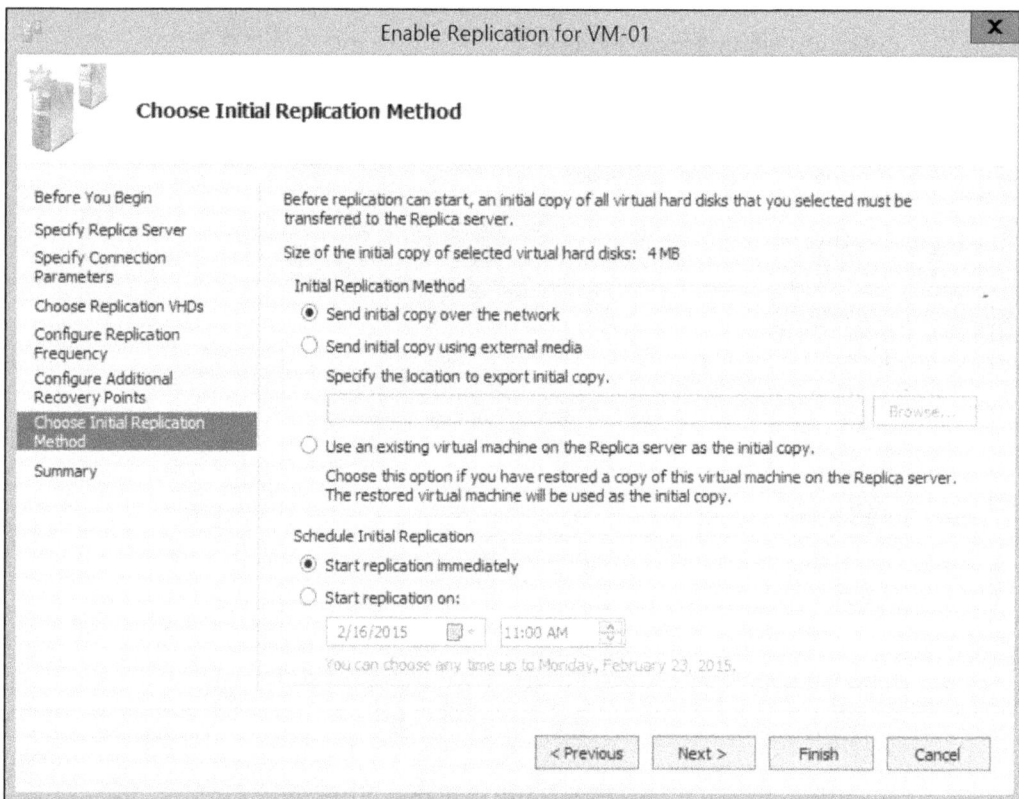

The problem with many Site Recovery solutions is in the initial Replica. This is because in regular operation, only the changed block storages will be transferred for the Replica host. However, the initial replication process has to move the entire VM storage to the other side. In Hyper-V Replica, there are three methods that can be used to initiate the replication:

- **Send initial copy over the network**: This option will transfer all the VM disks over the network.

- **Send initial copy using external media**: In this option, you have to indicate an external medium, and Hyper-V will generate a copy of the VM. On the Replica host, a VM with no content will be created, and you have to manually import the content generated by the source host. After you import this content, Hyper-V will sync the contents, which can move a large amount of data. This is still, for sure, less than the regular copy.

- **Use an existing virtual machine on the Replica server as the initial copy**: In this option, you have to indicate a VM on the Replica host that is a backup of the VM that you imported to be used as a base image for the Replica VM. Only the necessary storage blocks will be sent on the initial replication.

In this case, we will select the first option and click on **Next >**. On the **Summary** screen, click on **Finish** to initiate the replication. If the Virtual Switch on which the VM is connected does not exist on the Replica server, the following warning will be shown:

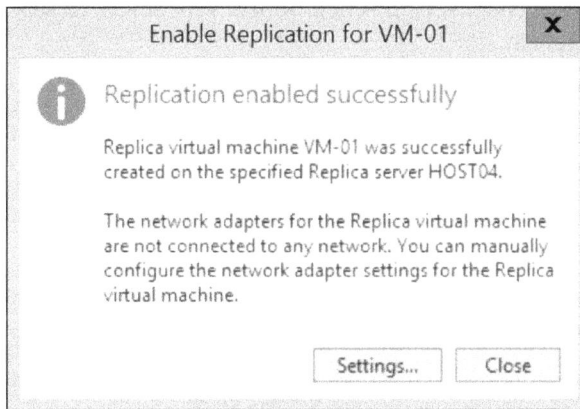

You can click on **Settings...** and change the network configuration. In our case, we will explain the network considerations later in this chapter. Right now, click on **Close**.

Once the replication configuration is done, you will see the replication progress under the status of the VM on Hyper-V Manager. You can also click on the **Replication** tab at the bottom to check the replication, as shown in this screenshot:

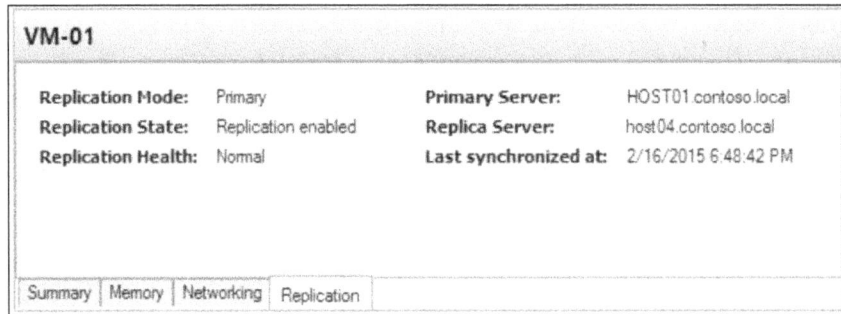

To check the replication status, right-click on the VM, select **Replication**, and click on **View Replication Health....**.

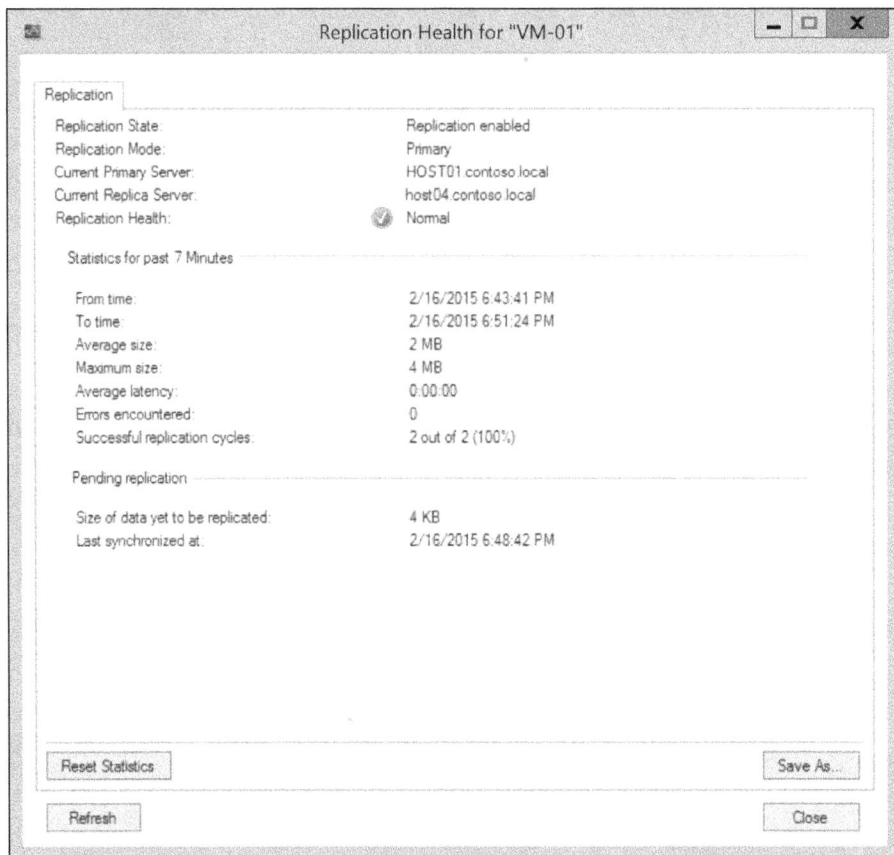

As you can see from the preceding screenshot, you can check multiple pieces of information from **Replication Health**, such as **Replication Health** itself, the average size of the replication, latency, and successful replication cycles.

It is important to note that if you choose initial replication through the network, the information shown under **Average size** and **Maximum size** will be impacted. The recommendation in this case is to click on **Reset Statistics**.

To enable VM replication using PowerShell, use the following cmdlet:

```
Enable-VMReplication -AuthenticationType Kerberos -
ReplicaServerName Host04 -ReplicaServerPort 80 -VMName VM-01
```

The preceding command will enable replication for VM-01 on the Host04 Replica server using Kerberos on port 80. Notice that, unlike GUI, this will not start the initial replication automatically. To start the replication, you can use the following command:

```
Start-VMInitialReplication -VMName VM-01
```

This will initiate the replication for VM-01. There are many other commands that can be used to manage the VM replication using PowerShell. You can see some of them in the list of Hyper-V cmdlets at https://technet.microsoft.com/en-us/library/hh848559.aspx.

# Testing Hyper-V Replica

When checking the Replica health, you can see whether the replication is okay and whether you will be prepared to fail over in the event of a disaster. However, it is always important to test your environment to see what happens when you try to start the Replica VM.

In a Disaster Recovery (DR) environment, it is usually difficult to test the environment. This is because you can't turn on the Replica environment without stopping the production environment. Furthermore, once you start the VM, it will retain all of the network configuration from the primary site. If you're failing over the VM to a different site — a DR site — you are probably using a different IP range, and you probably want the Replica VM to be able to communicate with this new DR site.

With all of this in mind, Microsoft configured Hyper-V Replica in such a way that you can test the Replica VM without stopping the original VM. This is the **Test Failover** process. To test the Replica VM without affecting the original VM, you will have to configure the Replica VM. Open **Hyper-V Manager** on the Replica host, right-click on the Replica VM, and open **Settings....** Expand **Network Adapter** and click on **Test Failover**, as shown in this screenshot:

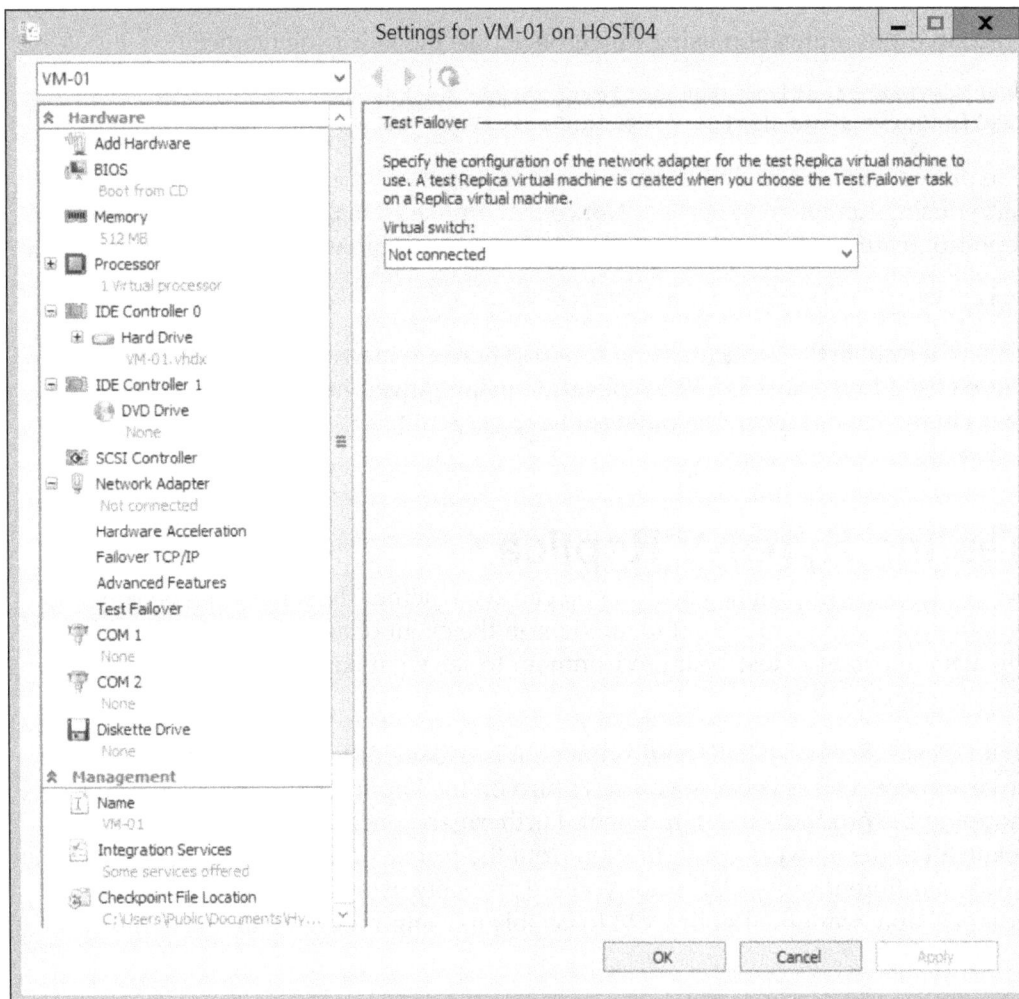

In this setting, you can change the VM Virtual Switch when testing the failover. When you test the failover, a Checkpoint will be created and the VM connection will be redirected to **Virtual switch** indicated here. This can be a **Private**, **Internal** or **External** Virtual Switch. The goal here is not to let the VM initiate on the same network as the original one. In this way, you can test the VM on **Test Failover**, and once you finish the tests, you can discard the test VM. Another important feature is **Failover TCP/IP**, as shown in the following screenshot:

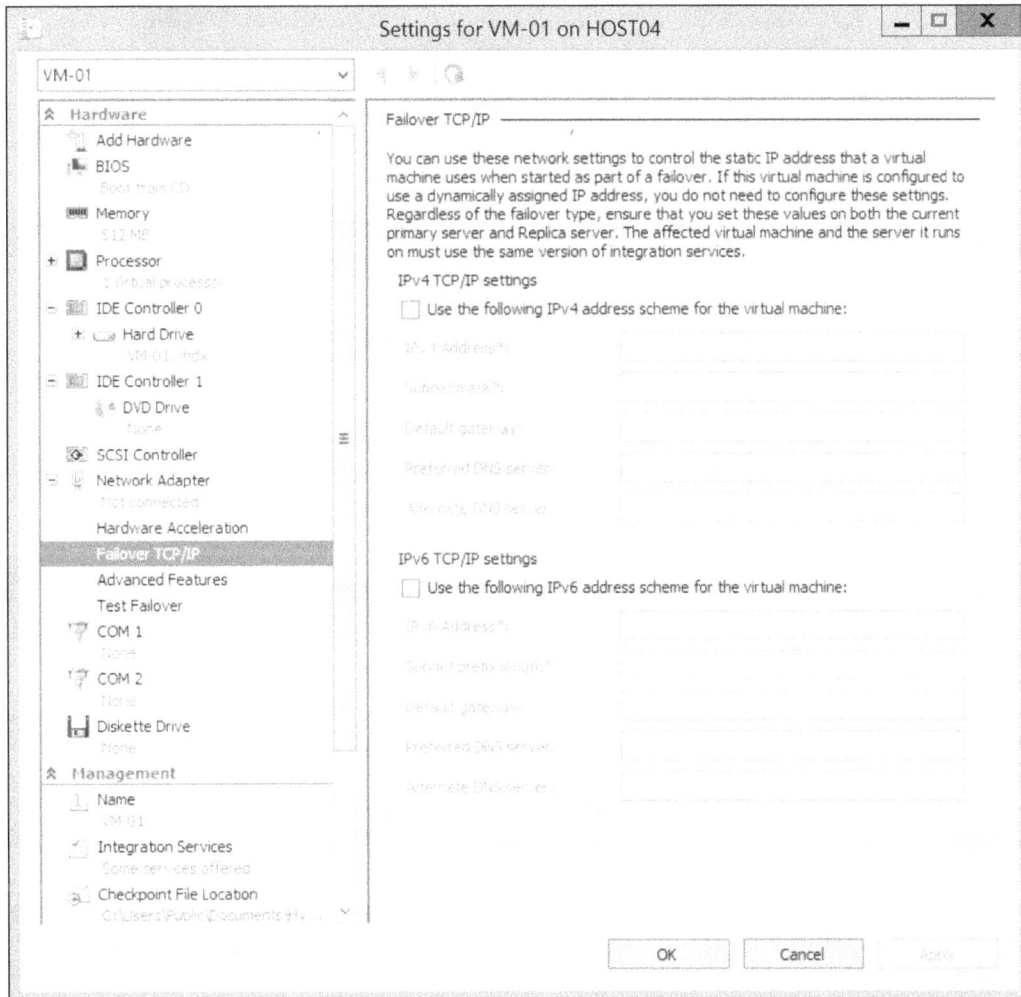

The preceding setting will change the IP address (IPv4 and IPv6) if the VM is failed over. This feature is important, as you might have different network IP ranges on different sites. This feature requires Integration Services on the guest OS. After configuring **Test Failover** and **Failover TCP/IP**, click on **OK**.

To test the failover, right-click on the VM, select **Replication**, and click on **Test Failover...** You will be prompted to select a recovery point, as shown in this screenshot:

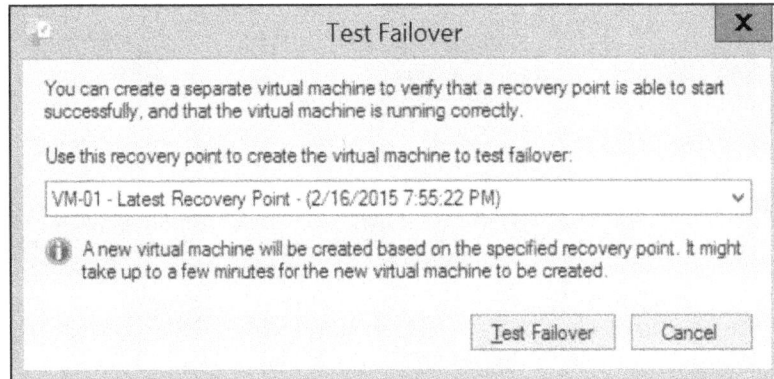

Select the appropriate recovery point and click on **Test Failover**. You will see that a new VM with the Test (**VM-01 - Test** in this case) label will be created, like this:

Right-click on this new Test VM (**VM-01 - Test**), and then click on **Start**. This will initiate the test. Once you've finished the test, you can right-click on the Replica VM, select **Replication**, and click on **Stop Test Failover**. Confirm the Stop Test Failover process in the warning message by clicking on **Stop Test Failover**. You will see that the Test VM (**VM-01 - Test**) will be deleted and will be merged with the Checkpoint on the Replica VM.

To test the VM failover using PowerShell, you will have to use three cmdlets:

```
Start-VMFailover -AsTest -VMName VM-01 -ComputerName Host04
```

The preceding command will initiate the Test Failover on VM-01. Notice that you have to specify the Replica server as -ComputerName. If you specify the source host, the process will fail:

```
Get-VM -ComputerName Host04 *Test* | Start-VM
```

The command you just saw will start the test VM on Host04, which is the Replica server. Notice that the command will return all the VMs with Test on VM name. If you have multiple VMs to test, check whether you want to perform the operation on all of them:

```
Stop-VMFailover -VMName VM-01 -ComputerName Host04
```

The preceding command can be used when you've completed the tests. This will delete the Test VM and complete the Test Failover.

# Failing over a VM

We always try to avoid it, but there are moments when a disaster happens. If you've replicated a VM, you can failover that VM to the Replica server. Before we continue, it is very important for you to understand the impact of failing over a VM to a different site:

- You are probably using a different IP range on this DR site. Although Hyper-V Replica can change the IP address of the VM, there are scenarios in which you can still lose connectivity with the VM. An example of this is when an application is binding the IP address directly. Another example is when a system has the IP address of the VM in the cache. Until the cache information is flushed, the *old* IP address will be used.

- When you fail over the VM, all of the traffic from the clients to the VM will be redirected to this DR site, or Datacenter. It is important to plan the links accordingly to avoid poor network performance.

- When you fail over the VM to a different site and the clients start using it, you will have to plan the rollback, which is basically the same process for creating the Replica VM. This impacts the network consumption from the DR site to the original site. Also, you will have to fail over the VM back to the original site, which will take the VM offline during the failover process.

- The Hyper-V Replica feature should be planned as part of a major plan that contemplates more than technical issues. If you're facing a disaster, it means that the location on which the VM was hosted has probably been compromised. A major plan should contemplate evacuation, transportation of people to a new location, and many other items. This plan is called a **Business Continuity and Disaster Recovery (BCDR)** plan.

- Because of all the preceding consequences, a disaster is never automatically established. Large organizations usually have a committee that will be consulted. In the event of a major disaster, they will invoke the BCDR, which contemplates Hyper-V Replica.

After going through all of these consequences, to initiate the failover process, go to the Replica server, open **Hyper-V Manager**, right-click on the Replica VM, select **Replication**, and click on **Failover...**.

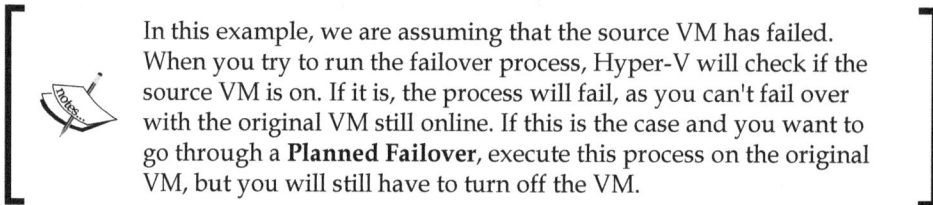

> In this example, we are assuming that the source VM has failed. When you try to run the failover process, Hyper-V will check if the source VM is on. If it is, the process will fail, as you can't fail over with the original VM still online. If this is the case and you want to go through a **Planned Failover**, execute this process on the original VM, but you will still have to turn off the VM.

You will be prompted to choose a recovery point, just as in the Test Failover process. Select the appropriate recovery point and click on **Failover...**. You will notice that the VM will initiate under a Checkpoint, which is the recovery point that you selected.

# Reversing the replication

Now that you've failed over the VM to the DR site, this VM is the source VM—from the content point of view. Technically, it is still a Replica VM, but it has the most updated information. Right now, you have two options:

- If you've completely lost your primary site in a disaster, such as a hurricane or earthquake, you can remove the replication from the Replica VM. This will transform the VM into a regular VM, and you can initiate the Replica process to another location, just as we did before. Another alternative is the next option.

- If you have not lost your primary site and want to fail back the VM, you can use the **Reverse Replication** process. This process lets you reverse the replication to the original host or another new host. After running this process, this VM will become the primary VM.

To use the first option, right-click on the VM, select **Replication**, and click on **Remove Replication**. This will merge the Checkpoint to the VM and transform the VM into a regular VM.

To use the second option, right-click on the VM, select **Replication**, and click on **Reverse Replication...**. This will initiate the regular Replication wizard, which you've already used. The difference here is that the information of the original host will be informed as the default Replica server. You can inform a new Replica server or keep the original one. After finishing the Reverse Replication Wizard, this VM will become a primary VM, with a Replica VM on the other host.

To go back to the initial configuration, you will have to perform a failover, planned or not, and configure the Reverse Replication again. In this case, as you will probably use the Planned Failover, you will have another benefit. When you right-click on the primary VM (in our case, the VM we want to be the Replica VM), select **Replication**, and click on **Planned Failover...**, you will see the following screen:

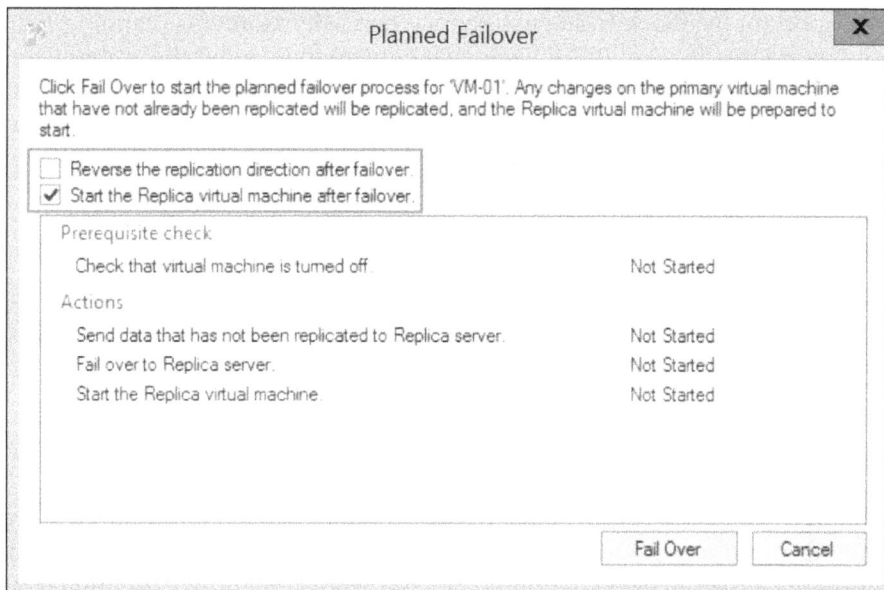

As you can see, **Planned Failover** lets you configure the Reverse Replication right away. With that, once the failover is done, the replication will come back to the original state.

To perform these operations using PowerShell, use the following cmdlets:

```
Start-VMFailover -VMName VM-01 -ComputerName Host04
```

The preceding command will start the failover process on `VM-01` on `Host04`, which is the Replica server:

```
Stop-VMReplication -VMName VM-01 -ComputerName Host04
```

The command you just saw can be used if you want to completely remove the replication from the failed-over VM:

```
Complete-VMFailover -VMName VM-01 -ComputerName Host04
```

The preceding command will complete the failover process and eliminate the Checkpoints on the failed-over VM. Now look at the following command:

```
Set-VMReplication -VMName VM-01 -Reverse
```

This will initiate Reverse Replication on the indicated VM.

## Extended replication

Another important feedback from customers when Microsoft was planning Hyper-V Replica on Windows Server 2012 R2 was that customers wanted the ability to create a third location for the VM. This is basically a Replica VM of the Replica VM. This is an important feature for companies that host VMs from customers, but they have to maintain a Replica of their own environment.

To extend the replication, right-click on a Replica VM, select **Replication**, and click on **Extend Replication...**. This will initiate the Extend Replication wizard. This wizard is the same as the Enable Replication wizard you saw earlier.

To perform this operation using PowerShell, use the `Enable-VMReplication` cmdlet, as already shown in the *Hyper-V Replica* section in this chapter.

# Summary

In this chapter, you learned how to configure and operate two important features of Hyper-V: Share Nothing Live Migration and Hyper-V Replica. You also learned how to configure the authentication methods for Live Migration, how to operate it, and how to perform Storage Live Migration.

Furthermore, you learned how to prepare for disasters with Hyper-V Replica, and that it is a part of major business continuity plans. You saw multiple ways of testing a replication and how to properly fail over the VM. Additionally, you saw how to reverse a replication process to restore the environment, and how to extend a replication for a hosting environment.

In the next chapter, you will go through a polemic topic—running your AD on a virtual environment.

# Virtualizing Active Directory Domain Controllers

So far, you have learned many features in Hyper-V itself, and you have been given tips on planning your applications on a virtual environment. It is beyond the scope of the book to cover the details of applications, because each application will have its own tricks in a virtual environment, assuming the virtual environment has any influence at all.

It is true that, in many cases, lack of planning or knowledge of the virtual environment will result in poor performance, which is usually held to be due to the virtual environment itself. It is not. The virtual environment requires precise planning that in many cases has nothing to do with the application, but the application can be impacted.

Databases, mail servers and web servers are examples of virtualized workloads that require proper planning, but above all of these one workload is the most controversial of all: Active Directory.

The usual questions are:

- Can I virtualize Domain Controllers (DCs)?
- Can I virtualize all my DCs or keep at least one physical DC?
- Does Hyper-V support virtualized DCs?
- Does a virtual DC require any different administration?
- Can I virtualize my DCs on a cluster environment?

Throughout this chapter, we will answer all of these questions and give you details on how to manage a DC on a virtual environment. Keep in mind that the objective here is to provide you with guidance on how to properly manage an Active Directory environment, not to teach you how Active Directory works. With that said, in this chapter we will cover:

- Active Directory virtualization concepts
- DC database configuration
- Time synchronization and virtual DCs
- Virtual DCs and Checkpoints
- Active Directory and Cluster service
- Virtual DC cloning
- Virtual DCs and Hyper-V Replica

# Active Directory virtualization concepts

A Domain Controller running on a VM is, theoretically speaking, just like a regular physical computer, as far as Active Directory is concerned. That means that you will manage this Domain Controller with the same tools as a regular DC. In fact, if you're managing Active Directory, you're probably familiar with the Active Directory Users and Computers snap-in, the `ntdsutil` command line tool, and many other tools, and you know that these tools allow you to manage a DC remotely, regardless of whether it is a physical or virtual computer.

So, why is a virtual DC so controversial? After reading this chapter, you will find that most of the issues with a virtual DC are because of the bad use of resources on a virtual environment. As you have learned so far, using the correct virtual hardware—that is, using the Hyper-V features—and correctly configuring the application, which in this case is Active Directory, are part of the administration process. In many companies, the administration of Active Directory and the virtual environment is a separate job function or role. It is not unusual to find different roles inside the IT department. This segregation can often lead to the bad administration of applications which requires a careful and closer look.

In an environment like that, imagine that your virtual DC is experiencing slow performance issues. Who do you blame in this case? The virtual environment shows that the performance counters are okay. The guest OS logs have no information on this. With all of this, many times what happens is that when two different teams can't work together to find a solution to a problem, a myth is established. One of the greatest myths on virtualization is concerns Active Directory. Ask anyone, and the answer will probably be "You can't have all your Domain Controllers virtualized".

Well, this chapter will show you that you can. Let's start by taking a look at a problem that is, most of the time, caused by the lack of knowledge of the Active Directory admin: the Domain Controller database.

# Domain Controller database configuration

If you are familiar with Active Directory, you have probably promoted a server to DC at least once. If so, you know the wizard on which you configure the Domain Controller. There is one step on that wizard that most admins simply ignore. Let's take a look at the following screenshot:

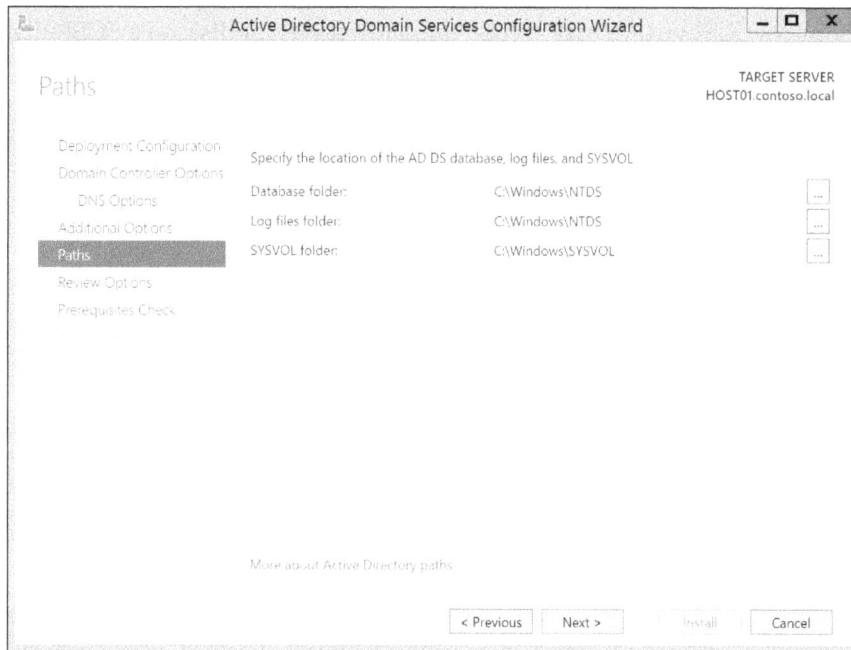

The preceding screenshot is the step in the DC promotion process at which you choose the location of the Active Directory **Database folder**, **Log files folder**, and **SYSVOL folder**. A regular admin will simply use the default location. There is, however, a more profound analysis to be made here.

Active Directory uses the **Extensible Storage Engine** (ESE) mechanism on its database. This ESE mechanism uses a technique to avoid integrity problems on the database caused by power loss or any other abrupt power-off—un-buffered writes to the database. In addition, the mechanism will try to disable the disk write cache on the volume hosting the DC database. As you can see from the preceding screenshot, the database will be placed in the C:\Windows\NTDS folder. As you learned earlier, the system/boot disk on a Generation 1 VM is an IDE virtual controller.

The problem with the IDE virtual controller is that the mechanism explained earlier requires a SCSI emulation mode that supports **Forced Unit Access** (**FUA**), which will pass these un-buffered writes to the host OS. If the SCSI emulation mode is not supported, on IDE virtual controllers it is not, you should manually disable the write cache on the guest OS.

However, instead of doing this, the recommended action is to host the DC database on a disk in a SCSI virtual controller, which supports FUA. In this case, you should add an additional disk to the virtual DC and, in the DC promotion process, change the default location to a disk hosted on a SCSI virtual controller.

If you have already installed the DC using the default location, you should change the location to a SCSI virtual disk. To do that, add a virtual disk on a SCSI virtual controller, so that the configuration will be like this:

After adding the virtual disk, you will have to go through the process of creating a new volume inside the guest OS. After preparing the volume for the database and logs, the recommendation is to create a folder for the files. In our example, we will create a directory E:\NTDS. Then, we will stop **Active Directory Domain Services** or restart the server in Active Directory Restore Mode and use the following commands on the ntdsutil command line tool:

> Before continuing with the following process, make sure you have backed up your Active Directory environment and that you are able to restore it, if necessary.

This will open the ntdsutil command line tool:

```
C:\> ntdsutil
```

This will activate the NTDS instance on the ntdsutil tool:

```
ntdsutil: activate instance ntds
```

This will open the file maintenance menu on ntdsutil:

```
ntdsutil: files
```

This will move the database file to the indicated directory. Make sure that the indicated directory is on a SCSI virtual disk:

```
file maintenance: move db to E:\NTDS\
```

This will move the log files to the indicated directory. Make sure that the indicated directory is on a SCSI virtual disk:

```
file maintenance: move logs to E:\NTDS\
```

With the previous commands, you are able to move the database and logs to a new location on a SCSI virtual disk.

If you are using a Generation 2 VM, all of the previous things do not apply, as the Gen2 VM uses only SCSI virtual controllers that support FUA. Keep in mind, however, that an Active Directory database should not be stored on the OS drive.

# Time synchronization and virtual DCs

Another important aspect of Active Directory is the Time synchronization. Time synchronization on an Active Directory environment plays a critical role as the entire replication process relies on it.

As an Active Directory admin, you should know that since Windows Server 2000, Active Directory has used a multi-master replication process. It means that you can write information on any Domain Controller, except the **read-only domain controller** (**RODC**). However, a single DC performs some functions on Active Directory. These are **Flexible Single Master Operations** (**FSMO**). The FSMO includes operations such as changing the Active Directory schema, which is performed by the Schema Master FSMO, and other operations that are performed by a single DC on the environment.

One of the FSMOs is the PDC (former PDC emulator). The function of the PDC prior to Windows Server 2012 was to emulate a Primary Domain Controller for compatibility with Windows NT **Backup Domain Controllers** (**BDC**). Since Windows NT is not supported and you cannot have these BDCs on your Active Directory environment these days, the PDC plays other roles. One of these is to be the primary overall timekeeper on an Active Directory environment. All other Domain Controllers will synchronize their time with the PDC. Moreover, all domain-joined computers will synchronize their time with the DC on which they are authenticating. Everything works fine, until you realize your virtualized Domain Controllers are not able to maintain the correct time.

As you learned in previous chapters, the guest OS uses Integration Components to enable features for Hyper-V to interact with this guest OS. One of the features enabled by default when the IC is installed is **Time synchronization**, as you can see when you open the VM **Settings...** on **Hyper-V Manager**:

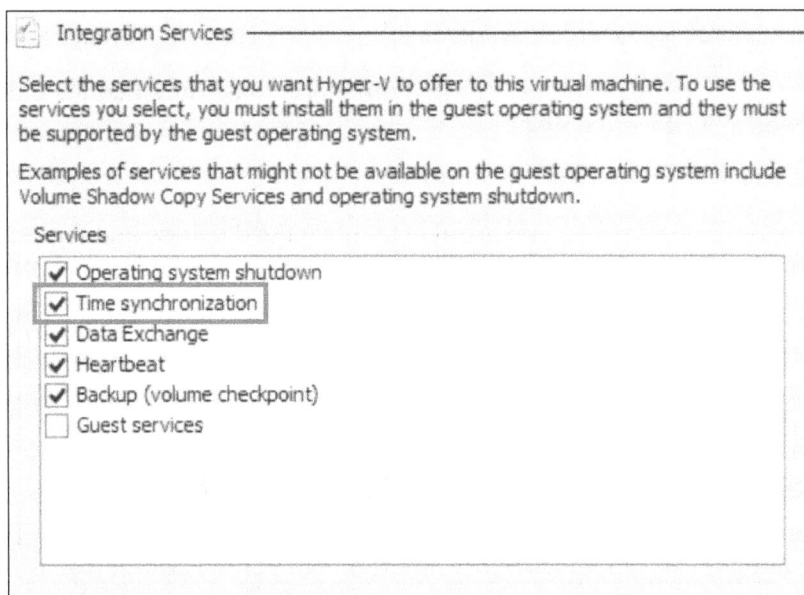

The **Time synchronization** feature on the IC uses the time of the host to set the time on the guest OS. Since the IC starts to work when the guest OS is starting up, the guest OS will use the host time. If you try to change the time manually on the guest OS, the IC will work before the host OS is able to synchronize the time through Active Directory, and the guest OS will receive the host time again.

To avoid this situation, you must disable the **Time synchronization** feature on the **Integration Services** configuration for the VM that is a DC.

# Virtual DCs and Checkpoints

This is another important problem that is caused by lack of knowledge of the virtual DC admin. In fact, this can cause a huge problem with your environment. To understand the problem, let's take a look at how synchronization happens in an Active Directory environment:

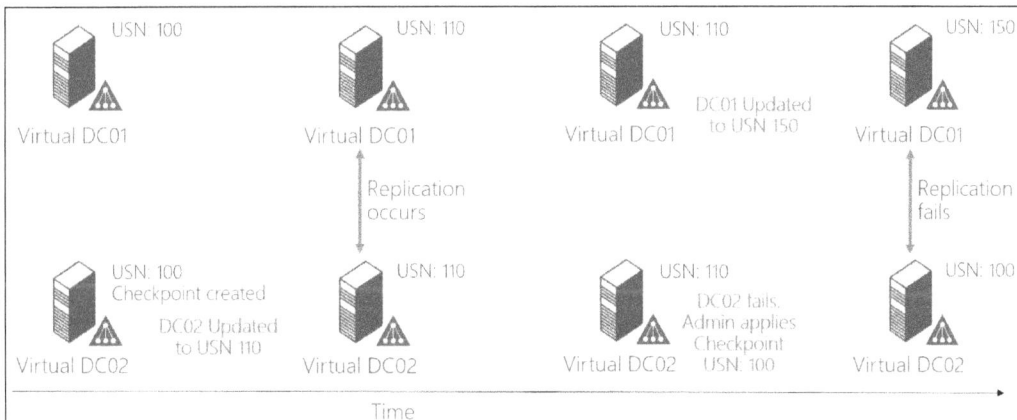

The replication process on an Active Directory environment uses an **Update Sequence Number** (**USN**) to identify whether the Domain Controller needs to be updated or not. If the DC01 USN value is 110 and the DC02 USN value is 100, than the registries from 100 to 110 must be updated on DC02. DC02 accepts the updates as it checks that it is not authoritative for the most updated information. However, when you apply a Checkpoint on for a DC, the DC believes it is authoritative for that information and will not accept replications from the other DCs. In this case, DC02 will continue to work, providing authentication to the network, but will not be supplied with the latest information available, and will remain that way. In this case, you will see many replication errors on the guest OS event viewer.

This is how Active Directory worked until Windows Server 2012. If you are running a Windows Server 2008 R2, or any earlier version of Windows Server as a Domain Controller (or, if you are running Hyper-V on Windows Server 2008 R2 or a earlier version), the earlier condition will apply. In fact, if this is the case, you cannot apply a Checkpoint (remember that it was called a Snapshot in earlier versions) on a virtual DC under any circumstances. If you find a situation like that, follow the instructions in the official article on how to solve this problem at `https://technet.microsoft. com/en-us/library/virtual_active_directory_domain_controller_ virtualization_hyperv(WS.10).aspx#usn_and_usn_rollback`.

On Windows Server 2012, Microsoft introduced a new feature on Windows Server Active Directory and Hyper-V. This new feature permits the Domain Controller to understand when a Checkpoint has been applied and to allow for the USN to be updated and the replication process to occur correctly. To understand that, let's see how it works:

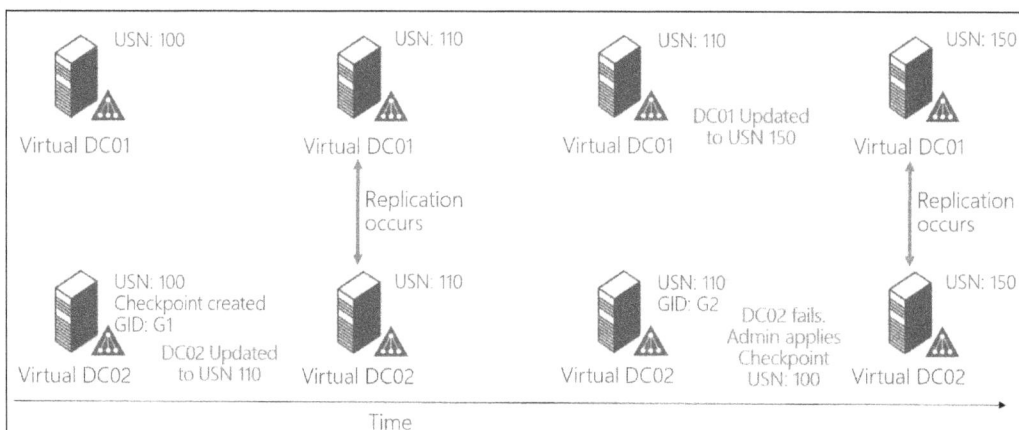

As you can see, there is a new attribute on the virtual DC—Generation ID. This attribute is written on the DC database and is independent from the regular Active Directory replication. A Windows driver inside the guest OS maintains this attribute, so Hyper-V can interact with it every time a Checkpoint is created or applied.

In the preceding process, a Generation ID is written when a Checkpoint is created for virtual DC02. When the admin applies the Checkpoint, the Generation ID is compared and Hyper-V informs the guest OS that a new Generation ID was created. With that, the USN is able to follow the regular replication process.

Right now, a regular Active Directory admin would be asking, "What is the minimal domain and forest functional level for this to work?"

In fact, the functional level for this feature is Windows Server 2008 R2. Note, however, that it will only work on Windows Server 2012 or 2012 R2 virtual Domain Controllers running on Hyper-V 2012 or 2012 R2, so you will have to prepare the domain to receive at least one Domain Controller running Windows Server 2012 or 2012 R2.

# Virtual DCs and Cluster service

At this point, you might feel that having a virtual DC is not that complicated, as long as you keep an eye on everything we've discussed until now. However, until Windows Server 2012, it was not possible to virtualize all the Domain Controllers—the exception was the Cluster service.

The Cluster service, until Windows Server 2012, was extremely reliant on the Active Directory service. For the Cluster service to start, the Active Directory service should be online. If all the Domain Controllers were hosted on a Cluster service and that Cluster service stopped for any reason, the virtual DC was not able to boot and consequently, the Cluster service was also unable to start.

Prior to Windows Server 2012, if you really wanted to virtualize all the DCs on a Cluster service, you had to split the DCs on two different clusters, trying to avoid the aforementioned scenario. It all changed with Windows Server 2012.

In Windows Server 2012, Microsoft changed the way the Cluster service works. If you check the Cluster service configuration, you will see the following:

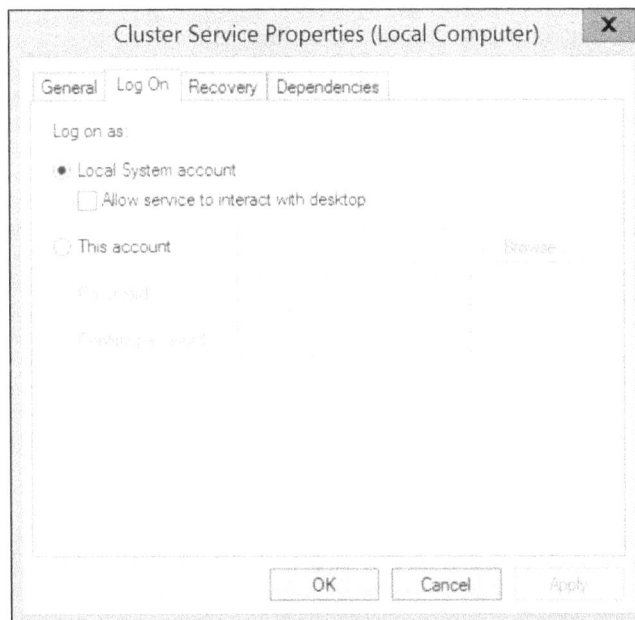

As you can see from the preceding screenshot, the Cluster service is able to start without a domain credential. Note that this does not mean that all the features of the cluster will work without having Active Directory online. The benefit here is that the Cluster service will start regardless of the Active Directory state. With the Cluster service online, the virtual DC can start and in a few moments all the services will be back online.

On Windows Server 2012 R2, Microsoft took another step towards removing the dependency of Active Directory on the Cluster service, and now you can create a totally Active Directory-detached cluster. Since the scope of this book does not include cluster configuration itself, if you need to create a detached cluster, read the official article at `https://technet.microsoft.com/en-us/library/dn265970.aspx`.

With all that has been presented so far, you can see that it is possible, on Windows Server 2012 and 2012 R2, to have all of your Domain Controllers virtualized and benefit from the virtualization features. There is one facilitator of the virtualization environment, however, that Active Directory was never able to benefit from — the rapid deployment of servers based on previous screenshots. With Windows Server 2012, Microsoft decided to change the game.

# Virtual DC cloning

A regular virtual environment has multiple benefits for administrators in respect of day-by-day tasks. One of these benefits is the rapid deployment of servers based on pre-configured images. Active Directory, however, has never benefited from it, since the Domain Controller database cannot be *sysprepped*.

With Hyper-V on Windows Server 2012, Microsoft decided to add this benefit and included a new feature on Active Directory to help administrators rapidly deploy new Domain Controllers on the environment by cloning these DCs.

The cloning process works in four main steps:

1. Granting the source DC the permission to be cloned.
2. Running the `Get-ADDCCloningExcludedApplicationList` cmdlet.
3. Running the `New-ADDCCloneConfigFile` cmdlet.
4. Creating the virtual DC clones using the export/import process.

# Granting the source DC the permission to be cloned

For the process to be completed, you will need a source DC to be used as an image for the cloned DCs. The source DC must be a member of the **Cloneable Domain Controllers** group on Active Directory. To perform this operation, open **Active Directory Users and Computers**, locate the source DC object under the **Domain Controllers** container, and add the **Computer** object to the group. The result will look as shown in the following screenshot:

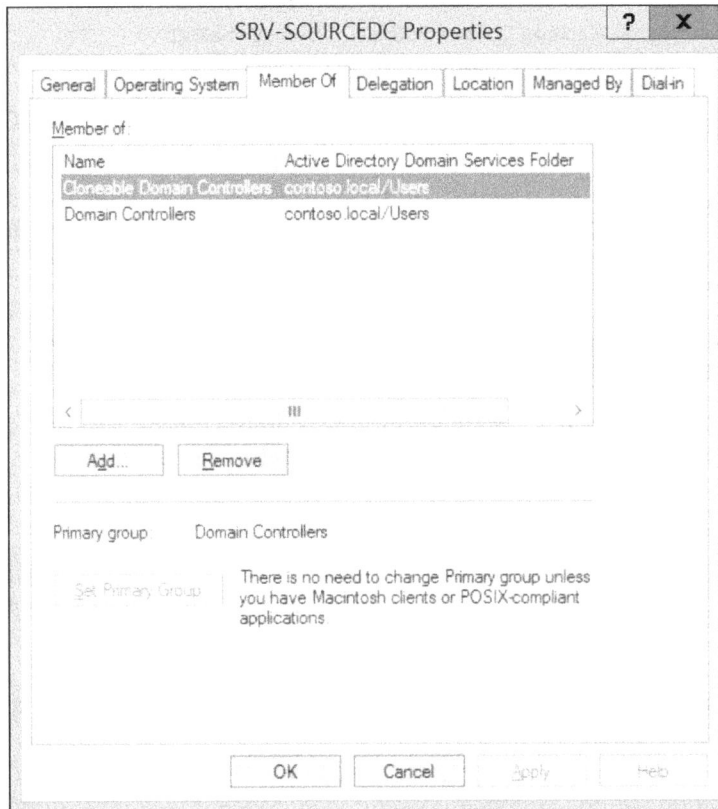

# Running the Get-ADDCCloningExcludedApplication List cmdlet

The purpose of the Get-ADDCCloningExcludedApplicationList cmdlet is to identify possible applications on the source DC that are not eligible for cloning. This cmdlet will generate a list that will be used in the next step, as a *go-no-go* action.

To run the following cmdlet, open the **Active Directory Module for Windows PowerShell**. With the module open, run the following cmdlet on the source DC:

```
Get-ADDCCloningExcludedApplicationList
```

The preceding command will list all the applications that cannot be cloned. You can check with the software vendor if there is any way for the application to pass the test, or you can choose to remove the application and run the cmdlet again. Once there are no applications listed, you can run the following cmdlet:

```
Get-ADDCCloningExcludedApplicationList -GenerateXml
```

## Running the New-ADDCCloneConfigFile cmdlet

Now that the applications have been tested, you can generate the XML file that will state the configuration for the cloned Domain Controller. On the cmdlet to be used, you can specify the configuration of the cloned DC. Use the following cmdlet:

```
New-ADDCCloneConfigFile -Static -IPv4Address "192.168.100.36" -
IPv4DNSResolver "192.168.100.10" -IPv4SubnetMask "255.255.255.0" -
CloneComputerName "SRV-DC03" -IPv4DefaultGateway "192.168.100.1" -
SiteName "Default-First-Site-Name"
```

The preceding command will create a configuration file on the default location C:\Windows\NTDS\DCCloneConfig.xml with all the configuration indicated in the command: IP address, DNS server, gateway, computer name, and site name.

> The process in this section shows you how to create the XML file for the destination DC. If you have to create multiple DCs, you will have to go through this process again for each DC.

If the output is successful, you can proceed to the export/import process.

# Creating the virtual DC clones using the export/import process

To initiate the process, make sure that the source DC is powered off and that there are no Checkpoints on the VM. On **Hyper-V Manager**, right-click the VM and click **Export...**:

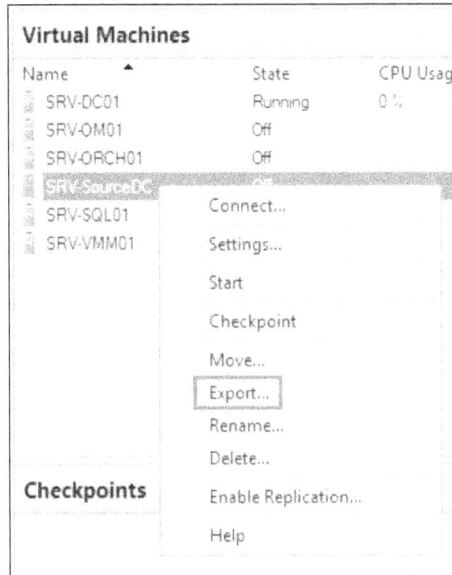

In the **Export Virtual Machine** dialog box, type a location to host the exported VM. You will need to copy the content of the folder to the other Hyper-V Host on which you want to host the new clone DC:

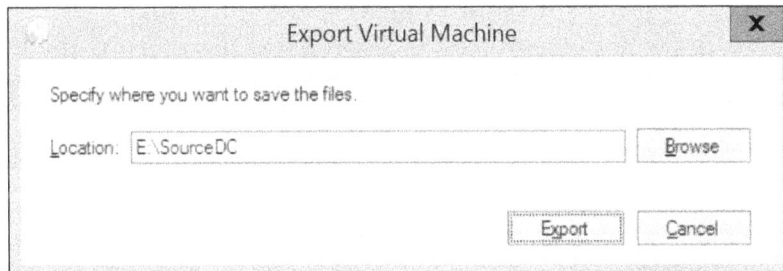

Click **Export** to start the Export process. After the Export process finishes, copy the folder to the Hyper-V Host that will host the new clone DC.

On the other Hyper-V Host, open **Hyper-V Manager** and click **Import Virtual Machine...** on the left-hand side of the screen. Click **Next >** on the wizard:

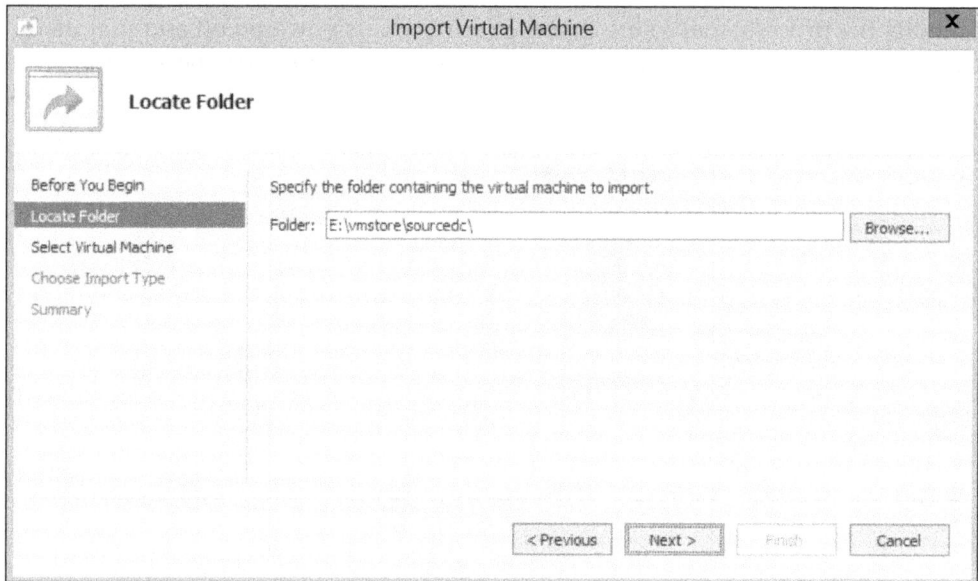

Type the location of the folder in which the VM resides and click **Next >**:

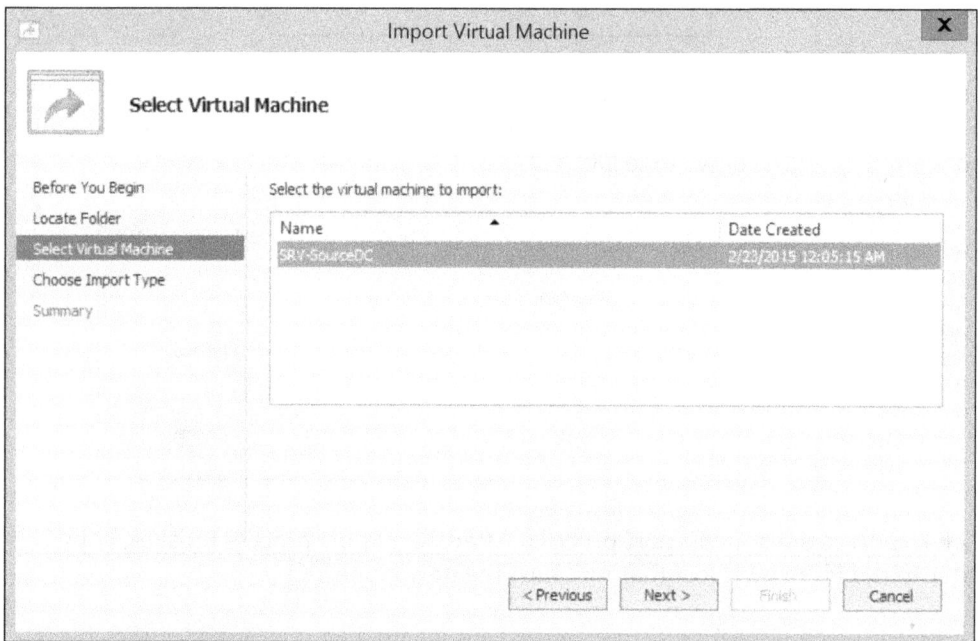

In the **Select Virtual Machine**, confirm that the VM name is displayed under **Name** and click **Next >**:

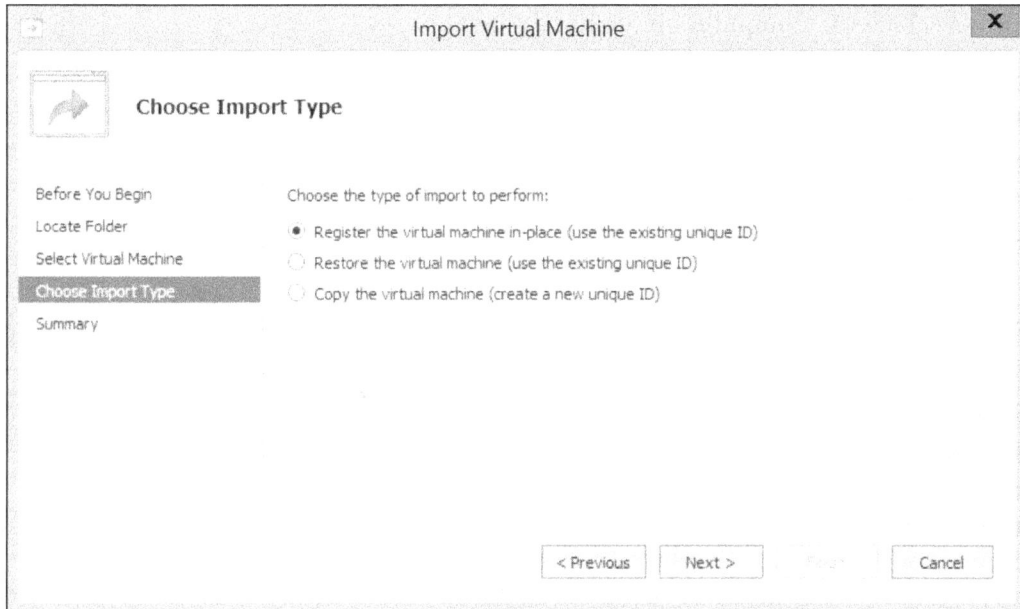

These options will be explained in *Chapter 11*, *Protecting Your Virtualization Environment*. For the moment, click **Next >** and **Finish** to finalize the import process. After the import process finishes, you can start the new clone VM. Make sure the source VM is also powered on before starting the new clone VM, and also that the PDC FSMO DC is on.

After initializing the new clone VM, you will see the cloning process:

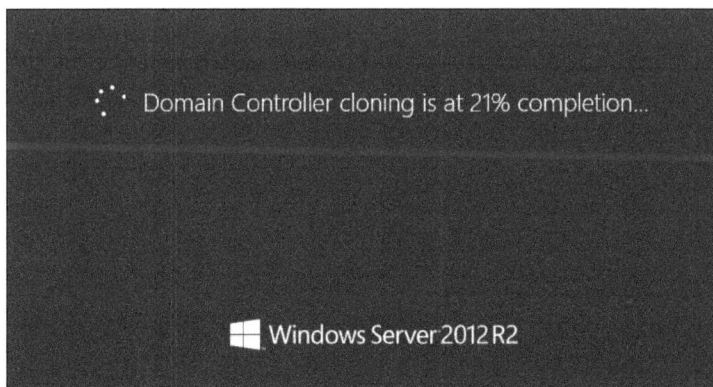

After the process is completed, the VM will initiate with the information configured on the XML file generated in the previous step. You can confirm that the process succeeded by accessing **Active Directory Users and Computers** and confirming that the new clone DC **Computer** object was created.

# Virtual DCs and Hyper-V Replica

In the *Chapter 8, Implementing Live Migration and Replica*, you learned about the Hyper-V Replica feature. Now that you know the feature, and since we are talking about Active Directory, it is time to ask, "Does it make sense to have a replicated virtual DC?"

In fact, many administrators, on the pretext of protecting such an important VM as a Domain Controller, replicate the virtual DC to another Datacenter/site. Although this can be used if you lose the primary VM, it is not so effective. This is because the Replica process, as you already learned, is an asynchronous replication. As an asynchronous replication, this process will have the same issues as the Checkpoint as explained earlier in this chapter. In fact, if you replicate a VM, the `GenerationID` attribute will be used just like the Checkpoint process, to allow the virtual DC to receive USN updates and replication from the other DCs. Keep in mind that only Hyper-V on Windows Server 2012 and a virtual DC running Windows Server 2012 support the `GenerationID` attribute.

Only Windows Server 2012 virtual DCs are supported in a Hyper-V Replica scenario. Earlier versions of Windows Server running on the virtual DC will not be able to replicate the changes since the last information and will cause replication errors on the environment.

On an Active Directory environment, there is a much simpler way to prevent a failure on a DC and recover it on another site—just add another DC, virtual or not, on the other site.

For a complete list of supported and unsupported scenarios, read the official article at `https://technet.microsoft.com/en-us/library/dn250021.aspx`.

# Summary

In this chapter, you learned how to manage an Active Directory virtual DC with Hyper-V. You learned the concepts behind having a virtual DC. You also learned that the database of a virtual DC must be placed on a SCSI virtual disk for better performance and data loss prevention. Further, you've seen how Time synchronization impacts on the virtual DC and the whole Active Directory environment. Also, you learned how a Checkpoint can impact the entire replication process on a virtual DC and that Windows Server 2012 with Hyper-V offers a mechanism to avoid this issue.

Moving on, you've seen that the Cluster service and virtual DCs can coexist, and that you can have an Active Directory-detached Cluster service on Windows Server 2012. Further, you learned how to clone a virtual DC and how it makes the DC deployment process easier for the administrator. To finish the chapter, you learned how Hyper-V Replica and Active Directory work and that, in many cases, it makes no sense to replicate a virtual DC.

All of the information that we discussed is part of a more detailed article that is available at `https://technet.microsoft.com/en-us/library/jj574191.aspx`. In the next chapter, we will cover the basics of a Virtual Desktop Infrastructure.

# 10

# Implementing a Virtual Desktop Infrastructure

So far, you have learned a lot about Hyper-V. You learned about its configuration, settings, tips and tricks, and how to manage Hyper-V VMs. In the previous chapter, we started to understand how a virtual environment can impact an application, in that case Active Directory. In this chapter, we will see how the virtual environment can actually change even the approach to the clients.

In the early days, from the client machine's perspective, performance was a problem in running client applications. When client hardware started to evolve, technologies such as mainframe no longer made sense. Over time, many architectures changed the balance for client machines: server/client, web services, and so on.

If you think about it, the point has always been: "Where is the processing going to happen, the datacenter or the client machine?" If the client machine is able to perform the necessary process in a viable time, then there is probably no reason to transfer this overhead to the datacenter. However, datacenter hardware has evolved as well, as you know. Add to this the fact that you can provide extremely low-cost hardware to the client (such as a thin client, which is a very small form factor with a relatively low performance hardware) that confers tremendous benefits in many scenarios, as thin clients are easy to set up and replace. There are many more benefits.

One of the caveats of having a thin clients is that, although you can actually provide the necessary application to the client, because this application resides on a server that is on the datacenter and will be accessible from Remote Desktop, for example, you can't provide a full, rich experience for this client. A thin client usually runs an embedded version of Windows or a light version of a Linux OS. This OS has a Remote Desktop client that can access the applications that the client will need. The OS will not, or should not, be presented to the client, since the OS on which the application is running is a Windows Server OS running the application and presenting it through **Remote Desktop Protocol** (**RDP**). Of course, thin client scenarios are not the only ones that can benefit from it, but they are probably the ones who get the most benefit.

Using thin client, and the introduction of virtualization to the datacenter, has enabled a new scenario: the **Virtual Desktop Infrastructure** (**VDI**).

In this chapter, we will cover:

- VDI overview and comparison
- Getting started with Microsoft VDI
- Pooled and dedicated VMs
- User Profile Disks
- RemoteFX

# VDI overview and comparison

The VDI environment on a Microsoft deployment is dependent on another well-known technology: **Remote Desktop Services** (**RDS**), formerly known as **Terminal Services** (**TS**). The reason for this dependence is that Microsoft decided to use the RDP protocol to present the VM to the client machine, since that is a well established technology. Additionally, on Windows Server 2012 both VDI and RDS evolved to provide a better user experience to the client.

On Windows Server 2008 R2, Microsoft introduced a number of new features for RDS, such as Web Access, Connection Broker, virtualization host, and others. It is not in the scope of this book to go into these new features in any depth. However, as some of these features will influence the VDI environment, here is a quick reference on the new features for RDS that work together with VDI:

- **Remote Desktop Web Access**: This feature will create a web page that displays the applications or VMs that the user can access. Web Access can also be used to publish the applications on a Session Host to the Start menu.

- **Connection Broker**: The server running this feature is responsible for ensuring that the user will always connect to the server on which a connection was established before. This ensures that if a user has an application or VM running in a server and needs to reconnect to the application or VM, it will reconnect to the same server.

- **Virtualization host**: This feature must be installed on the Hyper-V Host, and will allow the RDS system to manage the VMs and the access to these resources.

In a VDI scenario, these features will work together to provide access to the VMs from the client machines. Here is a high-level architecture of a VDI scenario with Hyper-V and RDS:

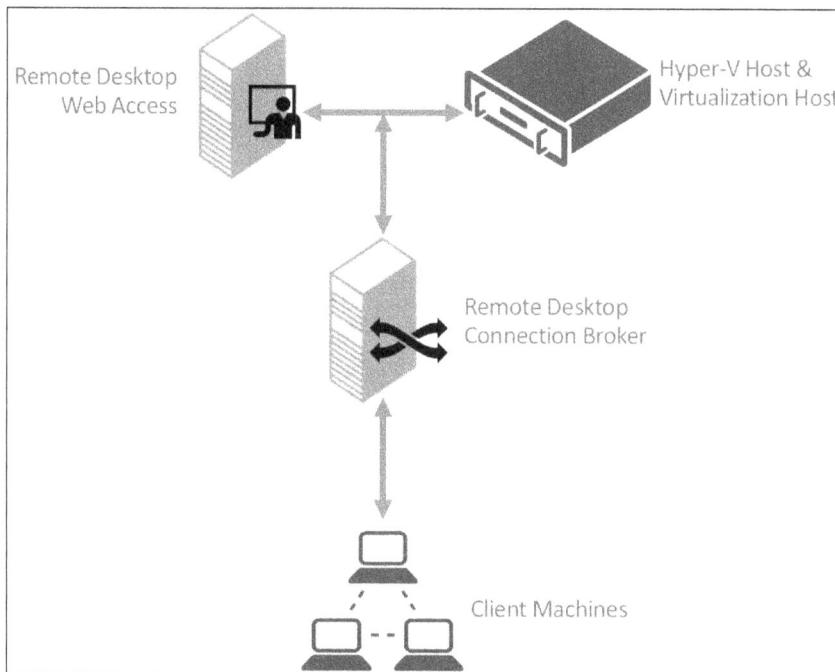

The preceding figure represents the most basic architecture of a VDI environment with Hyper-V and RDS. Note that all of the roles can be implemented with load balance and failover. Another important aspect is that, for a small scenario or a testing environment, you can combine all the roles on a single host.

This architecture is almost the same as a Session-based environment. The difference is that, on the Session Host environment, you will have a Session Host instead of a virtualization host.

The major question—which choice is the best for your environment?—can be answered by the following comparative table:

| | Session Based | VDI |
|---|---|---|
| Technology | RDS | RDS + Hyper-V |
| Scalability | High number of users per server | Low number of users per server |
| Isolation | • Session-based isolation<br>• OS is shared by the users<br>• Users runs with standard privileges | • Hypervisor isolation<br>• Each user will have its OS environment<br>• User can have administrative privileges |
| Protocol | **Remote Desktop Protocol (RDP)** | **Remote Desktop Protocol (RDP)** |
| User experience | User runs on a Windows Server environment | User runs on a Windows Client environment |
| Application compatibility | Windows Server compatibility | Windows Client compatibility |

As you can see, the foundation technology for a Session Host and VDI is the same. However, the objectives are completely different. A Session-based environment focuses on the application experience and the client user usually has full Windows client experience on their own machines. A VDI environment, on the other hand, will provide the full Windows client experience on the VM so the user can have, even with a thin client, the experience of a complete desktop.

# VDI characteristics

Don't imagine that a VDI environment can be the solution for all cases; there are some on which it is recommended, and others for which it isn't.

A VDI environment has the following characteristics:

- Deploys Windows Client OS in VMs on secure and centralized server hardware. This improves business continuity, data security, and desktop lifecycle management.
- Enables users to access and run desktop and applications wherever the user is located. This will provide desktop location independence and improves business productivity.
- IT can focus on a user-centric approach, as opposed to the regular infrastructure focus, improving user productivity.

Additionally, a VDI environment has the following benefits:

- Consistency on OS image delivery and a consistent user experience
- Processing is executed on the datacenter instead of the user machine
- Better hardware provisioning and management on the client side
- Better troubleshooting of application compatibility

However, there are some cases where VDI is not the best solution:

- Client machines have the necessary hardware for executing the applications.
- Client applications require specific hardware support, such as GPU for graphical applications. Although this requirement can be suppressed with RemoteFX, not all servers have this resource available.
- If most of your support tickets are not related to client hardware, a VDI environment will not help you lower the number of tickets on support.

# Getting started with Microsoft VDI

In order to better understand how the VDI environment works with Hyper-V and RDS, let's get started on the deployment process. In this example, we will use a single machine to host all the roles for RDS and Hyper-V. It is important to remember that this is only recommended on small or test environments.

To start, open **Server Manager** and, on the top left, click on **Manage**. Click on **Add Roles and Features**. Click on **Next >** on the wizard. You'll be prompted to install regular Windows Server Roles and Features or an RDS:

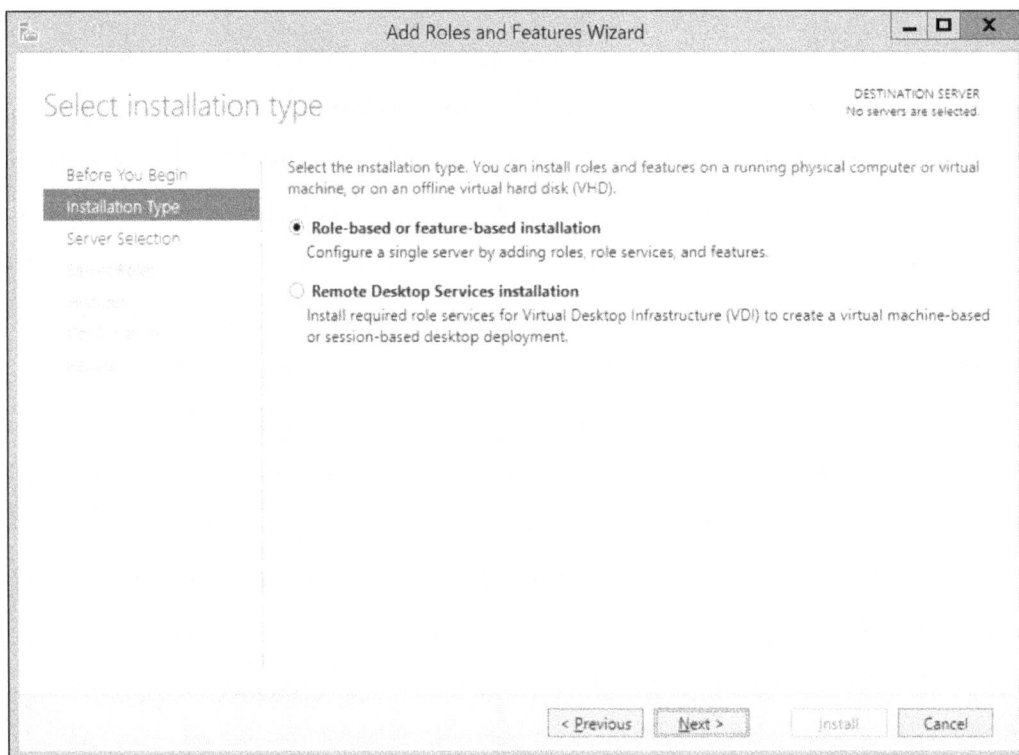

Select **Remote Desktop Services installation** and click on **Next >**:

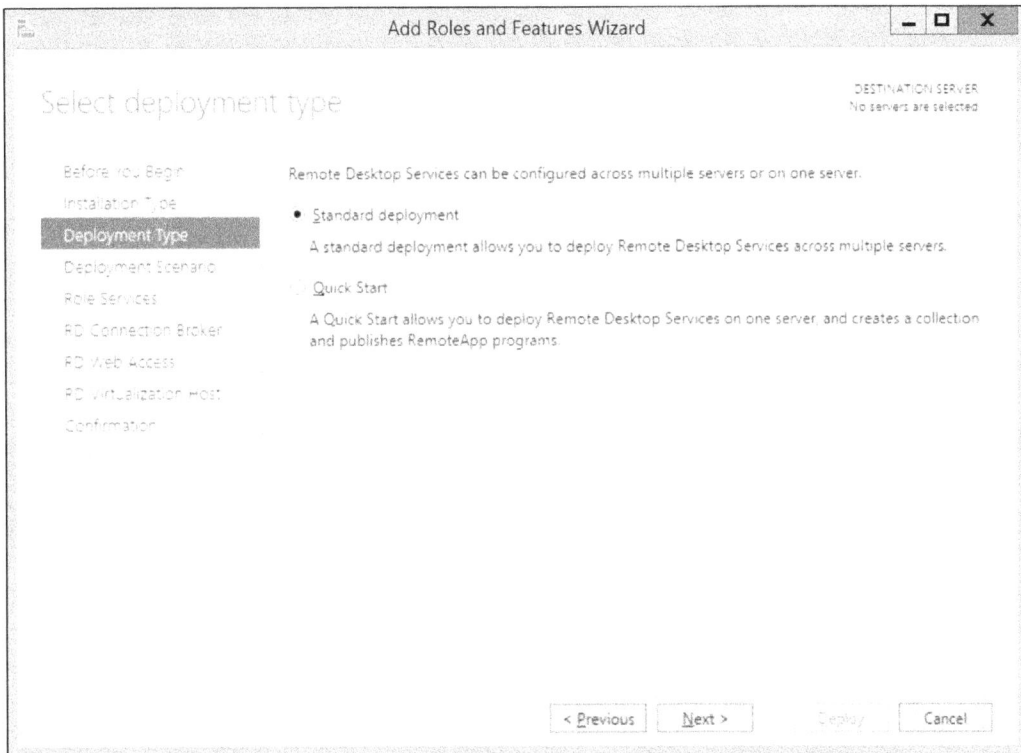

Now, you have to choose between **Standard deployment** and **Quick Start**. Let's explore the differences between these options:

- **Standard deployment**: This option will allow you to choose more options during the wizard. In this option, you can choose different servers for the Web Access, Connection Broker, and virtualization host roles. Also, you can choose to create (or not) a new Virtual Switch on the virtualization host.

- **Quick Start**: This option is recommended for small and test environments. In this option, you will indicate a server on which all the RDS roles will be installed. Also, you will have to indicate a virtual desktop template to be used as your first collection. After the Quick Start deployment finishes, you will be ready to start using the VDI environment, but with a simple environment. It is important to state, however, that you can change the settings after the wizard finishes.

In our case, we will select **Standard deployment** and click on **Next >**:

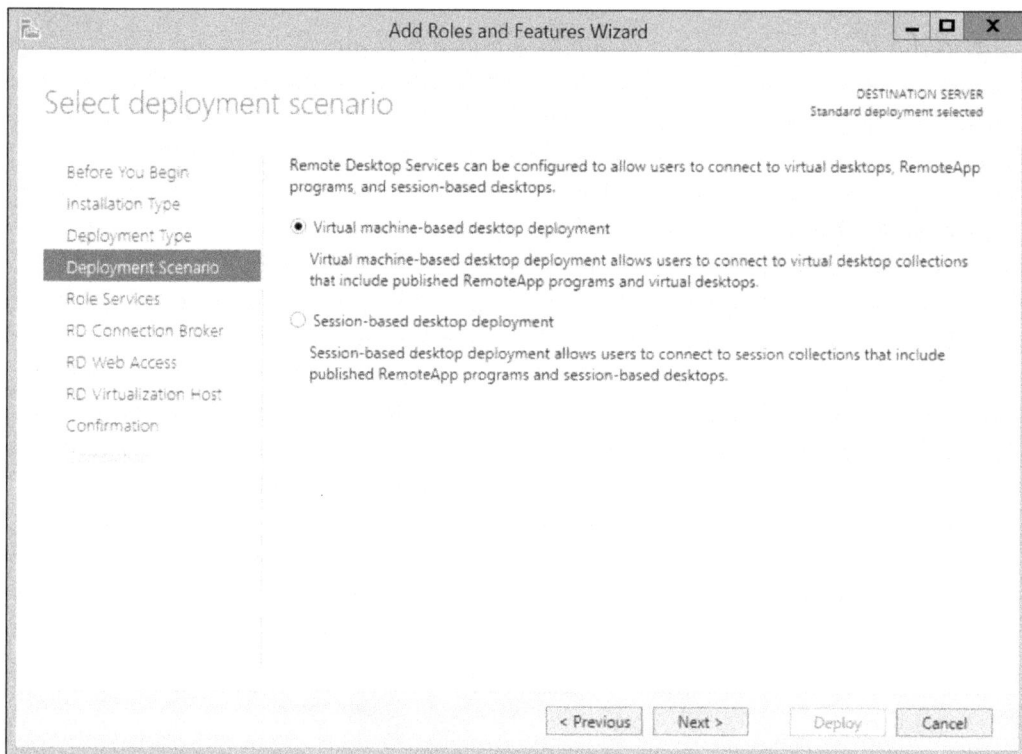

Now you have to select whether you are installing a **Virtual machine-based desktop deployment**, which is the VDI environment, or a **Session-based desktop deployment**. Select **Virtual machine-based desktop deployment** and click on **Next >**:

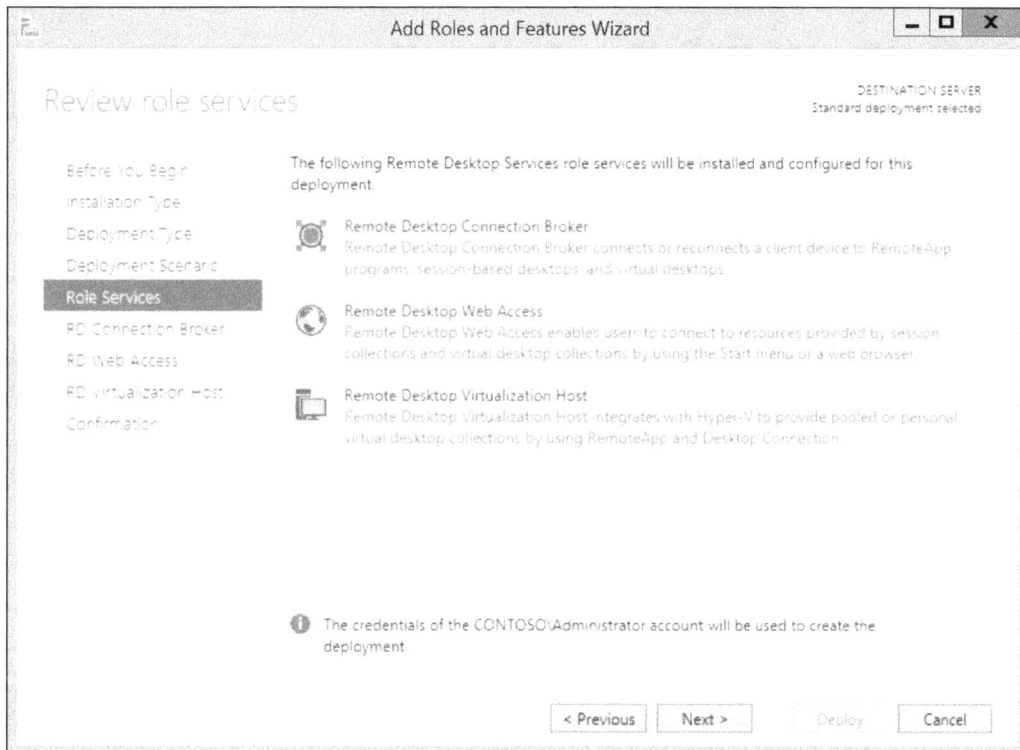

Here, you are presented with the RDS roles that will be installed via this wizard. Click on **Next >**:

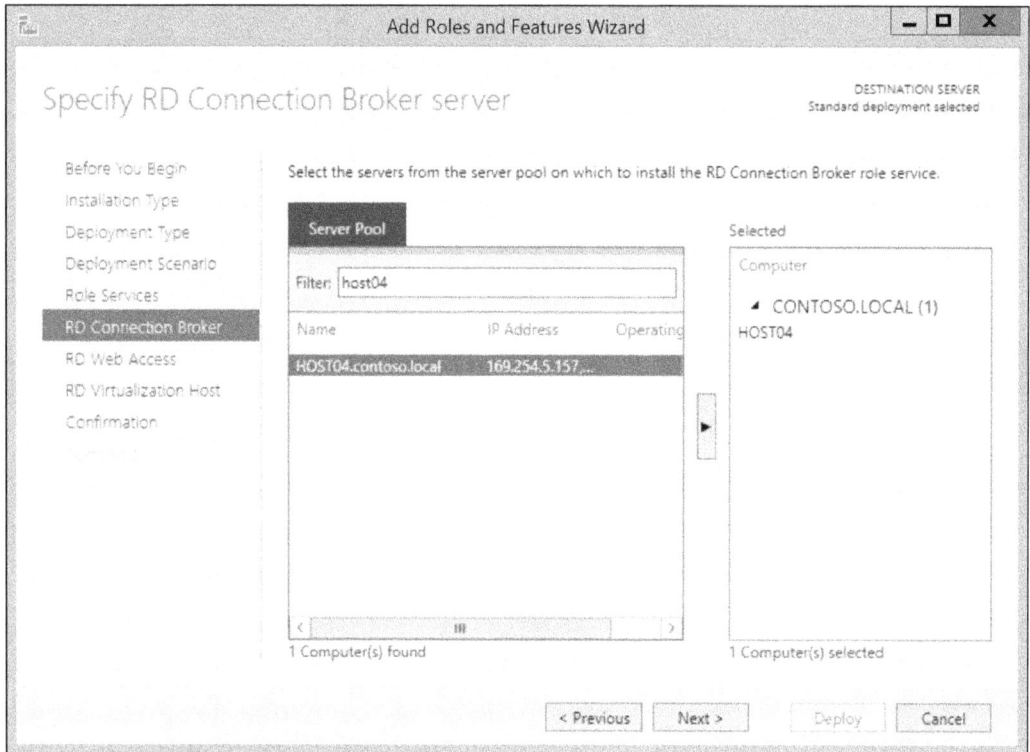

The first server role is **RD Connection Broker**. Select the server you want to install this role on and click on **Next >**:

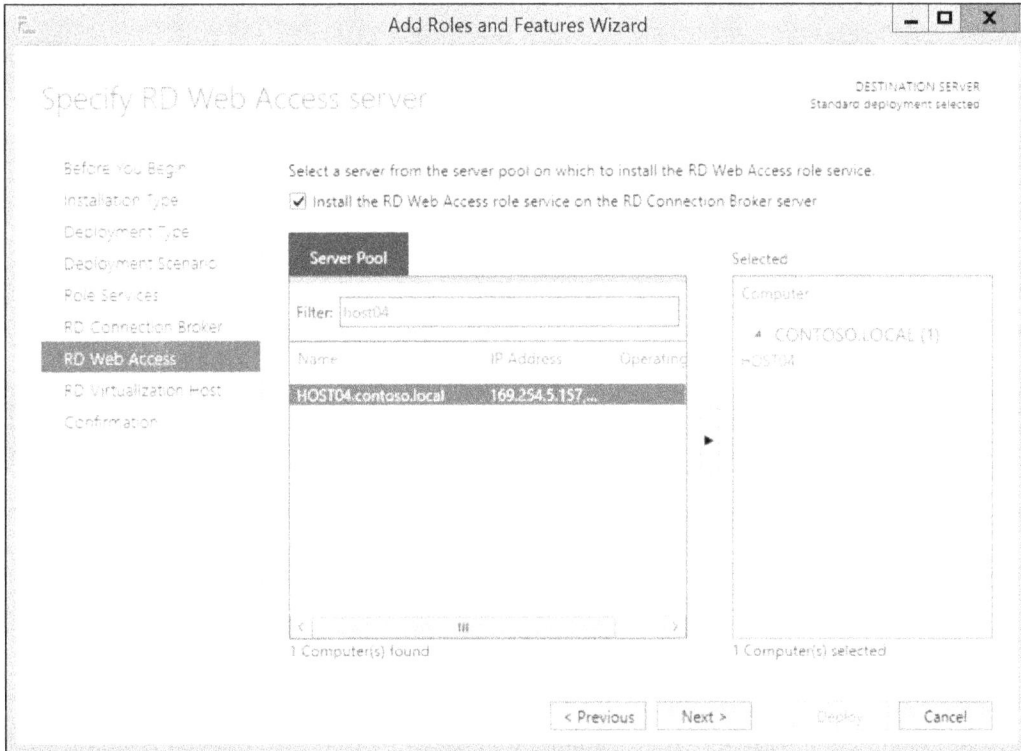

Now, you can select the **RD Web Access** role. If you are installing the role on the same server, you check the **Install the RD Web Access role service on the RD Connection Broker server** checkbox. After indicating the server, click on **Next >**:

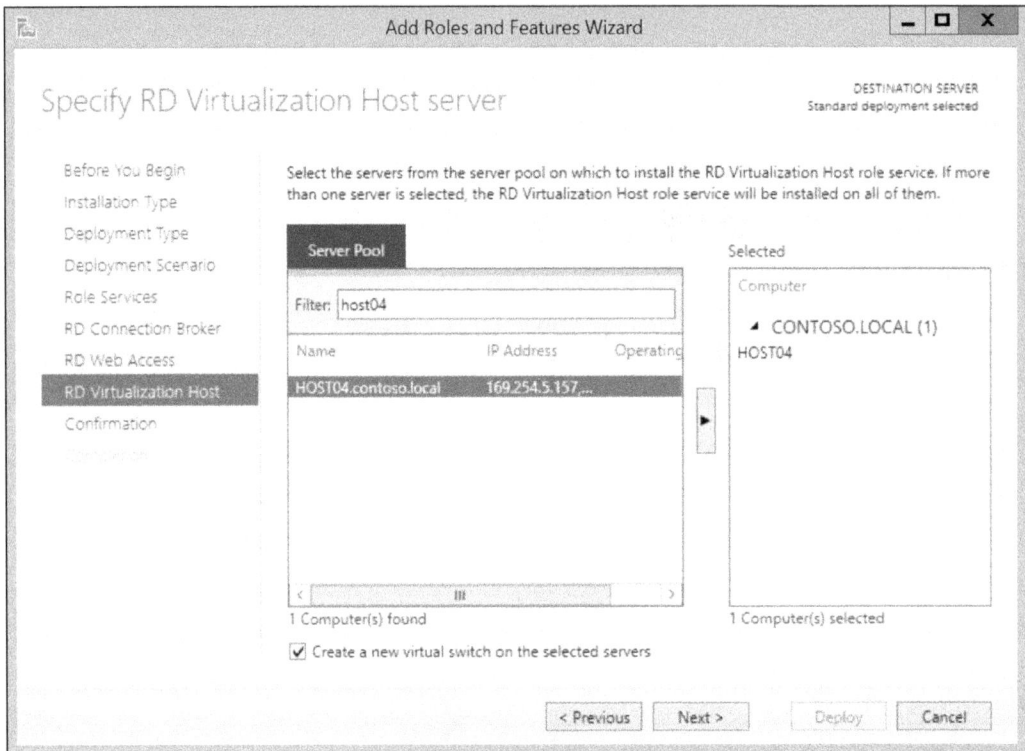

Now, you will specify the Hyper-V server on which you want to install the
**RD Virtualization Host** Server role. Note that you can check the **Create a new
virtual switch on the selected servers** checkbox. If you're not sure about the host
networking and you want to create the Virtual Switch later, just leave the checkbox
clear. After selecting the Hyper-V Host, click on **Next >**:

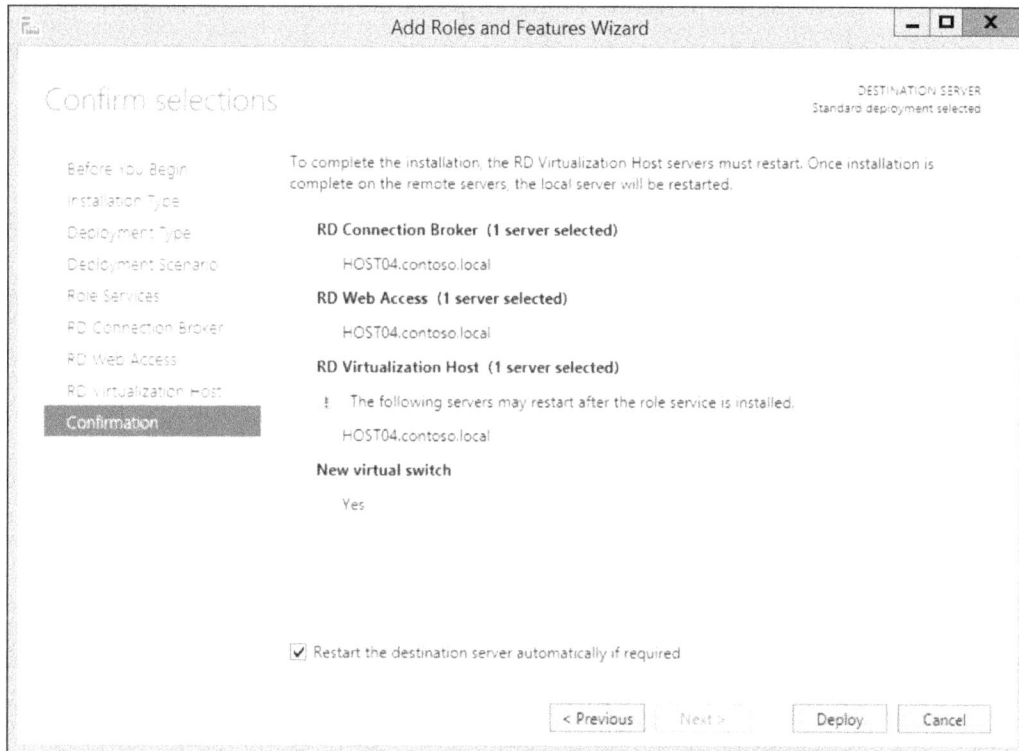

Review the information on the **Confirm selections** page. Note that the **RD Virtualization Host** will have to restart during the role service installation. Check the **Restart the destination server automatically if required** checkbox and click on **Deploy**:

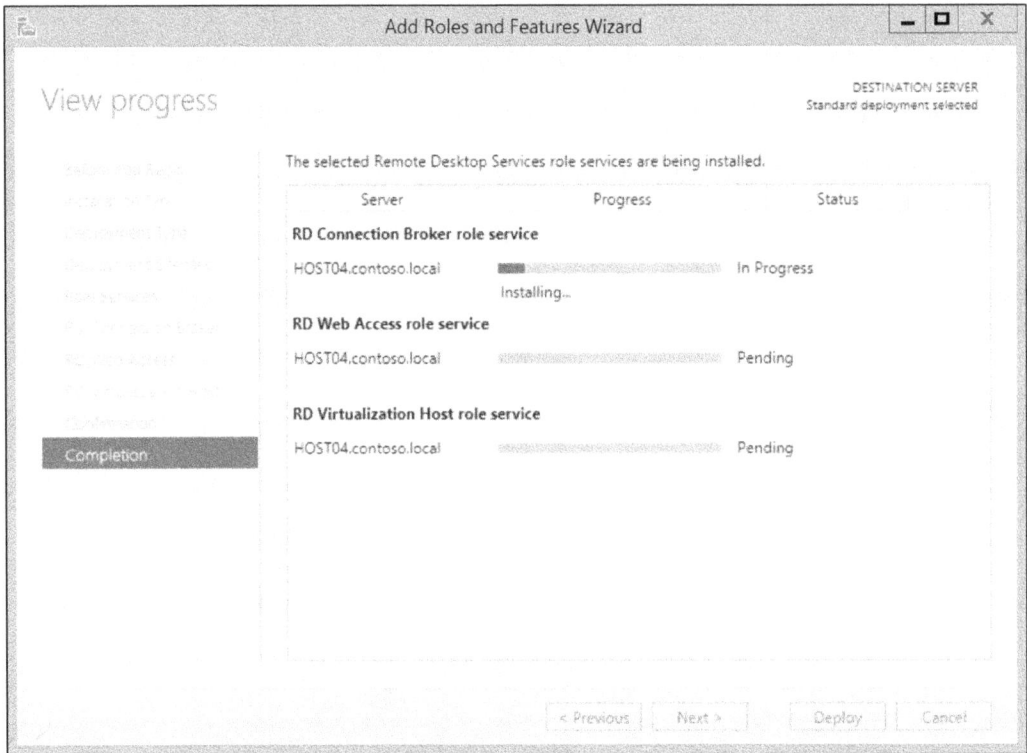

You can follow the installation progress on the wizard. Note that during the RD Virtualization Host installation, the host will be restarted.

When the process finishes, you will see the following screen:

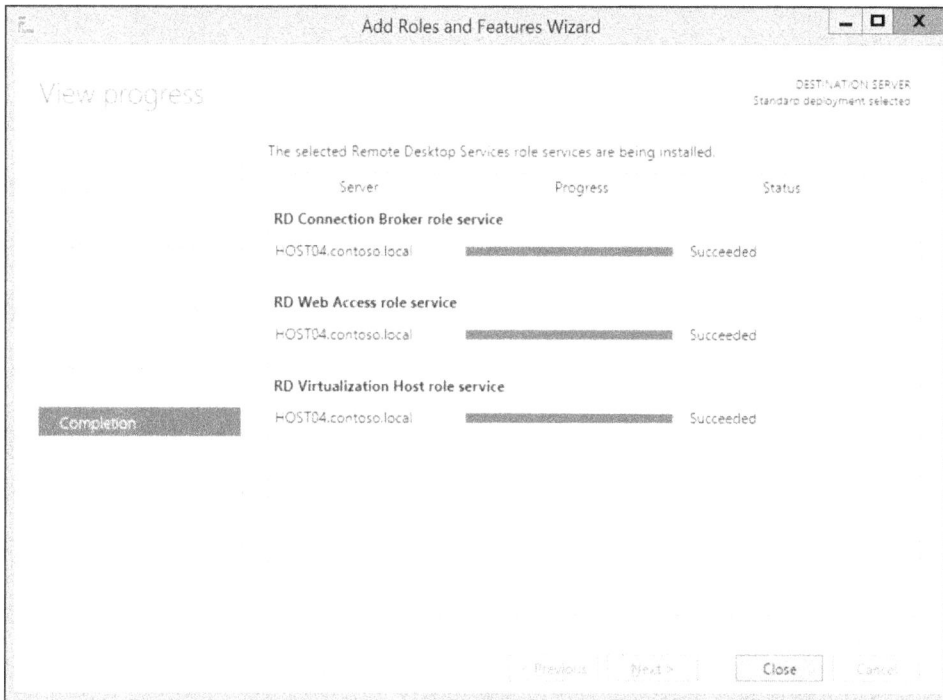

Click on **Close** to finish the wizard. On the **Server Manager**, you will see the following:

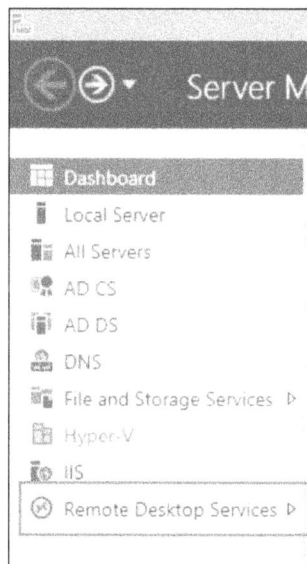

To perform the same installation using PowerShell, use the following cmdlet:

```
New-RDVirtualDesktopDeployment -ConnectionBroker Host04 -
WebAccessServer Host04 -VirtualizationHost Host04 -
CreateVirtualSwitch
```

The preceding command will install all the role services on `Host04` and will create the Virtual Switch on Hyper-V.

There are additional RDS configurations on Server Manager that you should go through before creating VM collections. The administrator should configure a Licensing Server, a certificate for the Web Access and other items. Since these tasks are RDS-related, they will not be covered in this book. You can find out more information from the official article about RDS at `https://technet.microsoft.com/en-us/library/hh831447.aspx`.

Now that the installation has finished, you can start by creating the first collection, but before doing so, there is a concept you need to understand.

# Pooled and Personal VMs

An important aspect of VDI is to understand which clients are going to use the VMs you publish through RDS. Different clients require different VMs. Because of that, there are two options in publishing VMs: Pooled and Personal.

Pooled VMs are VMs for users that need to access a certain application but will not need to use the OS itself and/or save files on the VM. A Pooled VM is usually used on kiosk machines, or where the user needs to use an application that runs on a Windows Client OS, so session-based is not an option. A Pooled VM works in a non-persistent fashion. That means that the VM will return to the original state after the user logs off the VM. The Pooled VM lifetime works like this:

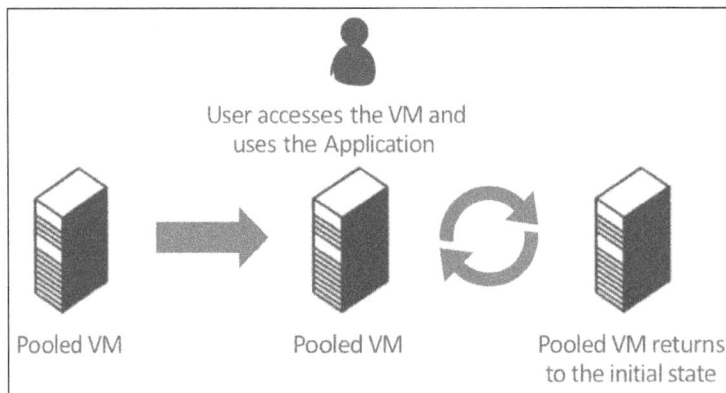

User accesses the VM and uses the Application

Pooled VM → Pooled VM ↻ Pooled VM returns to the initial state

Note that, after the user logs off, the VM is recycled and is available for another user to use. It is important to calculate how many VMs will be available given the number of users. For example, if you will have ten users, you don't need ten VMs available, but you need to make sure that all concurrent users can access the VMs. In this case, if you have ten users and you predict that about three users will use the VMs at the same time, you can have three or four VMs on the collection.

Personal VMs, on the other hand, are the opposite of Pooled. Personal VMs are, as the name says, dedicated to a user. The given user is the only one allowed to use that VM. Additionally, the VM is in a persistent-mode, which means that the VM will remain the same way when the user logs off or if the VM is powered off.

# Creating a Pooled VM collection

Before we get started, it is important to point out that you will need a VM template. A VM template is a VM that runs the Windows Client and is the base image for all the VMs that will be created on the collection. This VM must be a Windows 7/8/8.1 VM that has the latest Integration Components installed and has been sysprepped. The idea is to install all the necessary applications on the VM that the users will be able to use. This VM must be located on the Hyper-V Host/RD Virtualization Host in the `C:\RDVirtualDesktopTemplate` folder. Additionally, the VM network must be connected to the Virtual Switch created by the RDS deployment process and it must have at least 1 GB of virtual RAM.

A collection is a set of VMs that represents the Virtual Machines that the users will be able to connect to. These VMs, on a Pooled collection, will result in the same VM image.

To create a Pooled VM collection, open **Server Manager**, select **Remote Desktop Services** in the left-hand side menu. The following screen will be presented:

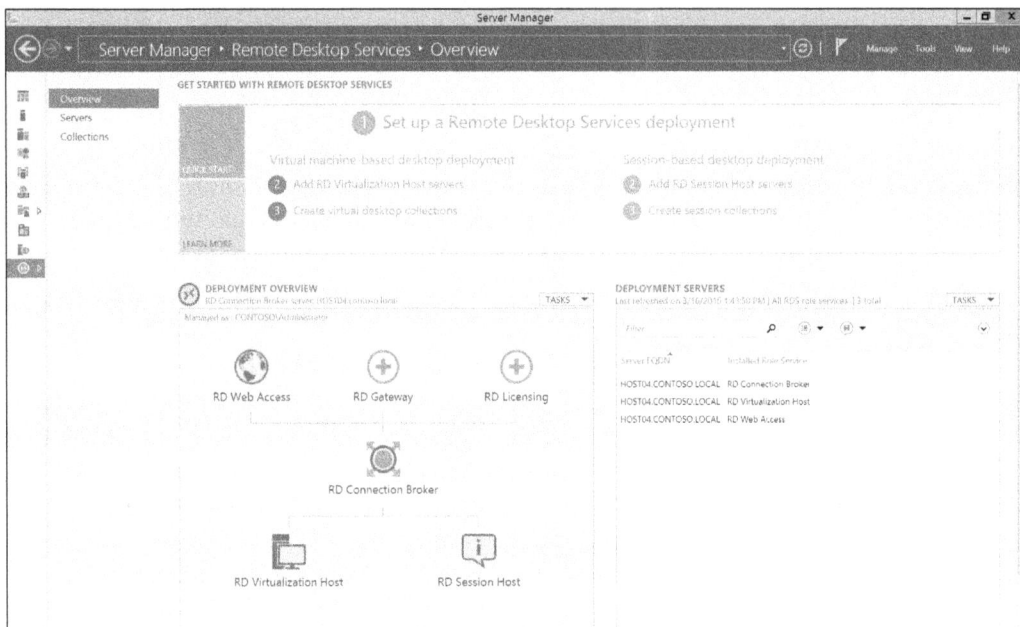

In this screen, you can edit the RDS Deployment, check the RDS Servers, and perform other RDS-related tasks. To create the Collection, click on **Collections** in the left-hand side menu.

On the **Collections** pane, click on **TASKS** and click on **Create Virtual Desktop Collection**.

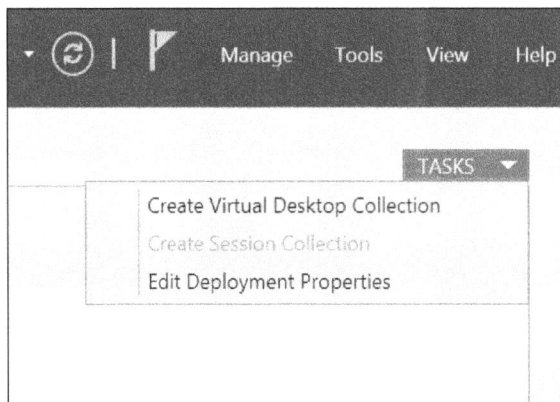

On the **Create Collection** wizard, click on **Next >**. Insert the **Collection Name** and click on **Next >**:

Now, you will have to select between Pooled and Personal virtual desktops. In this case, we will select Pooled virtual desktop collection. Make sure the **Automatically create and manage virtual desktops** checkbox is marked as you want to automate this process when the wizard finishes. If you do not check this checkbox, you will have to manually create the VMs and associate them manually:

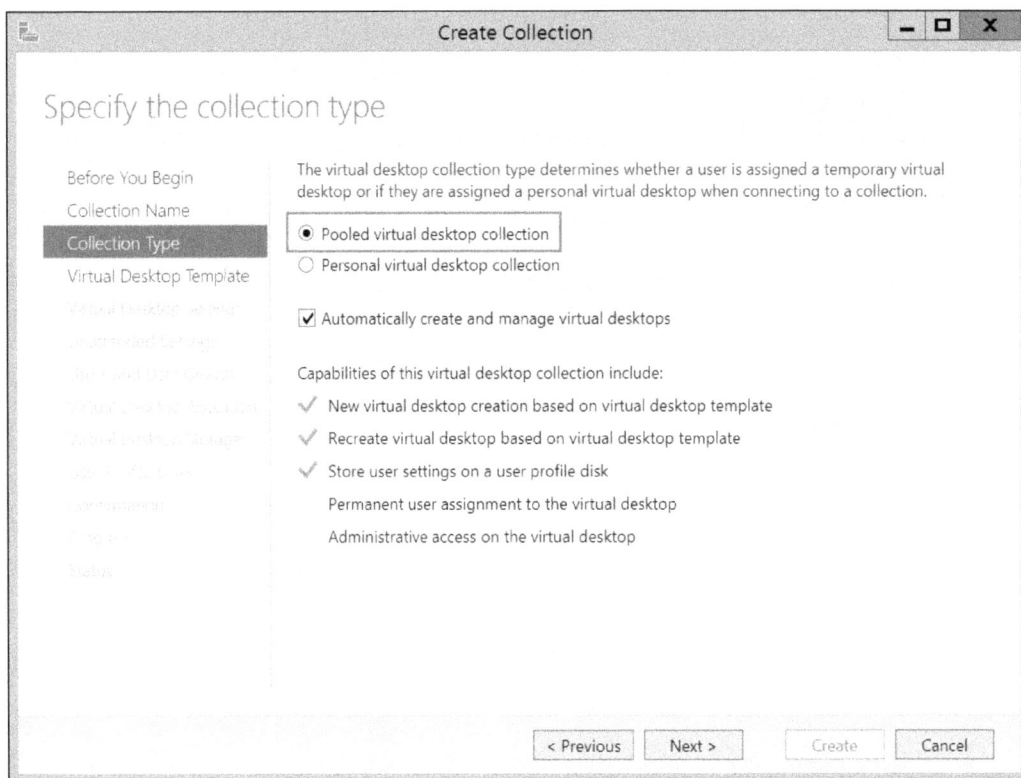

If you correctly created the VM as stated earlier on the `C:\RDVirtualDesktopTemplate` folder, the VM will be listed as shown in the following screenshot. If you have more than one VM template, select the appropriate one and click on **Next >**:

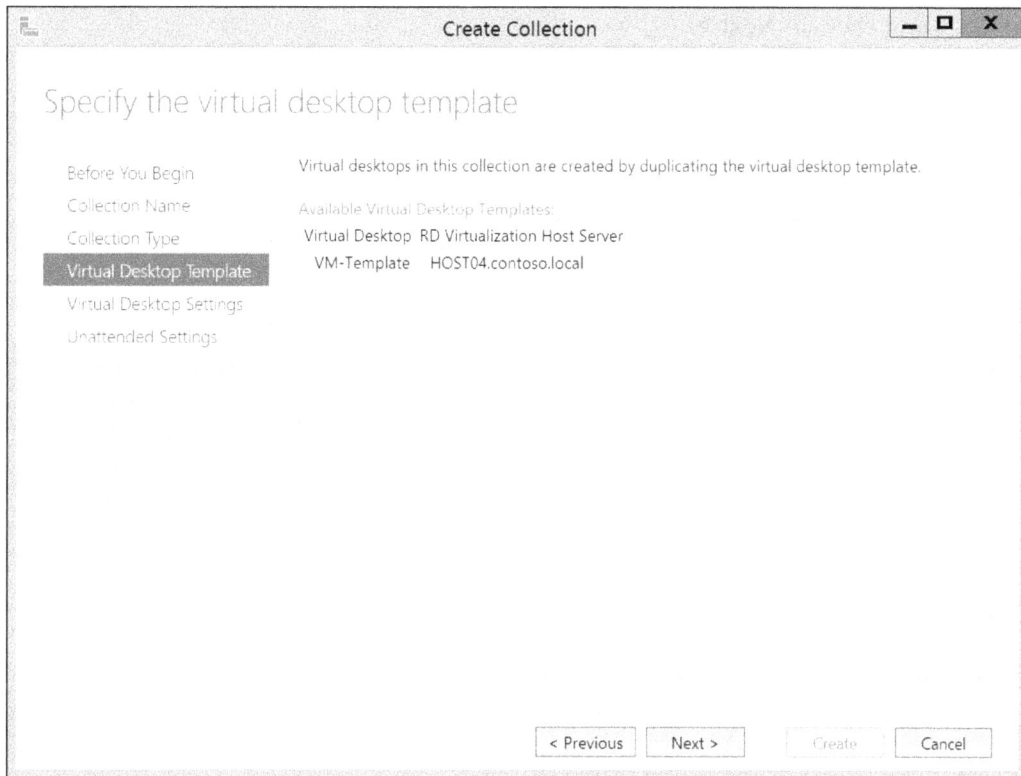

The wizard will have to run the Sysprep process on the VM template. There are two options for running it. You can specify the installation settings using the **Provide unattended installation settings** option or you can choose **Use an existing Sysprep answer file**. In this case, we will use the default **Provide unattended installation settings** and click on **Next >**:

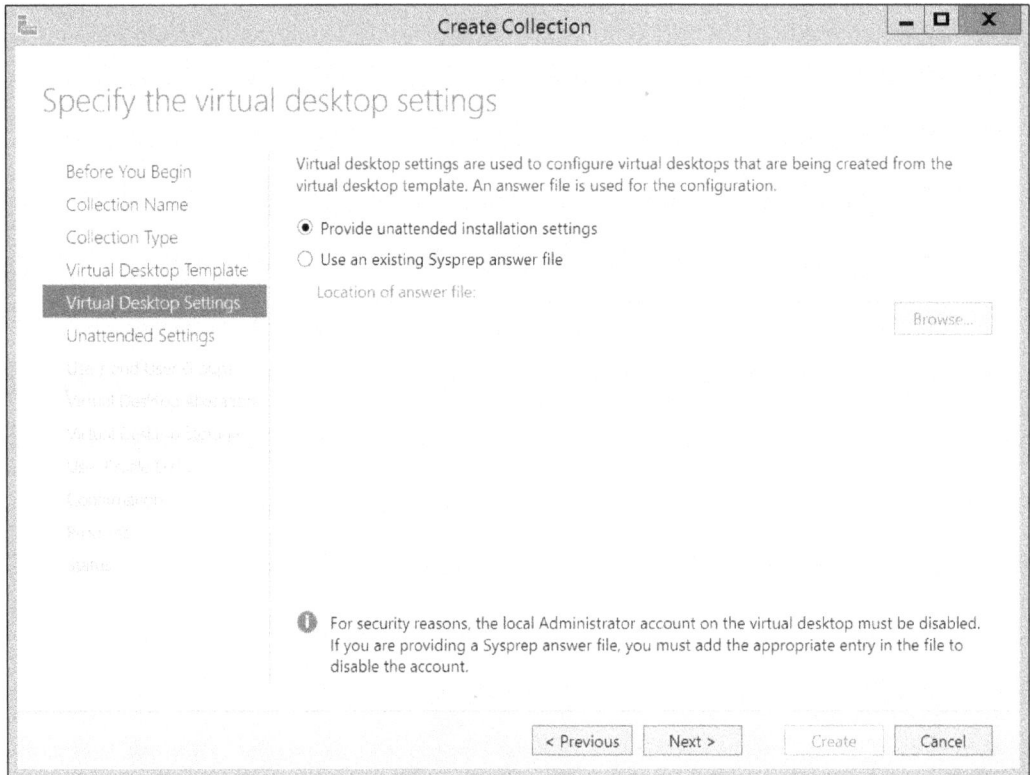

Next, you will have to specify the time zone for the guest OS and the **Organizational Unit (OU)** on which the computer objects for the VMs on the collection will be placed. It is important to place the Computer objects on a OU that has the correct **Group Policy Objects (GPO)** applied:

On the **Specify users and user groups** screen, you can specify which users or groups will have access to the VMs on this collection. By default, the **Domain Users** group is associated. It is highly recommended that you specify a group that has the required access. Additionally, you can specify how many VMs will be placed on the collection, as explained earlier, and a prefix and suffix for the VM names on the collection. After specifying the correct parameters, click on **Next >**:

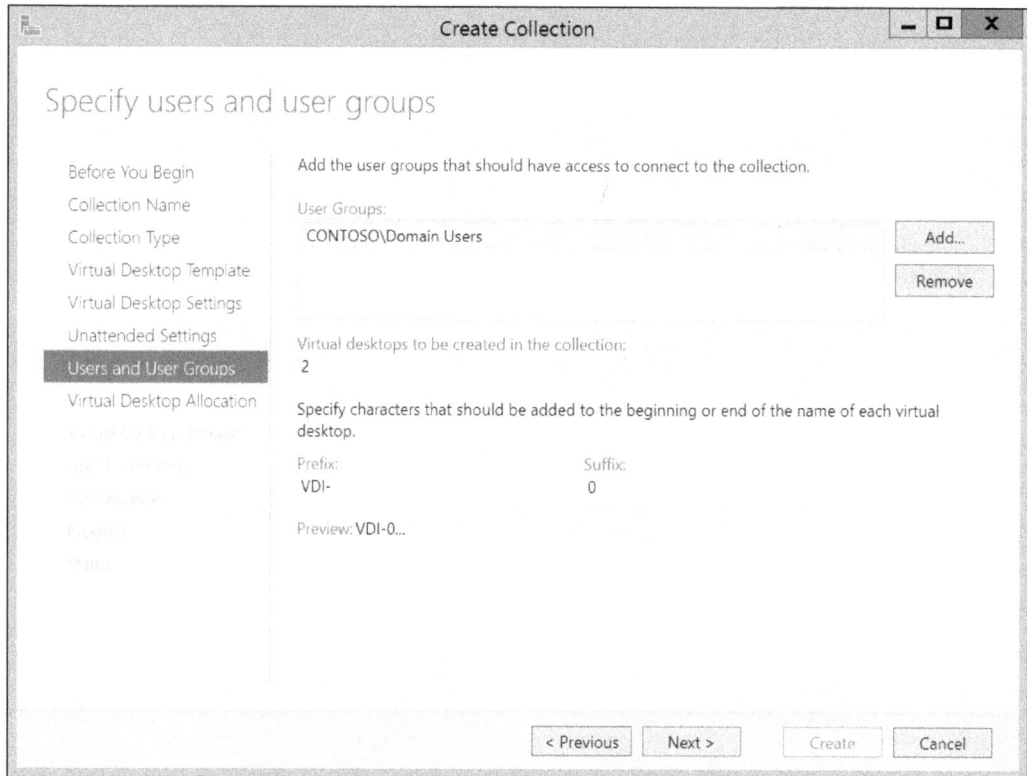

If you have more than one RD Virtualization Host, you can split the VMs on the collection across these hosts by changing the setting in the **New Virtual Desktop** column. Click on **Next >** after specifying the values:

Now you have to specify the storage location for the VM disks. It is important to specify a location that has the necessary free space as is reliable. After specifying the location, click on **Next >**:

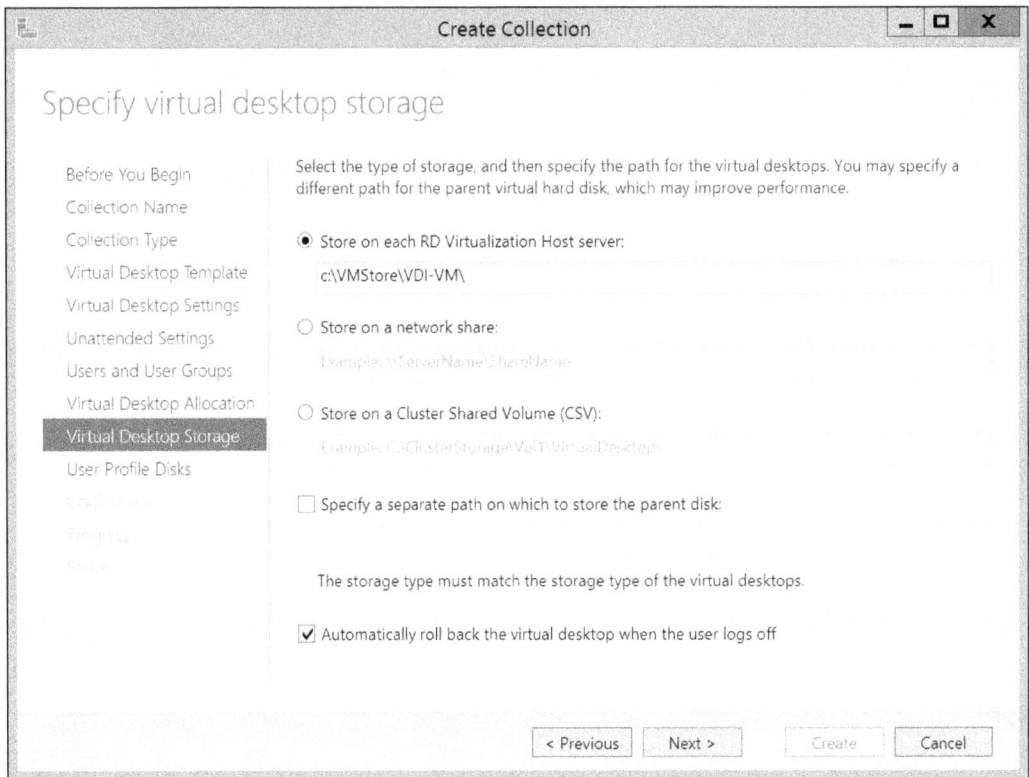

The **User Profile Disks** feature allows the user to store data on a separate disk. This feature will be explained later in this chapter. Click on **Next >**:

On the **Confirmation** page, review the information and click on **Create**. Wait for the process to finish. Review the completion page and click on **OK**. In **Server Manager**, select the new collection and you will see all the settings for it:

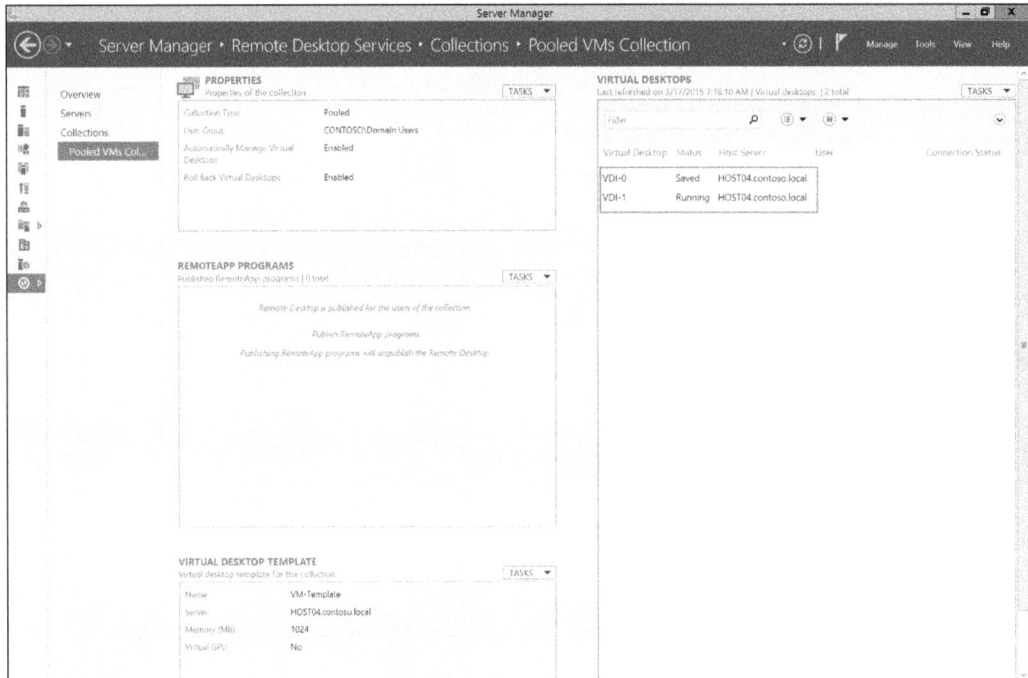

Note that, on the preceding screen, you can change the settings of the collection, see the status of the VMs on the collection, publish RemoteApp programs, and manage the virtual desktop template, which will be explained later in this chapter.

Now that the collection is running, you can open the RD Web Access website by opening the URL, `https://RDWebAccessServerFQDN/RDWeb`:

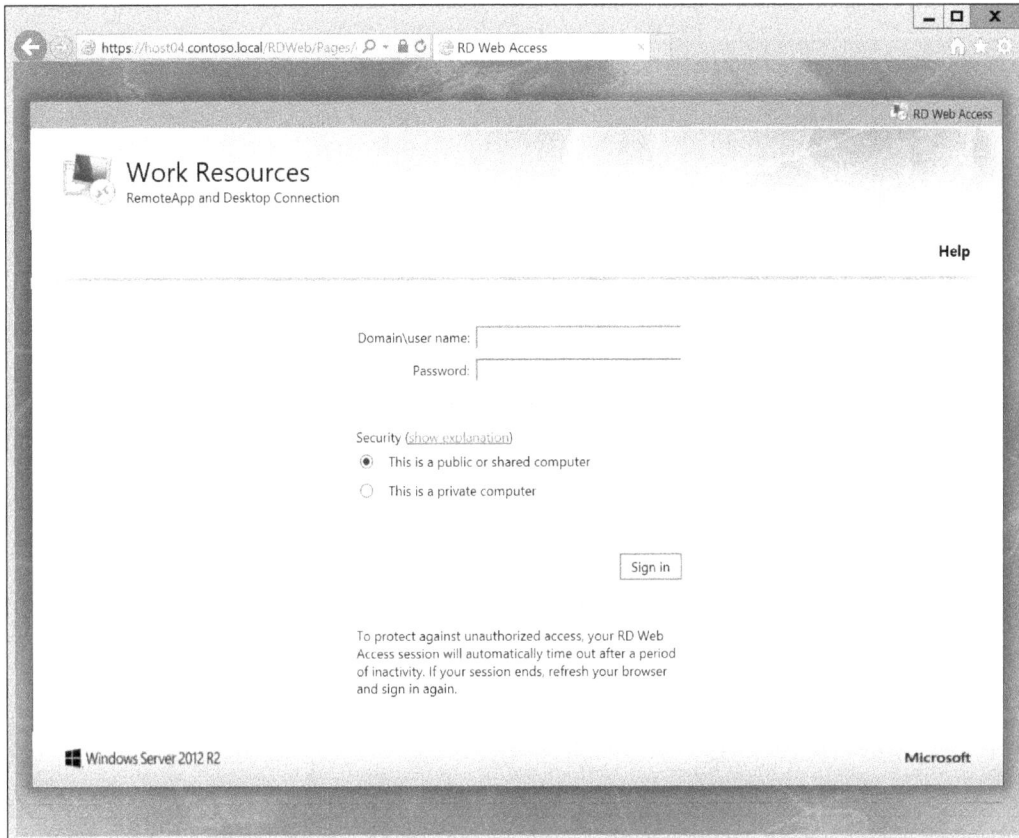

You will need to log on to the website using the appropriate credentials.

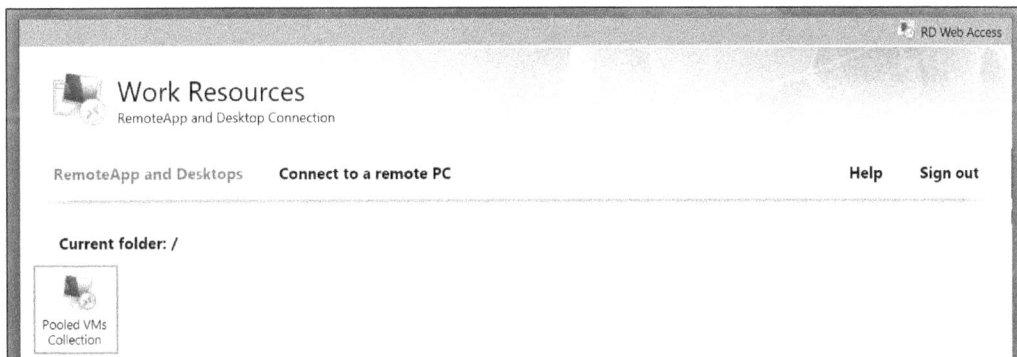

On the Web Access site, you will see the collection you created. Click on the collection and follow the regular Remote Desktop process to open the VM:

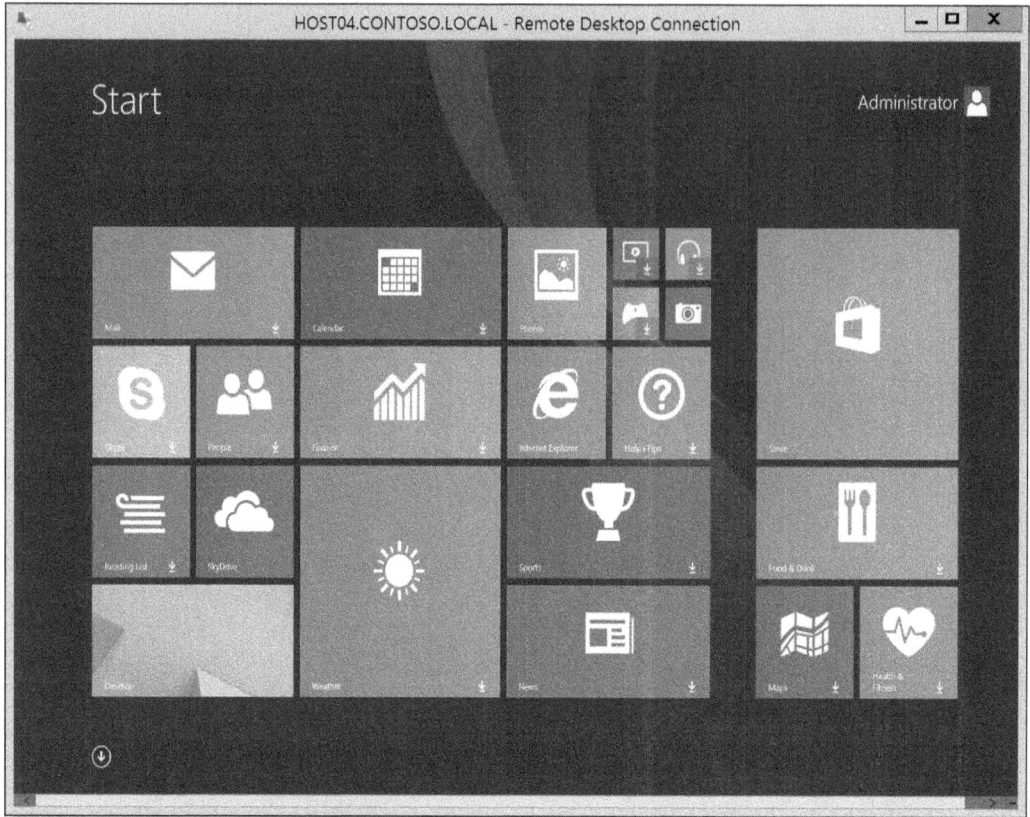

Now, the user is able to use the full desktop image and the applications installed on it. When the user logs off the VM, you can see the recycling process on Hyper-V Manager:

The restoring process will revert the VM to its original state, since this is a Pooled VM collection.

To create a Pooled VMs collection using PowerShell, use the following cmdlet:

```
New-RDVirtualDesktopCollection -CollectionName "Pooled VMs
Collection" -PooledManaged -VirtualDesktopTemplateName "VM-Template"
-VirtualDesktopTemplateHostServer "host04.contoso.local" -
VirtualDesktopAllocation @{"VDI-0.contoso.local"=1;"VDI-
1.contoso.local"=2} -StorageType LocalStorage -UserGroups
"contoso\domain users" -ConnectionBroker "host04.contoso.local" -
VirtualDesktopNamePrefix "VDI-0" -VirtualDesktopPasswordAge 31
```

The preceding command will create the exact collection as created on the GUI. The only difference between the command and the process on the GUI is that you can specify the password age. On the GUI, this will be done as a default configuration and, if you have a different security policy, you can use the cmdlet to configure it.

# Creating a Personal VM collection

During the process for creating the Pooled VM collection, you've seen that the process to create both collection types will start with the same wizard. The differences will start on the following screen:

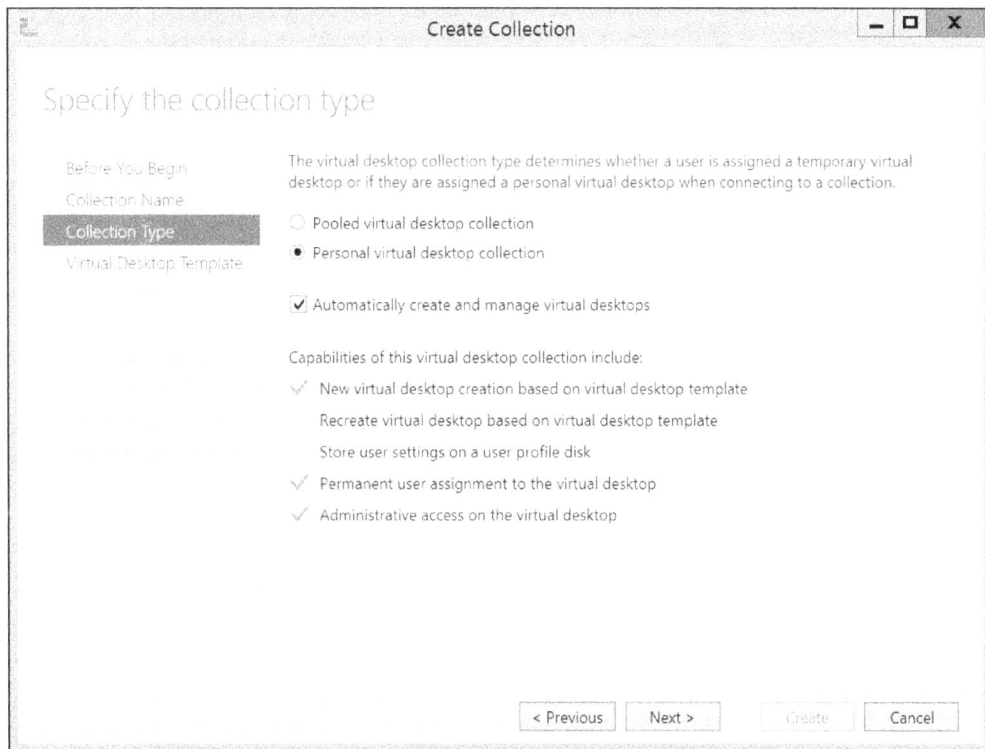

In the preceding screen, select **Personal virtual desktop collection** and click on **Next >**. Ensure that **Automatically create and manage virtual desktops** is checked.

In the following screenshot, you have the option to choose whether VMs will be created for users once they log on to the RD Web Access website and request access to a VM on the collection, or whether VMs will be manually created. If you want to automate the process, select **Enable automatic user assignment**. Keep in mind that, if you have a high number of users and this option is selected, you will see a large number of VMs on your environment and you will need to provide the necessary resources. If you want to prevent this situation, select **Disable automatic user assignment**. By selecting this option, you will have to manually create VMs for the user. Another important aspect of the following screen is that you can configure the user that will use the VM as a local administrator on the VM. This will allow the user to have full access on the guest OS:

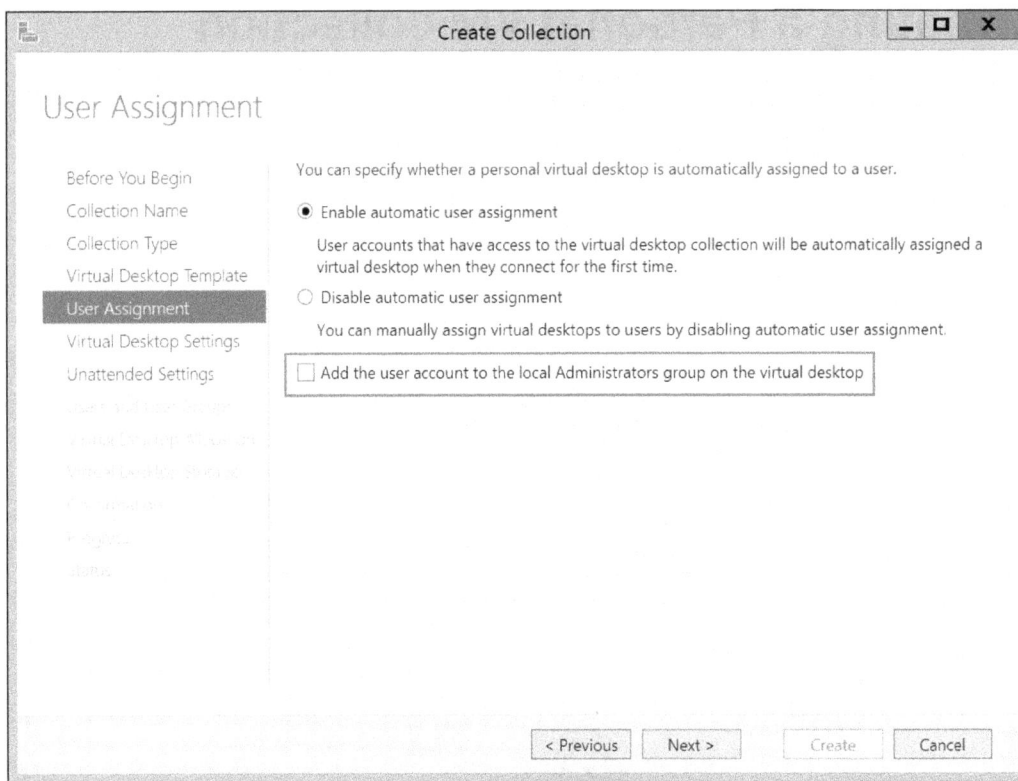

All other steps on this wizard are the same as those already shown in the Pooled VMs collection wizard. Follow the wizard and provide all the parameters. On the **Confirmation** page, review the information and click on **Create**. Wait for the process to finish and click on **Close**.

After the collection has been created, you can open the RD Web Access website and access the collection VM. Unlike Pooled VM collections, this Personal VM collection will not revert the VM state to the original. In this case, the VM will be in the state the user left it in.

Another important fact you may want to know is which VM was assigned to each user. You can see this information in the **Virtual Desktop** section on **Server Manager**:

| VIRTUAL DESKTOPS | | | | | TASKS ▾ |
|---|---|---|---|---|---|
| Last refreshed on 3/17/2015 9:41:35 AM | Virtual desktops | 2 total | | | | |
| Filter | | 🔍 | ⬛ ▾ ⬛ ▾ | | ⌄ |
| Virtual Desktop | Status | Host Server | User | Connection Status | |
| VDIPSN-0 | Running | HOST04.contoso.local | CONTOSO\arose | Disconnected | |
| VDIPSN-1 | Saved | HOST04.contoso.local | | | |

Another way to find that information is by running the following cmdlet:

```
Get-RDPersonalVirtualDesktopAssignment -CollectionName "Personal VMs
Collection" -ConnectionBroker Host04.contoso.local
```

The preceding command will return all users assigned to a VM on the Personal VM collection.

```
Get-RDPersonalVirtualDesktopAssignment -CollectionName "Personal VMs
Collection" -ConnectionBroker Host04.contoso.local -user
contoso\arose
```

The preceding command will return the VM assigned to the specific user.

# User Profile Disks

As you've seen with Personal VMs, when the user logs off from the VM all the data remains on the VM. That includes not only the application data and other files created on the VM, but also user profiles. If the user creates or stores any data in the user profile folder, such as documents or desktop folders, these files will not be lost when the user logs off. On Pooled VMs, it is exactly the opposite. When the user logs off the VM on a Pooled VM, all data on the entire VM will be lost, as the VM will return to its original state.

To avoid this behavior on a Pooled VM, you can use a feature introduced in Windows Server 2012 specifically for Pooled VMs that is called User Profile Disk.

The User Profile Disk is a disk separated from the VM disk that will be used exclusively for hosting the user profile. With that, the user data and files are kept on every session, even with the VM returning to its original state.

You can enable User Profile Disks on a Pooled collection while creating the collection, as shown earlier, or by opening it in **Server Manager** and editing the collection settings:

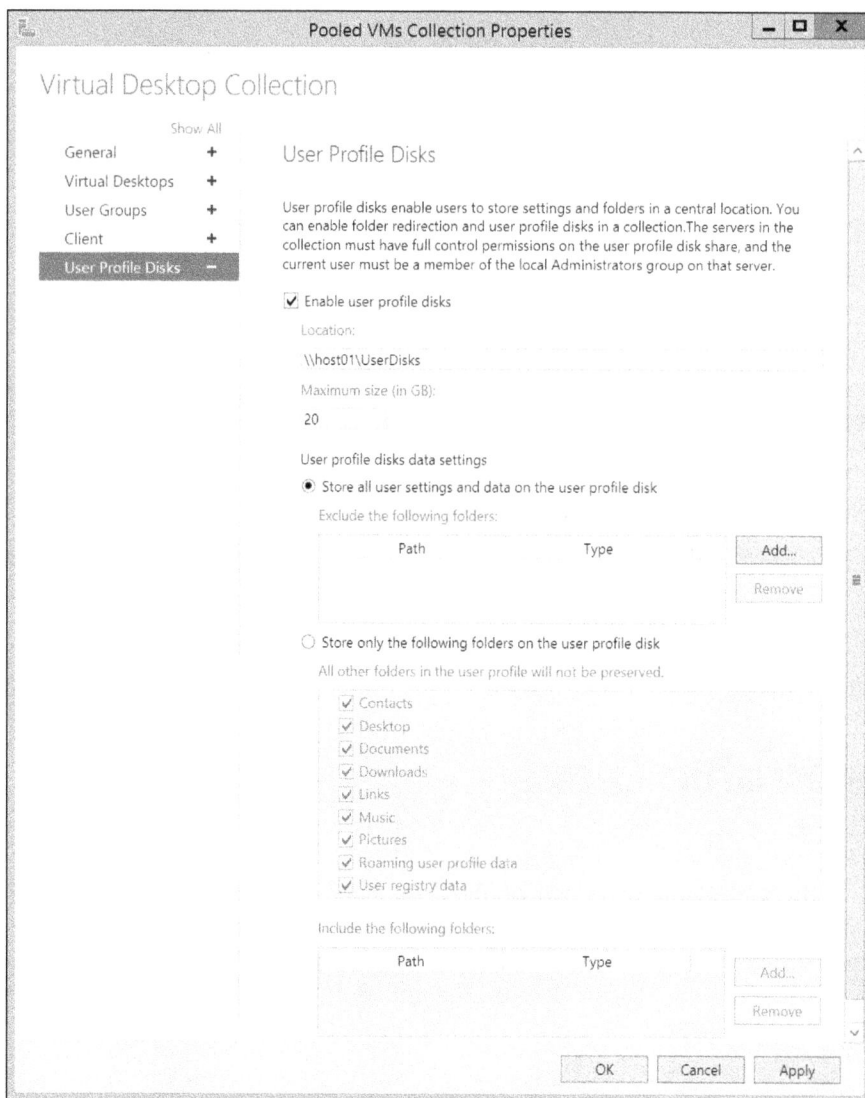

On the preceding screen, you can enable the User Profile Disk and set the maximum size of the disk for each user. Additionally, you can choose to store all the user profile data or specific folders of the user profile. With both options, you have the additional option to include or exclude a specific folder, which can be an actual folder outside the user profile data.

To perform the same operation with PowerShell, run the following cmdlet:

```
Set-RDVirtualDesktopCollectionConfiguration -CollectionName "Pooled
VMs Collection" -DiskPath \\host01\UserDisks -EnableUserProfileDisks
-MaxUserProfileDiskSizeGB 20 -ConnectionBroker host04.contoso.local
```

The preceding command will enable User Profile Disks using the indicated parameters for disk path and disk size. All other parameters are omitted and will be in the default configuration. For more information on how to set the User Profile Disk by using PowerShell and also how to manage a collection with PowerShell, check the official article at https://technet.microsoft.com/en-us/library/jj215467.aspx.

# RemoteFX

When you start a VDI project, you will probably go through a phase in which you will identify users who will use the VDI environment and those who will use a regular machine with all the applications installed and running locally. In this phase, one of the concerns about users who are going to use this VDI environment centers around the performance of the applications on the VMs.

Ensuring that all the VMs perform viably is critical for the success of your VDI implementation. However, some aspects require more than simply calculating how much hardware will be required from the RD Virtualization Hosts. One example of this is users with applications that require a GPU with 3D Graphics processing power to run application such as AutoCAD.

On a VM, the guest OS will have access to a synthetic driver for Video Adapter, which does not provide all the GPU processing power and features. By default, a scenario resembling the earlier scenario is not possible. With that in mind, Microsoft released a new feature called RemoteFX in Service Pack 1 of Windows Server 2008 R2.

RemoteFX allows the VM to use all the power and features of the physical GPU installed on the host machine. There are some requirements, however, for this to work properly:

- The processor on the host must support SLAT.

- The vendor of the GPU must provide the device driver and this must be installed on the host OS. The generic device driver cannot be used for RemoteFX.

- The GPU must support DirectX 11 and **Windows Device Driver Model (WDDN)** 1.2.

- If more than one GPUs are installed for RemoteFX, the GPUs must be identical.

- If you plan to live-migrate the VM using RemoteFX, both hosts must have the same GPU.

To get started with RemoteFX, open Hyper-V Manager and open the **Hyper-V Settings...**. In Hyper-V Settings, click on **Physical GPUs**:

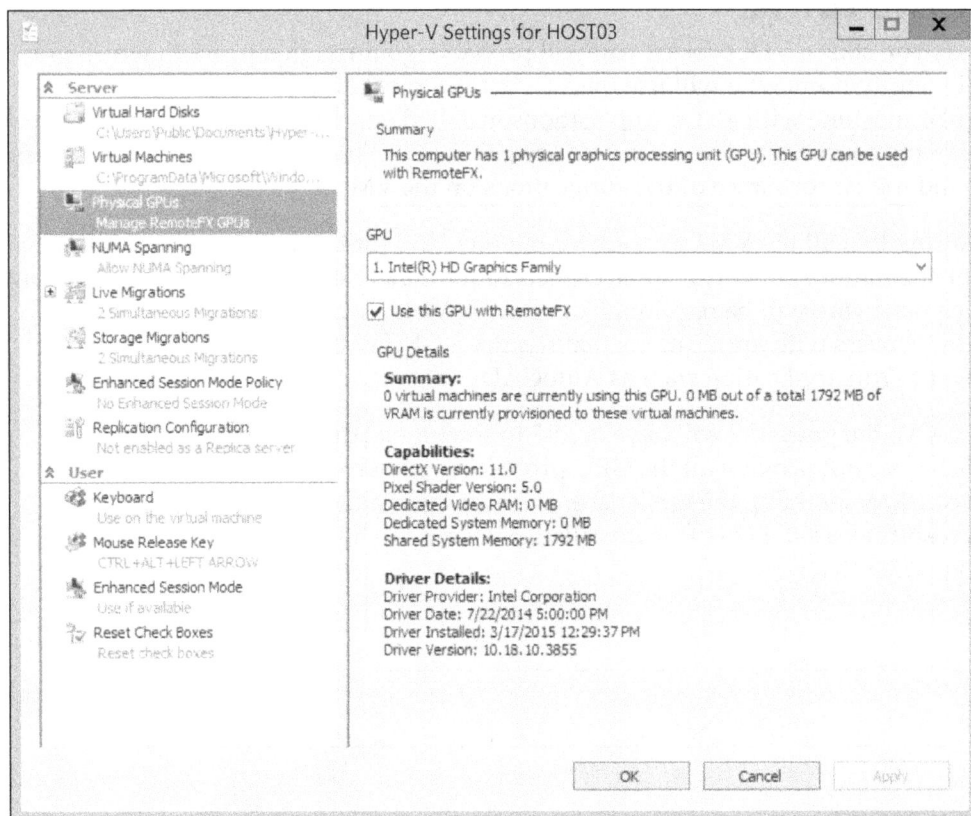

The preceding screenshot shows that a GPU that meets the requirements was found and is available for the VMs. Now, you have to add a new RemoteFX Video Adapter on the VMs. Open the VM **Settings...** and, on the **Add Hardware** page, select **RemoteFX 3D Video Adapter**:

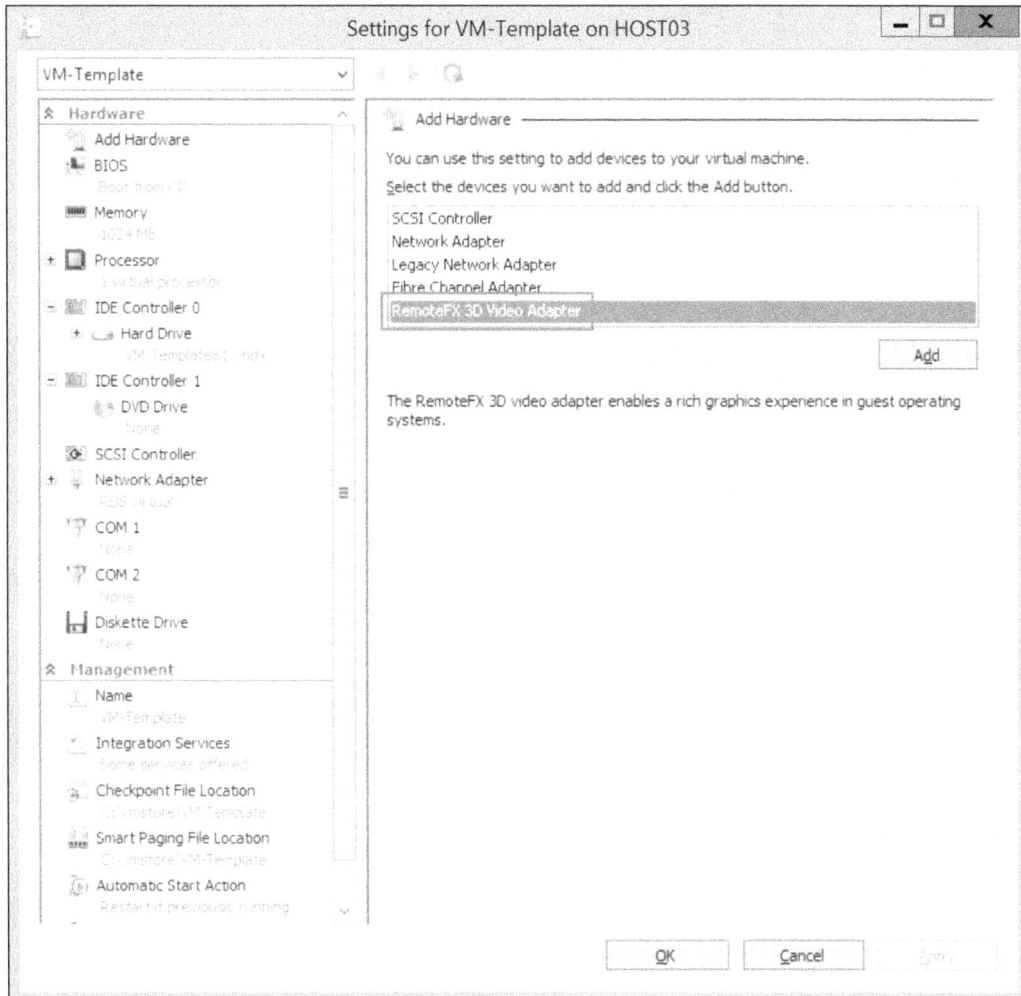

For the RemoteFX 3D Video Adapter, you can specify the maximum number of monitors that the user will be able to use on the Remote Desktop connection and the maximum monitor resolution:

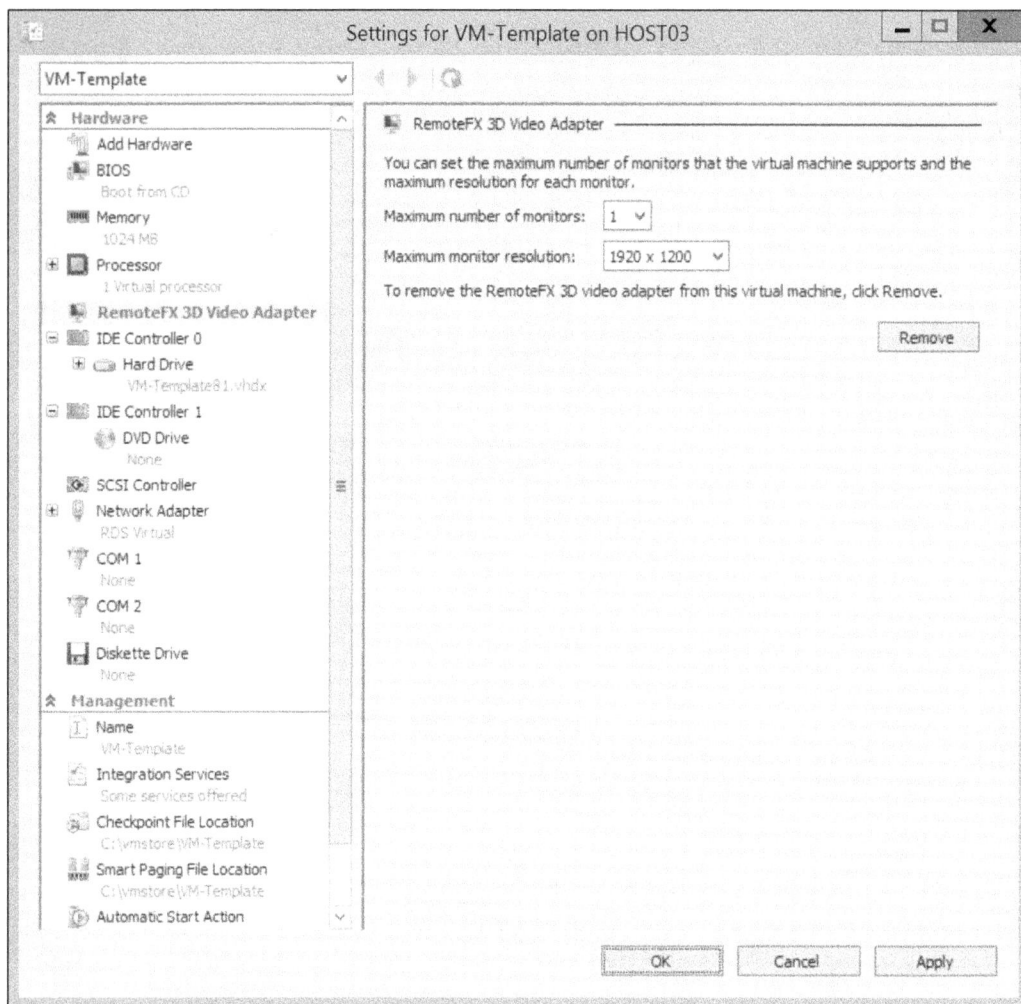

After selecting the appropriate settings, click on **OK** to add the adapter. To check if the RemoteFX 3D Video Adapter was added successfully, open **Device Manager** inside the guest OS and check the Video Adapter:

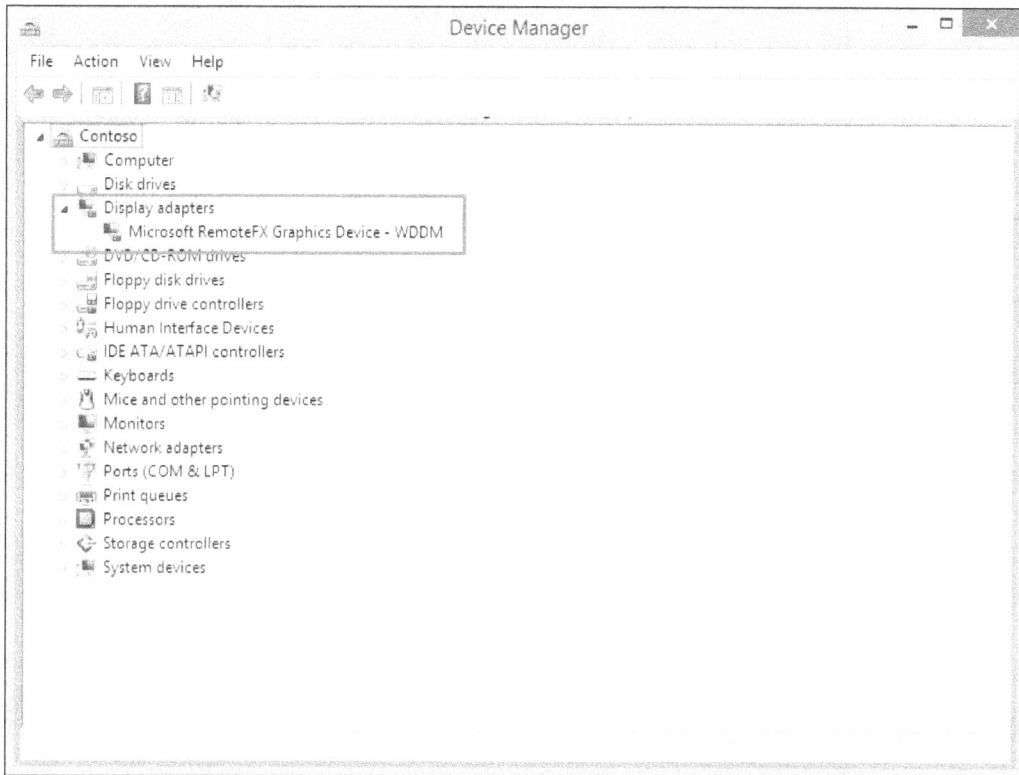

Now, you can use this VM as the template for the VMs in the Pooled or Personal collections. It is important to state, however, that RemoteFX is not tied to VDI. You can implement a RemoteFX-enabled VM on a regular environment in the same way as in a VDI environment.

# Recreating the VM template

When your VDI environment is established and everything is working, you will probably face a painful situation, especially with Pooled VMs. After a while, it is very common that the base image, or the VM template, becomes outdated, either because there have been many Windows updates, or because the application itself needs to be updated.

On a Personal VM collection, as the VM progress is being saved, you can simply update the VMs and everything will work just fine. However, on a Pooled VM collection, the VM state is reverted to its original state and all the changes, including updates to the SO and application, will be reverted.

To work with this situation, you can update the base image, or VM template. There are many options to do so—for example, tools such as MDOP, System Center Configuration Manager, System Center Virtual Machine Manager, and many others. Actually, you can even attach the VHD/VHDX to a host and add/remove files from the VM. The fact is that we are not going to cover these options in this book as they are within the scope of regular client management processes, which are probably in place in your organization.

After you have updated this template, however, there is a process on RDS to help you update all the VMs created by this template. To go through this process, open the collection in **Server Manager**, open **TASKS** on the **Virtual Desktop Template** menu, and select **Recreate All Virtual Desktops**:

**VIRTUAL DESKTOP TEMPLATE**
Virtual desktop template for the collection

| | | TASKS ▼ |
|---|---|---|
| Name | VM-Template | Recreate All Virtual Desktops |
| Server | HOST04.contoso.local | |
| Memory (MB) | 1024 | |
| Virtual GPU | No | |

The **Recreate All Virtual Desktops** wizard will detect the newest template in the environment and this template will be available for selection. Select the appropriate template and click on **Next >**:

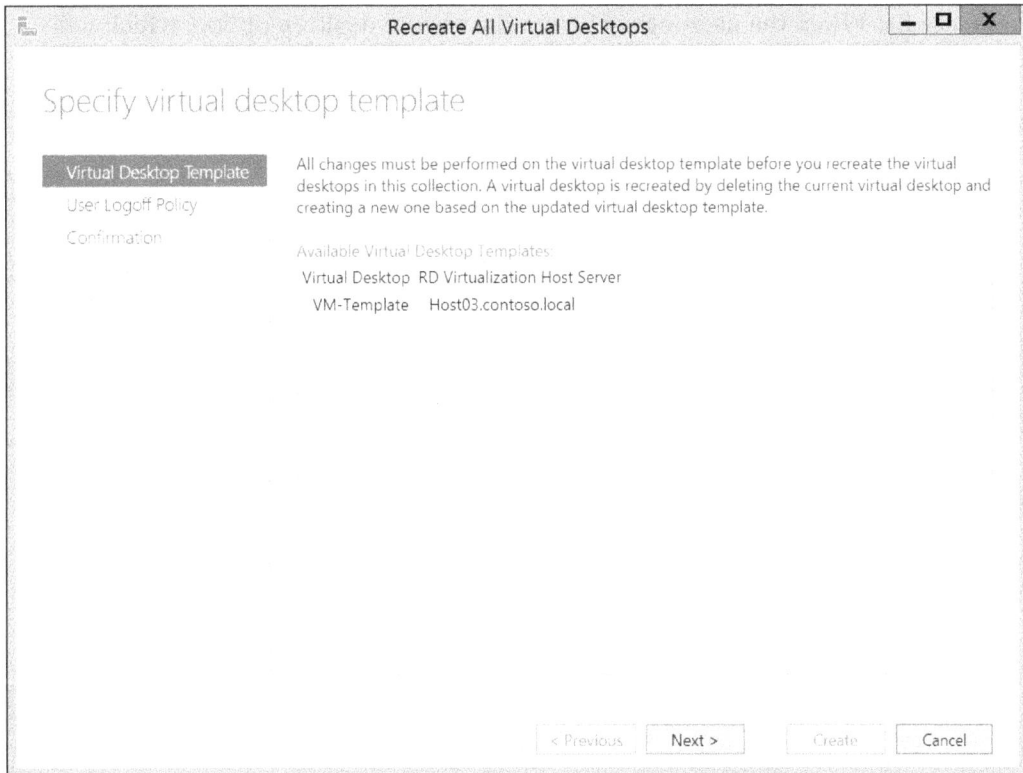

Now, you can select **User Logoff Policy**. This policy is important as it will dictate how fast the process is going to happen and also, on the other hand, how the users will be impacted. The first option, **When the user logs off from the virtual desktop**, is less impactful for the user, but can take longer to finish all the VMs. In this case, you set the period on which the update must be applied and the user will be prompted to logoff for the update to happen.

The **Based on schedule** option will force the users to log off immediately or in line with a specific schedule, depending on the subsidiary option you select. This option will speed up the VM update but will have a higher impact on the users logged on to the machines.

The general recommendation for the updates is to balance how important the update is for the environment. If it is a critical update that must be installed immediately, use the **Based on schedule** option. In this option, you can even schedule the update for a non-working hour. If the update is not critical and users can continue using the VMs, use the **When the user logs off from the virtual desktop** option, which will not impact user productivity and you can set your goal for the update to be on every machine, allowing the user to finish his/her job without any rush. After selecting the appropriate option, click on **Next >**:

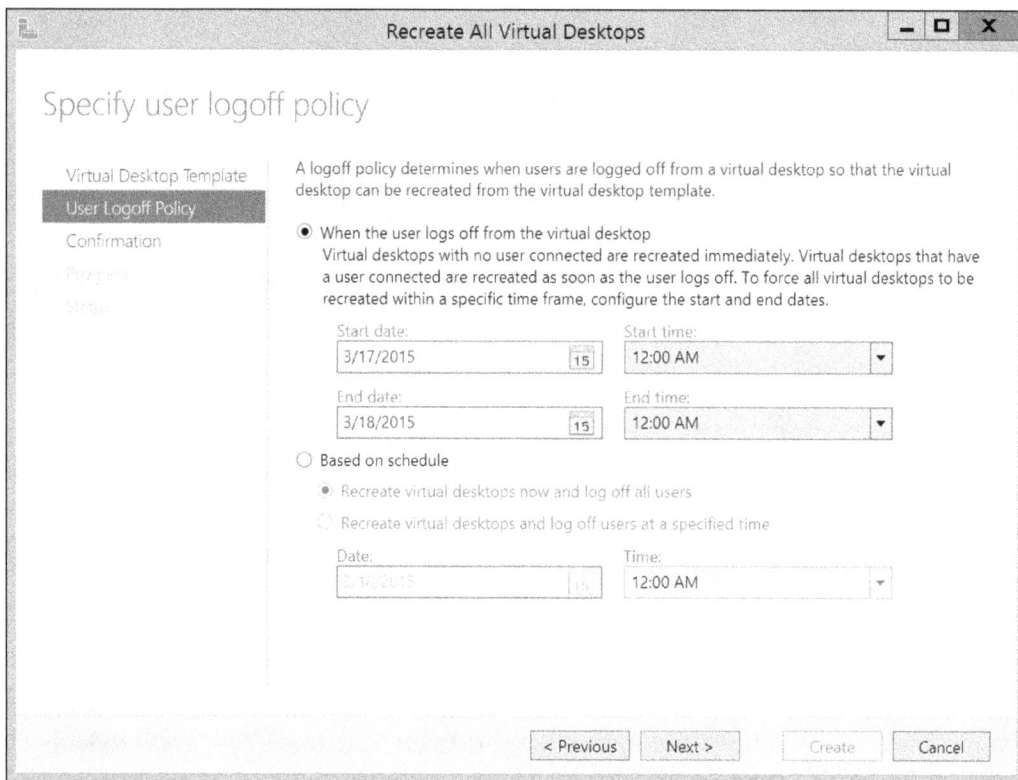

On the **Confirmation** page, review the information and click on **Create**. Wait for the process to finish. When the process finishes, click on **Close**. Now, the selected option will initiate the update process on the VMs, as configured in the previous step.

# Summary

In this chapter, you learned how Hyper-V can work along with Remote Desktop Services to provide a robust VDI environment. We covered the differences between a VDI-based and a session-based environment and its peculiarities. You also learned that a VDI environment must be planned and not all scenarios are ideal for VDI.

Moving forward, you learned how to implement a RDS environment with a RD virtualization host/Hyper-V Host and the other RDS roles necessary for the VDI environment.

You explored the difference between a Pooled and a Personal collection and how it will impact the clients using the VDI environment. Additionally, you learned how to deploy each collection and what its specific characteristics are.

In the final sections, you learned two important features of VDI administration: RemoteFX and all of its requirements, and how to recreate the VM template to perform an update on the VMs.

In the next and final chapter, we will cover how to protect your virtualization environment with the backup/recovery tools on Windows Server.

# 11
# Protecting Your Virtualization Environment

Last but not least. This phrase is excellent for this final chapter. During the journey to this last chapter, you learned many Hyper-V concepts and features. Some of these features can help you to protect your environment from a disaster, such as HA with a failover cluster and Hyper-V Replica. None of these features will protect your virtualization environment from data loss, though.

Note that HA will only protect against host hardware failure. You can even use the failover cluster to monitor application health inside the VM, but there is nothing to be done if a file is deleted, or if the VM disk crashes.

Hyper-V Replica is an excellent choice to recover the VM as fast as you can when a disaster occurs on the datacenter. With Hyper-V Replica, you can run an exact copy of the VM, at a given point in time, on another host on a different site. Hyper-V Replica can't, however, easily recover files to a different location. Also, Hyper-V Replica requires communication between sites and an entire virtualization environment in the replica site.

At the end of the day, a backup solution is your best option, the last man standing, to help you recover the information you need as quickly as possible. And it does not require much.

Of course, there are many backup solutions on the market. Even Microsoft delivers a very robust backup solution with System Center Data Protection Manager. These solutions focus on large deployments with large amounts of data to be backed up. Additionally, these solutions are, usually, centralized solutions. This means that you will have dedicated backup server(s) to back up all the servers on the network. There is, however, a need to provide a simple and affordable solution for small and medium deployments. That solution is Windows Server Backup.

Now, even if Windows Server Backup is not a solution in your case, there is a new feature to help you recover VM data: you can simply export the powered-on VM and import it on another host, or simply attach the disk to a Windows Server or Client.

In this last chapter, we will cover the following topics:

- Windows Server Backup overview
- Incremental backups
- Backing up your host and VMs
- Restoring your host and VMs
- Import and export VMs

# Windows Server Backup overview

Before I tell you how Windows Server Backup works, it is important to tell you a story. If you have been administering Windows Server environments for a long time now, you are probably familiar with NTBackup.

NTBackup was the backup solution on Windows Server until Windows Server 2003 R2. Until Windows Server 2003 R2, NTBackup was a native, in-place solution to back up all system data, native applications, such as Active Directory, and other network resources.

When Microsoft launched Windows Server 2008, many administrators realized NTBackup was not there. A myth was created that Windows Server did have a backup solution. The reason why NTBackup was not there is that NTBackup was part of a partnership from Microsoft with a company called Veritas. This company was bought by Symantec by the time Microsoft was developing Windows Server 2008, and this partnership ended. Without the NTBackup solution available, Microsoft developed a new, extremely simple backup solution, which is the Windows Server Backup. The reason for the myth about Windows Server Backup was because, unlike NTBackup, Windows Server Backup is not installed by default. You have to install Windows Server Backup if you want use it. As the new "Roles and Features" approach was not familiar to Windows Server admins, the myth was created. With all of this, Microsoft realized a more robust approach to a backup solution was necessary and the first release of System Center Data Protection Manager was launched.

Nowadays, Windows Server Backup has evolved and many features were introduced on each new release of Windows Server. In fact, one of the areas of investment on Windows Server Backup was Hyper-V.

# Getting started with Windows Server Backup

As explained, Windows Server Backup is not installed by default. You will have to install it by using Server Manager. When adding a new feature, as already explained in previous chapters, select **Windows Server Backup** from the list of features available:

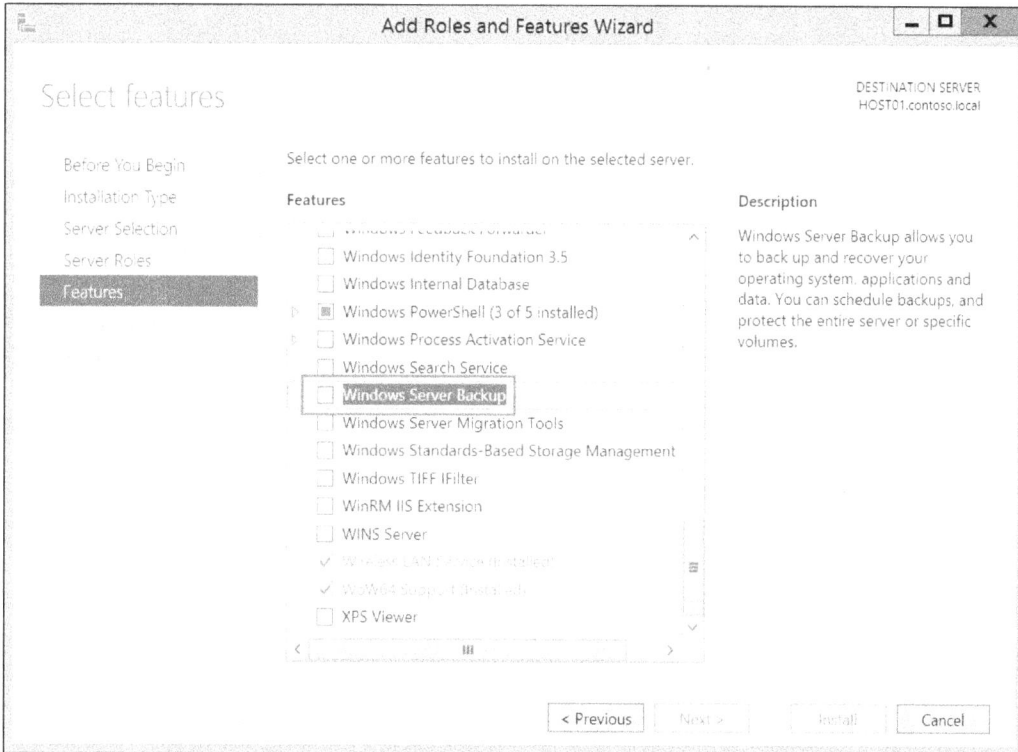

Follow the steps to install the feature and click on **Install**. There is also the possibility of using PowerShell to install the Windows Server Backup feature. You can use the following cmdlet:

```
Install-WindowsFeature -Name Windows-Server-Backup
```

When the installation finishes, you can open the Windows Server Backup snap-in:

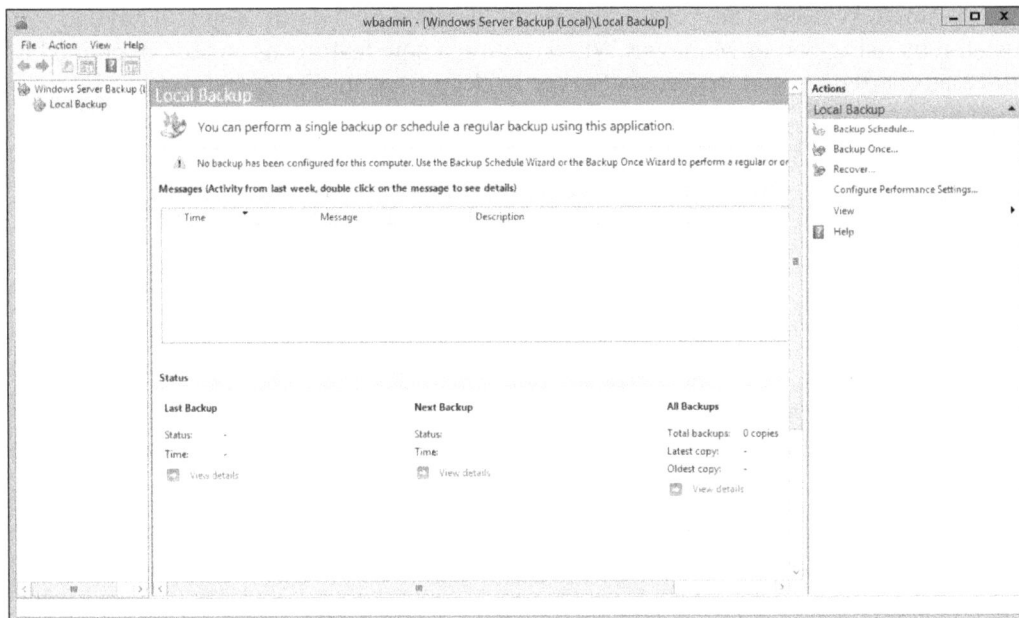

## Incremental backups

One of the major improvements in Windows Server Backup is the incremental backup feature. A regular incremental backup backs up the changes from the last backup and so on until the next full backup.

The problem with this approach is that, although it will use less space than the regular full backup, it will still add a considerable amount of data to the backup catalog. On Windows Server 2012, the incremental backup feature works like this:

Let's imagine you have a Hyper-V environment with a single VM, with a single disk, and you want to backup this VM. You schedule a full backup every Sunday and incremental backups on Monday and Tuesday.

On the Sunday backup, your volumes will be like this:

| VM | Before backup | During backup | After backup |
|---|---|---|---|
| VM-01 | VM VHD | VM VHD + Differences 1 | VM VHD + Differences 1 |

On Windows Server 2012 R2, when a new incremental backup occurs on a VM that already has an incremental backup, the old incremental backup is merged to the disk to save space on the disk. The Monday backup, in this case, will be like this:

| VM | Before backup | During backup | After backup |
|---|---|---|---|
| VM-01 | VM VHD | VM VHD + Differences 1 (Merged) + Differences 2 | VM VHD + Differences 2 |

As you can see, the Differences 1 incremental backup was merged to the VM disk. However, Hyper-V will maintain a catalog of this backup so you can still use it as a recovery point (much like a checkpoint) when recovering a backup. On Tuesday, the backup will be like this:

| VM | Before backup | During backup | After backup |
|---|---|---|---|
| VM-01 | VM VHD | VM VHD + Differences 2 (Merged) + Differences 3 | VM VHD + Differences 3 |

Now imagine that you have to recover the VM on Friday. You will see something like this:

| VM | Backups available to restore |
|---|---|
| VM-01 | Full |
| | Differences 1 |
| | Differences 2 |
| | Differences 3 |

# Backing up your host and VMs

To start a backup process on Windows Server Backup, open the Windows Server Backup snap-in and click on **Backup Schedule**.

> There is a **Backup Once** option that allows you to create a single backup. Note that this option is a one-time shot and is usually used on test environments and backup tests. A regular backup solution should use the **Backup Schedule** option.

On the **Backup Schedule** wizard, click on **Next >**. On the **Select Configuration** tab, you will need to choose between **Full Server** and **Custom**. The **Full Server** option will back up all partitions available, including system reserved, boot, system state, and so on. Additionally, it will back up all the applications, such as Hyper-V and its VMs. If you want to be sure that you can recover all host data, you can choose this option. Keep in mind that this option might be backing up unnecessary information.

The **Custom** option lets you choose what you really want to back up. We will choose this option, so you can have an idea of what is being backed up:

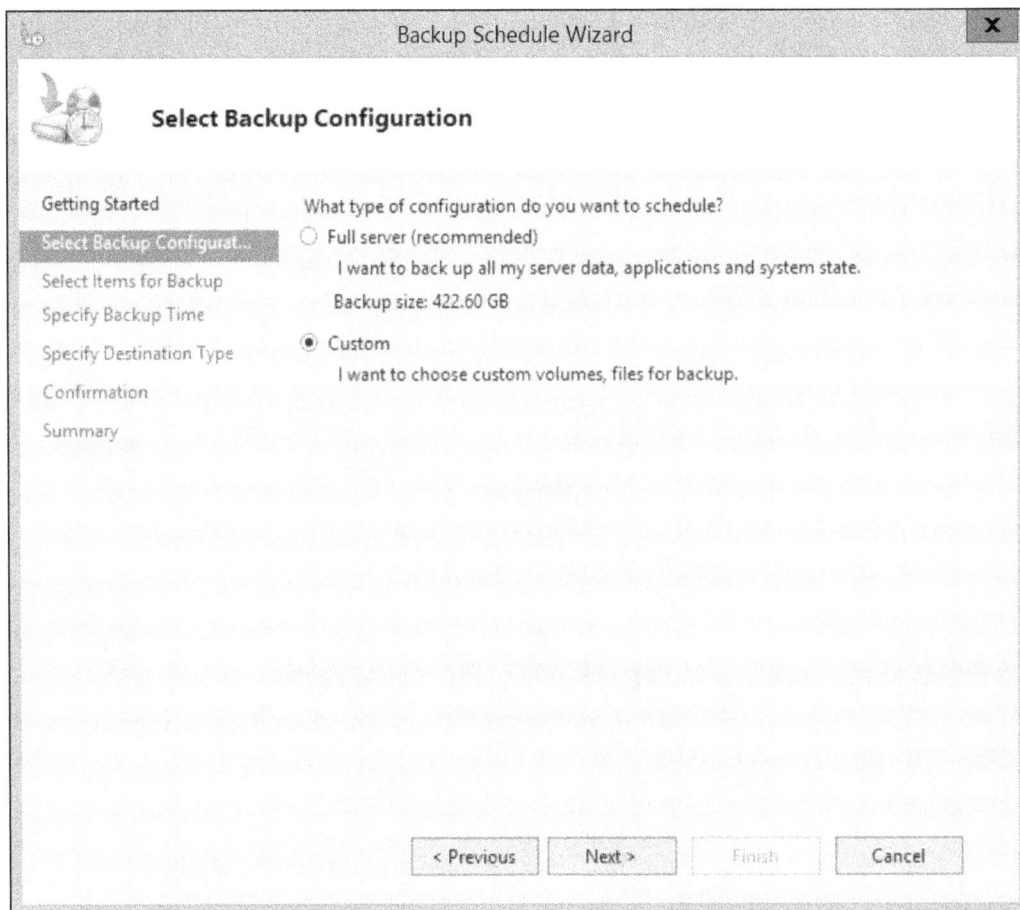

Click on **Add Items**:

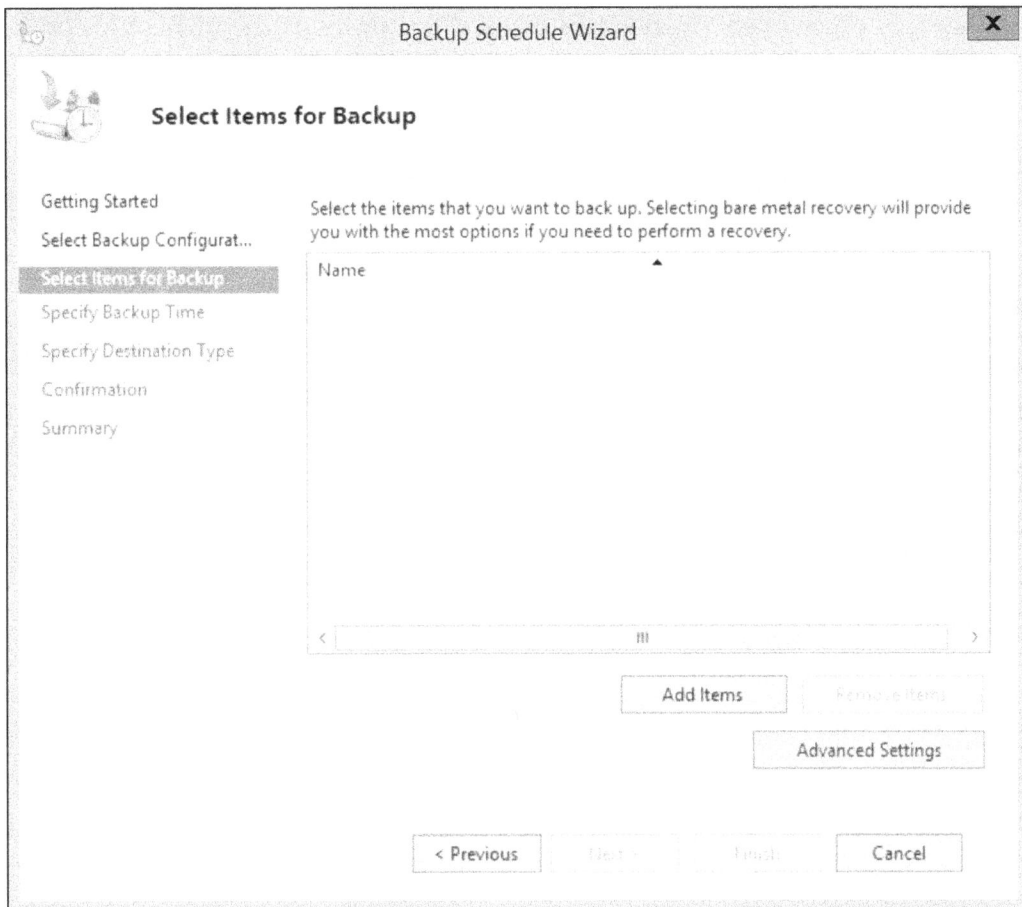

Now, you can choose which items you want to back up. From the host perspective, you can choose the **Bare metal recovery** option to make sure you can recover the entire host. Different from the **Full server backup** option, **Bare metal recovery** selects all the necessary information, but no unnecessary information, to recover the host, as in the following example, the E: drive.

From the VM perspective, you can expand the Hyper-V application and select the VMs you want to back up. When you select the VMs, Windows Server Backup will back up all the associated VHD/VHDX files and the physical disks on the VM. The **Host Component** option should also be checked whenever you back up a VM. This option will back up the VM configuration files. If you do not check this option, you will not be able to recover the entire VM, only the associated VHD/VHDX files and physical disk contents. Select the appropriate options and click on **OK**:

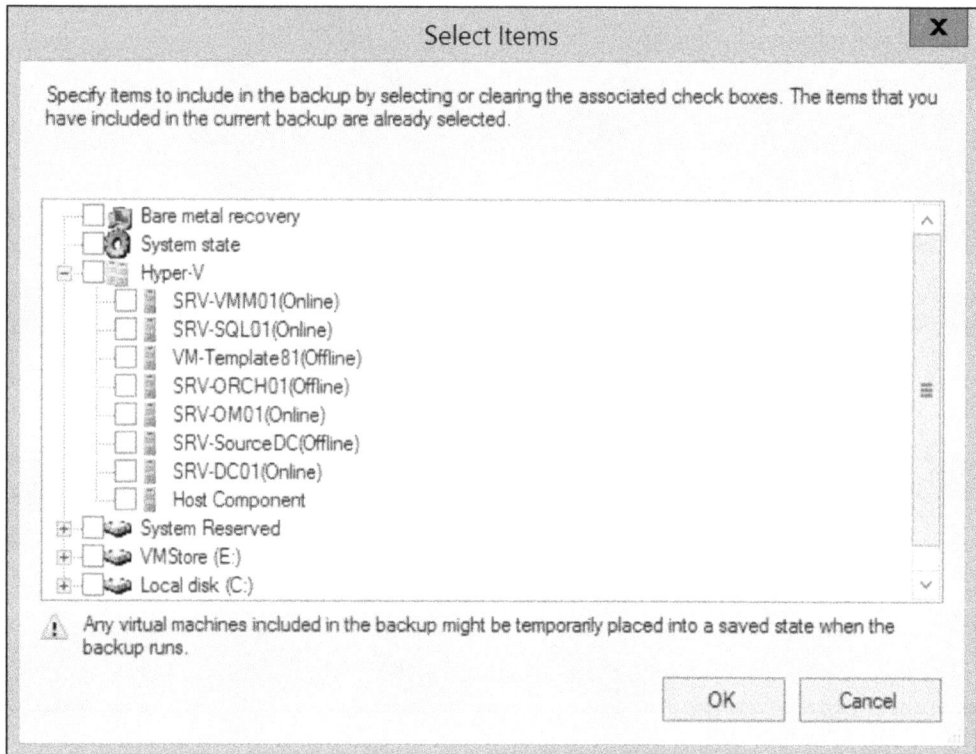

Now, you can review all the items that will be backed up. Click on **Advanced Settings**:

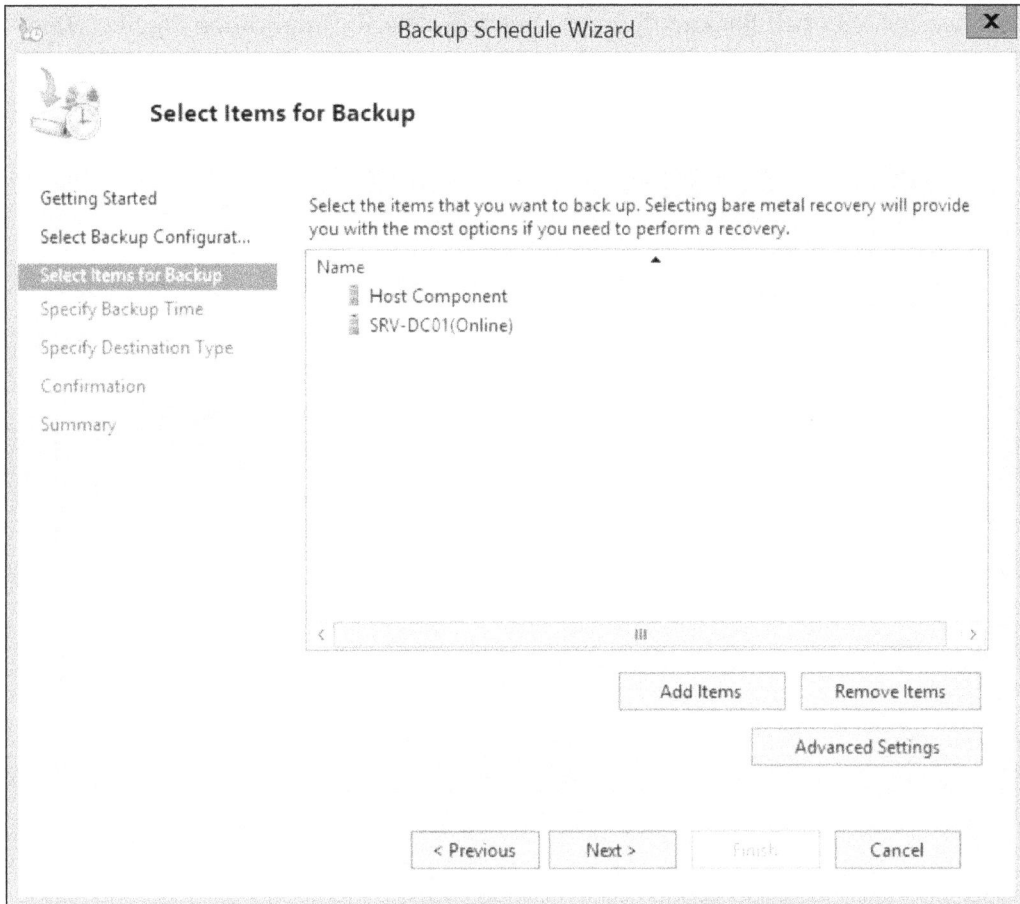

On the **Advanced Settings** window, you can click on the **VSS Settings** tab to change the VSS configuration on the host. If you're not using another backup solution in this host, use the **VSS full Backup** option as this will clear the application log files after the backup finishes. On the **Remove Items** tab, you can also check the items you want to exclude from the backup. Click on **OK** and then click on **Next >**:

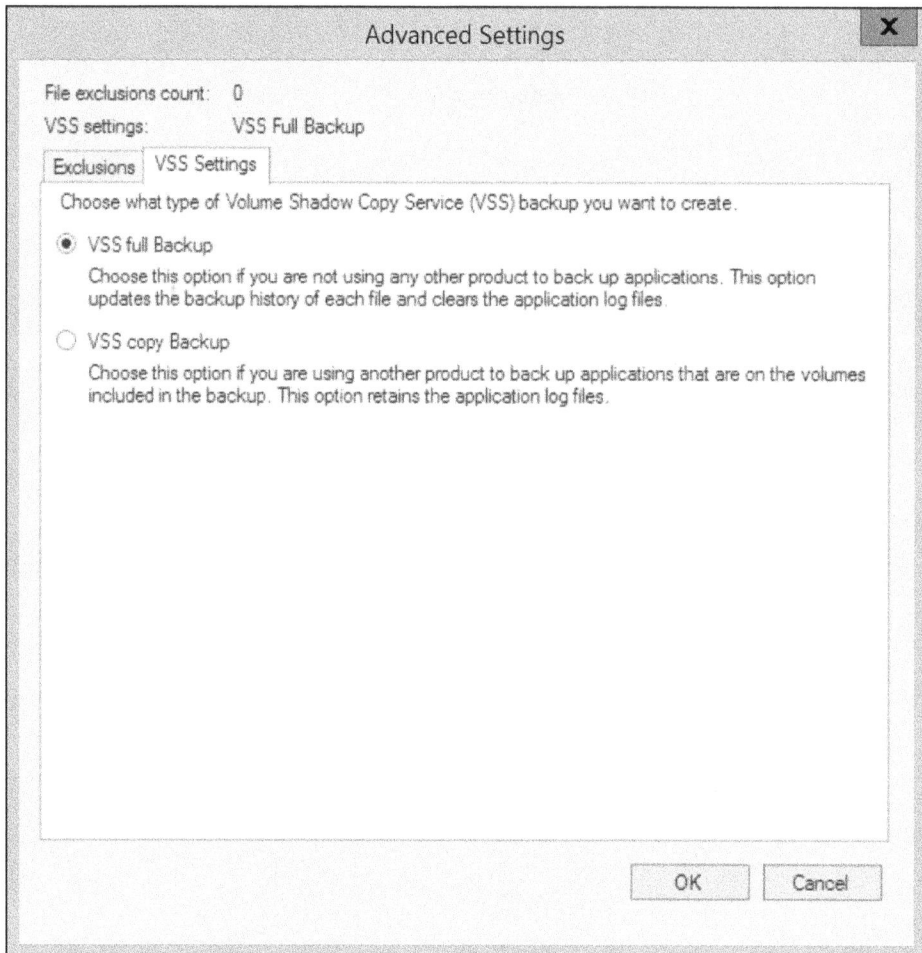

Now, you can specify how many backups you will create per day and at what time the backup job will run. Select the appropriate option and click on **Next >**:

On the **Specify Destination Type** page, you can choose between using a dedicated disk, using a regular disk, and using a network share to store the backup data.

The **Back up to a hard disk that is dedicated for backups (recommended)** option will erase everything on the disk you choose and dedicate this disk to the Windows Server Backup application.

The **Backup to a volume** option will create a folder on the indicated disk to store the backup data but will not erase the other disk data.

The **Backup to shared network folder** option will use an SMB share to store backup data. In this case, we will use the second option and click on **Next >**:

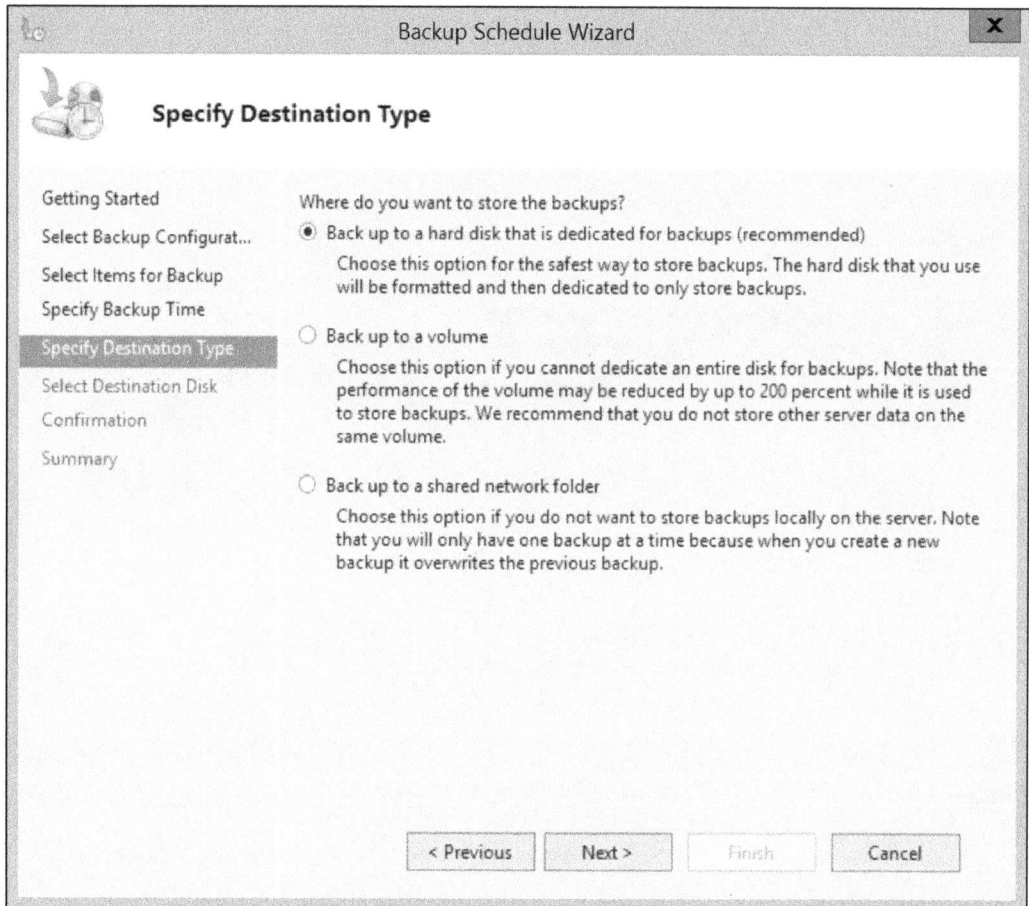

If you selected the **Back up to a shared network folder** option earlier, be aware that the following warning will appear, stating that each backup will erase the previous one, resulting in no backup history:

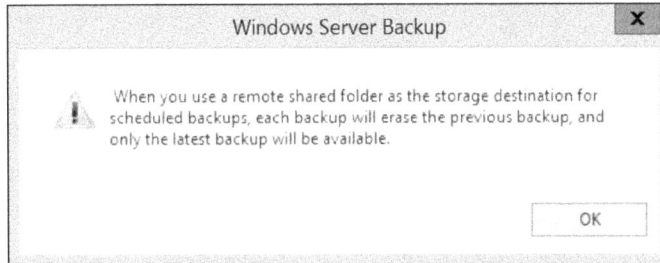

In the **Select Destination Volume** dialog box, click on **Add** and select the appropriate disk. After selecting the disk, click on **OK**:

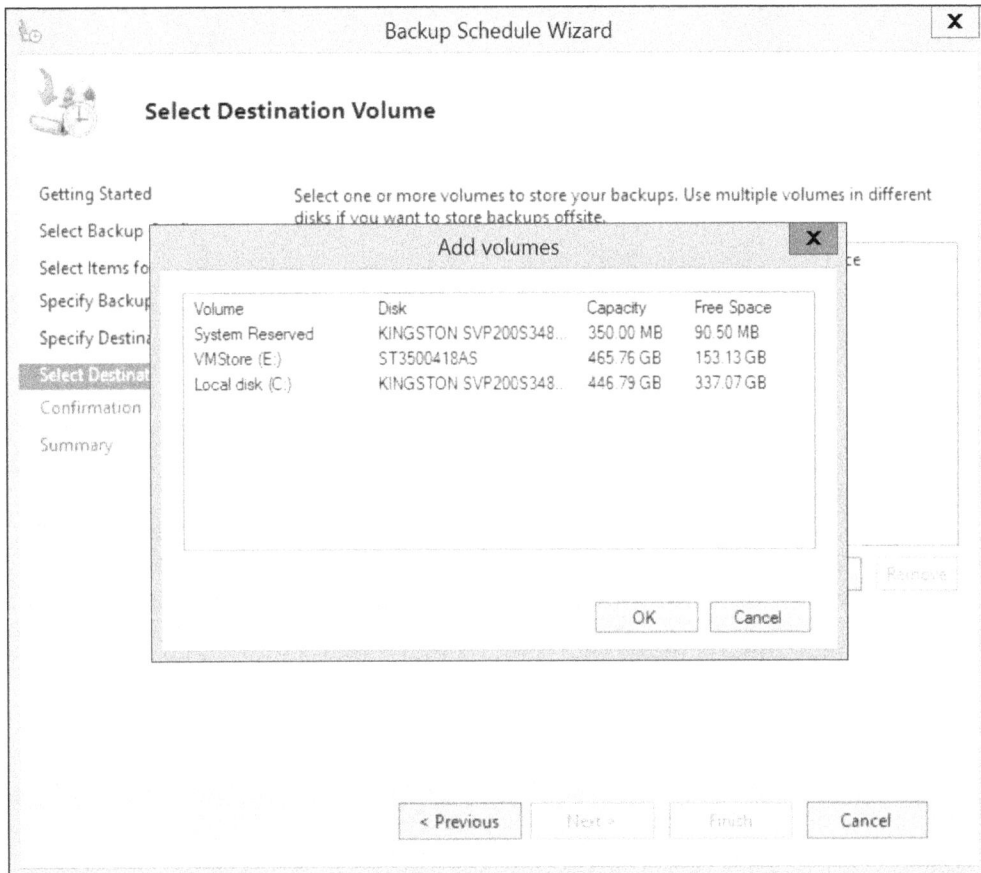

Check the information and make sure the selected disk has enough disk space to back up all the selected information. Click on **Next >**:

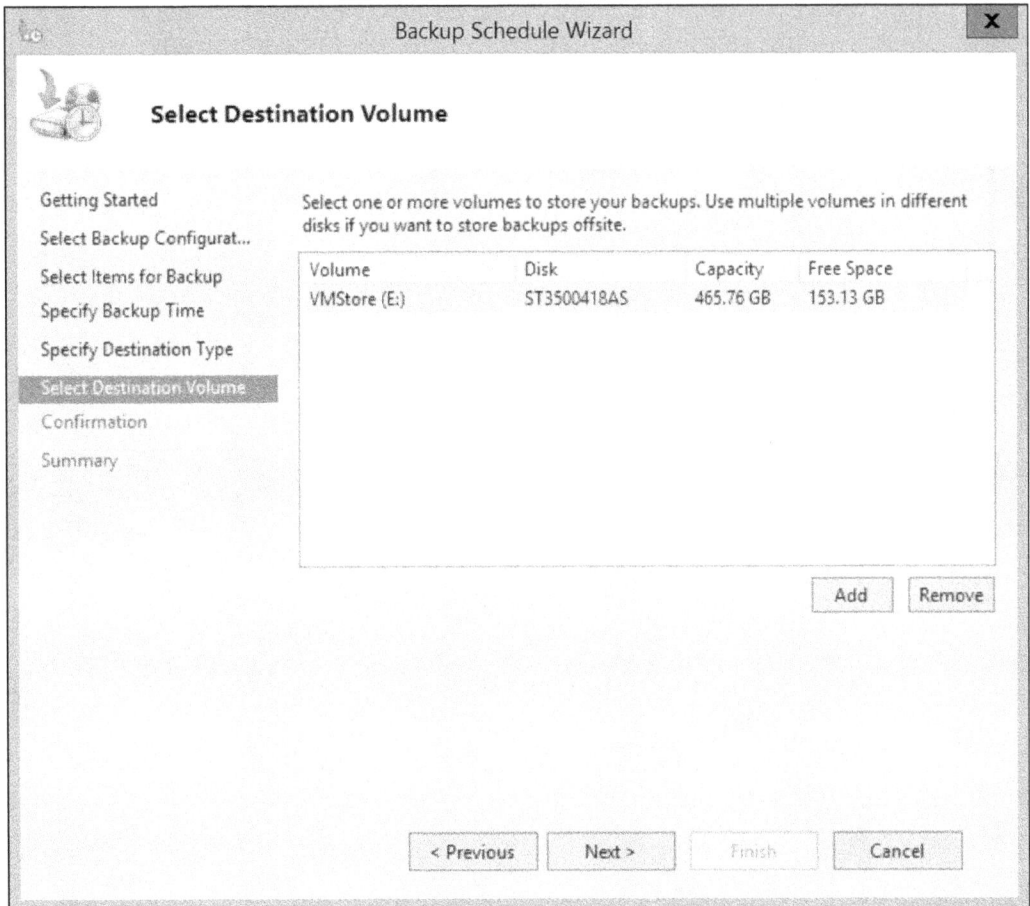

| | Backup Schedule Wizard | | X |
|---|---|---|---|

**Select Destination Volume**

Getting Started
Select Backup Configurat...
Select Items for Backup
Specify Backup Time
Specify Destination Type
Select Destination Volume
Confirmation
Summary

Select one or more volumes to store your backups. Use multiple volumes in different disks if you want to store backups offsite.

| Volume | Disk | Capacity | Free Space |
|---|---|---|---|
| VMStore (E:) | ST3500418AS | 465.76 GB | 153.13 GB |

Add    Remove

< Previous    Next >    Finish    Cancel

Review the **Confirmation** page and click on **Finish**. When the backup schedule is successfully created, the following message will be shown:

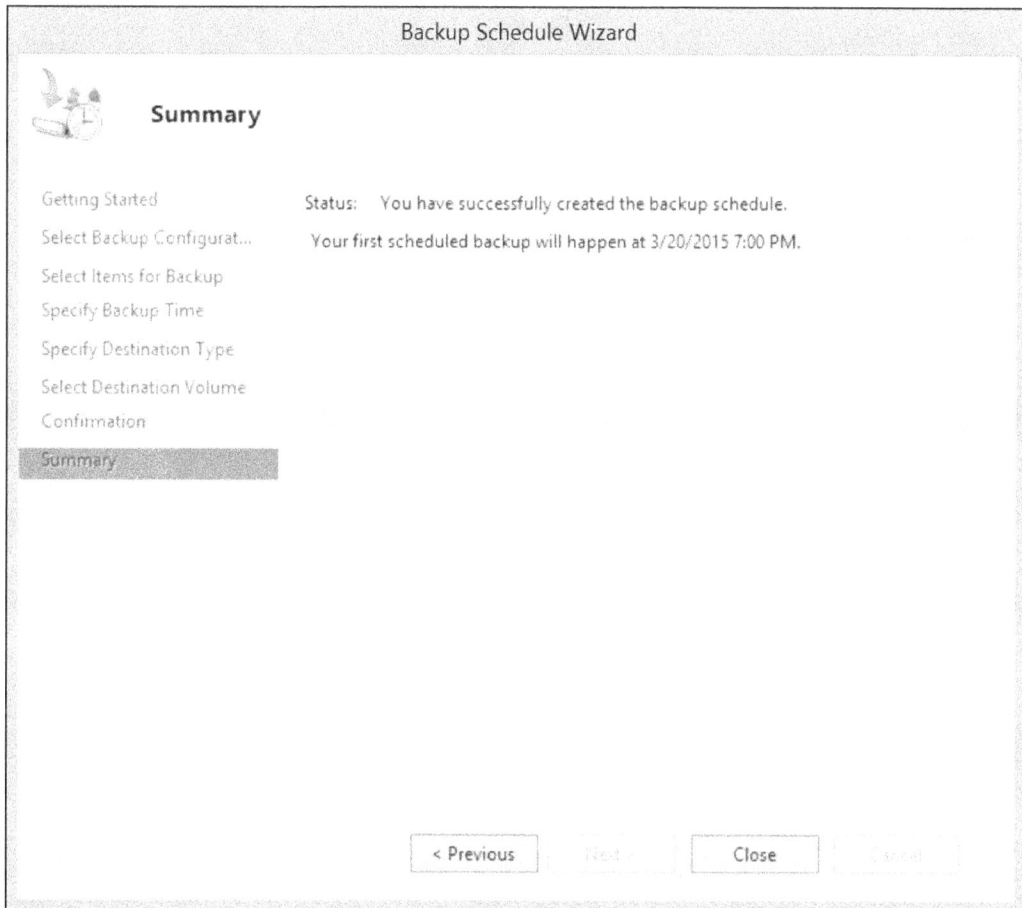

When the backup process starts, you can see from Hyper-V Manager that the backup job is running with the Hyper-V VSS application:

**Virtual Machines**

| Name | State | CPU Usage | Assigned Memory | Uptime | Status |
|------|-------|-----------|-----------------|--------|--------|
| SRV-DC01 | Running | 0 % | 1024 MB | 00:00:00 | Backing up... |
| SRV-OM01 | Running | 0 % | 4096 MB | 3.06:09:19 | |
| SRV-ORCH01 | Off | | | | |
| SRV-SourceDC | Off | | | | |
| SRV-SQL01 | Running | 3 % | 2048 MB | 3.06:30:31 | |
| SRV-VMM01 | Running | 0 % | 2048 MB | 3.06:09:16 | |
| VM-Template81 | Off | | | | |

When the backup job finishes, you will see the following information on the Windows Server Backup snap-in:

**Local Backup**

You can perform a single backup or schedule a regular backup using this application.

**Messages** (Activity from last week, double click on the message to see details)

| Time | Message | Description |
|------|---------|-------------|
| (i) 3/19/2015 9:00 PM | Backup | Successful |
| (i) 3/19/2015 7:51 PM | Backup | Successful |

**Status**

| **Last Backup** | **Next Backup** | **All Backups** |
|-----------------|-----------------|-----------------|
| Status: ⊛ Successful | Status: Scheduled | Total backups: 2 copies |
| Time: 3/19/2015 9:00 PM | Time: 3/20/2015 7:00 PM | Latest copy: 3/19/2015 9:00 PM |
| ▸ View details | ▸ View details | Oldest copy: 3/19/2015 7:51 PM |
| | | ▸ View details |

You can also see more details on the backup. Click on **View details** under last backup:

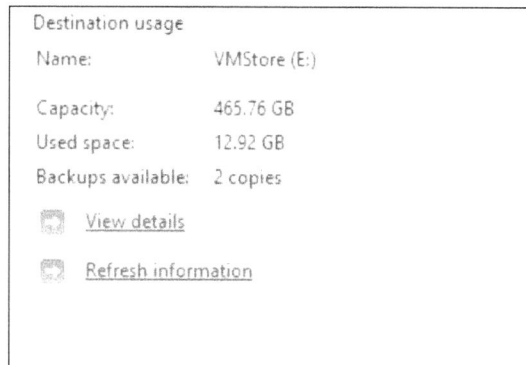

```
Destination usage

Name:                 VMStore (E:)

Capacity:             465.76 GB
Used space:           12.92 GB
Backups available:    2 copies

     View details

     Refresh information
```

As you can see from the following screenshot, Windows Server Backup will provide detailed information on how much space the backup is using, backup copies, and so on:

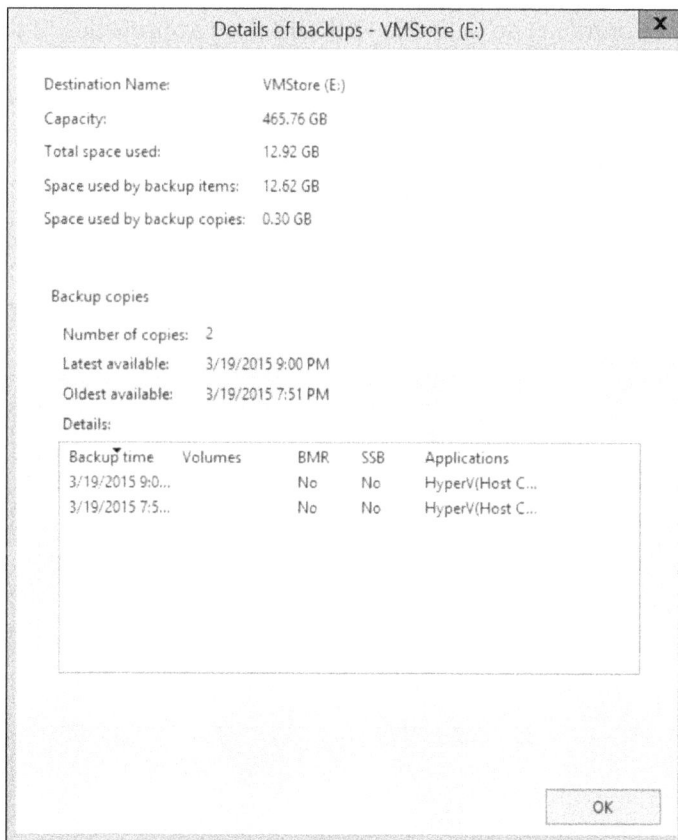

```
Details of backups - VMStore (E:)                    X

Destination Name:            VMStore (E:)
Capacity:                    465.76 GB
Total space used:            12.92 GB
Space used by backup items:  12.62 GB
Space used by backup copies: 0.30 GB


Backup copies

  Number of copies:  2
  Latest available:  3/19/2015 9:00 PM
  Oldest available:  3/19/2015 7:51 PM
  Details:

  Backup time   Volumes    BMR    SSB    Applications
  3/19/2015 9:0...          No     No     HyperV(Host C...
  3/19/2015 7:5...          No     No     HyperV(Host C...




                                              OK
```

On Windows Server 2012, there are PowerShell cmdlets to manage Windows Server Backup. However, if you've been a Windows Server admin for a long time, you are probably familiar with the command line option to do so. If you want to check out the PowerShell cmdlets, refer to the official article at `https://technet.microsoft.com/en-us/library/jj902428.aspx`. In this demonstration, we will use the following commands to manage Hyper-V with Windows Server Backup:

```
WBADMIN START BACKUP -backupTarget:E: -hyperv:"SRV-DC01"
```

The preceding command will back up the `SRV-DC01` VM on the `E:` disk.

The following command will get the backup versions that are hosted on the `E:` drive. The result of this command will show the version identifier for the backup. This information will be needed in the recovery process:

```
WBADMIN GET VERSIONS -backupTarget:E:
```

# Restoring your host and VMs

Restoring the environment can be made with different approaches. If you lost your host, you have the ability to restore the VMs on another host, by simply adding the backup catalog to that host. You can also try to restore the entire host. This is a more complex process, and requires you to have either the full server backup or the bare metal recovery backup.

This last alternative can be initiated by booting up the host with the Windows Server setup disk and selecting the **Repair your computer** option:

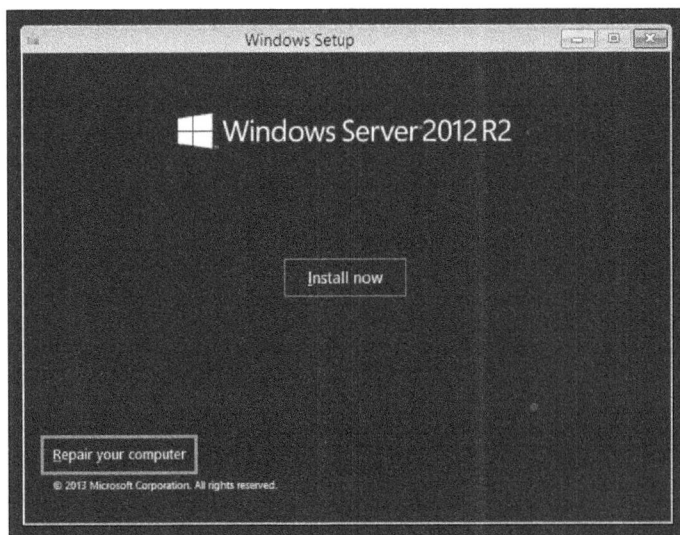

Select the **Troubleshoot** option:

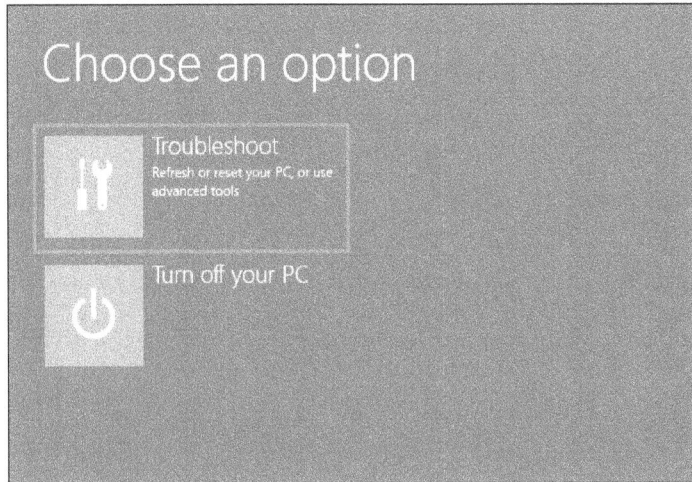

If you select **System Image Recovery**, the wizard will try to find, on any attached disk or DVD, the recovery image generated by the Windows Server Backup:

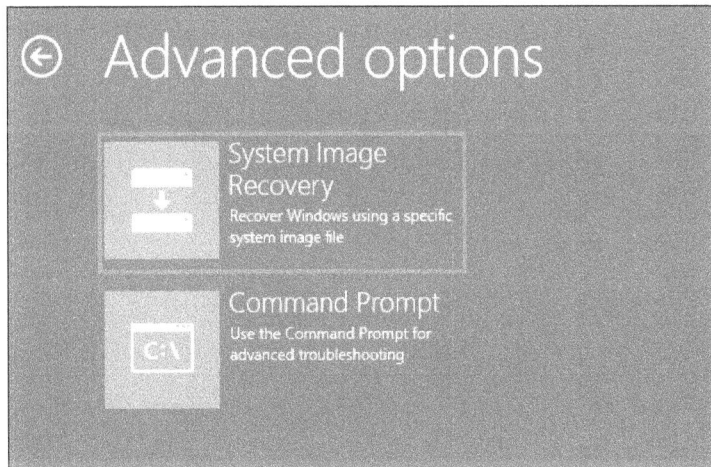

Select the appropriate image and follow the instructions to perform the host restore. You can find more information on how to perform the restore of the entire host in the official article at `https://technet.microsoft.com/en-us/library/cc755163.aspx`.

Recovering the VM, on the other hand, is much simpler. You can use the Windows Server Backup, by selecting the **Recover** option.

On the **Recovery Wizard** window, select whether the backup is already on the host catalog or whether this is a backup from another host and you want to add it to the catalog. In our case, the catalog is already listing the backup we created on the previous step. We will select the first option and click on **Next >**:

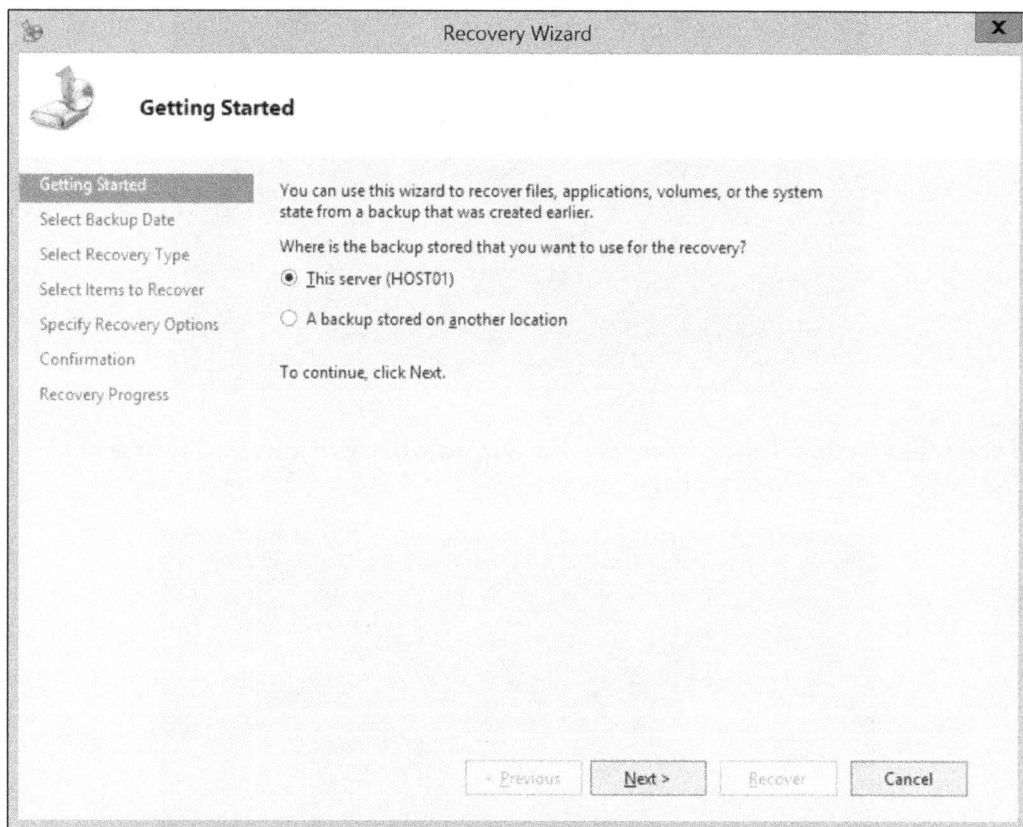

In the **Select Backup Date** screen, the backup catalog will present you with the oldest backup date available and the newest one. Based on this information, you can select the date of the backup you want to restore. Once you select the date on the calendar, you can select the backup time on the drop-down menu. Select the appropriate date and time and click on **Next >**:

The **Select Recovery Type** screen lets you choose from these three options as shown in the following screenshot:

- **Files and Folders**: This option will let you select the VM files, such as VHD/VHDX, and recover its files to the original location or a different location. This option will not recreate the VM itself; it will just recover the VM files.

- **Hyper-V**: This option will effectively recreate the VM on Hyper-V. This is the option we will choose; we will explore the alternatives ahead, after clicking on **Next >**.

- **Volumes**: If you backed up an entire volume, you can restore it by selecting this option.

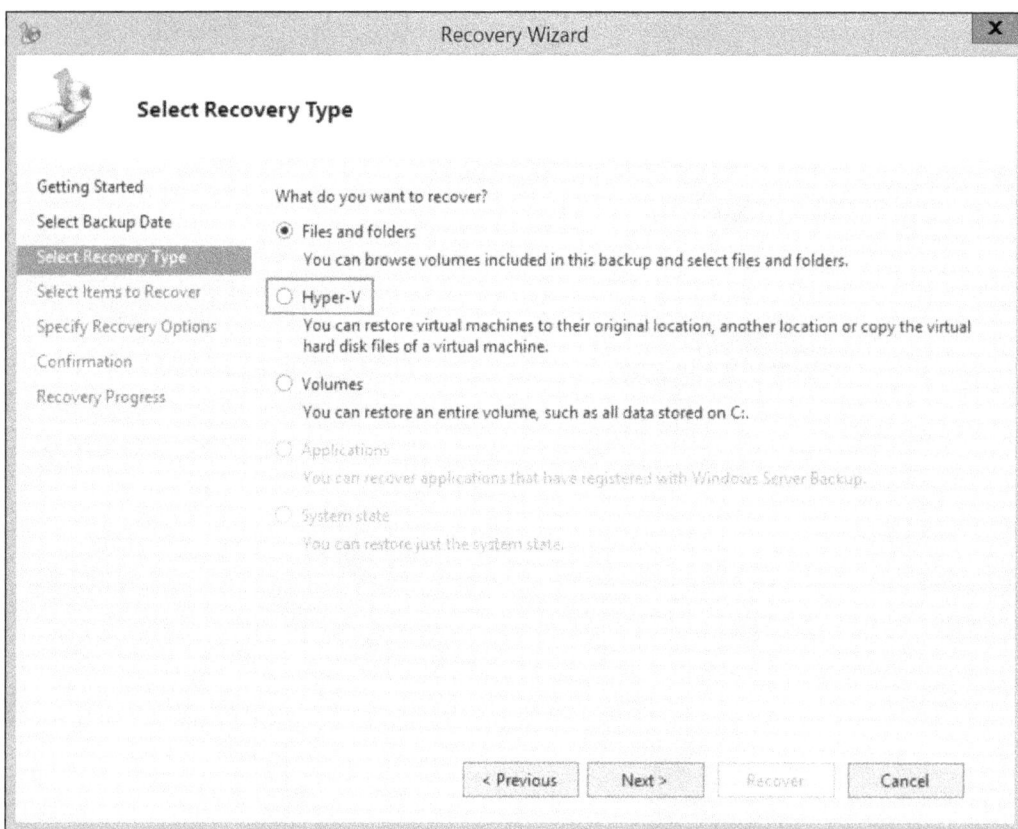

In the **Items to Recover** screen, you can choose the VMs you want to recover by selecting the items under **Hyper-V**. Select the VM you want to recover and the **Host Component** option (this will recover the necessary components of the host to recover the VM) and click on **Next >**:

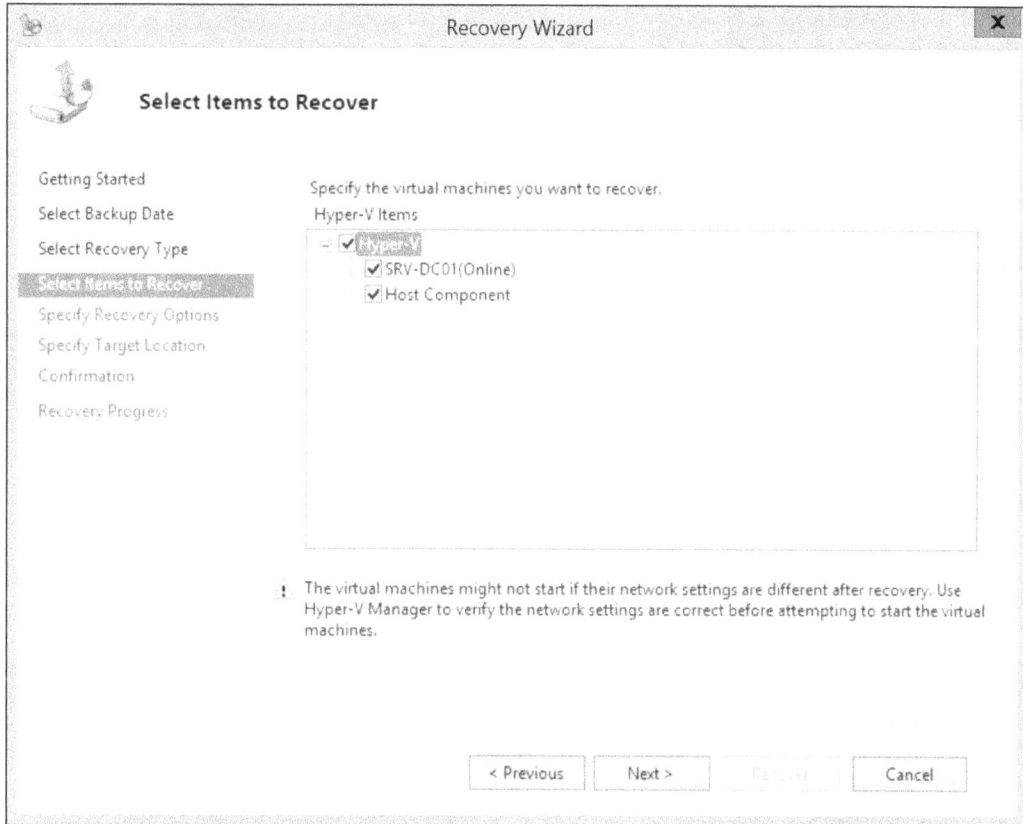

In the **Specify Recovery Options** screen, you have the following alternatives:

- **Recover to original location**: This option will recreate the VM on Hyper-V, if the VM is not created. If the VM is already created, the VM will be rolled back. This option will use the original folder of the VM to restore the VM files.

- **Recover to alternate location**: Like the previous one, this option will recreate the VM on Hyper-V, if the VM is not created. If the VM is already created, the VM will roll back. However, this option will use an alternate folder to recreate the VM files.

- **Copy to folder**: This option will not recreate the VM. Instead, it will just copy the VM files to the indicated folder so that you can manually recreate the VM later.

In this case, we will select **Recover to original location** and click on **Next >**:

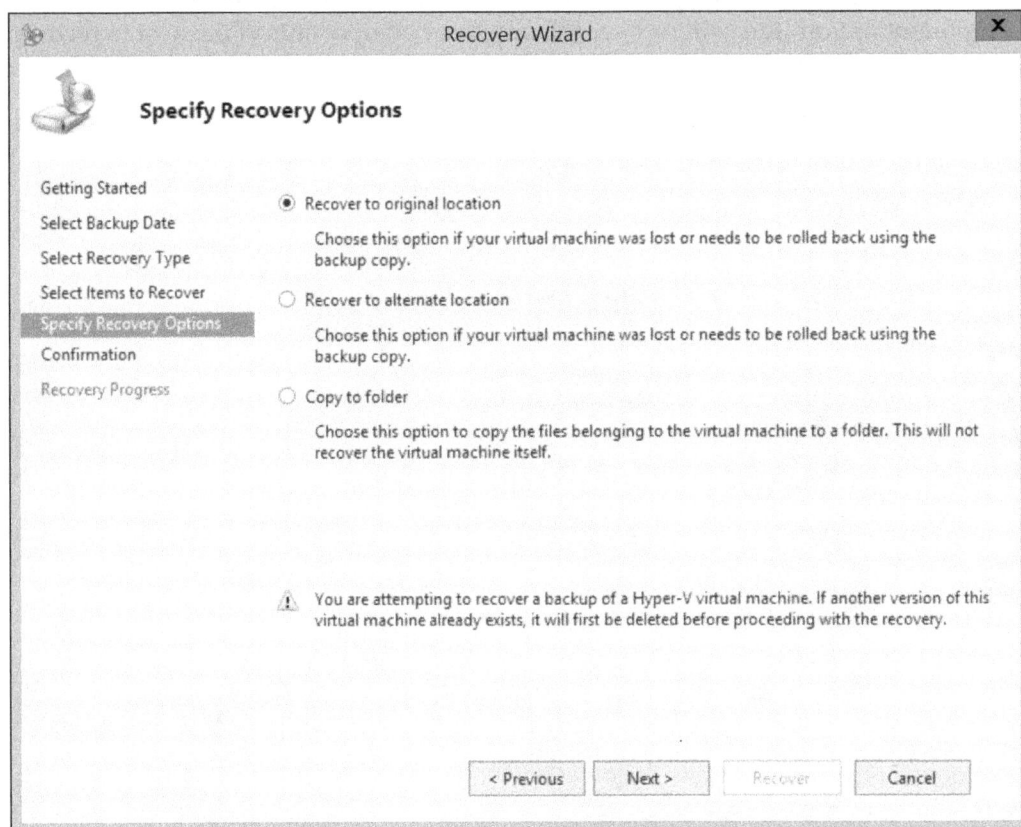

On the **Confirmation** page, review the information and click on **Recover**. Check if the restore process succeeded. To finalize, open Hyper-V Manager and check if the VM was recreated.

Just like the backup process, there is the option to use the command-line tool to restore the VM:

```
WBADMIN GET ITEMS -version:03/20/2015-04:00 -backupTarget:e:
```

The preceding command will detail the backup information about a specific backup job identified by the version. The version information was obtained earlier in this chapter.

```
WBADMIN START RECOVER -version: 03/20/2015-04:00 -itemType:hyperv -
items:"SRV-DC01" -backuptarget:e:
```

The preceding command will recover VM SRV-DC01 to its original location, just like on the GUI. You can find more information on how to use the WBADMIN command-line tool in the official article: https://technet.microsoft.com/pt-br/library/cc754015(v=WS.10).aspx.

# Import and export VMs

Another interesting alternative solution for data loss, though it's important to mention that it isn't a substitute for the backup process, is the import and export process.

The export wizard will create a copy of the VM on a different location. When you export a VM, a folder with all the VM structure is created, containing all the VM files and the VM virtual disks. With this, you can recover the VM in the exact state as at the moment of export. Additionally, you can import it on another host.

Another important aspect of the import and export process is that, on Hyper-V on Windows Server 2008 R2, if you did not export the VM, you can't import it again. On Windows Server 2012, Microsoft changed the VM settings so you can import the VM folder, on the same host, even if you forgot to export it before. You need, however, to export the VM to import it on another host. One more new feature is that now you can export a running VM. On Windows Server 2012, you had to stop the VM before exporting it.

To export a VM, perform the following steps:

1. Open Hyper-V Manager, right-click on the VM you want to export, and click on **Export...**:

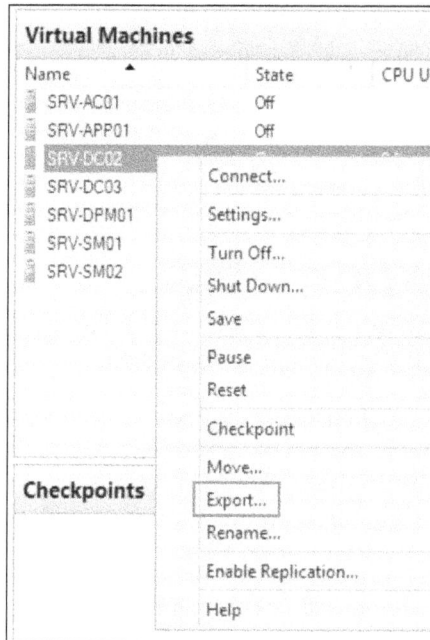

2. Enter the location where you want to export the VM and click on **Export**:

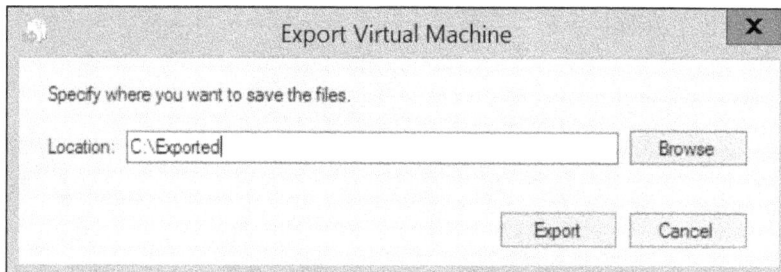

3. You can follow the export process:

| Name | State | CPU Usage | Assigned Memory | Uptime | Status |
|------|-------|-----------|-----------------|--------|--------|
| SRV-AC01 | Off | | | | |
| SRV-APP01 | Off | | | | |
| SRV-DC02 | Running | 0 % | 1024 MB | 2.12:51:40 | Exporting (92%) |
| SRV-DC03 | Off | | | | |
| SRV-DPM01 | Off | | | | |
| SRV-SM01 | Running | 8 % | 4096 MB | 2.12:51:06 | |
| SRV-SM02 | Off | | | | |

To import a VM on another host, perform the following steps:

1. Copy the exported folder to a location that the new host can access and, in Hyper-V Manager, click on **Import Virtual Machine**. In the **Import Virtual Machine** wizard, click on **Next >**. Click on **Browse...** to select the VM folder:

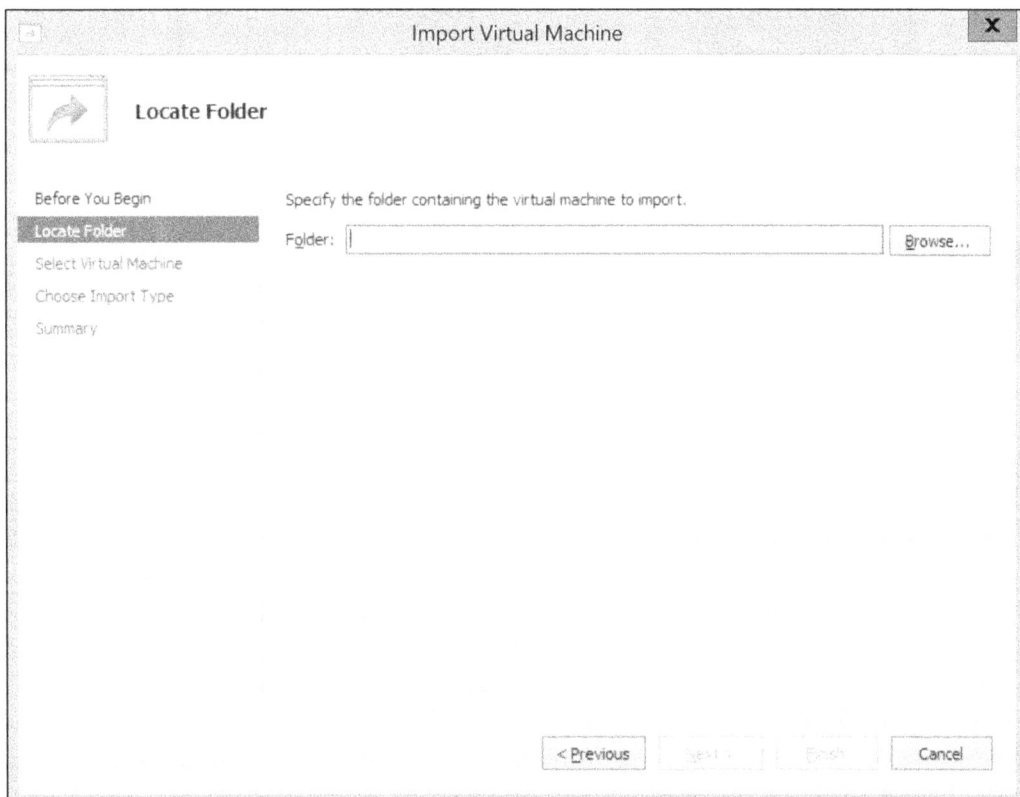

2.  Make sure you select the VM folder. Click on **OK** and then click on **Next >**.

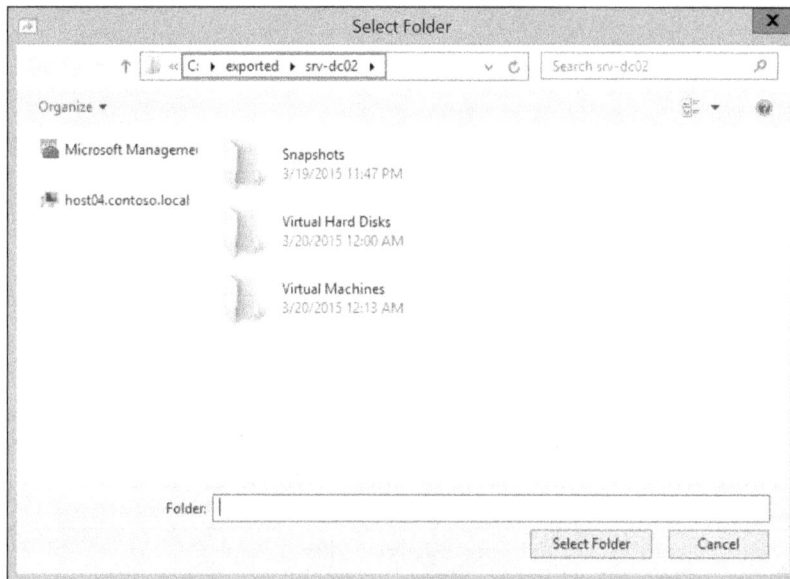

3.  If you selected the wrong folder, the wizard won't be able to find the VM information. If you selected the right folder, the VM information will be shown, as displayed in the following screenshot. Click on **Next >**:

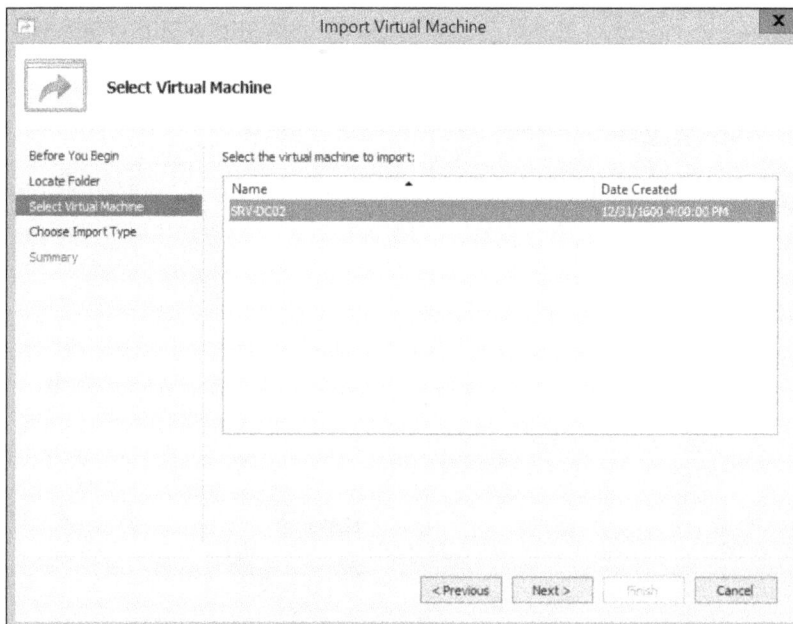

4. Now, you have three options to import the VM(see the following screenshot):
   - ° The first option will use the VM on the folder indicated, maintaining the unique ID of the VM
   - ° The second option will give you the ability to copy the VM folder to a different location, but will still maintain the unique ID
   - ° The third option will also allow you to copy the VM folder to another location, and will create a new unique ID for the VM

5. Since in this case the VM is already in the correct place, we will use the first option and click on **Next >**:

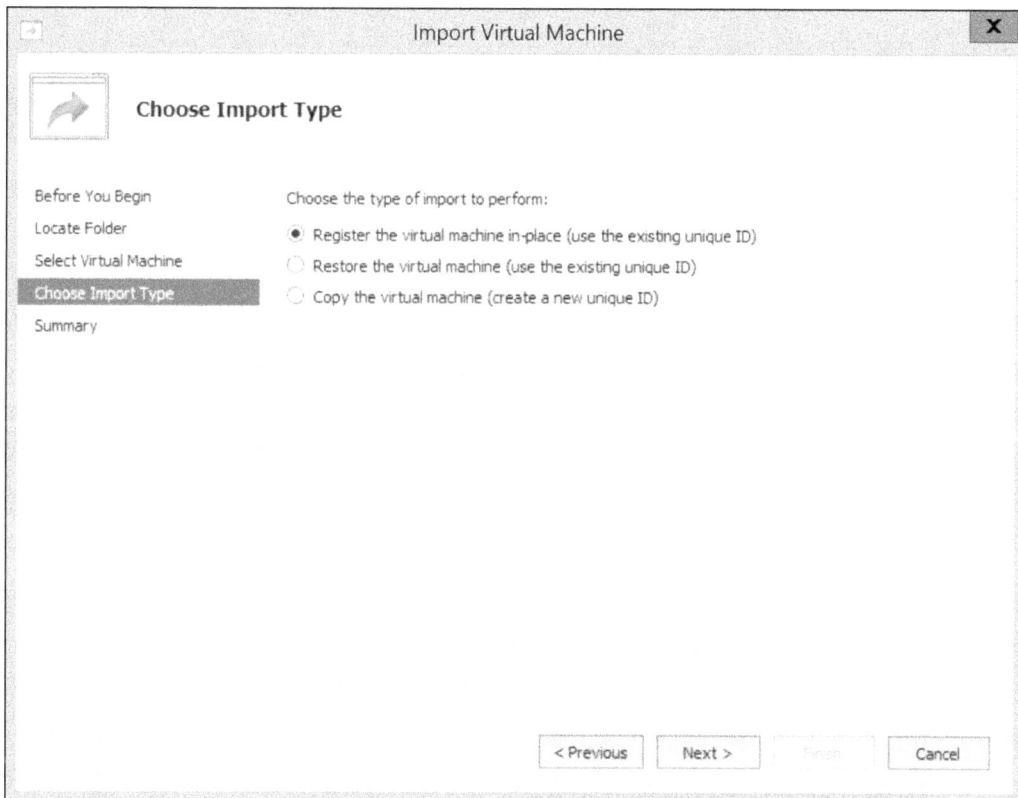

Import Virtual Machine  [X]

**Choose Import Type**

Before You Begin
Locate Folder
Select Virtual Machine
**Choose Import Type**
Summary

Choose the type of import to perform:

● Register the virtual machine in-place (use the existing unique ID)
○ Restore the virtual machine (use the existing unique ID)
○ Copy the virtual machine (create a new unique ID)

[ < Previous ]  [ Next > ]  [ Finish ]  [ Cancel ]

6. Since the VM was exported while still running, you may have errors in the import process if the processors of the hosts are different. This is exactly what you have already learned with Live Migration. To continue, you have the option to delete the saved state of the VM. Keep in mind that this will discard all the unsaved data inside the VM.

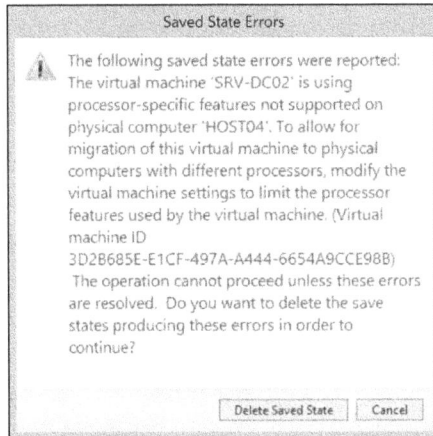

7. A new feature in the import process on Windows Server 2012 is that Hyper-V will check for mismatch configurations such as virtual networks. In the case below, the virtual switch on which the VM was connected to the original host does not exist in this host. In previous versions of Hyper-V this resulted in an error during the import process. Now the wizard lets you choose a different virtual switch for the VM. Select a virtual switch and click on **Next >**:

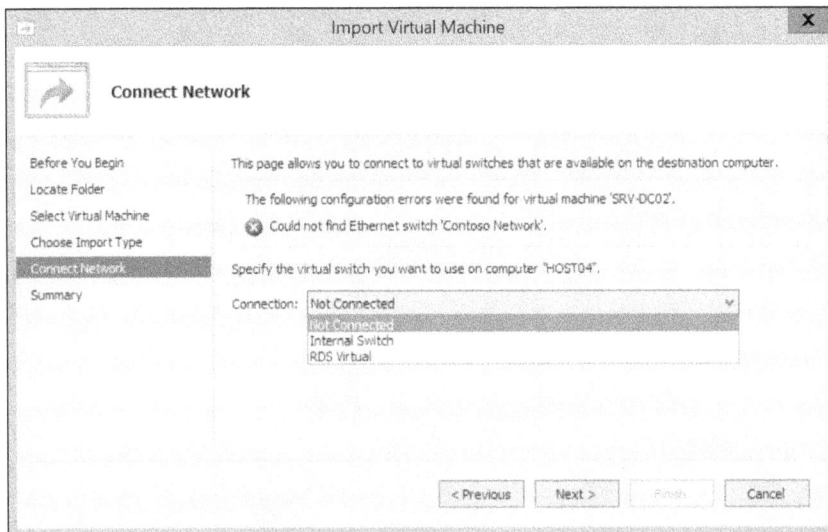

8. Review the **Summary** information and click on **Finish** to initiate the import process. The VM will be shown on Hyper-V Manager after the import process.

# Summary

In this final chapter, you learned how to protect the virtualization environment with Windows Server Backup. You learned how Windows Server Backup evolved from NTBackup and what the backup and restore options for the Hyper-V host and VMs are. You learned to use the new incremental backup feature on Windows Server 2012 and saw how it saves space for backup data.

Moving on, you learned that importing and exporting can be useful mechanisms for avoiding loss of data from VMs, and that you can import the VM on a different host. Also, you've seen that, if the host has different parameters from the original host, the import process lets you resolve the mismatches to correctly import the VM.

With all of that we end this book, hoping that you now have a strong background in Hyper-V and are well prepared to go out and get to grips with a production environment. Good luck!

# Index

## Symbol

## C

## D

Data Center Bridging (DCB)  97
Datacenter Edition, of Windows
        Server 2008 and 2008 R2  54, 55
Datacenter Edition, of Windows
        Server 2012 and 2012 R2  56, 57
Data Execution Prevention (DEP)  9
Differencing disks
  about  170
  using  170, 172
Direct Attached Storage (DAS)  107
Domain Controller
  database, configuring  259-261
DSC
  about  173
  Pull mode  173
  Push mode  173
  reference link  173
Dynamic Memory
  about  14, 15
  configuring  15, 16
  Memory buffer  16, 17
  Memory weight  17-19
  Smart Paging  19
Dynamic Quorum  187

## E

Enlightened Child Partition  7
Execute Disable Bit  9
Extensible Storage Engine (ESE)  259

## F

failover cluster
  configuring  177-185
  installing  177-185
  overview  176, 177
Fibre Channel over Ethernet (FCoE)  97
Fibre Channel Protocol (FCP)  108
file types, VM
  AVHDX / AVHD  47
  BIN  47
  VHDX / VHD  47
  VSV  47
  XML  47

Flexible Single Master Operations
        (FSMO)  262
Forced Unit Access (FUA)  260
Fully Qualified Domain Name (FQDN)  111

## G

Generation 1 VM  146, 147
Generation 2 VM
  about  146, 147
  modifications  146, 147
  reference link, for modifications  147
graphical user interface (GUI)  21
Group Policy Objects (GPO)  297
guest cluster
  about  212
  shared VHDX, presenting to  213-215

## H

Hard Disk Drive (HDD)
  about  102, 103
  RAID recommendations, for
        virtualization  103, 104
Hardware Acceleration
  IPsec task offloading  92, 93
  SR-IOV  93
  Virtual Machine Queue (VMQ)  91, 92
highly available VM
  creating  196-200
  managing  200
  startup priority, setting  200-202
host
  backing up  323-336
  considerations, for installation  22, 23
  licensing, with Hyper-V Replica  61, 62
  licensing, with Linux VMs  62, 63
  reference link, for restoring  337
  restoring  336-343
Host Storage
  4K disk  126
  about  102
  clustered iSCSI Target  124, 125
  DAS  107
  HDD  102
  implications  125
  local disks  105-107
  local storage  105-107

## M

## N

## O

## P

## Q

# R

RAID recommendations, for virtualization
  about 103, 104
  RAID 0 104
  RAID 1 104
  RAID 5 104
  RAID 10 104
  RAID 50 104
  RAID 60 104
RDS CAL 68
read-only domain controller (RODC) 262
Recovery Points, VM 245
Remote Desktop Protocol (RDP) 276
Remote Desktop Services (RDS)
  about 67, 68, 276
  reference link 290
Remote Desktop Web Access 276
Remote Direct Memory Access (RDMA)
  about 97
  URL 97
RemoteFX
  about 309
  enabling 310-313
  requisites 310
Remote Server Administration
    Tools (RSAT)
  about 39-41
  URL 39
Reverse Replication 254
Rings 3

# S

SAN
  about 108
  Fibre Channel (FC) 108
  iSCSI 108-113
Scale-Out File Server (SOFS) 125
SCSI-3 Persistent Reservation 180
Second Level Address Translation
    (SLAT) 7, 9
server consolidation 2
Server Core 31
Server Message Block 3 (SMB3)
  about 113-125
  SMB Direct 114

SMB Direct, URL 114
SMB Multichannel 114
SMB Multichannel, URL 114
Server Message Block (SMB) 113
Session Based
  versus VDI 278
Session Host environments 68
shared VHDX
  about 212
  presenting, to guest cluster 213-215
Share Nothing Live Migration
  about 218
  configuring, with PowerShell 227
  enabling 219-222
  Kerberos authentication, configuring 222-225
  Performance options, configuring 226
Smart Paging 14, 19
Software Assurance (SA) 52
Solid State Drive (SSD)
  about 102, 103
  RAID recommendations, for
    virtualization 103, 104
Standard Edition, of Windows Server 2008
    and 2008 R2
  about 53
  scenarios 58
  using 58
  versus Enterprise Edition 53
Standard Edition, of Windows Server 2012
    and 2012 R2 56, 57
states, BPA
  error 42
  information 42
  warning 42
storage
  configuring, for Hyper-V Cluster 192-195
Storage Area Network. *See* SAN
Storage replication 125
Sysinternals tool 9
Sysprep 167
Sysprepped VMs
  about 167
  creating 168-170
System Center Virtual Machine Manager
    (SCVMM) 28, 145

## About Packt Publishing

Packt, pronounced 'packed', published its first book, *Mastering phpMyAdmin for Effective MySQL Management*, in April 2004, and subsequently continued to specialize in publishing highly focused books on specific technologies and solutions.

Our books and publications share the experiences of your fellow IT professionals in adapting and customizing today's systems, applications, and frameworks. Our solution-based books give you the knowledge and power to customize the software and technologies you're using to get the job done. Packt books are more specific and less general than the IT books you have seen in the past. Our unique business model allows us to bring you more focused information, giving you more of what you need to know, and less of what you don't.

Packt is a modern yet unique publishing company that focuses on producing quality, cutting-edge books for communities of developers, administrators, and newbies alike. For more information, please visit our website at www.packtpub.com.

## About Packt Enterprise

In 2010, Packt launched two new brands, Packt Enterprise and Packt Open Source, in order to continue its focus on specialization. This book is part of the Packt Enterprise brand, home to books published on enterprise software – software created by major vendors, including (but not limited to) IBM, Microsoft, and Oracle, often for use in other corporations. Its titles will offer information relevant to a range of users of this software, including administrators, developers, architects, and end users.

## Writing for Packt

We welcome all inquiries from people who are interested in authoring. Book proposals should be sent to author@packtpub.com. If your book idea is still at an early stage and you would like to discuss it first before writing a formal book proposal, then please contact us; one of our commissioning editors will get in touch with you.

We're not just looking for published authors; if you have strong technical skills but no writing experience, our experienced editors can help you develop a writing career, or simply get some additional reward for your expertise.

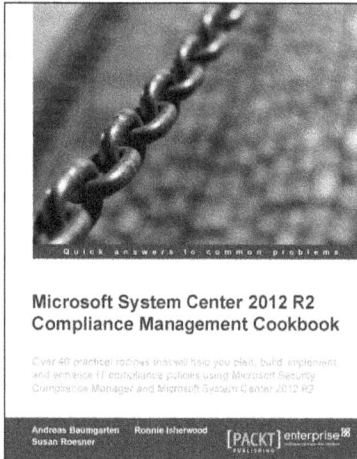

Microsoft System Center 2012 R2 Compliance Management Cookbook

Microsoft System Center 2012 R2 Compliance Management Cookbook

Over 40 practical recipes that will help you plan, build, implement, and enhance IT compliance policies using Microsoft Security Compliance Manager and Microsoft System Center 2012 R2

Andreas Baumgarten   Ronnie Isherwood
Susan Roesner     [PACKT] enterprise 88

# Microsoft System Center 2012 R2 Compliance Management Cookbook

ISBN: 978-1-78217-170-6            Paperback: 284 pages

Over 40 practical recipes that will help you plan, build, implement, and enhance IT compliance policies using Microsoft Security Compliance Manager and Microsoft System Center 2012 R2

1. A step-by-step guide filled with practical recipes that will show you how to start your compliance project using Microsoft System Center and other supporting technologies.

2. Demystify the compliance deployment myth; bridge the gap between IT, audit, and compliance programs.

3. Maximize your return on investment using the System Center product components.

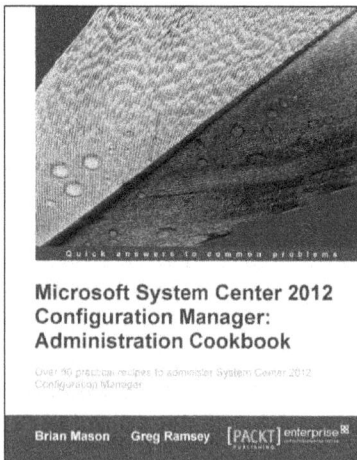

Microsoft System Center 2012 Configuration Manager: Administration Cookbook

Over 50 practical recipes to administer System Center 2012 Configuration Manager

Brian Mason   Greg Ramsey   [PACKT] enterprise 88

# Microsoft System Center 2012 Configuration Manager: Administration Cookbook

ISBN: 978-1-84968-494-1            Paperback: 224 pages

Over 50 practical recipes to administer System Center 2012 Configuration Manager

1. Administer System Center 2012 Configuration Manager.

2. Provides fast answers to questions commonly asked by new administrators .

3. Skip the why's and go straight to the how-to's.

Please check **www.PacktPub.com** for information on our titles

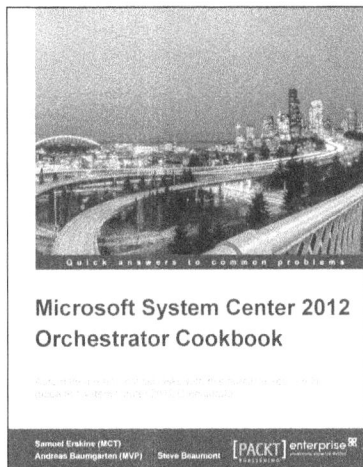

## Microsoft System Center 2012 Orchestrator Cookbook

ISBN: 978-1-84968-850-5        Paperback: 318 pages

Automate mission-critical tasks with this practical, real-world guide to System Center 2012 Orchestrator

1. Create powerful runbooks for the System Center 2012 product line.

2. Master System Center 2012 Orchestrator by creating looping, child and branching runbooks.

3. Learn how to install System Center Orchestrator and make it secure and fault tolerant.

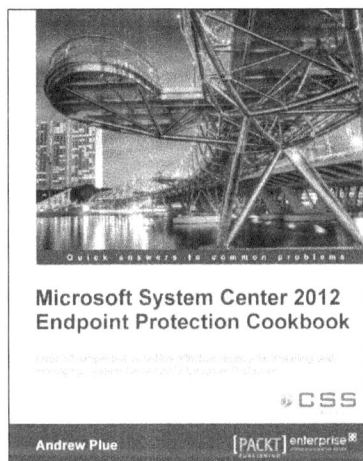

## Microsoft System Center 2012 Endpoint Protection Cookbook

ISBN: 978-1-84968-390-6        Paperback: 208 pages

Over 30 simple but incredibly effective recipes for installing and managing System Center 2012 Endpoint Protection

1. Master the most crucial tasks you'll need to implement System Center 2012 Endpoint Protection.

2. Provision SCEP administrators with just the right level of privileges, build the best possible SCEP policies for your workstations and servers, discover the hidden potential of command line utilities and much more in this practical book and eBook.

3. Quick and easy recipes to ease the pain of migrating from a legacy AV solution to SCEP.